God's Final Word

Discovery House Publishers

Books, music, and videos that feed the soul with the Word of God

Box 3566 Grand Rapids, MI 49501

God's Final Word
Understanding Revelation

by

Ray C. Stedman

with

James D. Denney

God's Final Word
Understanding Revelation
Copyright © 1991 by Ray C. Stedman

Library of Congress Cataloging-in-Publication Data

Stedman, Ray C.
    God's final word: understanding Revelation / by Ray C. Stedman
with James D. Denney.
    p.   cm.
    Includes bibliographical references.
    ISBN 0-929239-52-0
    1. Bible. N.T. Revelation—Commentaries. I. Denney, James D.
II. Bible. N.T. Revelation. English. New International. 1991. III. Title.
BS2825.3.S686 1991
228'.077—dc20   91-33778
                                         CIP

Discovery House Publishers is affiliated with
RBC Ministries, Grand Rapids, Michigan 49512.

Discovery House books are distributed to the trade exclusively
by Barbour Publishing, Inc., Uhrichsville, Ohio 44683.

Printed in the United States of America.

06 07 08 / CHG / 14 13 12

Other books by Ray C. Stedman

Authentic Christianity

Body Life

From Guilt To Glory (2 volumes)

How To Live What You Believe

Is This All There Is To Life?

Man Of Faith: Learning From The Life Of Abraham

Psalms Of Faith

Spiritual Warfare

Talking To My Father

Waiting For The Second Coming

Contents

Chapter One

Behind the Scenes of History

Revelation 1

The book of Revelation is the scariest book in the Bible. Yet it is also one of the most comforting, reassuring, and exhilarating books in the Bible.

Why is it scary? Well, just imagine having your home shaken and broken to splinters by a devastating 8.0 earthquake. Then imagine huddling in a shelter as bombs rain down upon your city with deafening explosions, lung-searing smoke, and blistering fire. Imagine the horror of being surrounded by plague, of watching friends and family falling sick, moaning, dying. Imagine the eerie sight of strange creatures descending from the sky, settling over the whole earth, killing people by the hundreds and thousands.

Now imagine experiencing not just one but *all* of these horrors at the same time. That is just part of the terrifying, electrifying, awe-inspiring swirl of events that make up the book of Revelation.

And yet, as I said, the book of Revelation is also one of the most comforting and exhilarating books in the Bible. It pictures a time when there will be a glorious new heaven and a new earth, a time when God will dwell with human beings, when there will be universal peace and an end to all sorrow. Jesus will wipe every tear from our eyes, and there will be no more death, nor mourning, nor crying, nor pain.

As we attempt to place ourselves amid this dizzying vortex of terrors, miracles, and wonders that are prophesied for the end of this age in the book of Revelation, we have to agree with Dr. Earl Palmer, who observed, "This remarkable book is both hard to understand fully and impossible to forget."[1]

Perhaps the most striking and profound aspect of this book is its relevance and importance to our lives in these closing days of the twentieth century. The book of Revelation is not just a musty piece of parchment from a bygone age, nor is it merely a collection of mysterious, symbolic images for some future age. The book of Revelation is vibrant, alive, and profoundly applicable to the times in which you and I live.

The "Bookends" of the Bible

It is no accident that the book of Revelation appears as the last book of the Bible. Revelation gathers all the threads of theme and historic events contained in the rest of the Bible, weaving them into a seamless whole. The entire scope of human history—and of eternity itself—comes into brilliant focus in the book of Revelation.

Someone has rightly observed that the book of Genesis and the book of Revelation are like two bookends that hold the entire Bible together. In Genesis we have the story of the origin of human sin; in Revelation we have the complete and final victory over sin. Genesis presents the beginning of human history and civilization; Revelation presents the end of both. In Genesis we learn the beginnings of God's judgment and His grace toward mankind; in Revelation we see the awesome result of His judgment and the triumph of His grace. The great themes of these two books are intricately intertwined.

Have you ever been to a major airport and watched the people get off the planes? You may see a crowd of people wearing shorts and flowered shirts, with leis around their necks. Aha, you think, these people just arrived from Hawaii. You may see another crowd of people lugging raincoats and umbrellas, with faces wreathed in gloom like an overcast day. They are just off the plane from Seattle.

In much the same way, as you work your way through the book of Revelation, you recognize the identifying features of the great themes of the Bible, and it is easy to tell in which Old Testament books those themes originated. Here we catch an echo of Daniel, there an aroma of Joel, and elsewhere we find nuggets from Isaiah and Ezekiel. In Revelation, we see very clearly the organic unity of the Word of God.

A "Sign-ificant" Book

The first three verses of Revelation form a prologue or preface which tells us the purpose of the book, the importance of the book, and the spirit or attitude in which it is to be read:

1:1–3 *The revelation of Jesus Christ, which God gave him to show his servants what must soon take place. He made it known by sending his angel to his servant John, who testifies to everything he saw—that is, the word of God and the testimony of Jesus Christ. Blessed is the one who reads the words of this prophecy, and blessed are those who hear it and take to heart what is written in it, because the time is near.*

There are two words in this paragraph that reveal to us the special nature of this book: it is called a *revelation* and a *prophecy*. The Greek word which is translated "revelation" is *apokalupsis*, which literally means "an unveiling." A revelation removes the veil which obscures our understanding, it unravels the mystery, it makes the meaning plain.

Accordingly, as we move through the book of Revelation, we will find many mysteries made clear. We will learn why evil persists on the earth, and what the ultimate fate of evil will be. The mystery of godliness will also be explained, so that we can discover how to live a godly, righteous life in the midst of a broken, evil world. Many other mysteries will be unveiled in this book of *apokalupsis*, of revelation.

And then there is the other word used to describe the book of Revelation: "Blessed is the one who reads the words of this *prophecy*." This is a book that deals in predictions. It deals with people and events which lie in the future. Powerful personalities are waiting to make their entrance on the stage of human events. Extraordinary circumstances are waiting to unfold as the juggernaut of history rumbles toward its fateful consummation. We will meet these personalities and witness these events in the book of Revelation.

The book is called the "revelation of Jesus Christ," and John says that Jesus Himself "made it known by sending his angel to his servant John." The English phrase "made it known" actually has a deeper meaning in the original Greek, where instead of three words there is just one Greek word, *semaino*. This word should be translated "signified"—or, if you want to really get the true sense of this word, pronounce it aloud: "sign-i-fied." In other words, Jesus made His revelation known to John by signs or symbols. Once you grasp the symbolic "sign-ificance" of this book, you can begin to understand and apply the book of Revelation.

Revelation is a book of symbols, and these symbols are important. Symbols help to simplify difficult concepts and to clarify things which are baffling or murky. I once heard of a boy who tried to explain to his little brother what radio was like. He said, "You know that a telegraph is a long wire that runs between two cities. It's like having a big dog with his tail in Los Angeles and his head in San Francisco. If you step on his tail in Los Angeles, he barks in San Francisco. Now a radio is the same thing—only you don't have no dog!" This boy tried his best to clarify an idea with the use of symbols—though I doubt his brother was any more enlightened as a result.

The book of Revelation, however, uses symbols with great precision and clarity. The weird beasts and strange persons of Revelation are all symbols of things which are real and literal. As we journey together through the pages of this book, I think you will be surprised to see how many seemingly difficult images and events in the book of Revelation become clear.

The key to understanding the symbols of Revelation is recognizing that almost all of these symbols have been given to us elsewhere in the Bible. If you try to read Revelation without any understanding of the rest of the Bible, you are doomed to confusion. But if you use the rest of the Bible as a guide and interpreter of the symbols of Revelation, most of these symbols immediately become understandable.

A Book from the Mind of God

Who is the author of the book of Revelation?

At first glance, the answer might seem to be John. But look again. John writes that this book is "the revelation of Jesus Christ, *which God gave him*," and which Jesus in turn made known to John. The author of Revelation is *God Himself!* John was certainly involved in the process of producing this book, but it truly had its origin not in the mind of John, but within the Godhead, in the mind of God the Father. The Father revealed it to the Son, who in turn made it known to a human being named John.

Why did God the Father have to give this revelation to Jesus the Son? Remember that in Matthew 24:36 Jesus said that though He understood many of the events of the last days of the age, He did not know the time when these events would happen. This knowledge, He said, belonged only to the Father. Now, of course, since Jesus is risen and glorified, He knows all that the Father knows, but while on earth the timing of these events was unknown even to Jesus Himself.

So God the Father gave this revelation to Jesus, who in turn entrusted it to John by means of an angel. Thus, while all Scripture is inspired by God, the book of Revelation occupies a unique place in the Bible, because no other book of the Bible has been given to us in this way. John's role in the writing of this book is virtually that of a secretary taking dictation John is the writer, but God is the Author of the book of Revelation.

But who is this man John, whose pen has preserved for us this awesome and powerful vision of the future? In verse 4 he simply identifies himself as "John." By comparing Revelation with other Scriptures and by examining the traditions of the early church, we can be reasonably sure that the author is John the apostle, the brother of James, the son of Zebedee, the beloved friend of Jesus, author of the gospel and three letters that bear his name. Certainly, there are Bible scholars who disagree, but when we compare the style, content, and structure of Revelation with that of the other writings of the apostle John, it is difficult to come to any other conclusion.

John probably wrote this book near the end of his life, at around A.D. 94 to 96. He was an old man, likely in his eighties, when this vision was given to him. The book is addressed to seven selected churches located in the Roman province of Asia, which today is part of the nation of Turkey.

As we begin our journey through the vision God gave to John, notice the inspiring promise we find at the outset: "Blessed is the one who reads the words of this prophecy, and blessed are those who hear it and take to heart what is written in it." God has promised all the readers of this book—including you and me—a special blessing if we read, hear, and take to heart the words of this prophecy.

What kind of blessing? I believe the Lord is promising that we will find comfort, guidance, and assurance, even through such times of upheaval and fear as described in Revelation. The 1990s are troubled, confused times, filled with temptations, pressures, and anti-Christian philosophies—and the days will grow darker as we near the conclusion of history. But the person who understands the book of Revelation will have a faithful guide through the tumult and confusion of this dying age.

The Key Number of Revelation

Once, during a trip to England, the renowned Indian mathematician Srinivasa Ramanujan was visited at his hotel by the English mathematician J. E. Littlewood. As the two men settled into their chairs to share tea together, Littlewood remarked, "You know, on the way over here, I happened to notice the number of the taxicab was 1729. I thought to myself, 'That is certainly a dull number.' I hope it's not an unfavorable omen for our visit."

"Oh, but you're quite mistaken, my friend," said Ramanujan. "In fact, 1729 is quite an interesting number! It is the smallest number expressible as the sum of two cubes in two different ways!"

Numbers which would escape the notice of you and me hold a strange fascination for mathematicians. Similarly, we find there are certain numbers which hold a fascinating significance in the book of Revelation.

1:4-8 *John,*

To the seven churches in the province of Asia:

Grace and peace to you from him who is, and who was, and who is to come, and from the seven spirits before his throne, and from Jesus Christ, who is the faithful witness, the firstborn from the dead, and the ruler of the kings of the earth.

To him who loves us and has freed us from our sins by his blood, and has made us to be a kingdom and priests to serve his God and Father—to him be glory and power for ever and ever! Amen.

Look, he is coming with the clouds, and every eye will see him, even those who pierced him; and all the peoples of the earth will mourn because of him. So shall it be! Amen.

"I am the Alpha and the Omega," says the Lord God, "who is, and who was, and who is to come, the Almighty."

Note, first of all, the greeting, "Grace and peace to you from him who is, and who was, and who is to come." These words describe God the Father as the Lord of all time and all eternity. His name in Hebrew, *Yahweh,* means "I Am." In English, "I Am" sounds like a statement in the present tense, but in Hebrew it contains *all* the tenses used in Revelation 1:4—in effect, "I am he who is, and he who was, and he who is to come."

Next we come to the key number of Revelation, the first of a series of *sevens:* "and from the seven spirits before his throne." Why is the number *seven* significant in Revelation? Because, whenever you encounter seven of anything in this book, it is a symbol of completeness and perfection.

Who is signified by the "seven spirits before his throne"? Here we find the first of many echoes from Old Testament prophecy. In Isaiah 11:2, the prophet speaks of the Spirit of God coming upon the Messiah:

> The Spirit of the LORD will rest on him—the Spirit of wisdom
> and of understanding, the Spirit of counsel and of power, the
> Spirit of knowledge and of the fear of the LORD. . . .

In this passage the Spirit of God is described in a sevenfold way. He is (1) the Spirit of the Lord, (2) the Spirit of wisdom, (3) the Spirit of understanding, (4) the Spirit of counsel, (5) the Spirit of power, (6) the Spirit of knowledge, and (7) the Spirit of the fear of the Lord. So the "seven spirits" of Revelation 1:4 are a symbol of the Holy Spirit in His sevenfold completion, perfection, and fullness.

This greeting of grace and peace comes from God the Father, the eternal "I Am"; from the Holy Spirit; and from Jesus Christ, the central figure of Revelation, who is introduced in threefold fashion as (1) the faithful witness, (2) the firstborn from the dead, and (3) the ruler of the kings of the earth.

He is called "the faithful witness" because what He says is true and reliable. When He speaks, He utters absolute, trustworthy reality. In a confusing, chaotic, dying world, Jesus is the Way, the Truth, and the Life. He is the truth-teller.

He is called "the firstborn from the dead" because of the resurrection. Though there were others (such as Lazarus, whom Jesus called forth from the tomb at Bethany) who died and were raised again, they were merely raised to the same earthly life they had before. Eventually, they died again and were buried. Only Jesus was raised to eternal, incorruptible glory. It is this same eternal, incorruptible life that Jesus gives to those who believe in Him. He is the life-giver.

He is called "the ruler of the kings of the earth" because He has ultimate sovereignty over the whole world. There are many rulers and leaders who claim to be sovereign in their own countries, but Jesus exercises ultimate authority over them all. He is the great law-maker, the king of kings.

So, in this passage, Jesus is introduced in threefold fashion as the *truth-teller*, the *life-giver*, and the *law-maker*.

The First Doxology

This introduction is followed in verses 5 and 6 by a threefold doxology to (1) "him who loves us," (2) who "has freed us from our sins by his blood," and (3) who "has made us to be a kingdom and priests to serve his God and Father." This is the first doxology of the book of Revelation, a paean of praise to God, which concludes, "to him be glory and power for ever and ever! Amen." This is a powerful declaration, and its three essential themes deserve closer examination.

First theme: *He loves us*. This is a statement in the present tense. It's an amazing fact. Despite all our foolishness, waywardness, selfishness, and sin, the Lord Jesus loves us. He is always on our side.

Years ago, while I was traveling in the state of Virginia with Dr. H. A. Ironside, we met a man who was rector of an Episcopal church. This man told us the story of his conversion to Christ. I've never forgotten that story.

He was a student at England's Cambridge University when D. L. Moody was invited to speak to the students. He and a number of other students were furious that such a distinguished institution as Cambridge would invite Moody—an unschooled American preacher—to give a lecture. Moody murdered the king's English so badly that he is said to have pronounced the word "Jerusalem" in only one syllable!

The night of Moody's appearance, the group of rebellious students sat in the very front row, waiting for just the right time to humiliate Moody with jeers and mocking. Just before Moody was to speak, the great gospel singer and composer Ira B. Sankey stood and sang. As he sang, the restless audience grew quiet and respectful. Immediately after the song and without introduction, Moody stepped up on the platform, pointed his finger at the young men in the front row, and said, "Young gentlemen, don't ever think God don't love you, for He do!"

It was perhaps the most ungrammatical sentence ever uttered on the Cambridge University grounds. Yet there was such power in Moody's face, in his voice, and in his straightforward declaration of God's love that the young men in the front row dared not jeer and mock as they had planned. Moody went on to speak of the love of Jesus for a lost human race—a love that compelled Jesus to go to the cross and die an agonizing death in our place. In the course of his talk, he repeated those ungrammatical but awesomely powerful words, "Young gentlemen, don't ever think God don't love you, for He do!"

Concluding his reminiscence of that meeting, the Episcopal rector looked first at Dr. Ironside, then at me, and he said, "In those moments, I saw myself in a different light. By the end of that meeting, I gave my heart to Jesus Christ."

That is how John wants us to see ourselves in relationship to Jesus Christ: *He loves us*, in the present tense, despite our rebellion and sin. When the truth of this statement begins to seep into our hearts, then our lives—like the life of this Episcopal rector—can be transformed.

Second theme: *He has freed us from our sins by His blood*. Jesus breaks the shackles of sin and destructive habits in our lives. He sets us free from the addictions and dependencies which harass us, enslave us, and chain us down. It is true that many Christians continue to struggle with evil habits even after coming into a relationship with Christ. Some struggle with drug or alcohol dependency, some with selfish attitudes or sexual temptations, some with an angry temper or a malicious tongue. But the blood of Christ gives us the *power* to break the chains of sin—if we will but turn the control of our lives over to Him. As in the words of the old hymn,

> He breaks the power of cancelled sin,
> He sets the prisoner free;
> His blood can make the foulest clean;
> His blood availed for me!

Third theme: *He has made us to be a kingdom and priests to serve His God and Father.* We are all sinners, estranged from a holy and just God because of our sin. The role of a priest is to bridge the alienation between the people and God, to bring the people near to God again. In the Old Testament, priests explained the meaning of sacrifices, called the people to repentance, and thus brought the people near to God.

Today, *all* believers are called to perform the function of a priest. Do you ever think of yourself as a priest? It's a high and holy calling, given to us by Jesus Himself.

We are to reach out to others in their pain and lostness. We are to explain to them the sacrifice that Jesus has made on their behalf. We are to share with them the fact that God loves them and longs to draw them to Himself, to heal their loneliness and alienation. For this reason, Jesus has made all believers, including you and me, to be a kingdom of priests.

The Splendor of His Coming

Some years ago, I was visiting with a number of rabbis in Southern California. The subject of our discussion was the differences between Judaism and Christianity.

"You know," one rabbi said to me, "when the Messiah comes, we Jews will say, 'Welcome!' But you Christians will say, 'Welcome back!'"

"And what will the Messiah say?" I asked.

"I think," the rabbi replied without missing a beat, "He will say, 'No comment.'"

In Revelation 1:7, the Lord is introduced to us not only in terms of who He is, His attributes and His glory, but also in terms of what He will do in the future: "Look, he is coming with the clouds." This is the focal point of human history, the single event toward which all human events—and heavenly events as well—are moving. One day Jesus Himself will break through the skies, and He will appear again in glory, just as when He left the earth. His coming will have planet-wide impact, for, as Revelation 1:7 says, "every eye will see him."

This account of Jesus' return accords with that of Matthew 24:30. There, Jesus said, "At that time the sign of the Son of Man will appear in the sky, and all the nations of the earth will mourn. They will see the Son of Man coming on the clouds of the sky, with power and great glory."

No one will miss this spectacular event, not even those without televisions. He will appear everywhere, and He will be visible to everyone in the world at once. In 2 Thessalonians 2:8, Paul calls this event "the splendor of his coming," or, more literally, "the outshining of his *parousia*" (*parousia* is the Greek word which describes the future presence of Jesus on earth).

Jesus' appearance will be so unmistakable that even the Jews will recognize Him. John tells us, "even those who pierced him; and all the peoples of the earth will mourn because of him." This is a reference to the prophecy in Zechariah 12:10–13:6, where we are told that when the Messiah appears, those who pierced Him shall look upon Him and mourn greatly. The Jews shall ask Him, "What are these wounds on your body?" and He will say, "The wounds I was given at the house of my friends."

From these passages, I have to conclude that my rabbi friend was mistaken when he said the Jews would say, "Welcome!" when Messiah comes. I am convinced that even they will say, "Welcome back!" because they will see Him, they will know Him, and they—along with all the peoples of the earth—will mourn, knowing that the Messiah has visited this planet once before, that He was despised, rejected, and crucified.

One of the great puzzles of history is the fact that the Jewish people have so resolutely turned their backs on the evidence that Jesus is their promised Messiah. At the beginning, of course, the early church was almost entirely Jewish, but over time, increasingly more non-Jewish converts came into the church, while the number of Jewish converts dwindled to a trickle. Why? Because the Jewish people are "blinded" (as Paul so convincingly argues in Romans 9 through 11) by long-standing unbelief.

But Jewish unbelief will not last forever. The day will come when the Jewish people will recognize—and mourn—their Messiah. They will mourn, just as all the peoples of the earth will mourn, because of the tragic and terrible way they have treated Jesus and His work for all mankind upon the cross.

The Alpha and the Omega

The nineteenth-century English clergyman William Lisle Bowles was a prolific and much-admired poet. He was often asked to autograph copies of his poetry collections. On one occasion, while visiting in the home of his friend Tom Moore, he presented a Bible to Mrs. Moore as a gift. She was so pleased with the gift that she asked Bowles to inscribe it, which he did. After the poet left the house, Mrs. Moore opened the Bible to the flyleaf and was surprised to discover that he had absentmindedly written, "To Mrs. Moore, with cordial wishes, from the Author."

In these opening verses—the "flyleaf" of the book of Revelation— God takes the pen in His own hand and signs the book with His own signature: "I am the Alpha and the Omega, says the Lord God," using the first and last letters of the Greek alphabet to symbolize the beginning and end of all things. He continues, describing Himself in this inscription as the One "who is, and who was, and who is to come, the Almighty."

In no other book of the Bible do we find this wonderful imprimatur of God. When we read these words, we are reading a copy autographed by the Author Himself!

The Prisoner of Patmos

The first chapter of Revelation concludes with John's explanation of how and where he received this prophecy from God.

1:9–20 *I, John, your brother and companion in the suffering and kingdom and patient endurance that are ours in Jesus, was on the island of Patmos because of the word of God and the testimony of Jesus. On the Lord's Day I was in the Spirit, and I heard behind me a loud voice like a trumpet, which said: "Write on a scroll what you see and send it to the seven churches: to Ephesus, Smyrna, Pergamum, Thyatira, Sardis, Philadelphia and Laodicea."*

I turned around to see the voice that was speaking to me. And when I turned I saw seven golden lampstands, and among the lampstands was someone "like a son of man," dressed in a robe reaching down to his feet and with a golden sash around his chest. His head and hair were white like wool, as white as snow, and his eyes were like blazing fire. His feet were like bronze glowing in a furnace, and his voice was like the sound of rushing waters. In his right hand he held seven stars, and out of his mouth came a sharp double-edged sword. His face was like the sun shining in all its brilliance.

When I saw him, I fell at his feet as though dead. Then he placed his right hand on me and said: "Do not be afraid. I am the First and the Last. I am the Living One; I was dead, and behold I am alive for ever and ever! And I hold the keys of death and Hades.

"Write, therefore, what you have seen, what is now, and what will take place later. The mystery of the seven stars that you saw in my right

hand and of the seven golden lampstands is this: The seven stars are the angels of the seven churches, and the seven lampstands are the seven churches."

Here, even in the first chapter of Revelation, we discover truth imparted in the form of symbols. Jesus is described in a way that is not intended to convey His actual physical appearance but various aspects of His character, His attributes, and His role.

The setting for the vision John received is a tiny island in the Aegean Sea. This island, called Patmos, is only about four miles wide and six miles long, located just off the coast of Turkey. It was a dreary little place in John's day, containing a stone quarry, some mining excavations, and very little else. John had apparently been banished to Patmos by the Romans in order to silence his preaching—hence his statement that he was there "because of the word of God and the testimony of Jesus." John was a prisoner on Patmos.

On one Sunday morning (or "the Lord's Day," as John calls it), John was "in the Spirit." This does not mean that John was in some state of religious ecstasy, but rather that he was worshiping God and meditating on God's greatness and majesty. It is the state of mind and spirit that Jesus described in John 4:24 when He said, "God is spirit, and his worshipers must worship in spirit and in truth."

While John was in this worshipful attitude, a voice like a trumpet said, "Write on a scroll what you see and send it to the seven churches." Upon hearing this voice, John did what you or I would have done: he turned to find the source of this powerful, trumpetlike voice. What he saw was the Lord Himself, standing among seven golden lampstands, holding seven stars in His hands. Note the significance of the number seven again, the number of completeness.

John's Encounter with the Lord

Now let's look at each of the symbols which characterize John's vision of the Lord Jesus:

1. Jesus is dressed in a long robe, bound across the chest by a golden sash, a priestly garment symbolizing His role as the Great High Priest. In Scripture, gold symbolizes deity. This robe with its golden sash speaks of the fact that Jesus is a priest who is Himself God. He is the Lord, sovereign over all of history, healing the breach between God and man.

2. His head and His hair are white. These are symbols used in the book of Daniel to denote wisdom and purity.

3. His eyes are like blazing fire, from which nothing can be hid. Fire speaks of judgment.

4. His feet are like bronze, glowing in a furnace. Again, the image of furnace-hot fires of judgment.

5. His voice is like the sound of rushing waters, like the roar of the surf as it dashes against the rocks. The sound of His voice is the sound of power, inspiring our awe.

6. The sword which comes out of the mouth of Jesus is clearly the Word of God, by which Jesus reveals truth to us.

7. His face is like the sun shining in its strength. The brilliance of the sun symbolizes the burning intensity of truth.

Perhaps as John looked upon the brilliant face of the risen Lord, he recalled a time during the Lord's earthly ministry, when John, Peter, and James stood together with Jesus on a high mountain in northern Israel.[2] There, as they prayed together, the face and garments of the Lord suddenly shone with a whiteness like nothing ever seen on the earth. This is the event which theologians call the *transfiguration* of Jesus. In 2 Peter 1:16–18, Peter recalled the transfiguration and said that it was a preview of the future coming of Jesus.

Perhaps this vision of Jesus in Revelation 1 explains an interesting episode at the end of the gospel of John. In John 21, Jesus commissioned Peter with the words, "Feed my sheep," then prophesied that Peter would one day die a martyr's death. At this point, Peter indicted John, and said, "Lord, what about him?" Peter wanted to know what sort of death was prophesied for John. And Jesus replied, "If I want him to remain alive until I return, what is that to you? You must follow me." Because of a misunderstanding of this conversation between Peter and the Lord, word went out among the disciples that John would never die until the Lord returned.

Here, in Revelation 1, is the explanation: John did remain alive to see the coming of the Lord. He foresaw the Lord's coming as an event in history, but he saw it in the form of a vision from God. Though historical tradition holds that John died at the age of ninety and was buried in Ephesus, he did live to see the coming of the Lord. He saw the Lord's coming in symbols of priestly garments, of brilliant light, of blazing fire, of thunderous sound, of supreme power, purity, wisdom, and holiness.

Throughout the remainder of Revelation, we will see other symbolism employed to describe various aspects of Jesus' character, power, and position. In chapter 5, He will appear as a lamb—and also as a lion. In chapter 19, He will appear as a rider on a great white horse. He is a bridegroom coming for His bride in chapter 21. But it is the image of

Jesus which John describes in chapter 1 that is the most startling and graphic of all.

Before such an awesome sight, what could John do, what could any human being do, but fall at the feet of Jesus as though dead? Who could remain standing before such a vision? This, indeed, is the reaction of every human who experiences the kind of profound encounter with the living God that John experiences in Revelation 1. John's reaction is identical to that of Isaiah when he sees the Lord seated on a throne, high and exalted, with the long train of His robe filling the temple.[3] John's reaction is the same as that of Job when he is awed and humbled in the presence of God.[4]

And as John lay prostrate before the feet of Jesus, the Lord did something that was completely typical and characteristic of Him: He reached down and *touched* John! He placed His right hand on the trembling shoulder of the beloved disciple.

As you read through the gospels, you see that Jesus was always touching people. When He healed a leper, He touched him. When He restored sight to the blind, He put His hands upon their eyes. Now, in Revelation 1, Jesus touches His friend John and reassures him with the words, "Do not be afraid." He is saying to John, in effect, "I am your friend, not your enemy. I am the First and the Last. I set the boundaries of time and history. All people and all events are enclosed within the limits that I have determined in my sovereignty. I hold the keys of death and hell, the keys of both physical death and spiritual death. I am sovereign over all that is, so you have nothing to fear, my friend."

"Write!"

Having reassured John, Jesus then commissions him. "Write, therefore," says the Lord, "what you have seen, what is now, and what will take place later." Notice that Jesus gives him a three-part writing assignment. First, John is to write what he has seen, which is that vision we have just examined, recorded in Revelation 1.

Second, John is to write "what is now." That is, he is to write seven letters to seven churches about existing conditions in those churches. These letters comprise Revelation chapters 2 and 3.

Third, John is to write "what will take place later." This is the prophetic vision of the future contained in Revelation chapters 4 through 22. These are the three divisions of the book of Revelation, as given to us by the Lord Himself. If we will follow these divisions carefully, we will be able to understand God's message to us in this challenging, rewarding, symbol-laden book. That, of course, is our goal as we keep before us God's promise from verse 3, "Blessed is the one who reads the words of this prophecy, and blessed are those who hear it and take to heart what is written in it, because the time is near."

The point of the first chapter of Revelation is to focus our attention on Jesus. He is the central figure of Revelation, just as He is the central figure of all history. Our lives can never be lived realistically, triumphantly, and joyously without reference to Him. We, as Christians, are called to live as though we see Him who is invisible. He is the One we must take to work with us each day. He is the One who will be beside us as we drive our cars, as we go to sleep, as we face our trials, as we experience our joys. He is the source of our courage, our peace, our wisdom, our forgiveness when we sin, our help in time of need.

In this first chapter of Revelation, John takes up the commission given him by Jesus and performs it with dramatic force: he elevates our hearts and focuses our attention upon Jesus, upon who He is and what He is doing in human history. The Lord, through His servant John, has lifted the veil from the obscured face of the future. He invites us to look behind the scenes of history and see the great and awesome things He is doing— and is about to do!—upon the earth, and within each individual life.

So come with me. Let's venture a step closer and look upon the face of Tomorrow.

Chapter Two

Seven Letters to Seven Churches

Overview: Revelation 1:19 Chapters 2 and 3

The Austrian composer Franz Joseph Haydn was a man with a cheerful disposition, despite the fact that he was married to an exceedingly bitter and malicious woman. She continually belittled both Haydn and his music. Several times, purely out of spite, she stole the only existing copies of his musical scores from his desk and destroyed them.

Haydn spent much of his career traveling around Europe—partly because his talents were in such demand throughout the Continent, but also because travel gave him time away from his disagreeable wife. During one extended visit to England, an acquaintance visited Haydn in his rented room in London. This friend noticed a large stack of unopened letters on Haydn's desk and asked the composer why he did not open his mail.

"All of those letters are from my wife," Haydn jovially explained. "We write to each other every week, but I do not open her letters, and I am quite sure she does not open mine."

In Revelation chapters 2 and 3 we find a stack of letters, seven in all, which have largely lain ignored and unopened by the Christian church over the years. As one Bible scholar laments, "Many casual worshipers in

Christian churches today who are quite familiar with the Sermon on the Mount are not aware of the existence of these seven messages of Christ."[1]

I find that many people tend to skip over these seven letters to the churches, so eager are they to hurry on to those juicy, action-packed, blood-and-thunder sections of Revelation. We would rather hear about the great cataclysms of the last days than be confronted with the urgent challenge of our own present moment. How tragic!

These seven letters to seven churches are powerful letters, burning with urgency. Their message is still as vital and timely today as when first written. So many ills of our churches in the 1990s could be cured if we would only listen with attentive ears to the message Jesus gave us through the pen of John nearly 2,000 years ago.

In these letters, our Lord outlines for us His plan for the church. He shows us that He has set His church in the midst of the world. It is His instrument to impact and direct the course of human history. Jesus calls the church "the light of the world" and "the salt of the earth." The apostle Paul calls it "the pillar and ground of truth." That is the mystery and the mission of the church. God intends the church to exert tremendous influence over the affairs of the world.

These seven letters set forth His eternal "game plan." So it's a grievous mistake to slight the crucial importance and timely relevance of these letters. They are filled with both warning and encouragement to churches that are struggling with sin and complacency within, and persecution without. In these letters, our Lord teaches the church how to live as light in a darkening world while also confronting the sin and error that threatens the health and life of the church.

A Sevenfold Pattern

As we approach these letters, two questions occur to us: (1) Why are only *seven* churches addressed? (2) Why *these* particular seven?

The only satisfactory answer is that these are seven representative churches. They were carefully selected to represent not only the spectrum of churches that existed in the first century A.D., but the spectrum of churches that exist now, at the close of the twentieth century.

There were many churches in the province of Asia at the time John wrote this letter. Other churches could have been chosen. In fact, many other churches were better known—churches such as Colossae, Tralles, and Manisa. But the Lord chose these seven churches because they represent conditions that have prevailed throughout church history, from the beginning to the end.

In other words, there are seven basic types of churches that exist in any period of church history. Every church that truly knows Jesus as Lord can be recognized as fitting one of these seven models at some particular moment in its history. By either repentance or disobedience, a church may change from one classification to another of these seven basic types—but it can always be found somewhere within this sevenfold pattern.

Moreover, as many Bible scholars have pointed out, these letters also serve as a preview of the entire history of the church, from its beginning to its consummation. They represent seven stages or key periods in church history. This view is suggested by verse 1:3, which calls the entire book of Revelation a "prophecy." This prophecy includes chapters two and three as well as the rest of the book.

As we've previously noted, seven is the number of completeness. These seven letters, then, constitute our Lord's complete overview of the church, stage by stage, from beginning to end.

We must never forget that *all* of Revelation was written for these seven churches. Each church—not just one particular church from chapter 2 or 3—is expected to know and understand the entire book. As we explore these seven letters we will briefly trace the different historical periods of the Christian church, while also carefully examining what the Lord says to each of these seven historical churches.

Somewhere in this sevenfold list we will find your church and mine.

The Light of Truth

Light has a special significance throughout the Bible. The first words of God ever recorded in Scripture are the words He spoke at Creation: "Let there be light!"[2] And the findings of science confirm the significance of light in the created order. Astronomer Carl Sagan says that in the first moments after Creation "space was brilliantly illuminated" and did not become dark as we now see it until much later.[3] A science book published by Encyclopaedia Britannica reports that the early universe "was flooded with a light that was denser than matter."[4]

In Scripture, *light* appears as a symbol of God's Word,[5] of God's truth,[6] of God's righteousness and justice,[7] of God Himself[8] and His Son Jesus Christ.[9] In Matthew 5:14 and 16, Jesus used the symbol of light to describe us, His followers, and the impact we are to have upon the world. "You are the light of the world," He said. "Let your light shine before men, that they may see your good deeds and praise your Father in heaven."

In Revelation 1, light again is used as a powerful symbol. Jesus is described in this passage as holding seven bright stars in His right hand, and He is surrounded by seven golden lampstands. In verse 19 the Lord commands John,

> Write, therefore, what you have seen, what is now and what will take place later. The mystery of the seven stars that you saw in my right hand and of the seven golden lampstands is this: The seven stars are the angels of the seven churches, and the seven lampstands are the seven churches.

Note that a lampstand is not the light. It is the *bearer* of the light. A light-bearer holds the light so that the light itself can shine forth, illuminating its environment. The light, of course, is the truth God reveals to the world in Jesus Christ.

The world is full of learned men, of prestigious universities, of libraries that are great repositories of knowledge. Yet, despite the great accumulation of knowledge our race has amassed over the centuries, there are many truths which are unknown to man in his natural state. One place where these truths may be found is in the church, the light-bearer, the lampstand. Only in the church can mankind find the moral and redemptive light which alone can illuminate this darkening world. As members of the church, you and I are called to uphold that light and reflect it into every corner of our society.

The church is not just a holy huddle where we gather to escape the pressures of a hostile world until the Lord returns. The church is called to *move out*, to penetrate the world with the white-hot rays of God's truth. We have a powerful influence to exert and exercise in the world, and that's what these seven dynamic letters are all about.

Angels in the Church

In his bestselling novel *This Present Darkness*, Frank Peretti describes a praying, faithful community of believers called Ashton Community Church. Unseen by human eyes, this church is guarded from satanic evil by shining beings in white with swords at their sides, bearing such names as Scion, Krioni, Signa, and Triskal. These beings are angels, guarding and ministering to the church.

And while Peretti's depiction of angels as something out of an Italian Renaissance fresco—winged, clad in flowing white robes, bearing swords—may seem at times a little quaint and melodramatic, the seven letters of Revelation clearly suggest that churches *do* in fact have angels. Each of these letters is addressed to the *angel* of that particular church.

Many Bible scholars struggle over this statement. What is meant by "the angel of the church"?

It is true, as some Bible commentators note, that the word in the original text for "angel" could also be translated "messenger," which some would suggest means the pastor of the church.

In other parts of the New Testament this word in the original language does mean "messenger" rather than "angel"—but it does *not* have that meaning anywhere else in Revelation. Everywhere this word appears outside of chapters 2 and 3, it definitely refers to an *angel*—a heavenly being.

Moreover, as you carefully examine the structure of the church in the New Testament you never find a church governed by just one human leader. Leadership in the first-century church appears to have been plural—elders and pastors—and it is only in later centuries that men placed churches under the authority of a single leader. So it seems highly unlikely that these letters in Revelation are directed to a single human "messenger" or pastor.

Remember that in Hebrews angels are called "ministering spirits, sent forth to serve the heirs of salvation"—that is, Christians like you and me. It seems likely, therefore, that in those invisible but utterly real dimensions of spirit, there are angels assigned to each church to help the leaders and the congregation know what is on God's heart.

I am convinced that the "angel" or "messenger" addressed in Revelation 2 and 3 is *not* a human leader or pastor. I believe these seven letters are addressed to the *angels* of the seven churches—heavenly beings responsible for guiding the human leaders of each church.

Letters to History

It was Christmastime in 1945 at the White House. President Harry Truman strolled into one of the rooms of the family quarters only to find his wife feeding old letters, one by one, to a merry fire in the fireplace. "Bess, dear!" Harry exclaimed. "What are you doing?"

"Burning some old letters, dear."

"But those are letters I wrote to you over the past thirty years!" Harry protested. "Think of the history!"

"I *have*," Bess replied with a wink.

When you think of all the letters in the New Testament—the many letters of Paul, the epistles of Peter, James, and John, and these letters from the heart of our Lord to the seven churches in Asia—do you ever wonder if the human writers of these letters stopped to think of the history, the 2,000 years of church history that would follow, the millions and millions of believers who would someday read those words? Perhaps not. But I do know that God, when He inspired these letters, was thinking not only of the moment in which they were written, but of the centuries of history to come. That is why these ancient letters continue to live and breathe and give life to the church in our own era, as in every previous era.

You and I are making history. We are the latest links in an unbroken chain of church history that extends all the way back to the time of Jesus and His disciples. The letters of the Bible, including these seven letters to seven ancient churches, were written with history in mind. Future history. Our history, yours and mine. A history filled with computers and electronic media and space travel—and the unchanging human condition, the age-old problems of the human spirit.

So let us now turn to the first of these seven letters. If we have ears to hear, let us listen to what the Lord has to say to the churches—and to you and me.

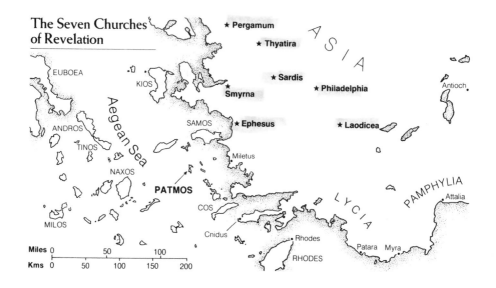

The Seven Churches of Revelation

Chapter Three

The Church That Lost Its Love

Revelation 2:1–7

W hen Daniel Webster was but a struggling young lawyer in Portsmouth, New Hampshire, he became acquainted with a lovely, delicate young woman named Grace Fletcher. She was his first love, the first woman he had ever given his heart to, and he was deeply devoted to her. Grace's father, a clergyman, allowed young Webster to call on Grace in their home. Webster spent many hours holding skeins of silk for her while she unknotted the thread so that it could be sewn. It didn't matter to him what they did together, as long as he could be near her.

On one of his visits to Grace's home to help her unknot her silken thread, Webster waited for just the right moment to speak what was on his mind. Finally, the moment came. Grace's father and mother stepped out of the room for a few moments, and Webster knew it might be a long time before they would be alone again. Screwing up every ounce of his courage, Webster said, "Grace, we have been untying these silken knots for many weeks together. I think it is time we tie a knot which will not be untied for a lifetime."

Speechless, her eyes wide, her heart tripping, Grace watched as Webster took up a piece of red ribbon and began to tie an elaborate knot in the middle of it. Then he handed the ribbon to Grace. She took it and added several more intricate loops, completing the difficult knot. This silent act was the ceremony of their engagement.

Soon afterward, Daniel Webster married Grace, a marriage which lasted until her death, 21 years later. Webster eventually remarried and lived on for many years, but he never lost his affection for his first love. Following his own death in 1852, a box was found hidden among his personal effects. Inscribed upon the box were the words "Precious Documents." Within the box were the letters he and Grace had exchanged during their courtship and marriage. They were well-worn, as if they had been often removed from the box, read, then replaced and hidden again.

And there was one other memento in Daniel Webster's box of memories: a length of red ribbon, still tied in an intricate knot.

This is a beautiful story of a man who never lost his affection for his first love. And in many ways, it is a parable of how our love for Jesus Christ should be: devoted, loyal, fond, tender, filled with remembrance, thankfulness, and yearning. Do you remember the first time you fell in love? Do you recall that feeling of always wanting to be near the object of your love, to simply bask in the presence of that person?

In Revelation 2:1-7, we meet a church that once loved Jesus that way. But tragically, at the time that we encounter this church in Revelation, the fondness, the remembrance, the yearning of that first glow of love had faded. Instead of a church that is ardently in love with its Lord, we find a church that has lost its love.

The Ephesian Story

2:1–3 *"To the angel of the church in Ephesus write:*

These are the words of him who holds the seven stars in his right hand and walks among the seven golden lampstands: I know your deeds, your hard work and your perseverance. I know that you cannot tolerate wicked men, that you have tested those who claim to be apostles but are not, and have found them false. You have persevered and have endured hardships for my name, and have not grown weary."

The first thing the Lord impresses upon the Ephesian church is that He is the Lord of *all* the churches. He holds the seven stars in His right hand, and He walks among the seven lampstands. He is in control of the angels of the churches, and He is directly observing the lampstands, the churches themselves, as He walks through their midst.

The city of Ephesus was one of the most important cities in the Roman province of Asia, a center of wealth and commerce and a crossroads of travel and trade, much like San Francisco or New York in our own era. Ephesus was a center of worship for the pagan goddess Artemis (also called Diana), and the world-renowned Temple of Artemis was located there. This temple was longer than two football fields, and was considered one of the seven wonders of the world. Its ruins can still be visited today.

The church at Ephesus was planted by the apostle Paul. You can read of its founding in Acts 19. When Paul came to Ephesus on his third missionary journey he discovered a number of disciples living there who had been given a smattering of truth by Apollos, the great orator of the early church. At the time Apollos had been at Ephesus he had known only the ministry of John the Baptist, so when Paul found these disciples at Ephesus the good news of the life, death, and resurrection of Jesus Christ was unknown to them.

Paul asked the Ephesian disciples if they had received the Holy Spirit, and they replied that they did not know the Holy Spirit had been given. So Paul explained to them about Jesus, and they believed and were baptized by the Spirit and in water. Thus the church at Ephesus was born.

Some time later Paul spent two years in Ephesus, teaching and building up this body of believers. Later he sent Timothy to the Ephesian church to ground them even more firmly in God's Word. Paul's two letters to Timothy were written while Timothy labored in Ephesus. There is even a tradition (though it is not confirmed in Scripture) that John, after writing the book of Revelation, also went to Ephesus and spent the closing days of his life there.

So the church at Ephesus was rich in church history, having enjoyed the ministering presence of some of the most prominent charter members of the Christian faith.

An Appraisal and an Appeal

This letter to the Ephesians—like the other six letters to follow—consists of both an *appraisal* and an *appeal*. There is an affirmation of what is good, plus an admonition against what is wrong. There is also an appeal for those who have fallen away to repent and return to true faith, and a spiritual promise to those who hold fast.

The Lord finds three things to affirm in the Ephesian church. First, they are committed and hardworking. "I know your deeds, your hard work and your perseverance," He says. The Ephesian Christians are activists, not couch potatoes. They take their faith seriously and put it to work. They tell others about their faith. They minister to human needs. They reach out to the homeless and the outcasts. They are busy people, and the Lord says that is good.

Second, the Ephesian Christians have sound, orthodox doctrine. The Lord commends them highly for this: "I know that you cannot tolerate wicked men, that you have tested those who claim to be apostles but are not, and have found them false." Their faith was well defined and well defended. They exposed and opposed false teachers.

And there were, unfortunately, plenty of false teachers around. In Acts 20, Paul says his final goodbye to the Ephesian elders, and he warns them to expect such teachers to come and seduce the Ephesian Christians away from true faith. He warns them to watch out for such "wolves"—and to oppose them. In Revelation 2:2, the Lord commends the Ephesian church for heeding Paul's advice.

Such "wolves" are still around today, prowling among the flocks with doctrines that are subtly yet fundamentally skewed from the truth. Certainly there are many godly, Christ-centered, biblical teachers and preachers who lead congregations, preach on radio or television, have thriving audiocassette ministries, or write books. But there are also "wolves" who do these same things. Every Christian must be on guard against deceptive doctrine. The words of every preacher, teacher, and author—including the words in the book you are holding in your hands—*must* be subjected to the pure light of God's Word.

When you do this some people will say you are being judgmental. Yet the Scriptures command us to judge what is right—and what is not right. "Test everything," says 1 Thessalonians 5:21. "Hold on to the good. Avoid every kind of evil." Similarly, in Revelation 2:2, the Lord commends and approves the Ephesian Christians for testing and judging what is right and what is wrong.

Third, the Lord commends the Ephesian Christians because they have "persevered and have endured hardships for my name, and have not grown weary." The Ephesians were not quitters, even when the going got tough. Up to this point in the letter, the Ephesian church is getting an A+ grade. But the other shoe is about to drop.

And Now the Bad News . . .

It's the old "good news, bad news" story. In verse 4, our Lord uses that fateful word *yet*. He commends the Ephesians for A, B, and C—*yet* there's the matter of D.

2:4–6 *"Yet I hold this against you: You have forsaken your first love. Remember the height from which you have fallen! Repent and do the* *things you did at first. If you do not repent, I will come to you and remove your lampstand from its place. But you have this in your favor: You hate the practices of the Nicolaitans, which I also hate."*

Now we learn there is serious trouble in the Ephesian church. Yes, there is much to applaud about this church—*yet* there is also something tragically wrong. "You have forsaken your first love," says the Lord.

So serious is this situation that the Lord says, in effect, "If you don't fix this problem, I'll have to *remove your lampstand.*" This doesn't mean that individual members of the church will lose their salvation or lose the grace of God. Rather, it means that this church will lose its ability to shed the light of truth. No matter how hardworking, persevering, and orthodox this church may be, if it loses its first love it will cease to have an illuminating impact on the world.

This first-century warning of our Lord has been fulfilled again and again in thousands of churches down to and including our own age of the 1990s. All across the world, everywhere you turn, you find church after church where congregations continue to meet, sermons continue to be preached, hymns continue to be sung, good works continue to be done— and yet there is no impact, no fire, no light. The lampstand has been removed. The community which surrounds such a church goes on about its business, blithely ignoring whatever is said and done within that quaint little building with the cross on the roof. That church has become irrelevant. So has its message. Its light has failed.

Our First Love

What does the Lord mean, "You have forsaken your first love"? What is our first love?

It is the love we felt for Jesus when we first came to know Him. It is that wonderful sense of discovery that He loves us, that He has delivered us, that He has freed us from our sins. Once our hearts went out to Him in gratitude. Once we had eyes for no one but the Lord Jesus.

Watch a young couple in love. See how they talk to each other, how they touch each other's hands, how their eyes meet! Talk to them and they probably won't even hear you. They are "spaced out." They are lost in each other. They are thinking only of the wonder of each other.

That is what it's like when a person first comes to Christ. His heart is filled with gratitude, with wonder, with amazement. "I have been *forgiven!*" he thinks. "Jesus died for *me!* God loves *me!* I can hardly believe it!"

Think of the times you've heard the testimony of a new Christian. Remember those tears of joy? Remember the trembling voice, the look of wonder on his or her face?

I have seen strong men — athletes, successful businessmen, political leaders — break down completely, unable to finish telling their own story, so overcome were they by the wonder of the fact that Jesus had come to live His life through them. Their lives had turned around 180 degrees. Their families had been rescued. Their sins had been forgiven. The love of Jesus is something new, fresh, heart-stopping, incredible. It is the feeling captured in the lines by Charles Wesley:

> Amazing love, how can it be
> That Thou My God shouldst die for me!

That is what "first love" is like.

How do we lose our first love? It happens very gradually, as our focus slowly, imperceptibly shifts from our love-relationship with Jesus to simply being busy for Him. Whereas we once delighted in serving others, singing God's praise, and studying His Word out of a wondering love for Him, we now begin to do these same things out of a subtly different motive. Now, instead of pleasing Jesus, we seek the approval of others. Our position, our status, our reputation in the church begins to matter more than our love-relationship with Jesus.

Without even noticing the change, we have lost something of our first love. The busyness, the religious activity, the pious jargon is all there — but the wonder and the intense love are gone. The light has failed. When this occurs to an entire church, then that church's lampstand is removed.

The Ephesian church trembled at the brink of this very precipice. Its light flickered, yet still shone — but for how much longer?

And could it be that you and I stand at this same brink, wavering alongside the Ephesian Christians, tottering, about to tumble off?

If so, how do we know? And how can we be rescued from such a fate?

Three Symptoms

The great English poet Alexander Pope lay on his deathbed with only a few days of life remaining. His doctor, meanwhile, was cheerily attempting to lift his spirits. "Why, Alexander," exclaimed the physician, "already your pulse is stronger, your breathing is easier, and the color is coming back into your cheeks. All the signs are completely encouraging. Soon you shall be out of that bed and back to work, as fit and robust as ever!"

"Here I am," Pope wheezed in reply, "dying of a hundred good symptoms."

So it often is with you and me. Just look at all the good symptoms in our lives—our busy religious activity, our faithful church attendance, our charitable giving and volunteerism. But could it be that we, like Alexander Pope, are "dying of a hundred good symptoms"?

Whenever Christians lose their first love, there are always telltale symptoms to watch for. I will list for you just three.

The first symptom of a fading first love is when *you lose that distinctive, glowing joy of the Christian life.* This symptom rarely shows on the outside. It's just something you know deep within you. Life becomes humdrum and routine. You listen to the Word of God or to a powerful sermon or to the testimony of a fellow Christian, and you feel you've heard it all already. Worship begins to be mechanical, routine, dull. This is a danger sign; heed it! It means you are beginning to lose your first love.

Second symptom: *you lose your ability to love others.* One of the great revelations of Scripture is that the reason we love others is because we have first been loved ourselves. When we lose that awareness of the amazing wonder of Jesus' love, it is almost inevitable that our love for others begins to fade. We become critical of others. We become complainers. We become more selective in our friendships, singling out only those who match up to our beliefs, standards, professional level, economic status. We lose our Christlike, indiscriminate, unconditional love for others—that kind of love we expressed in the days when our love affair with Jesus was warm and new and alive.

Third symptom: *we lose a healthy perspective on ourselves. Our* wants, *our* needs become more and more important in our thinking. Instead of concerning ourselves with what pleases God, we think only about pleasing ourselves.

When enough people in a church develop this symptom (and just a few is enough), the result is division and schism in the church. Instead of being focused on their love for Christ, and wanting to spread that love to others, they become focused on themselves, their own agendas, their own programs, their own interests. Self-centeredness sets in—and the light of the church flickers, falters, and fails.

These are the marks of a church that is gradually losing its first love—and this is what was happening to the church at Ephesus. The frightening thing is that there is nothing particularly unique about the Ephesian crisis. We have all been "Ephesian" in our faith at one time or another. I have. I'm sure you have, too. We know these symptoms all too well.

If the symptoms are not recognized early enough, if the disease of losing our first love goes untreated, then our light goes out. Our lampstand is removed. We cease to be light-bearers in our darkening world.

So what can we do? Is our disease treatable? Can we recover from the loss of our first love—or is the darkness inevitable?

Three Steps to Recovery

In His letter to the Ephesian church, our Lord gives three specific, practical steps to recovery: *Remember, repent*, and *return*.

First, *remember*. "Remember the height from which you have fallen," He says. Look back. Recall how you felt and how you responded when you first came to Jesus. Re-experience in your mind that sense of joy and wonder and closeness you felt when you first gave yourself to the living Christ. Re-experience that sense of inner support and strength that came to you in times of pressure and trouble. Recall the eagerness with which you went to the Lord in prayer. Warm your soul with the fond memory of the delight you took in fellowship with other believers, in hungrily devouring God's Word, in soaking up the preaching and exposition of that Word in church. Recall how you could hardly bear to miss a service, because each Sunday morning was an adventure of discovery of God's transforming truth for your life. "Remember the height from which you have fallen." Only then can you see how to undertake the journey back to that height.

Think back. Look back. Remember.

Second, *repent*. Change your mind—and change your life. That is what repentance means. Change your mind about what has taken the place of Jesus in your life. Renounce that ambition, that pride of position and reputation, that longing for approval that has replaced your original wondering love for Jesus. Many of the things you now do—your service in the church, your Sunday morning worship, your weekly Bible study, your outreach to others—will take on new meaning and fresh power from God as you replace your old prideful, self-centered motivation with a new, joyful, Christ-centered motivation.

Give up that critical spirit, that complaining attitude, that reliance on knowledge. Put Jesus back into the center of all you are and do. Allow the joy of your salvation and your amazement over God's love to permeate every endeavor you undertake.

Change your mind. Repent.

Third, *return*. "Do the things you did at first," says our Lord Jesus.

I will never forget an illustration which Dr. Robert Munger used during a pastors' conference at the Mt. Hermon Christian Conference Center near Santa Cruz, California.

Dr. Munger, who was then pastor of the University Presbyterian Church of Seattle, stood before us and drew a great circle on the blackboard. He put a big X in the middle of the circle, then turned to us and said, "As I look back on my pastoral ministry there were many years when Christ was here, like this X, at the center of all my endeavors. The Lord Jesus was real and vital to me. But in these past few years of my life, I feel I have drifted."

He turned and drew another X on the edge of the circle. "I've drifted," he said, "so that the Lord is no longer at the center but at the periphery. I want you all to know that I'm praying God will enable me to put Jesus back here," he tapped the center of the circle, "where He belongs. And I ask you to pray to that end for me."

I can testify that God answered Dr. Munger's prayers, and he has continued to be in fruitful service for the Lord. It was a moving and challenging experience to hear this man of God open his heart to us, and ask us to pray for him as he did what the Lord is calling you and me to do right now: repent and return to where you were before.

"Do the things you did at first," our Lord pleads with us. As we return to our Bibles, absorbing its truths with eager eyes; as we pray to God continually, trusting Him with all the issues of our lives, great and small; as we respond to others selflessly and compassionately out of a heart full of wondering love for the Lord Jesus; as we praise God from the depths of our hearts, full of gratitude for all He has done in our lives; as we sing praises to His name and meditate on His grace—*then* we are truly returning to our first love.

Are We Listening?

At the end of this confrontational and convicting passage, the Lord adds a comment which at first may seem puzzling and strange. "But you have this in your favor," He says. "You hate the practices of the Nicolaitans, which I also hate." What did Jesus mean?

Today there is some controversy as to who these "Nicolaitans" were. They are mentioned again in the letter to the church at Pergamum. I believe the Lord deliberately mentions the Ephesians' abhorrence of the practices of the Nicolaitans because this is the starting point for the recovery of the Ephesian church. Their spiritual fire has not entirely gone out yet, and Jesus points out to them that a coal still glows and may yet be fanned into flame. Here, in this one important respect, some of the fire of their first love remains: they hate the practices of the Nicolaitans.

As best we can tell from Scripture and the traditions of the early church fathers, the Nicolaitans were probably a sect that combined some aspects of the Christian faith with dictatorial leadership and loose sexual practices. They believed you could be Christian while your sex life reflected the unrestrained practices of the world.

In Revelation 2:6, our Lord says, in effect, "Return to your first love but retain your abhorrence of such practices, which I also hate. That is how to fan this remaining vestige of your first love into a brilliant flame once again. Start here—and return to the place you once were."

When we look at this letter from the viewpoint of church history, we see that many churches began to lose their first love in the period immediately following the death of the apostles. The "Ephesian" period of church history covers the years from A.D. 70, when the temple at Jerusalem was destroyed, to about A.D. 160, the middle of the second century. During that time, there were literally hundreds of churches that drifted away from a warm, accepting, compassionate ministry to the world, and toward a hard, formal, unloving institutional religion. The church became rife with conflict and theological arguments. Formalism and ritualism were on the rise.

In many ways, the dangerous drift of that period has come to characterize many churches in our own age. Instead of a loving, awe-inspired relationship with Jesus, we see critical spirits, religious ambition, and contentiousness abounding. Human endeavor, human dogma, and human achievement have superseded a pure love relationship with the living Lord.

So our Lord's message to the Ephesian church assumes as great (if not greater) urgency in our own darkening age.

2:7 *"He who has an ear, let him hear what the Spirit says to the churches. To him who overcomes, I will give the right to eat from the tree of life, which is in the paradise of God."*

"He who has an ear, let him hear. . . ." Do we have an ear to hear what God is saying to us? Are you and I really listening to this urgent message from the Spirit of God?

If we do, if we take the steps to remember, repent, and return to our first love, if we overcome and persevere in the original wondering love we first experienced when we gave ourselves to Jesus, then God will give us the right to eat from the Tree of Life.

Imagine it! The Tree of Life which was removed from us by sin in the book of Genesis, when Adam and Eve were cast out of the Garden of Eden, is now being offered to us again in the book of Revelation. In the concluding book of the Bible, the Word of God comes full circle.

As we shall later explore in detail, the Tree of Life appears in Revelation 22, when the new heaven and the new earth appear, with the Tree of Life in the midst of the New Jerusalem. The twelve fruits of the Tree of Life—one fruit for each month—are the food of the people of the city. You might even call it a "Fruit of the Month Club."

The Tree of Life is a symbol of our Lord Jesus. He feeds us and sustains us, and we draw our strength from Him. That is what He says to us in these verses. Feed on the Tree of Life. Listen to His words and obey them, and soon you will find that your spiritual life is flourishing. You will find yourself growing strong and resilient, even amid the pressures and struggles that come your way.

As a people, we "Ephesian" Christians are prone to drift from our first love. One hymn-writer put it this way:

> Prone to wander, Lord, I feel it.
> Prone to leave the God I love.

We are prone to forget the wonder of our Lord's self-sacrificing love for us. He is urgently, lovingly appealing to you and to me: *remember, repent*, and *return*.

The great English novelist and poet G. K. Chesterton had a reputation for absentmindedness. He relied upon his efficient and organization-minded wife to guide him in all his practical affairs, including his travel itinerary. Without her, he was literally "prone to wander."

Once, while on a lecture tour, he sent his wife a telegram which read, AM IN BIRMINGHAM. WHERE OUGHT I TO BE?

She wired back a single word: HOME.

May you and I find our way home to the safety, security, and warmth of our first love, the Lord Jesus.

Chapter Four

A Church under Pressure

Revelation 2:8–11

I t was a thriving seaport city more than 3,000 years before Christ was born, and it is still a thriving city today. During the time Revelation was written, it was a center of commerce, wealth, and architectural splendor, located about 40 miles north of Ephesus. The city fathers proclaimed it (with typical Chamber of Commerce humility) "the Pride of Asia."

Today it is the third largest city in Turkey and a major international trade center, as well as the home of the NATO southern command headquarters and the prestigious Aegean University. The city is now known as Izmir, but during the first century, when the book of Revelation was written, its name was Smyrna.

Smyrna. The name means "myrrh," a fragrant spice or perfume obtained when the tender bark of the flowering myrrh tree is pierced or crushed. It is a fitting name for the first-century church of Smyrna, which gave off a fragrance of Christ throughout the region because it was a church that was often pierced, often crushed, often afflicted.

The city of Smyrna was a center of idolatrous emperor worship. As early as A.D. 26, during the reign of Tiberius Caesar, a temple was erected to the emperor, and all the citizens of Smyrna—including Christians— were expected to worship the Roman emperor. If you were a Christian in Smyrna, you were called upon once a year to appear at the temple and either say, "Caesar is Lord," or, "Jesus is Lord." Those who refused to confess Caesar as their Lord were either imprisoned or put to the sword.

So Smyrna was a place of enormous oppression and persecution for the early church. This persecution was inflicted upon the church by the Roman government. And it was also inflicted upon the church by the Jewish community in Smyrna—a community that was fanatically hostile to the early Christian church.

These, then, are the circumstances of the church in Smyrna at the time the second letter of Revelation was written.

2:8–11 *"To the angel of the church in Smyrna write:*

These are the words of him who is the First and the Last, who died and came to life again. I know your afflictions and your poverty—yet you are rich! I know the slander of those who say they are Jews and are not, but are a synagogue of Satan. Do not be afraid of what you are about to suffer. I tell you, the devil will put some of you in prison to test you, and you will suffer persecution for ten days. Be faithful, even to the point of death, and I will give you the crown of life.

He who has an ear, let him hear what the Spirit says to the churches. He who overcomes will not be hurt at all by the second death."

That is our Lord's appraisal of the church of Smyrna. Clearly this was a church under oppression, under affliction, under severe pressure. To be a Christian in Smyrna was to exist in a twilight between two completely opposite extremes: (1) the rich, nurturing, loving fellowship of the Christian church family, and (2) the cruel and hostile surrounding society.

So as the Lord appraises the church at Smyrna—a church under pressure, living within two extremes—His message to them is a message that encompasses the extremes. He begins by identifying Himself to the Smyrna church as "the First and the Last," the One "who died and came to life again." Jesus was present at the beginning of Creation; He will be present at the end of history. He encompasses all the forces and events of the cosmos, including both death and life. The Lord's statement in Revelation 2:8 is reminiscent of His declaration to the disciples when He gave them the Great Commission in Matthew 28: "All authority in heaven and on earth has been given to me." He is the Lord of all heavenly and earthly forces.

Jesus is the Lord of all extremes, and of everything in between. It must have been a tremendous encouragement for the believers in Smyrna, who were enduring enormous persecution and pressure, to receive this reassurance from their Lord.

Jesus says, "I know your afflictions." The original Greek for *afflictions* in this verse conveys a sense of crushing, relentless pressure. From this word we get an image of a church caught in a vise and being slowly, cruelly squeezed.

Perhaps the closest analogy to what the believers in Smyrna were forced to endure would be the experience of the Jews in Nazi Germany during the 1930s. Their travel was restricted. Their shops were subject to frequent vandalism and looting. Their livelihood was destroyed. Their synagogues were defiled or destroyed. Their property was seized. They were humiliated, stigmatized, slandered, harassed, and physically assault-ed. Eventually, even their lives and their children's lives were taken.

So also the Christians in Smyrna were subject to the same kind of unrelenting pressure and affliction.

Poor—Yet Rich

Jesus then says to them, "I know . . . your poverty—yet you are rich." This is probably a reference to the economic deprivation the Christians in Smyrna faced as part of the overall pattern of persecution. Remember that Smyrna was an exceedingly prosperous city, one of the richest cities in Asia, so the "poverty" Jesus refers to could hardly have been the result of a recession or bad economic conditions. It was clearly caused by per-secution. The homes and shops of the Christians of Smyrna had probably been pillaged and their possessions taken—a common feature of early persecution. Perhaps these people—even those who were educated as teachers or doctors or lawyers—were forced to do menial labor for low wages just so they and their families could survive.

Yet, despite this picture of poverty and persecution, the Lord says to them, "You are rich!"

Poverty is a terrible thing which perhaps few of us have experienced firsthand. Since World War II, there have been periods of recession or double-digit inflation or stagnation, but nothing remotely like a genuine economic collapse. Yet until the last few decades economic depressions and panics were a fairly ordinary occurrence. Prior to the Great Depression, which began with the panic of 1929, there were major inter-national panics in the years 1797, 1820, 1835, 1857, and 1873. During such times, banks failed, factories closed down, commerce ceased. Thousands were out of work, homeless, and hungry. For the most part, the present generation has no conception of what real economic depres-sion is like.

I was a high school student during the Great Depression of the 1930s. We did not have much to eat, and we had no luxuries at all. We bought nothing but the basics, and almost never had new clothes to wear. We had nothing in the way of entertainment except a battery-operated radio (sparingly used) and whatever entertainment we could create on our own—street and sandlot sports, imaginative indoor games, and songs sung and stories told among ourselves.

We were, I suppose, poor. Yet I look back on those days as a wonderfully rich time of my life. We enjoyed each other. We laughed together. We experienced the simple joys of relationships and fellowship. We were rich in everything except material possessions.

Someone once captured what it means to be poor yet rich in the lines of a poem:

> I counted dollars while God counted crosses.
> I counted gain while He counted losses.
> I counted my worth by the things gained in store,
> But He sized me up by the scars that I bore.
> I coveted honors and sought for degrees.
> He wept as He counted the hours on my knees.
> I never knew till one day by a grave,
> How vain are the things that we spend life to save.
> I did not yet know, till a Friend from above
> Said, "Richest is he who is rich in God's love!"

There is a program on U.S. television called *Lifestyles of the Rich and Famous*. On this series, the luxury seemingly enjoyed by the rich is paraded before the viewers to ogle and desire. But as you look closely at the lives of the rich and famous you rarely discover a happy person among them. Riches do not make people happy. Many of the richest people in the world are extremely poor in the things that are truly important.

True riches, says the Lord, are those riches that are found within, where the heart is filled with grace and the love of God. "I know your poverty," He encourages the church in Smyrna, and all Christians who are poor, persecuted, and oppressed, "yet you are rich!" When our lives are full of rich relationships with other Christians and with God Himself, then we have riches indeed! That was the experience of the church in Smyrna.

A Smear Campaign

Jesus goes on to say, "I know the slander of those who say they are Jews and are not, but are a synagogue of Satan." There was a smear campaign being waged against the Christians in Smyrna! Lies were being spread about them. Their reputation was being ruined.

Historical records show that all manner of fraudulent and despicable stories were broadcast about Christians in the first century. Because Christians celebrated Holy Communion and talked about partaking of the body and blood of Christ, they were accused of being cannibals, of actually eating one another. You can imagine the horror and loathing that must have attached to the name "Christian" among those who heard such stories.

Because they refused to worship the gods who were enshrined in the pagan temples, they were called atheists and infidels. They were scorned by a world given over to idolatry.

Christians talked about being members of one another, of loving one another, so they were accused of engaging in sexual orgies. When they met together in homes for worship and fellowship, others accused them of indulging in obscene practices.

This slander was the cause of much of the suffering and persecution faced by the early Christians. It came, as Jesus tells us in this letter, from false Jews. That is, it came from people who were the physical, genetic descendants of Abraham, people who attended a synagogue in Smyrna, but who proved by the quality of their lives that they lacked the spiritual insight of their father Abraham. They scorned and slandered the truth. They hated and persecuted people whose only crime was loving God and loving one another. By persecuting the truth and being far removed from the true faith of Abraham, they were, in effect, "a synagogue of Satan."

If you've ever been the victim of slander you have at least a taste of what the Christians in Smyrna were forced to endure. There are few experiences in this life more frustrating and painful than the experience of having one's reputation destroyed. Often by the time you discover that someone is spreading lies about you, there is no way to set the record straight. Too many people have heard—and repeated!—the false report about you. The damage that is done by a smear campaign often cannot be undone.

A well-known Christian was once subjected to a campaign of lies, and he could do little to defend himself. One day, a friend approached this Christian leader and told him how much he hurt for him and sympathized with him over this trial of being slandered. Then he said, "Remember, at least they have not spit in your face yet."

Jesus could understand what the church at Smyrna was going through, for He had not only been lied about and verbally abused but His enemies had spit in His face. Moreover, they physically assaulted Him. They beat Him with rods. They mocked Him and pressed a crown of thorns onto His brow. Then they pierced Him and hung Him on a cross to die. If anyone understands what it means to be slandered, attacked, and abused without cause, it is Jesus.

And Jesus wanted the church at Smyrna to be encouraged and strengthened, for the pressure and persecution was going to grow *more intense*, not less. "Do not be afraid of what you are about to suffer," He told them. "I tell you, the devil will put some of you in prison to test you." Notice that this is the first mention of the devil in the book of Revelation. The Lord acknowledges that He who is the First and the Last is going to allow this to happen. The devil will cause some believers to be put in prison. Roman prisons were ghastly places where prisoners knew they could be hauled out of their cells and executed at any moment.

Encouragement for the Testing

But the Lord has three words of encouragement for those who will endure this severe form of persecution, three statements to strengthen and embolden the hearts of the believers in Smyrna:

First, He says, "The devil will put some of you in prison *to test you*." Many people interpret these words to mean that God seeks to learn how committed they are by this test. But this can hardly be the case since God already knows their hearts. He knows what we are able to endure even before we are subjected to it. The fact is, it is not God but we who learn from the testing we go through!

When we go through pressure or persecution or affliction or prison experiences it is we ourselves, not God, who learn from that test. We discover how much we have matured in Christ, and how trustworthy God is in times of trouble. Trials strip away our artificial and superficial supports and force us to lean on the only support that is truly reliable: the grace and strength of God Himself!

Second, He says that the persecution will last only a limited time. "You will suffer persecution," He says, "for ten days." What exactly does the Lord mean when He says "ten days"? We will examine that question more fully in a moment, but for now we can be encouraged to know that *the Lord sets the limits to our suffering.* The test will not last longer than we can endure. If the Lord says the test will last "ten days," then there is no force on earth that could make it last eleven days! The pressure under which the Smyrna congregation suffered would not last forever.

Third, He says, "Be faithful, even to the point of death, and I will give you the crown of life." We can be certain that "the crown of life" had a special significance to the Christians in Smyrna. The city was fronted by the coast of the Aegean Sea and flanked by a hill known as the Pagos. The crest of this hill was ringed by a circle of pagan temples, giving the appearance of a crown resting on the brow of the hill. Because of this crowned hill, the city of Smyrna was often called "the crown of Asia." This feature was a source of status and pride to the citizens of Smyrna.

But in the second letter of Revelation Jesus says that He will give to the Christians of Smyrna an even *better* crown—the crown of life, the enjoyment of eternal life in glory! These words of reassurance to the church in Smyrna remind us of Paul's statement in Romans that "the sufferings of this present moment are not to be compared with the glory that shall be revealed in us." And elsewhere Paul writes, "This light affliction, which is but for a moment, is working for us to produce an eternal weight of glory."

We are continually encouraged by the fact that these trials, testings, and pressures are producing something of eternal value in our lives.

The Age of Martyrs

As we discussed in chapters 2 and 3, each of the seven churches of Revelation represents a period of church history. According to this prophetic view the church in Smyrna represents a period called "The Age of Martyrs," which lasted from about A.D. 160 to the rise of the first "Christian" emperor, Constantine the Great, in A.D. 324. To call this period "The Age of Martyrs" is not to suggest that this was the only time in history when Christians have been martyred. Believers have suffered and died for their faith and their Lord from the earliest days right up to the present day. In fact, it might surprise you to learn that the century that has seen the most Christians put to death for their faith was not the first, second, or third century, *but our own twentieth century!*

But it was during the Age of Martyrs that Christians were persecuted in ways almost beyond our ability to describe or believe. Their bodies were torn apart, joint from joint, upon the racks. Their fingernails were pulled out. They were wrapped in animal skins and thrown into sports arenas to be gored by wild animals for the amusement of others. They were covered with tar, suspended in Nero's gardens, and set alight—grisly human torches to illuminate the festivities of the pagans. Other atrocities against the faithful, as gruesome or worse than those I've already mentioned, are described in *Fox's Book of Martyrs.*

One of the prominent early casualties of the Age of Martyrs was Polycarp, bishop of the church at Smyrna. As a young man Polycarp had personally known the apostle John. Perhaps he had even heard the vision of Revelation recounted from the lips of the apostle himself. Without question, Polycarp knew well the words of the letter from Jesus to the church in Smyrna: "Do not be afraid of what you are about to suffer. . . . Be faithful, even to the point of death, and I will give you the crown of life."

In A.D. 155, at the age of 86, Polycarp was brought before the Roman proconsul at Smyrna, who demanded that Polycarp take an oath renouncing Christ and placing his trust in "the Luck of Caesar." Polycarp refused. "Eighty-six years have I served the Lord Jesus," replied the bishop. "He has been faithful to me. How can I now be faithless to Him and blaspheme the name of my Savior?"

"Swear by the Luck of Caesar," the proconsul insisted, "or I will have you torn and eaten by wild beasts."

"Hand me over to the beasts," Polycarp calmly replied. "You will not change my heart. I tell you plainly that I am a Christian, even unto the death."

Enraged, the proconsul sent a messenger out into the city to proclaim that the bishop Polycarp had admitted to being a Christian. The messenger gathered a mob together in the arena of Smyrna. There the mob built a pyre of kindling, sticks, and planks, while clamoring that Polycarp be handed to them. The speed with which the bloodthirsty mob was assembled is clear evidence of the intense anti-Christian hatred that poisoned the city of Smyrna.

When Polycarp was delivered to the mob in the arena, several of the people brought forth hammers and nails with which to nail the bishop's hands and feet to the stake to keep him from struggling. "Put away those nails and let me be!" said Polycarp with such an air of authority that the men put down their hammers and nails. "The One who gives me strength to endure the flames will give me strength not to flinch at the stake."

As the wood was piled around his feet and ignited, Polycarp turned his eyes skyward and said, "O Lord God Almighty, Father of the blessed and beloved Son, Jesus Christ, I thank you for giving me this day and this hour, that I may be numbered among your martyrs, to share the cup of Jesus, and to rise again to life everlasting."

His "Amen" was wafted up in the flame and smoke of the pyre.

The Second Death

Let's look again at the Lord's promise to the church at Smyrna: "You will suffer persecution," He says, "for ten days." History tells us that there were ten separate periods of persecution in the Roman Empire. There were ten edicts of condemnation against the Christian church issued by Roman emperors, beginning with Domitian in A.D. 96 to Diocletian, the last emperor before Constantine.

In verse 11, the Lord appeals directly to each individual believer in the church of Smyrna:

"He who has an ear, let him hear what the Spirit says to the churches. He who overcomes will not be hurt at all by the second death."

To understand the term "second death" we need only to look near the end of Revelation, in chapters 20 and 21, where the phrase "second death" appears three times. There we are shown in vivid, graphic terms what is meant by "the second death." It is the terrible lake of fire, the symbol of the final judgment of all those who refuse the gospel of the grace of God. The second death was not originally prepared for humanity, but for the devil and the rebellious angels—yet it will be shared by those human beings who align themselves with the devil by refusing God's grace.

The "second death" involves complete, eternal separation from God, a torment of soul and spirit that is so devastating that it is depicted by the effect that fire has on the nerve endings of the human body. It is the fate demanded by those who say, "I don't want anything to do with God. I don't want God in my life." The God of love, of grace, of mercy, the God who gave us all free will, will at the final judgment give people what they have demanded all their lives—a total and complete separation from His love.

"If you listen to the message of this letter," says Jesus, in effect, "if you trust me in times of pressure and persecution, I will give you the gift of eternal life and you will have nothing to fear from the judgment of God. You will be kept safe from the second death."

This is the hope Paul rejoices in when he writes in Romans 8,

Neither death nor life, neither angels nor demons, neither the present nor the future, nor any powers, neither height nor depth, nor anything else in all creation will be able to separate us from the love of God that is in Christ Jesus our Lord.

Except for those believers who are alive when Jesus returns, we are all destined one day to die. Some people reading this book will die quietly in their sleep. Some are no doubt certain to go through great suffering, although the Lord has promised it will not be more than they can bear.

Some who read these words may even be martyred for their faith someday, just as Polycarp and so many other Christian saints of past and present ages have been.

Whatever happens, however death may come to us, we have the promise of Jesus that, as His faithful followers, we can never be hurt by the second death. So let us determine, as the believers of Smyrna determined, that we shall be faithful until death, no matter how or when that death shall come, secure in the fact that nothing, nothing, *nothing* in heaven or on earth will ever separate us from the love of God.

Chapter Five

The Church That Compromised

Revelation 2:12–17

I t has been said that Christians ought to live with a newspaper in one hand and a Bible in the other, for it takes one to understand the other. The newspaper records the visible events that take place across the face of the earth, day by day. The Bible looks beyond, to the invisible realm where the councils of God determine what events take place upon the earth—and also what is the *eternal* significance of those events. You cannot really understand life in all its scope and meaning unless you look into both realms.

There is no book in the Bible which more clearly discloses that invisible, eternal realm to us than the book of Revelation. As we open its pages we learn not only what will someday happen upon the earth, but we learn about what is happening now—and why. We learn the invisible, eternal counsel of God about how we are to live out our lives in the world and in the church.

In recent years the newspapers, news magazines, and television news reports have been focused on many of the same problems which are addressed in the Lord's third letter to the churches in Revelation—problems of scandal, immorality, and corruption in high places in the Christian church. For example, the second-highest-rated segment of ABC's *Nightline* show was one which featured an interview with a tel-evangelist involved in a major sex-and-hush-money scandal. These well-publicized religious debacles have brought shame, scorn, and disgrace upon the Christian church and the Christian gospel. So it also was in the church at Pergamum.

2:12–16 *"To the angel of the church in Pergamum write:*

These are the words of him who has the sharp, double-edged sword. I know where you live—where Satan has his throne. Yet you remain true to my name. You did not renounce your faith in me, even in the days of Antipas, my faithful witness, who was put to death in your city—where Satan lives.

Nevertheless, I have a few things against you: You have people there who hold to the teaching of Balaam, who taught Balak to entice the Israelites to sin by eating food sacrificed to idols and by committing sexual immorality. Likewise you also have those who hold to the teaching of the Nicolaitans. Repent therefore! Otherwise, I will soon come to you and will fight against them with the sword of my mouth."

Notice how sharply these words contrast with the Lord's previous message to the church in Smyrna. The church in Smyrna was enduring enormous pressure and persecution. The church in Pergamum was flirting with corruption and immorality.

It seems that the devil has two very effective weapons which he delights in using against the church: intimidation and/or enticement. He either seeks to make the church knuckle under—or he tries to tempt and lure the church into destroying itself. The church is hemmed in on one side by the violence and terror of a roaring lion, and on the other side by the cloying corruption of a fallen angel of light. The fellowship at Pergamum is fast being undermined by corrupt practices and corrupt teaching.

The Double-Edged Sword

In His letter, Jesus identifies Himself as the One having "the sharp, double-edged sword." As we previously discovered, the sharp, double-edged sword is a symbol of the Word of God, proceeding with power from the lips of Jesus. Because it is double-edged it cuts two ways. I believe this is a reference to the fact that the Word can cleave the skull so as to reach the mind, and it can also pierce the heart so that it can touch the emotions.

The Word of God awakens us to objective reality. It appeals to the thinking, reasoning dimension of our humanity. It speaks to the mind. By its light, we can see truth that would otherwise be hidden from our sight.

The Word of God is a reasonable book, through which God appeals to us, saying, "Come now, let us reason together."[1]

The Word of God also awakens feelings within us. It inspires our awe and our reverence. It touches us with the message of God's unconditional love and forgiveness toward us. It thus activates the will. It appeals to the soul and spirit. By its fire, our hearts are warmed and energized.

The emotional power of the Word of God was demonstrated on the day of Pentecost. Peter stood before a crowd in the Jerusalem marketplace and preached a message about Jesus Christ from two Old Testament books, the Psalms and the prophet Joel. After Peter had finished preaching the people who listened to him "were cut to the heart" and asked Peter and the other apostles standing with him, "Brothers, what shall we do?" In other words, "Tell us what we can do to be saved!" As a result, three thousand people found faith in Jesus Christ that day.[2]

Clearly, the Word of God has power to touch both the intellect and the conscience.

Where Satan Has His Throne

Pergamum was the Roman capital of the province of Asia, boasting a population of around a quarter of a million souls. Located about fifty miles north of Smyrna, it was a center of pagan idol worship and emperor worship. Jesus calls Pergamum the place "where Satan has his throne"—that is, the place where Satan rules. He also calls it the city "where Satan lives"—that is, where Satan has his headquarters.

Many Bible scholars think this is a reference to the great altar of Zeus which stood on a hillside overlooking the city. This altar was in the form of a great throne or chair, forty feet high. From almost any place in the city, you could look up and see what the Lord called "Satan's throne." Because Pergamum was such an influential center of pagan worship, the Lord portrayed it in His third letter as the very focus of satanic evil.

There is a fascinating historical footnote in connection with "Satan's throne" in Pergamum. In 1878, an archaeological team, working under the auspices of the Berlin Museum, began excavating in and around the site of ancient Pergamum. The team unearthed several fabulous historical finds, including a beautiful hillside terrace theater, a magnificent temple to the goddess Athena, and—most amazing of all—the great altar of Zeus, "Satan's throne" itself!

Considered one of the most valuable and intriguing artifacts of Hellenistic culture, the throne of Zeus is richly ornamented with carved figures from pagan mythology. It was removed from Pergamum and shipped to Germany where, for over a hundred years it has remained on display in the Pergamum Museum in East Berlin. Such sites as Hitler's bunker, the Nazi Reich Chancellery, and the pre-unification communist government's Palace of the Republic are all located within twenty-five miles of "Satan's throne."

Could there be some connection between Pergamum's satanic altar-throne and the black rise of Nazism or the gray oppression of East German communism? I leave that for you to judge.

The Lord's Affirmation of the Pergamum Church

The first half of the Lord's assessment of the Pergamum church is an affirmation of its strengths. He affirms the Pergamum believers because they have remained true to His name. They have refused to budge on the issue of who Jesus Christ is. They hold sound doctrine concerning the fact that Jesus is the God-man—not godlike, not half-man, half-God, *but fully God and fully man in one completely whole person.* Almost all the heresies from that day until our own day flow out of a corruption of this basic truth, out of a denial of the deity of Jesus.

Jesus also affirms the fact that the Pergamum believers risked their own lives for the faith. He says, "You did not renounce your faith in me, even in the days of Antipas, my faithful witness, who was put to death in your city—where Satan lives."

The name *Antipas* means "against all." We do not know much about this man, although he is said to be the first martyr under the Roman persecution in Asia. Tradition holds that Antipas was tortured to death, seared alive inside a hollow brass statue in the form of a bull which was heated until it glowed white-hot. That is the price Antipas paid for being true to his faith in Jesus Christ. He had to literally stand "against all."

The Lord's Rebuke of the Pergamum Church

The second half of the Lord's assessment of the Pergamum church is a rebuke for the serious errors that undermine the soundness of this church. One such error is what Jesus calls "the teaching of Balaam." This is a reference to Numbers 22 to 25, where Balaam, a false prophet, is hired by King Balak of Moab to place a curse on the nation of Israel. Balaam attempts to impose the curse, but every time he opens his mouth, out comes not a curse but a *blessing!* God would not let Balaam and King Balak curse His people.

Yet Balaam was so determined to achieve his evil purpose that he paid women from Moab and Midian to entice and seduce the men of Israel into sexual immorality. Because these women were worshipers of idols, they also seduced the Israelites into following their false gods. Thousands of Israelites suffered and died because of Balaam's error and Israel's sin.

So Jesus, in Revelation 2:14, warned the Christians in Pergamum not to be seduced by the same error. Peter issued the same warning when he wrote about those "with eyes full of adultery" who "seduce the unstable," who "have left the straight way and wandered off to follow the way of Balaam."[3]

The error of Balaam continues to threaten the church in our own day: it is the practice of pornography, adultery, fornication, and cohabitation (living together as husband and wife without the sanction of marriage). Many individual Christians, individual churches, and even some entire denominations openly tolerate or endorse such behavior, and the result is the same today as it was in Balaam's day: emotional, psychological, spiritual, and even physical damage to many lives. Those who engage in such behavior are invariably led away from God and closer to their own destruction.

Another error Jesus warns against is "the teaching of the Nicolaitans." In chapter 3, as we examined the Lord's letter to the Ephesian church, we saw that He affirmed the Ephesians for hating the *practices* of the Nicolaitans. The Nicolaitans, remember, were probably a sect that combined aspects of the Christian faith with loose sexual practices. There is also historical evidence that the Nicolaitans claimed to have a special relationship with God and special revelations from God. In other words, they claimed to be spiritually superior to other people and presumed to take the place of the Hebrew priesthood.

The name *Nicolaitans* means "conquerors of the people," and there is evidence in church history that the Nicolaitan cult did indeed "conquer" many Christians and even entire churches, leading them into error and destruction. Their doctrines appealed to both physical lust and sinful spiritual pride.

The teachings of the Nicolaitans can still be found today in churches where an "imperial pastor" is put on a pedestal and given a kind of spiritual supremacy over the laypeople. Such pastors claim to have a more intimate relationship with God. Such churches seem to view themselves as a theater filled with spectators, all watching the performance of their pastor.

But the Christian life is not a spectator sport. Rather, we are all expected to be players on the field, part of the game plan. A church can be likened to a football team. When we gather together on Sunday for worship, we are "in the huddle." We are there to learn the game strategy and to become motivated for the struggle of the game. Monday through Saturday, on the playing field of everyday life, we all do our part for the team, and for our ultimate Coach, the Lord Jesus. No one is on the sidelines or in the stands. We are all in the game.

How, then, should a church deal with such threats as the error of Balaam or the teaching of the Nicolaitans, whether in the present day or in the day of John the apostle? Jesus' reply was, in effect, you deal with error with a sharp, two-edged sword! "Repent," He said. "Otherwise, I will soon come to you and will fight against them with the sword of my mouth." The Word of God exposes both the error of immorality and the error of spiritual pride and priestly superiority. That is one reason why many churches in our time ignore the clear exposition of Scripture.

The Pergamum Stage of Church History

As we've previously seen, each of the seven churches of Revelation corresponds to a period of church history. The Pergamum stage is that period of time between the accession of Constantine the Great in A.D. 324 to the sixth century, when the era of the popes began. During that period of time, the great councils of the church—Nicaea, Constantinople, Ephesus, Chalcedon, and others—determined and canonized the true doctrine of the person of Jesus Christ—who He was and how He combined in Himself the full nature of God and of man.

But this was also the time of the first "marriage" between church and state, when Constantine made Christianity the official religion of the Roman Empire. In fact, the name *Pergamum* means "marriage" and comes from the same root word from which we get such words as *monogamy* and *bigamy*.

Despite the seemingly desirable goal of fostering the rise of Christianity by making it the state religion, Constantine was not an orthodox Christian. In fact, he adopted many pagan practices and brought them into the church where they became accepted. By this time in its history the church was enjoying considerable popularity. It had come to be viewed not so much as a family of faith, but as a formal, institutional, worldly kingdom, much like any other kingdom. As the church's political influence grew throughout the Pergamum period of history, its spiritual influence waned.

Symbols of Intimacy

At the close of His letter to the church at Pergamum, the Lord gives a special promise to the believers of that far-off place and time—but also to believers of our own time.

2:17 *"He who has an ear, let him hear what the Spirit says to the church-es. To him who overcomes, I will give some of the hidden manna. I will also give him a white stone with a new name written on it, known only to him who receives it."*

This promise is addressed to all those who heed the warnings of this letter, who are vigilant and faithful in the areas of sexual immorality, spiritual superiority, and spiritual pride. If you and I stand fast against the lure of corruption and the lust for power over others, Jesus promises that we will be given several things—secret things with a special significance.

First, He says He will give us "hidden manna." Second, He will give us a white stone. Third, upon that stone will be written a new name, known only to ourselves. Here is a beautiful symbolic picture of special intimacy with God.

Manna was the food from heaven with which Moses fed the people of Israel in the wilderness.[4] Jesus Himself is the food from heaven on which you and I may feed. In John 6, Jesus says, "I am the bread that came down from heaven." He is the "hidden manna." He is the food for the inner spirit—a food that others do not know about.

In John 4, the Lord sent His disciples into the city of Sychar to get food. When they came back and found He had been ministering to the woman at the well, He said, "I have food to eat that you know nothing about." Jesus fed upon the inner strength He found in His intimate relationship with God the Father. We find that same inner nourishing and strength when we experience true intimacy with God as we resist the lure of moral impurity and spiritual conceit.

Jesus also promises a white stone with our new name—a *secret* name—written upon it. The symbol of the white stone is significant because the Romans of John's time used it as a mark of special favor. The secret name written upon the white stone was, of course, another symbol of intimacy, of a special, intimate relationship with God.

A number of years ago, the well-known Christian author Elisabeth Elliot came to speak at Peninsula Bible Church, where I served as pastor. I had read several of her books, including one she wrote about her life with missionary Jim Elliot, who was martyred in Ecuador. In that book, she referred to herself as Betty a number of times, so while she was visiting at PBC, I called her Betty. After a while, she took me aside and said, "Could I ask a favor? Would you please call me Elisabeth? You see, Betty was Jim's private name for me."

I immediately understood. A private name is a special mark of intimacy. The name Betty was a mark of the special relationship Elisabeth

Elliot enjoyed with her late husband. She cherished that name and very properly wanted to preserve its special value. From that moment on, I called her Elisabeth.

If we know the Lord Jesus and if we keep our hearts pure from the corrupting influences of the world around us, He has promised to give us a new name, a secret name, a special mark of intimacy with Him. That name signifies not merely a change in what we are *called,* but a change in what we have *become:* We are new creatures, with a new nature, heirs to a new and exciting destination in eternity—a rich, warm, intimate relationship with Jesus Christ that goes on and on forever.

Chapter Six

The Worldly Church

Revelation 2:18-29

The beginnings of the modern city of Akhisar in western Turkey are shrouded in mystery. No one knows when it was founded. Once it was a little village named Pelopia, nestled in a fertile plain on the banks of the Zab River. Around 300 years before the birth of Christ, it became a Greek colony and was renamed Thyatira—the name by which it is known in the book of Revelation. During the time of the writing of Revelation, it was a Roman colony.

Located about 35 miles southeast of Pergamum, Thyatira was a small but bustling commercial center on the main road between Pergamum and Laodicea. In many ways, modern Thyatira, the Turkish city of Akhisar, is much like it was in the days of the apostle John. Akhisar is still a busy commercial center, and even in the 1990s its most important exports are essentially the same products that ancient Thyatira was known for: cotton and wool cloth, fruits, and dyes.

In fact, the word "dyes" may jog your memory if you are familiar with the New Testament, because in the book of Acts we are introduced to a woman named Lydia, who was led to the Lord by the apostle Paul in the city of Philippi. Lydia was a seller of purple dyes and dyed goods, and she originally came from the city of Thyatira.[1]

It might surprise you to know that Thyatira was a city in which trade unions were very important. You might think that trade unionism had its beginnings in the "sweat shop" factories and coal mines of nineteenth-century England and America, but the truth is that carpenters, dyers, merchants, clothmakers, and other trade workers had organized into fraternal guilds even before the time of Christ. In Thyatira the trades were so strongly unionized that it was difficult to make a living without being a guild member—a fact which will soon become very important in our study of the Lord's fourth letter in Revelation.

In this letter, Jesus begins with a word of affirmation.

2:18–19 *"To the angel of the church in Thyatira write:*
These are the words of the Son of God, whose eyes are like blazing fire and whose feet are like burnished bronze. I know your deeds, your love and faith, your service and perseverance, and that you are now doing more than you did at first."

I think it is significant that the title "the Son of God" appears in these verses for the first and only time in the entire book of Revelation. Some cults, sects, and nonbelievers claim that Jesus never said He was the Son of God, yet here is one of several New Testament passages where He clearly makes that claim.

In this passage Jesus stresses the fact of His deity and adds to the claim such potent, memorable imagery as "eyes . . . like blazing fire," and "feet . . . like burnished bronze." The picture of eyes like blazing fire suggests His ability to pierce the facades, disguises, and pretensions of His people. Nothing can be hidden from the hot gaze of His truth. The picture of feet like burnished bronze suggests His ability to trample sin and injustice underfoot, His authority to punish evil.

Both the eyes of blazing truth and the bronze feet of justice are needed at the church in Thyatira. Tragically, it is the most corrupt of the seven churches of Revelation.

An Attractive Church

The church at Thyatira was neither dead nor doomed to die. The Lord found many things to affirm in this church. "I know your deeds," He said, "your love and faith, your service and perseverance." These four qualities—love, faith, service, and perseverance—are inter-related.

Love leads to service. If you love God, you will serve His people. You cannot help it. Service is the visible sign, the outward expression of a heart full of love.

Faith leads to perseverance. If you have faith, you will persevere. You now understand that God is in control of all the circumstances of life and things will always work out for His good purpose. When you have faith you keep at your work. You do not quit.

Within the fellowship at Thyatira were many believers who loved God, who served His people, who had faith in His word, and who persevered. As they loved God and served others, the church grew. And, as the Lord observed, the church had grown in these qualities since its early days: "you are now doing more than you did at first."

That is the way churches grow: People are always attracted by the reality of Christian love, the heartfelt compassion of Christian service, the stirring hope of Christian faith, the challenging example of Christian perseverance. People who stand outside the church and see such qualities being lived out in the name of Jesus are like hungry children standing outside the window of an ice cream shop with their noses pressed against the glass. They earnestly desire what they see inside.

If you and I could stand among the believers in Thyatira, we would be marvelously impressed by all that we see: the busyness, the bustling activity, the personal warmth and caring of many wonderful people, the deep faith, the concern and care for others. It was a very attractive church—on the outside.

But something was dreadfully wrong deep within.

Jezebel

2:20–23 *"Nevertheless, I have this against you: You tolerate that woman Jezebel, who calls herself a prophetess. By her teaching she misleads my servants into sexual immorality and the eating of food sacrificed to idols. I have given her time to repent of her immorality, but she is unwilling. So I will cast her on a bed of suffering, and I will make those who commit adultery with her suffer intensely, unless they repent of her ways. I will strike her children dead. Then all the churches will know that I am he who searches hearts and minds, and I will repay each of you according to your deeds."*

Evidently, there was a woman in the church at Thyatira who was influential, domineering—and depraved. Jesus names her "Jezebel." That, of course, was not this woman's given name, but rather a name the Lord gave her to indicate her character. Jesus often renamed people according to their inner qualities, much as He renamed Simon, an ill-educated fisherman, to show that he would one day emerge as a "rock," as "Peter." Without question, everyone in the church at Thyatira knew who Jesus meant when He said "Jezebel." Equally without question, Jesus chose to give her the name of the most evil and loathsome woman in the Old Testament.

The original Jezebel in the Old Testament was the daughter of the king of Sidon, an ancient town in Lebanon that has been in the headlines of our own era as a major site of bloodshed and upheaval.2 Jezebel was the wife of King Ahab of the Northern Kingdom of Israel, and she is particularly noted for having introduced and made popular the worship of the pagan god Baal in Israel.

Baal was a fertility god, and the worship of Baal involved obscene sexual practices and temple prostitutes, both male and female. The worship of this demonic god spread throughout Israel because of Jezebel's influence, and she used her wealth to sponsor more than 800 false prophets of Baal.

It was Jezebel who attempted to murder the prophet Elijah after his famous encounter with 480 false prophets of Baal on Mount Carmel. There, you recall, the false prophets failed in their attempt to call down fire from their god Baal to consume a sacrificial bull. But when it was Elijah's turn, he called upon God, and God sent fire from heaven to consume not only the sacrifice upon the altar, but the wood fuel, the stones of the altar, the dust of the ground, and the water Elijah had poured upon it all. When Jezebel learned of the humiliation and defeat of Baal and the prophets of Baal, she threatened Elijah's life.3

Jezebel also murdered her neighbor Naboth so that her husband, the king, could seize the dead man's vineyard. Jezebel was a ruthless, godless, calculating, power-mad seducer of the people. According to Old Testament prophecy, her life ended when she was thrown from the palace window into the courtyard below. There her body was set upon by dogs, who licked up her blood.4

As we gain an understanding of what kind of evil woman the original Jezebel was we begin to see exactly what Jesus means when He calls the tyrant who dominates the Thyatira church by the name Jezebel. The Jezebel in Thyatira called herself a "prophetess," and there is nothing innately wrong with that. No Scripture forbids a woman from exercising the gift of prophecy per se. There were other prophetesses in the Bible, both in the Old Testament and the New. Philip, the Spirit-filled evangelist of the book of Acts, had four daughters who were prophetesses and who faithfully exercised their spiritual gift for the edification of the church.5

The problem with Thyatira's Jezebel was not that she was a prophet of the feminine gender, but that she was a false prophet. The Lord tells us what her corrupt teaching consisted of: seducing believers into tolerating, accepting, and engaging in immorality and idolatry.

"Business Is Business"

At this point we find the link between this evil woman Jezebel in the Thyatira church and the pervasive economic control of the Thyatiran trade unions. In order to make a living in Thyatira, a citizen of the city was required to join a union or guild. The membership of these guilds was comprised largely of pagans. The problem for the Christians in Thyatira was that the meetings of the guilds were mostly devoted to idol worship and the licentious debaucheries associated with the Greek culture's erotic idols.

The English Bible scholar William Barclay describes the dilemma of the Thyatiran Christians this way:

> These guilds met frequently, and they met for a common
> meal. Such a meal was, at least in part, a religious ceremony. It
> would probably meet in a heathen temple, and it would certain-
> ly begin with a libation to the gods, and the meal itself would
> largely consist of meat offered to idols. The official position of
> the church meant that a Christian could not attend such a
> meal.[6]

Here was the problem: These Thyatiran Christians had to belong to a union in order to make a living—yet belonging to the union meant they were pressured (and perhaps even required) to participate in immoral sexual practices and idol worship. So these Christians had to make a decision—a decision that in many cases came down to a raw choice between remaining faithful to God and simple physical survival for themselves and their families.

Worst of all, this Jezebel in the Thyatira church was teaching that it was all right for the Thyatiran believers to join the unions, to submit to the pressures of the surrounding evil culture, and that God would over-look their sin. Her philosophy was one we often hear these days whenev-er Christians want to excuse or justify an unethical or immoral business practice: "Business is business." If your Christian principles get in the way of your success in business, then it is those Christian principles that have to go. "I have to make a living, don't I?" is the plea of many. I've heard this argument many times. You've probably heard it, too.

Here again we see how powerfully applicable and relevant the book of Revelation is to our own time and problems. The Thyatira syndrome is closely paralleled by many churches in our era. There are churches which endorse homosexuality as an alternate lifestyle, churches which do not discipline their members who engage in sexual immorality, churches which allow pornography to go unchallenged in their midst.

But the Lord holds such churches accountable today, just as He did in the first century. His charge against them is, "You tolerate that woman Jezebel." This is a problem that church leadership must face today just as church leaders of the apostle John's era had to.

Notice that in the letters to the churches at both Pergamum and Thyatira the Lord links sexual immorality with idolatry. At first glance we may wonder what one has to do with the other. In fact, however, one inevitably leads to the other. Fornication and adultery are clear-cut violations of what the Word of God clearly commands. So when a person engages in sexually impure behavior, he or she deliberately violates the authority of God. Even if that person verbally professes to be a Christian, he or she is living a lifestyle in which God is no longer their God.

Now the link between immorality and idolatry becomes clear: If people reject the Lord's authority over their lives and if God is no longer God in their lives, *then they must find another god!* It is impossible for the human spirit to thrive without something to live for, something larger than itself—and that *something* is what a god is! Whatever makes your life worthwhile becomes your god. It may be the god of pleasure, of self-gratification, even of sexual self-indulgence. Or it may be the god of wealth, success, ambition, power, or fame.

The point is that we "enlightened," "modern," "sophisticated" people still have our idols, just as the ancients had. Our idols may not be carved out of wood or stone. But they are just as real, just as seductive, just as dishonoring and offensive to the one true God.

For most of us, our greatest temptation to idolatry can be found in our place of work—in the office, on the campus, at the store, on the road. It is there that we spend most of our waking hours, there that we invest so much of our self and our aspiration, there that we are under the greatest pressure to compromise and knuckle under to the corrupt standards of the dying world around us. As Earl Palmer reminds us,

> The most subtle challenge to faith does not usually originate in public amphitheaters but in the daily places where we earn the money we need to live. . . . A job that is worshiped is a job badly done. This is because we ask too much from the job we are doing—from the company, from the union, from the success of financial achievement. What the trades need, what professions need, what all deployments of our lives need is not our soul but our skill, not our worship but our hard work. When we once learn

this vital alignment of values, we will do better in our work, and have fewer ulcers too. Idolatries, whether of the dramatic amphitheater type or the low-grade office type, always make us sick.[7]

The Disease of Immorality and Idolatry

The punishment our Lord assesses against the corrupt teaching of Thyatira's Jezebel reflects the seriousness of the disease of immorality and idolatry. Notice that this punishment involves three parties.

First, there is Jezebel herself. Jesus says, "I will cast her on a bed of suffering." There is a note of irony and even sarcasm in this statement. A bed, in this instance, implies a place not of sleeping but of illicit sexual union. He is saying, in effect, "If it's a bed she wants, so be it—but it will prove to be a bed of pain, not pleasure." The "bed of suffering" is an inducement for Jezebel to recognize her sin—and to repent of it.

Second, there is a group of people around Jezebel who will also be subject to punishment. The Lord says, "I will make those who commit adultery with her suffer intensely, unless they repent of her ways." This is a reference to those who practice immorality and idolatry after the corrupt example of Jezebel.

The suffering Jesus refers to may well be a reference to sexually transmitted diseases. Gonorrhea and syphilis were common in the ancient world and are still with us today. In our own century, such sexually transmitted diseases as chlamydia, type II herpes simplex, and AIDS have been identified as the causes behind untold human suffering, from disfigurement, blindness, birth defects, and sterility to the most horrible, wasting form of death imaginable. I have known people dying of AIDS, and words are completely inadequate to express how horrifying and excruciating this disease is, both physically and emotionally.

Third, the Lord says, "I will strike her children dead." This is a reference not to physical children but to those who are spiritually the children of Jezebel—that is, those who have absorbed her teaching, who have lived their own lives by it, and who now teach others to do the same. The death Jesus refers to is, I believe, *spiritual* death, what He calls "the second death" in His letter to the church at Smyrna. The second death is the terrible destruction of the lake of fire.[8] This extreme form of punishment is merited by the "children" of Jezebel because their commitment to a lifestyle of evil, along with their corrupt teaching, makes repentance difficult and unlikely.

Judgment and Discipline

Does this mean that the Thyatira Jezebel and those around her are doomed? Is there still hope that they might repent and be spared from the judgment of God?

Yes. The Lord is gracious and always leaves the door of repentance and forgiveness open. The key phrase He uses in this passage is *"unless they repent of her ways."* As John recorded the Lord's words to the believers in Thyatira, there was still time for them to change their ways. But *would* they?

When people go through times of affliction or have a close brush with death as a result of sickness, accident, natural catastrophe, or war, they often come through such times with a new recognition of their own powerlessness and mortality. At such times people have an opportunity to think hard about their way of life — and about whether they should *change* their way of life. Such events may seem harrowing, frightening, or even punishing, yet God can use these events to shake us, rouse us, and shout "Wake up!" to us. He wants to use all the circumstances of our lives, both our pain and our joy, to draw us closer to Him.

God has attempted to reach the Jezebel in the church at Thyatira, giving her time to repent of her immorality. Jesus ultimately concludes, however, that she is unwilling to repent. She has hardened her heart. As a result, judgment must come. In verse 23, Jesus says, "Then all the churches will know that I am he who searches hearts and minds, and I will repay each of you according to your deeds."

The purpose of judgment and discipline within the church is *purification*. A pure church is a strong church. The more aware we are of our weaknesses and hidden areas of sin, the more alert we become to sin's destructive power in our lives. We are better able to arm ourselves against temptation and to guard ourselves against becoming conformed to the dying world around us. We can stand against the tide and swim against the current.

The church at Thyatira needed this kind of purification. So do many churches in our time. Tragically, there are all too few churches in our time that have the courage, conviction, and obedience to Scripture to undertake the purifying process of church discipline.

The process of church discipline derives from such passages as 1 Corinthians 5 and Matthew 18:15-17. It is used on those rare occasions when a church member is engaged in a pattern of behavior that is destructive to himself and to the purity of the church. At the top of the list of such behavior in 1 Corinthians 5 is sexual immorality, but the apostle

Paul also includes unethical business practices, idolatry, slander, substance abuse, and thievery as causes for church discipline. The motive for biblical church discipline is always two-fold: (1) love for the sinner himself, a desire to call him to repentance for his own spiritual welfare, and (2) love for the church, a desire to keep it pure, undefiled, and distinct from the sinful world around it.

Every church will someday know, says the Lord, that He is the one who searches hearts and minds and who repays each according to his or her deeds. A church that obediently practices self-purification will be repaid according to its good deeds and its purity. A church that must be forcibly purified by the Lord will be repaid according to the evil which it tolerated and condoned.

The original Greek phrase rendered "hearts and minds" in verse 23 would, if strictly translated, read "kidneys and hearts"—a phrase that would be jarring and meaningless to the modern mind. The translators simply chose a phrase that would convey the same sense to the modern mind that "kidneys and hearts" did to the ancient mind.

People in the first century regarded the kidneys as the source of feelings. If your kidneys were not working well, then you wouldn't feel good either. They viewed the heart as the seat of the will, of decision-making, of volition. So what the Lord means when He says that He searches "the kidneys and the hearts" is that our feelings are important, our deliberate choices are important, and each of us will be held responsible for his or her choices. We cannot shift the blame for our actions to anyone else. We are accountable to God.

The Devil's Millennium

We have examined the dynamics of the historic church of Thyatira and its relevance to our own lives and our churches today. Now let's take a *prophetic* look at the church of Thyatira and discover what age of church history this church symbolizes.

The Thyatiran church, remember, was the most corrupt of the seven churches. Accordingly, this church clearly symbolizes the darkest and most corrupt period of Christian history. It foreshadows the time from the sixth century to the sixteenth century—a thousand-year period that has been variously called "The Dark Ages," "The Middle Ages," and even "The Devil's Millennium."

It was a time when the institutional church had become very powerful and very corrupt. It defiled itself by combining pagan rites and magical practices with watered-down Christian teaching. Believers were taught to venerate and pray to images. The church was organized into a massive, intricate multi-level structure which more closely resembled worldly government than the simple servant-leadership we see exercised in the New Testament. The elite hierarchy of the church introduced practices which were unknown in Scripture or the early church. Religious authorities sought to dominate the political sphere of power.

During the sixth century the Bishop of Rome became accepted as the dominant figure in the church, and the office of pope came into being. For centuries the pope was more powerful than emperors and kings. On one occasion the pope summoned a German emperor to Rome and then forced him to stand barefoot in the snow for several hours before he would receive him. When the king was finally permitted to enter the presence of the pope, he was required to crawl on his hands and knees. Such was the power, arrogance, and corruption of the church during "The Devil's Millennium."

Yet, just as there were many within the corrupt church at Thyatira who loved God, who served His people, who had faith in His word, and who persevered, there were many Christians during "The Devil's Millennium" of church history who were equally faithful. The monasteries which flourished during this time served as hospitals and refuges for the sick, the poor, and the oppressed. Some of the most beautiful and enduring hymns and literature of our faith were written by devoted Christians of those days—Bernard of Clairvaux, Francis of Assisi, Thomas Aquinas, Meister Eckhart, Jan van Ruysbroeck, Catherine of Siena, and Thomas à Kempis, to name a few.

Yet these devoted, compassionate, faithful people were just islands of light in a sea of religious darkness. The "Thyatira stage" of church history could only be characterized as a period of incalculable oppression, corruption, and depravity. The evil influence of that period of history continues to reverberate in our own time, and it will culminate in a future time that is described for us in Revelation 17 and 18. There we will see the great harlot who rides the beast and who has assumed dominion over the kings of the earth.

It is a common notion among Bible commentators to identify the "harlot" only with the Roman Catholic Church, but I am convinced that this is a serious mistake. Although many of the doctrines, practices, and structures of the Roman Catholic Church are rooted in the "Thyatira stage" of church history, it is not the only branch of Christendom that suffers from these errors.

For centuries we Protestants have strongly differed with Rome over a number of issues, especially the "Three M's"—Mary, the Mass, and the Magisterium (that is, the form of government of the church). But you will find many of these errors also in the great Orthodox churches of the East, the Coptic church in Egypt, the Anglican and Lutheran churches of northern Europe, and many of the great Protestant denominations in America and around the world. In fact, the seeds of Thyatiran error are everywhere you look.

Wherever there are domineering, power-seeking "church bosses" like Thyatira's Jezebel; wherever Christians begin to accommodate themselves to the moral laxity and impurity of the surrounding society; wherever Christians slip into the idolatrous mindset of allowing ambition, self-gratification, and pride to remove God from the throne of their lives; wherever church structure becomes more important than Christian love, service, faith, and perseverance—at that point, that church, regardless of its denomination or its history, has become Thyatiran in character. The Lord will repay that church according to its deeds.

Hold On!

Now comes a sensitive and encouraging word, straight from the heart of the Lord to the hearts of those who remain faithful amid the corruption of the Thyatiran church.

2:24–25 *"Now I say to the rest of you in Thyatira, to you who do not hold to her teaching and have not learned Satan's so-called deep secrets (I will not impose any other burden on you): Only hold on to what you have until I come."*

Here, for the first time in Revelation, our Lord lays special emphasis on His coming. Notice, too, the phrase "Satan's so-called deep secrets." This indicates that when a church drifts away from its moral purity, it invariably drifts toward the things of Satan, toward mystical rites and occultic rituals.

People love to feel they are a part of something special and secret. They love to feel that they are the initiated, the knowledgeable, the ones who know what the "truth" is. As a result we are seeing a proliferation of mystical cults and movements arising across our society. The New Age movement seduces people by the thousands with its promise of "so-called deep secrets"—revelations from powerful spirit beings who can impart information that ordinary folk on the outside just don't have.

Notice how the Lord's reference to the deep secrets of Satan parallels Paul's words in 1 Corinthians 2:10: "The Spirit searches all things, even the deep things of God." It seems that whenever God has something good, Satan imitates it. The dark and hidden matters of Satan are his twisted imitation of the wonderfully deep truths in the Word of God.

The Lord's message of encouragement to the faithful in Thyatira is *Hold on*! "Only hold on to what you have until I come." He says in effect, "Do not let go of the truth. Do not let go of your moral standards. It may be difficult to live for Christ in a worldly and corrupt church, but remain faithful until I come."

To those who hold fast until His return, the Lord gives an inspiring word of promise.

2:26–27 *"To him who overcomes and does my will to the end, I will give authority over the nations—*

'He will rule them with an iron scepter;
he will dash them to pieces like pottery'—

just as I have received authority from my Father."

The Old Testament quotation in these verses is from Psalm 2, and it is a reference to the rule of the Messiah in the earthly kingdom called the Millennium.

There is an important distinction here. The "rule" of the Messiah during the Millennium should not be confused with His ultimate rule over the new heaven and new earth which follows the Millennium. Notice that the passage Jesus quotes says, "He will rule them with an iron scepter." Clearly, this is a description of a stern and authoritarian mastery. Then, "He will dash them to pieces like pottery," speaks of judgment and the breaking up of evil strongholds.

In the new heaven and new earth evil will be a thing of the past. There will be no rebellious subjects to rule with an iron scepter, no evil strongholds to be broken into pieces like pottery. As we shall see in later chapters, only righteousness dwells in the new heaven and new earth, and there will be nothing there except that which is pure and good.

Clearly, then, these verses refer to the earthly kingdom of the Millennium, in which the saints will share ruling authority with Christ. The Millennium will be a time when righteousness reigns, but it will also be a time when judgment must occur, for both sin and death will still exist.

The Morning Star

Finally, the Lord gives a beautiful symbol to the faithful believers in Thyatira.

2:28–29 *"I will also give him the morning star. He who has an ear, let him hear what the Spirit says to the churches."*

Have you ever stood outside and watched the rising of the morning star? Today we know the morning star as the planet Venus, second planet from the sun and the brightest object in the night sky. Depending on where it is in its orbital path, the morning star can be seen to rise as much as three hours before the sun. You must arise early, while it is still dark, while the sky is still jet-black. Then when the morning star appears over the horizon with its light second only to the moon in nocturnal brilliance, you will understand what an awesome symbol the Lord gives us in this passage.

In the last book of the Old Testament there is a prophecy regarding the return of Jesus Christ in power and glory: "But for you who revere my name, the sun of righteousness will rise with healing in its wings."[9] When He returns visibly to the earth Jesus will be like the noonday sun breaking through the gloom of the dark night of the world.

But before the sun rises, the morning star will appear. Later in the book of Revelation, Jesus says of Himself, "I am . . . the bright Morning Star."[10] So what Jesus is saying to the faithful believers in the corrupt church at Thyatira is that there will be two stages of the appearance of the Lord Jesus Christ. First He will appear as the morning star, shining brightly before dawn, coming for His own. Then, at a later period, He will appear as the shining sun, coming in all His power and glory, visible to all the world.

The promise of the morning star is in fact the promise of the Rapture or gathering of the church out of the world—the first such promise in the book of Revelation. Jesus will appear to collect all those who truly belong to Him, who have been guarded by the Spirit of God from the evils of the world around them.

This is not to say that those He takes are utterly sinless. Even the most faithful and devoted Christians sometimes fail and sin. The visible sign of their faithfulness and devotion, however, is the fact that they repent, they turn back to God, and they recover. These are the ones whose faith is real. Someone once said, "If your faith fizzles before you finish it's because it was faulty from the first!" True faith holds on until the end of life.

What an amazing reality awaits us! If you and I hold on until the end, we will receive the bright morning star, Jesus Himself. Whether we have died or still live when He returns for us, He will gather us together to be with Him.

But the story doesn't end there. We know that soon after the morning star rises, the sun will also rise—brilliant, powerful, visible to the whole world. Think of it: a new heaven is coming, and a new earth—and we will be alive with Jesus to see it!

Chapter Seven

The Church of the Zombies

Revelation 3:1–6

 t was one of the most depressing worship experiences I have ever had.

I was scheduled to preach in a church in a major city in Australia. I had never been to this church before, and I had no idea what to expect before I arrived.

The building was old and beautiful, fashioned out of stone and stained glass, topped with a sky-scraping spire, furnished with rich-looking carved pews, altar, and railings. An organ with enormous brass pipes filled the sanctuary with rolling swells of music.

The spacious, ornately decorated sanctuary could seat 800 worshipers, but only 35 mostly elderly worshipers were present. The choir consisted of seven elderly ladies, led by a woman who tried enthusiastically (if unsuccessfully) to coax a joyful noise from the ensemble. The organist mechanically played a few hymns, then picked up his sheet music and left.

As I awaited my time to preach I was aware that just outside this dying church a bustling city went about its business. People streamed by along the thoroughfare, totally unaware of—and untouched by—this church. Those within the church might as well have been worshiping inside a tomb. Today, whenever I read the letter to the church at Sardis I am reminded of that tragic, dying congregation in Australia.

Sardis was once one of the greatest cities of the world. It was at one time the capital of the ancient kingdom of Lydia, and today its ruins can be visited near the city of Izmir, Turkey. In the sixth century B.C., Sardis was ruled by a fabulously wealthy king whose name, Croesus, became a byword for unimaginable wealth. When I was young, millionaires were said to be "as rich as Croesus" (a phrase now replaced by "as rich as an Arab sheik").

Sardis was built on a mountain spur about 1500 feet above the valley floor. It was regarded as virtually impregnable against military assault. Many armies laid siege to Sardis, but only two—the Persians and Greeks—ever succeeded. Both victories were achieved by stealth, not force, because the overconfident military of Sardis failed to post an adequate guard by its "impregnable" walls. Both times, small bands of spies climbed the sides of the ravine and entered an unwatched gate. So if there is one observation we could draw about the character of Sardis, it is that the city possessed a smug, complacent spirit.

Christians in Name Only

The church at Sardis is the least favored of all the seven churches addressed by the Lord in Revelation. He can literally find *nothing* to commend in this church.

3:1 *"To the angel of the church in Sardis write: These are the words of him who holds the seven spirits of God and the seven stars. I know your deeds; you have a reputation of being alive, but you are dead."*

Remember that the way the Lord presents Himself to each church is a clue to what that particular church needs. In this passage He refers to Himself as the one "who holds the seven spirits of God and the seven stars." These images signify the Holy Spirit in His fullness and completeness. What the church at Sardis desperately needed was the Spirit, from whom all believers receive *life*.

They also needed to remember that Jesus is Lord of His church. It is not left to mere human beings to set up, run, and govern a church. These are the prerogatives of the Lord Himself, and the church at Sardis had forgotten this fact.

"I know your deeds," the Lord says to the church at Sardis. The life and character of a church is revealed in its deeds. And the deeds of the church in Sardis have been done not to please the Lord but to impress people. The church had built up a good reputation, but it was really dead and corrupt inside. The members of this church were, for the most part, not even believers.

Today we would call the Christians at Sardis "nominal Christians"— *nominal* from the root word for *name*. They were Christians in name only. Jesus told them, "You have a reputation [a name] of being alive, but you are dead." This indicates that the church at Sardis was made up largely of people who outwardly professed Christ, but who possessed no real spiritual life.

Unfortunately, such churches have only grown more numerous in our own day. It is churches such as these which have largely created a negative image of Christianity in the world today. People see the outward profession of Christianity and hear the pious-sounding words—but they see no life, no reality, to back it up. Someone once described such churches as full of "mild-mannered people, meeting in mild-mannered ways, striving to be more mild-mannered."

The Church of the Walking Dead

Calvin Coolidge, our thirtieth president, was an extremely quiet and reserved man. When questioned, he rarely answered in more than two or three words—a tendency which earned him the nickname "Silent Cal." The public saw him as a stiff and emotionless man, causing Alice Roosevelt Longworth to remark, "He looks as if he'd been weaned on a pickle."

In 1933, the radio airwaves crackled with the news of Coolidge's death. Columnist Dorothy Parker was in her office at *The New Yorker* when a colleague flung open the door and blurted, "Dottie, did you hear? Coolidge is dead!"

Endowed with a quick but acid wit, she shot back, "How can they tell?"

And as we stand under the hot glare of our Lord's letter to Sardis we have to look honestly within and ask ourselves, "Can anyone tell if we are alive or dead? Am I truly alive—or do I just have a reputation, a name, for being alive?"

The Lord's words to the church at Sardis are blunt and strong: "You have a reputation of being alive, but *you are dead*." What sort of image does that conjure up in your mind? I picture a church peopled with the walking dead. I picture scenes out of some awful Hollywood B-movie with a title like *Night of the Living Dead* or *I Married a Zombie*. And yet, a church full of zombie-like walking-dead Christians is a thousand times more terrifying to me than any old horror movie. Why? Because one of those walking corpses could be me. Or it could be you.

The letter to the "First Zombie Church of Sardis" is the most dire and somber of the seven. There are serious issues at stake in this letter—eternal issues. There was a time when the Sardis church was truly alive, quickened by the Spirit of God. The people in the Sardis church once served the needy out of a genuine love for Jesus. They worshiped out of a heart of devotion to their Lord. As a result, they won a reputation for being active and alive.

But as the book of Revelation was being written, the life had departed. A church that had once made an impact on its society had become a corpse—a walking, zombie-like corpse of a church that didn't have sense enough to consent to be buried. It continued to carry out its ghastly, hollow pretense of life.

Steps to Recovery

Dr. William Barclay has said, "A church is in danger of death when it begins to worship its own past, when it is more concerned with forms than with life; when it is more concerned with material than it is with spiritual things." I've seen many such churches; perhaps you have, too. Churches which exist only as shrines to past glories. Churches where "worship" consists of mechanically sung hymns and anemic rituals. Churches which celebrate appearances and reputation and distinctives rather than a jubilant, buoyant, living relationship with the God of the universe.

Notice the differences between Sardis and all the other churches addressed in Revelation 2 and 3. Ephesus lacked love, Sardis lacks life. In every other church, there is something happening, there is tension, there is even struggle and conflict. Tension and struggle may be unpleasant, but at least they are signs of life. The church in Sardis was so devoid of life that it actually had no struggles going on within it.

In this church we find no orthodox Jewish opponents of the church, even though there was a large Jewish population in Sardis. The Jews ignored the Christians because the Christians of Sardis were neutralized, impotent, dead.

There were no false apostles harrying the church at Sardis either. There were no Nicolaitans springing up like choking weeds, nor was there a seductive false prophetess as in the church at Thyatira. There was no struggle, no contending for truth in Sardis. There was only death.

What does a dead church need? Can a dead church like Sardis be resurrected? Yes—but there is no time to waste.

It's encouraging to notice that the Lord Jesus is the Lord of *all* the churches—even of the First Zombie Church of Sardis. He doesn't say, "I wash my hands of you." He says, "You are dead—but I am still your Lord, and I will show the way to recovery."

So let's examine the signs of death—and the steps to recovery and resurrection—that Jesus sets forth in His letter to the church at Sardis.

Wake Up!

Part of the lore that circulates in many theological seminaries is a tale concerning a seminarian with a bent for practical jokes. This seminarian, the story goes, was sitting in a class taught by an exceedingly boring professor. Noticing that the student in the next seat had fallen asleep, he thought to himself, "Aha! Now I'll liven things up a little!"

So, in the midst of the lecture, as the professor turned to jot a note on the chalkboard, the student leaned over to his sleeping friend and nudged him sharply. "Wake up, Tom!" he whispered, "class is over! The professor called on you to close in prayer!"

Shaken awake, the victim of the prank jumped to his feet and startled the professor and the class with the announcement, "Fellow students, let us pray!"

The Lord has a message for the church at Sardis—and for you and me. The message is, "Wake up!" and unlike the seminarian's message to his hapless seatmate, *this* message is no joke. It is an urgent alarm for a dead church to rouse itself back to life.

3:2–3 *"Wake up! Strengthen what remains and is about to die, for I have not found your deeds complete in the sight of my God. Remember, therefore, what you have received and heard; obey it, and repent. But if you do not wake up, I will come like a thief, and you will not know at what time I will come to you."*

The first need of a church that is dead or near death is to *wake up* to its desperate condition.

The words of Jesus' message to Sardis are sharp, staccato commands in the original Greek. They are like a slap in the face, a splash of cold water, a sniff of spirits of ammonia, a shout, an urgent cry of alarm:

"Wake up!"

In his letter to the Ephesians, Paul says, "Wake up, O sleeper, rise from the dead, and Christ will shine on you." This was the desperate need of the church in Sardis: Wake up! Honestly face your failure and spiritual dullness! Admit the futility of your self-serving religious activity! Catch a whiff of the reeking corruption of your way of life!

As Christians we must not shrink from the convicting words of the letter to Sardis. Rather, we must bravely face them and ask ourselves, "What has gone wrong with my spiritual life? Why does my worship and Christian service seem so dreary? Why does my church seem so lifeless and unattractive? Why don't people want to come?" As individual Christians and as collective bodies of believers, these are the questions that confront us in the letter to the church at Sardis.

"Wake up!" our Lord cries to us in our worldly lethargy and stupor. "Wake up *now*—or you may *never* wake up!"

Strengthen What Remains

If the first need of the church at Sardis was to rouse itself and wake up to its dying condition, the second is to *strengthen what remains*. Why does Jesus tell the Christians at Sardis to "strengthen what remains"? Certainly, the Lord found nothing to commend about this church. What, we wonder, was there left at Sardis worth strengthening?

But remember in verse 1, Jesus said, "I know your deeds." Clearly the church at Sardis was doing *some* good deeds, or else it wouldn't have had a reputation (however misplaced) for being "alive." The Christians at Sardis were doing good works, but these works were incomplete, unfinished. Their actions were right, but their motives were wrong. By doing the right things for the wrong reasons they robbed their good deeds of power. That is why the Lord says in verse 2, "Strengthen what remains and is about to die, for I have not found your deeds complete in the sight of my God."

The Christians at Sardis were like so many Christians today—busy doing good things, but doing them primarily to impress people. They were trying to enhance their reputation for being alive. But as Jesus warned them, even *these* good works, as incomplete and falsely intentioned as they were, were about to die. Soon the church at Sardis would end up bereft of even its flimsy reputation and phony good deeds.

"Strengthen what remains," says Jesus to the Sardis Christians. How? By setting their motives aright.

All through the Scriptures we see that God judges not merely our actions but the *intentions* of our hearts. Often, the same activity that is done out of love and gratitude toward God can also be done for reasons of our own pride and our desire to impress others. God is watching not only our behavior but our hearts, monitoring whether we are living to please ourselves or to please Him.

Mother Teresa, the Albanian nun who has given her life in service to the untouchables of India, once told an interviewer for *Time* magazine, "We try to pray through our work by doing it *with* Jesus, *for* Jesus, *to* Jesus. That helps us put our whole heart and soul into doing it. The dying, the crippled, the mentally ill, the unwanted, the unloved—they are Jesus in disguise." What a powerful motivation for Christian ministry! This is the vision the church of Sardis needed to recapture.

Remember, Obey, Repent

So the church at Sardis needed to *remember what they had heard.* Then they needed to *obey,* and, third, to *repent.*

At this point, I have to disagree with that fine Bible translation, the New International Version, and point out that verse 3 should not read, "Remember, therefore, *what* you have received. . ." but rather, "Remember, therefore, *how* you have received and heard; obey it, and repent."

What they had heard, of course, was the Christian gospel. They had heard the story of the life of Jesus, His death upon the cross on behalf of sinners, His resurrection, and the new life He offers to all who believe in Him. But what Jesus is talking about here is *how* they received it.

What Jesus is referring to is the ministry of the Holy Spirit. Remember that Jesus had said He is the one who holds the seven spirits. When these people first heard the gospel, they had heard it by the Spirit. The Word came to them in the power of the Spirit.

Many years ago I visited a large, well-known Methodist church in the Midwest. As I was waiting for the service to start I turned to the doctrinal statement in the back of the hymnal, a statement that originated with John Wesley, the founder of the Methodist movement. This statement came out of the Great Awakening when John Wesley, his brother Charles, and their colleague George Whitefield preached to thousands in the fields and streets of England.

As I examined that statement of faith, I pondered the fact that the gospel preached by the Wesleys and Whitefield was the same gospel the church has had for 2,000 years. Yet in the days of the Great Awakening the gospel went forth with extraordinary power—the power of the Holy

Spirit.

As I sat in that sanctuary the service began, hymns were sung, creeds were recited, Scripture was read, a sermon was preached. But the spirit of that service was cold, formal, and lifeless. I remember looking at the doctrinal statement and feeling grateful that the Methodist denomination continued to hold to the creed John Wesley had formulated during the world-shaking days of the Great Awakening. Yet I was also saddened as I left the sanctuary. For in this particular Methodist congregation, the fire was flickering, if it had not gone out altogether.

That was many years ago, and perhaps that church has recovered. I hope so. For that church once had a national reputation for being alive. Yet the church I visited that morning was spiritually dead.

How do you lay hold of the Spirit and revive a church—or an individual—who has become spiritually dead? Many Christians have the gospel, but do not seem to have the life-giving presence of the Spirit. How do we bring the Spirit's life back into our lives and our churches?

According to this letter from Jesus, there is only one way: *Remember, obey, and repent!* Look at yourself, your wrong outlook, your tainted motives. Recognize that all your prideful religious busyness is little more than a covering of filthy rags for your poverty and sin. Cast yourself upon the grace of the Lord Jesus, believe, and receive His grace. Let it take root in your heart, and then He will give you the life of the Spirit of God. That is what the Christians in Sardis needed. And that is what you and I need today as well.

Recover Your Hope

The fourth thing they needed at Sardis was to recover the hope of the Lord's return. "If you do not wake up," says the Lord, "I will come like a thief, and you will not know at what time I will come to you." The hope of the Lord's return is alluded to many times throughout the New Testament and particularly in the book of Revelation. But Sardis had lost its expectation of that coming.

Some friends of mine live in a two-story house, with bedrooms upstairs. One morning they came downstairs to find that while they had slept peacefully in their beds upstairs a thief had been very busy downstairs. Their silverware and many other costly items and furnishings had been stolen. They had heard nothing, because a thief never knocks, never rings the doorbell, never announces his presence. He enters silently, takes what he wants, then disappears again.

The Lord says that is what His coming again will be like—not His visible coming when He appears to establish His kingdom, when every eye will see Him, as described in Revelation 1:7. Rather, what Jesus describes here is the coming He mentioned in His great Olivet discourse in Matthew 24:43. There He says He will come suddenly, without warning, like a thief who comes to steal treasure in the night. That is how the *parousia,* the coming of the Lord for His church, will begin. He will take His true church suddenly out of the world. It will disappear from the world's sight.

Paul describes this event in 1 Corinthians 15, the great resurrection chapter, when he says, "Listen, I tell you a mystery: We will not all sleep [i.e., die], but we will all be changed—in a flash, in the twinkling of an eye." That is the dynamic hope of the church. The church is the great unrecognized treasure of the world, but the Lord will one day come as a thief and take it to Himself. That is what theologians have called the *Rapture* of the church (though *departure* of the church might be a better term).

The church at Sardis desperately needed to focus upon this elevating, emboldening, encouraging hope. Without this hope, the church was dead.

Winds of Reformation

In 1986, East German Communist party boss Erich Honecker declared that the Berlin Wall would stand for at least a hundred more years. Three years later that wall was pulled down in pieces. Beginning in the spring of 1989, the winds of reform and freedom swept through East Germany, Hungary, Czechoslovakia, Poland, and Romania.

As I watched these exciting, world-shattering events unfold on the evening news and on the front-page of my newspaper, I was reminded of the winds of reform and freedom that swept through Europe more than 400 years earlier during the Protestant Reformation. In the days of the Reformers—Martin Luther in Germany, Ulrich Zwingli and John Calvin in Switzerland, and John Knox in Scotland—the gospel of Jesus Christ spread like wildfire throughout Europe, and the cruel walls of spiritual bondage fell before the power of God's Word and God's Spirit.

What many people forget about the Reformation, however, is how rapidly its fire was quenched. Many of the churches founded by the Reformers began to die even within the lifetimes of the Reformers themselves. Why? Because the leaders of the Reformation made a serious error!

Yes, they had correctly and wisely steered Christendom back to a focus on salvation by grace through faith in Jesus Christ. But they made a grievous mistake when they linked the authority and oversight of the church with the civil government of the country in which they lived. Luther looked to the German princes for protection against the power of Rome. Zwingli tied the church to the ruling state in Switzerland. Calvin attempted to establish a theocratic government in the city of Geneva. So also did Knox in Scotland.

The result was a system of state churches spreading across the continent of Europe. Today these state churches are almost uniformly dead, like the church in Sardis.

I had an opportunity to see what the spiritual life of a state church is like when I toured northern Germany, Denmark, Holland, England, and Scotland in 1965. I met many laypeople and clergymen in these countries. The laypeople were uniformly dissatisfied with the stagnant atmosphere in their churches. The clergymen were frustrated by the fact that their duties as state-employed civil servants robbed them of time to prepare sermons and preach the Word of God.

"I simply have no time," said one pastor in Copenhagen, tears brimming in his eyes, "I have to baptize all the babies that are born, marry all the couples, and bury everyone who dies in the parish. I have no time to study." As someone put it, these state-employed pastors are so busy "hatching, matching, and dispatching" their parishioners, they have no time to feed them the life-giving Word of God! I'm sure there are a few genuine believers in these cold and lifeless churches, but I am equally certain that *most* of these parishioners are people with a reputation for being alive, yet who are spiritually dead.

In the historical overview provided by the seven letters of Revelation, the church at Sardis represents that period of church history from the last half of the sixteenth century (immediately following the Reformation) to about the middle of the eighteenth century, the beginning of the Great Awakening. It was a time of great darkness and death in Christendom. The light was not entirely gone, but it was failing until the moment the Spirit of God rekindled the light through men like the Wesleys and George Whitefield.

Those Who Overcome

In every age in history and in Sardis-like "dead" churches, there are usually a few faithful believers. It is to these faithful few that the Lord delivers a special promise.

3:4–6 *"Yet you have a few people in Sardis who have not soiled their* *clothes. They will walk with me, dressed in white, for they are worthy. He who overcomes will, like them, be dressed in white. I will never blot out his name from the book of life, but will acknowledge his name before my Father and his angels. He who has an ear, let him hear what the Spirit says to the churches."*

White garments are always a symbol of redemption in Scripture. In Revelation 7, we will read of a great multitude who emerge from the great Tribulation, and who have "washed their robes and made them white in the blood of the Lamb." Clearly, white garments are a sign of being redeemed and saved by the grace of God. Remember the words of the Lord in Isaiah 1:18—"Though your sins are like scarlet, they shall be as white as snow; though they are red as crimson, they shall be like wool."

In Sardis, and in other dead churches, there are usually a few believers who walk with Jesus, dressed in white. God calls them "worthy"—not for any works of righteousness they have done, but because they are covered by the righteousness of Jesus.

These, then, are the models for those in the church who wish to be "overcomers," as mentioned in verse 5. And to these believers, the Lord promises three things:

1. They will be dressed in white,
the righteousness of Jesus.

2. Their names will not be blotted
out of the Book of Life.

3. Jesus will acknowledge them
before His Father and the angels.

Here, the Lord calms the fears of the redeemed. To anyone who worries that he might lose his salvation and the grace of God, Jesus says, in effect, "Those who place their trust in me rather than in their own efforts, those who are covered by my righteousness, *can never be blotted out of the Book of Life.* Their names are written in indelible ink and sealed with the seal of my own promise."

I recall, as a young pastor, visiting a much beloved and respected Presbyterian pastor in the San Francisco Bay area of California. He was a godly man in his 90s. When I sat down to visit with him, I found he was deeply troubled by the fact that he was nearing the end of his life. He wondered if he was really a Christian after all. Older people are often troubled by such doubts. Our Lord knows that, so He gives us these reassuring words in Revelation, "I will never blot out his [your] name from the book of life."

That word *never* in the original text is the strongest negative possible in the Greek language. To convey the true force of this word the passage should actually be rendered, "*I will never, ever, under any circumstances,* blot out your name from the Book of Life!" Added to that, these words should be underlined, italicized and set in headline-size type! That's how total and all-encompassing this wonderful reassurance truly is.

And when, in eternity, the book of our lives is opened, and everything we have done in our earthly lives comes spilling out—the good, the bad, and the ugly—Jesus will be there to acknowledge us before the Father and the angels. "None of that matters," He will say. "This one is covered by my blood, my righteousness. This one wears white garments. This one is mine." That is what Jesus promised in Matthew 10, and that is what He promises to those who remain faithful in Sardis—and to those who remain faithful today.

Church attendance is good, but church attendance won't save you. Church membership is good, but church membership won't save you. Giving money to the church is good, but giving won't save you. Activity in the church—teaching, serving, leading, witnessing—all of this is good, but being active in the church won't save you.

You can only be saved when you repent of your self-reliance and self-will and self-centered pride. You can only be saved when you place your trust in the One who settled it all for you on the cross.

We who have ears to hear, let us hear what the Spirit says to the First Zombie Church of Sardis—and to us.

Chapter Eight

The Little Church That Tried

Revelation 3:7–13

Most people know that the name *Philadelphia* means "brotherly love." English religious and civic leader William Penn founded the historic American city by that name as a place where he and his fellow Quakers could worship in freedom. He took the name for his "city of brotherly love" from an obscure city in Asia Minor. That ancient biblical city is remembered primarily because of a letter that was addressed there during the first century A.D., a letter from the Lord Jesus Christ, the sixth letter of the book of Revelation.

The biblical Philadelphia was located about 28 miles southeast of Sardis. It was the youngest of the seven cities of Revelation, having been founded about 150 B.C. by King Attallus Philadelphus of Pergamum. The name *Philadelphus*, meaning "lover of a brother," was actually a kind of nickname. King Attallus was noted for the great affection and admiration he had for his brother Eumenes, and the city of Philadelphia was named in his honor.

In A.D. 17, Philadelphia and a number of cities in the region were devastated by a massive earthquake. Philadelphia suffered more than the rest in that it was not only leveled in the initial quake, but it continued to be jolted by serious aftershocks for years afterward. Many were killed and injured in this lengthy "season" of earth tremors.

The Roman emperor Tiberius Caesar helped Philadelphia rebuild after the earthquake. In gratitude to him, the city changed its name to

Neocaesarea (meaning "New Caesar"), a name it bore for a number of years. The history of this city and the suffering the Philadelphian people endured during the years of earth tremors are important to understanding the Lord's message to the church in Philadelphia.

No Complaints

The church in Philadelphia is unique among the seven churches in that it is the only church against which the Lord registers *no complaint*—not one. Here is a church that *delights* the Lord! I suppose each of us wishes his or her church could be like the church in Philadelphia.

As we take a close look at the Lord's message to the believers in Philadelphia, notice the unusual way He addresses this church, as compared with the other six churches of Revelation.

3:7 *"To the angel of the church in Philadelphia write:*

These are the words of him who is holy and true, who holds the key of David. What he opens no one can shut, and what he shuts no one can open."

In all the letters except this one, the Lord vividly describes Himself, using symbols from John's first vision of Him in Revelation 1. In this letter, however, Jesus makes no reference to that vision. Instead, He uses other titles to describe Himself. First He tells the Philadelphian believers *who He is*. He says He is the one who is *holy*. That means He is morally perfect and His character is without flaw. He also says He is the one who is *true*. That means He is genuine, objective reality, the one who is behind all that truly exists. That is *who* Jesus is.

Jesus also tells the Philadelphian believers *what He does*. He "holds the key of David." This is a reference to an incident in Isaiah 22. In the days of King Hezekiah there was a palace courtier (the modern equivalent would be a chief of staff) named Shebna. He dishonestly used the power of his position to enrich himself. He was, in effect, a scam artist. So the Lord pronounced judgment on Shebna, declaring that he would be sent to die in disgrace in Babylon and that a godly man named Eliakim would take his place. The words of the Lord in Revelation 3:7 are an echo of the prophecy of the Lord upon Eliakim in Isaiah 22:22—"I will place on his shoulder the key to the house of David; what he opens no one can shut, and what he shuts no one can open."

When the Lord, in His letter to the Philadelphian church, applies these same words to Himself, He is saying that His will cannot be opposed. He governs all events in the history of this planet. He will open some doors and close others. The doors He opens will remain open. The doors He closes are inalterably locked. No power on earth can contravene what He has determined.

A Church with a Little Power

The Lord then tells the Philadelphian church how He will use His power to open and close doors.

3:8 *"I know your deeds. See, I have placed before you an open door that no one can shut. I know that you have little strength, yet you have kept my word and have not denied my name."*

The image of open and closed doors has been powerfully employed elsewhere in the New Testament. The apostle Paul used this imagery to describe his missionary efforts. On his second missionary journey, he attempted to go into the province of Asia to preach the gospel, but was disallowed by the Holy Spirit—a shut door. Then he tried to go into Bithynia, on the southern shore of the Black Sea, but again was not allowed by the Lord—another shut door.

But when Paul came to Troas he received a vision of a man from Macedonia beckoning to him, and from this vision he learned that the Lord had opened the door for him to enter Europe. Paul's commitment to enter that open door changed the course of the entire Western world, affecting all of civilization since that time. Because of that open door into Europe, Paul took the Christian faith north and west through Europe and into Italy. Thus the Christian gospel gained a major beachhead in Europe from which it eventually launched itself around the world.

Later, in 1 Corinthians 16:8, Paul writes, "But I will stay on at Ephesus until Pentecost, because a great door for effective work has opened to me, and there are many who oppose me." Ephesus was the capital of Asia, a region that was once a door tightly shut against Paul. But later, as he penned these words to the Corinthians, that door was wide open, and Paul chose to stay there to make the most of his opportunity.

In recent years, we have seen doors that were locked and barred for decades being suddenly flung open to receive the gospel. Against all human calculation and completely without warning, doors have opened in Poland, Germany, Romania, Czechoslovakia, Yugoslavia, Hungary, and the Soviet Union. In these countries, millions of people—starved for hope, truth, and meaning in their lives—are responding to the Christian gospel. In these countries, the door is open, and fresh, fragrant air is sweeping in.

At this point I have to make a correction to the New International Version's text: "I know that you have little strength." This is not what the Greek text says. The NIV takes one continuous thought and breaks it in two, which I think is unfortunate. I believe a more faithful rendering of this entire thought would be:

> "I have placed before you an open door that no one can shut *because* you have a little power and have kept my word and not denied my name."

There is a cause-and-effect principle at work here. The Lord opened a door for the Philadelphian church *because* this church had fulfilled certain conditions: *because* they had "a little power," *because* they had kept the word of the Lord, and *because* they had not denied His name. When a church fulfills these conditions, a door for ministry is always opened.

The Philadelphian church had "a little power"—that is, it had discovered to some degree the power of the Spirit. The Lord is talking here not about human strength, but about *spiritual* power. This is the kind of power that comes from faith, from expecting God to act. The Philadelphian church was comprised of people who sensed that God could act in human events, and they looked for an opportunity, a way to respond, a door for ministry and service and evangelism to the world around them. They sought to bring others through that open door and into a rich and fulfilling relationship with Jesus Christ.

To me, Ephesians 2:10 is in some ways the most exciting verse in the New Testament. The apostle Paul says, "For we are God's workmanship [also translated "masterpiece"], created in Christ Jesus *to do good works,* which God prepared in advance for us to do." That is why you have been made and saved by Jesus Christ: *to do good works,* works of help, mercy, kindness, witness, love, comfort, counsel, and strength.

Then notice that Paul adds the phrase, "which *God prepared in advance* for us to do." God in His foreknowledge and His love has made us and prepared for us the opportunity of doing works of love and service to others. When you are confronted with a need—from a child with a skinned knee to a neighbor who has just lost a spouse to a friend dying of cancer—you may feel that you have an insignificant role to play. But as you respond to that need it becomes an open door through which ministry—God's ministry, through the power of His Spirit—may flow. As you continue responding to such opportunities, you will be challenged, encouraged, and blessed, and the lives of those all around you will be changed.

The Lord does not say to the believers in Philadelphia, "You are weak," or, "You are powerless." Rather, He says to them, "You have a little power." He is stressing the fact that the Philadelphian believers have untapped potential for doing good works. This statement of the Lord's underscores the fact that most churches scarcely realize the power they have for ministry. Each of us in the body of Christ has been given spiritual gifts, and the responsibility to use those gifts to bless others and meet human needs. Yet how few of us really exercise our spiritual gifts as God truly intended!

What vast untapped potential resides in a single congregation, or in a single believer, when there is a willingness to utilize the gifts of the Spirit! That is why the Lord suggests to the believers in Philadelphia, "You have a little power—not much, but some." He is hoping they will grow in using that potential for ministry.

The *presence* of the Holy Spirit has been promised to every believer without any conditions whatsoever. But the *power* of the Spirit is given only to those believers who actively choose to *keep His Word* and *not deny His name*. These two dynamics are crucial to the ministry of every believer and every church.

God always plants His Word at the heart of His church. A church that is faithful and pleasing to God is a church that preaches, teaches, studies, knows, and lives out His Word. The Word of God is not just for pastors or elders or Sunday school teachers. Every individual believer in the church is to know and obey God's Word.

Beyond the Word of the Lord stands the Lord Himself. The Word points us to the reality of a relationship with God Himself. That is why Jesus commended the Philadelphians not only for keeping His Word but for being faithful to His name. An old hymn puts it this way:

> Beyond the sacred page I seek Thee, Lord.
> My spirit pants for Thee, O Living Word.

It is the Word of God that enables us to know the character of Jesus, to have fellowship with Him, to build His character into our own lives. His name is to be the identifying mark upon our lives. As non-Christians watch us live out our faith amid the stress and pressure of the real world, they are to see the imprint of the name of Jesus in all that we do.

When Jesus is present with us throughout each day, and when our lives serve to reflect the life and character of Christ, then doors of ministry open before us. This is true of each believer in an individual sense, and it is true of entire churches.

The Synagogue of Satan

Some years ago, I was discussing the future of Israel with a rabbi. During our talk, he said something to me I will never forget. "You are a premillennial evangelical," he said, "and I am a Jew." (The word *premillennial* refers to Christians who believe that Jesus the Messiah will literally return to rule over Israel during the future Millennium in fulfillment of Old Testament promise and prophecy.) "You premillennial Christians," he continued, "are the only Christians we Jews can really talk to."

I was intrigued. "Why is that?" I asked.

"Because," he replied, "you believe there is a future for Israel. That enables us to communicate with you. So many other Christians have just written us off; they have written Israel off, and we have nothing in common with them."

This rabbi's comments underscore the fact that when you truly reflect the love and compassion of Christ, and when you truly understand the promises to Israel in the Old Testament and how they relate to the prophecy of Revelation, you have something in common with Jews anywhere. You can communicate with them, and they will respect what you say and do.

As we come to verse 9, we will see that our Christlike love, together with our reverence for the Word of God, gives us an open door for ministry to the Jews.

3:9 *"I will make those who are of the synagogue of Satan, who claim to be Jews though they are not, but are liars — I will make them come and fall down at your feet and acknowledge that I have loved you."*

Here is the Lord's promise that He will use His power to subdue the enemies of the Philadelphian believers. Their enemies will respect the Philadelphian church and openly acknowledge God's blessing upon them.

In this verse a phrase from the letter to Smyrna appears again: the "synagogue of Satan." As in the Smyrna letter, this phrase refers to those Jews who claim to be spiritual descendants of Abraham, yet who persecute Christians and reject the truth. Though they are physically descended from Abraham, their attitude is far removed from Abraham's faith. During His earthly ministry the Lord Jesus repeatedly opposed the "synagogue of Satan," the spiritually arrogant scribes and Pharisees who claimed to be Abraham's children. Jesus' message to them was harsh but true: "You are of your father the devil."

The church in Philadelphia, like most churches of that early era, was composed largely of Jews who had converted to Christianity. So the hostile Jews of the "synagogue of Satan" were actually persecuting other Jews—converted Jews—because of their beliefs. In His letter, Jesus reassures the mostly-Jewish Christians at Philadelphia, "I will make [those Jews who persecute you] . . . fall down at your feet and acknowledge that I have loved you."

How? What will cause the anti-Christian Jews to bow before the believers in Philadelphia and acknowledge God's blessing on the church? Answer: they will see the church respond to their opposition with love, courage, and an intimate knowledge of God—a knowledge these nonbelieving Jews do not possess, even though they have the Scriptures. Their hearts will be changed as the Christians of Philadelphia exhibit the results of a special and supernatural relationship with the living Christ.

What was true for the first-century Christians in Philadelphia is true for you and me today. Today, Jews are far more persecuted than persecutors. The plague of anti-Semitism continues to threaten the Jews worldwide, and the nation of Israel continues to survive while encircled by enemies. But though there is no Jewish oppression of the church today as there was in the first century, there are many Jews who harbor deep resentment against Christians. This resentment is rooted in the fact that many past persecutions of Jews were carried out by so-called "Christians."

I have a friend named Tuvya Zaretsky. He is Jewish, and as a child was raised to distrust Christians and to hate the Christian gospel. The name of Jesus was anathema to him. The very subject of Christianity filled him with an intense loathing and anger.

Today, however, Tuvya Zaretsky is a changed man, a devoted Christian who is always eager to share his faith in Jesus Christ. He now works with Jews for Jesus in San Francisco.

What made the difference? His heart was changed by the loving, caring example of genuine Christians, living out the Word of God and the lifestyle of Jesus. At a crucial point in his life he met some Christlike people who were willing to minister to him, listen to him without judging or arguing, and accept him despite his anger and hostility. Gently and gradually they loved my friend Tuvya into the kingdom of God.

As we live out the lifestyle of Jesus under the authority of God's Word the Lord opens doors of ministry even among those who are hostile and unreceptive to our message.

A Triumphant Promise

In verse 10, the Lord gives the Philadelphian church a word of amazing encouragement and promise.

3:10 *"Since you have kept my command to endure patiently,¹ I will also keep you from the hour of trial that is going to come upon the whole world to test those who live on the earth."*

Here is a clear reference to what Jesus, in Matthew 24, called "the great distress." It will be a time of worldwide upheaval the like of which has never been known in human history. Those who remember such events as World War II, the Cuban Missile Crisis, the assassination of President Kennedy, or the Desert Storm conflict in Iraq have only barely tasted the uncertainty, the horror, the sorrow, and the fear of the coming Tribulation. There will be slaughter, atrocity, terror, and panic on a scale that beggars our ability to imagine, and we will encounter vivid descriptions of that time in the coming pages of Revelation.

The Great Tribulation is coming, the Lord says, "to test those who live on the earth." This phrase is widely misunderstood to refer to all those who are residents of the planet. But no, "those who live on the earth" are metaphorically those who live as though this life is all there is, who have their minds set upon the things of the earth, who are materialistically minded.

The amazing promise of verse 10 is that the church will be *delivered* from that hour of trial. "I will also *keep* you from the hour of trial that is going to come upon the whole world," says the Lord. So the church will be *kept* from the time of trial, caught up and removed even before the Great Tribulation begins. This is the promise of the departure of the church, which Paul describes so beautifully in 1 Thessalonians 4:16-17:

> For the Lord himself will come down from heaven, with a loud command, with the voice of the archangel and with the trumpet call of God, and the dead in Christ will rise first. After that, we who are still alive and are left will be caught up together with them in the clouds to meet the Lord in the air. And so we will be with the Lord forever.

And as we shall see, there are many signs which indicate that the fulfillment of this wonderful promise may be very close at hand today.

The Philadelphia Stage of Church History

Viewed from the standpoint of Christian history, the church at Philadelphia symbolizes a very rich and shining era: the Great Awakening of the eighteenth and nineteenth centuries, following the decline of the Reformation church.

It was during this "Philadelphia" stage of history that the Moravian Brethren began meeting in small groups for prayer, catching the vision for what God could do in the world, and eventually sending Moravian missionaries throughout the world.

In England the Awakening began with the Puritan Movement. The Puritans included John Bunyan, author of *Pilgrim's Progress*, and John Newton, writer of so many great hymns of the faith, including "Amazing Grace." The Awakening also encompasses the great Wesleyan Revival and George Whitefield's preaching throughout England and in America.

In America the Great Awakening was characterized by men like Jonathan Edwards, the American Puritan theologian who strongly advocated Christian missionary activity. It included the Methodist circuit riders, who rode horseback from church to church, preaching the gospel up and down the eastern seaboard and eventually moving out across the western plains.

I am personally indebted to a circuit rider named Brother Van who came to the territory of Montana soon after it became populated in the Montana gold rush. He went into the saloons and mining camps, preaching the gospel, winning hundreds to Christ, planting churches throughout the state, many of which are still there. I was for a while a member of a church founded by Brother Van and knew people who knew him well.

The Great Awakening was a time of tremendous missionary activity. During this time, William Carey in England got a vision of the desperate spiritual need in India. He went there and planted the gospel, and a powerful outreach for Christ was born in India. Also from England, Robert Moffet and his famous son-in-law, David Livingstone, took the gospel into untouched regions of Africa.

The American missionary Adoniram Judson pioneered a major outreach into Burma. Hudson Taylor took the gospel into inland China. David Brainerd gave his life on the American mission field at the age of 29, living, caring, and witnessing among native Americans.

This was the time when so many of the great evangelists of church history emerged: George Whitefield, John Wesley, Charles Haddon Spurgeon, Charles Finney, and Dwight L. Moody. Out of the ashes of a deteriorating Reformation, God's Spirit brought forth new light and new life, a new and vibrant awakening throughout the Christian church.

All of the great people, events, and movements of the Great Awakening were foreshadowed by the church at Philadelphia in Asia Minor. Even while so many other surrounding churches were sinking into death and decay, the Philadelphia church was coming marvelously alive.

Coming Soon

In early 1942, just a few months after the disastrous attack on Pearl Harbor, the United States was suffering another bitter military setback: the Philippines were about to fall into the hands of the Japanese invaders. General Douglas MacArthur, who had led a courageous delaying action for several months, realized that defeat on the field of battle was inevitable. Reluctantly and sadly, he ordered American forces to withdraw.

On March 11 he stood with the Pacific surf lapping at the cuffs of his trousers and made a promise to the Philippine people: "I shall return." In 1944, MacArthur kept his promise and liberated the Philippines. Those events are a part of history.

Nearly two thousand years ago, our Lord Jesus left the shores of this planet. He made a promise to return. His promise is a part of our history, and His return is our future hope.

3:11–13 *"I am coming soon. Hold on to what you have, so that no one will take your crown. Him who overcomes I will make a pillar in the temple of my God. Never again will he leave it. I will write on him the name of my God and the name of the city of my God, the new Jerusalem, which is coming down out of heaven from my God; and I will also write on him my new name. He who has an ear, let him hear what the Spirit says to the churches."*

What a tremendous promise, so simply stated! "I am coming soon."

Hearing this promise, many people ask, "How can Jesus say that? This letter was written almost 2,000 years ago. The church has been expecting Him ever since. He still has not come. How can He say, 'I am coming soon'?"

The answer is to see this promise in its proper context. The Lord has just referred to "the hour of trial," the Great Tribulation. In His Olivet Discourse in Matthew 24, He vividly depicts that time as the most terrible upheaval in the history of the planet. He describes a darkened sun, the moon not giving its light, stars seeming to fall from the heavens, and men's hearts failing as they look in fear on the things coming to pass upon the earth. It is in relationship to *that* event that Jesus says He is coming soon. As that event draws near, His coming will be even sooner.

As world events grow more tense, violent, and climactic, we need to hear again the Lord's promise that He is coming soon. As the attention of the entire world grows continually more focused on events in Israel and the Middle East we should focus our attention on the Lord's reassuring promise. He Himself said, "When these things begin to take place, stand up and lift up your heads, because your redemption is drawing near."[2]

In view of the Lord's promise to return soon, a question logically occurs to us: "How should we then live? What should our lives be like as we expectantly wait for the Lord's return?" To this, Jesus replies: "Hold on to what you have, so that no one will take your crown." As times get harder, it becomes increasingly more difficult to be a Christian. As the world becomes more and more hostile to Jesus and the people who bear His name, as it casts off Christian values and plunges headlong toward moral and spiritual destruction, there will be increasing pressures on us to compromise. We will find ourselves tempted to let go of what we have, to lose our grip on God's Word, to deny the Lord's name, to yield to worldly desires and ambitions.

Amid these temptations the Lord says, "Hold on to what you have. Don't allow the desire for status, for prestige, for material possessions, for wealth, for self-gratification to become central in your thinking. Don't let anyone take your crown."

Now, the Lord is not referring here to a loss of salvation. The "crown" is a symbol of God's eternal reward—although not in the sense that we usually think of a reward. This reward from God is not like a paycheck, a bigger mansion in heaven, a plaque or a trophy, or a pat on the back. This reward is profoundly *more* than any of our paltry, earthbound conceptions of "rewards" could match. The reward, the crown, is the opportunity for even *greater* service for God! It is the privilege of knowing God and being given opportunity to serve Him both now and in the eternal ages!

As James I. Packer has said well,

> The Christian's reward is not directly earned; it is not a payment proportionate to services rendered; it is a Father's gift of generous grace to His children, far exceeding anything they deserved. Also, we must understand that the promised reward is

not something of a different nature tacked on to the activity being rewarded; it is, rather, the activity itself—communion with God in worship and service—in its consummation.3

This is the truth Paul teaches in 1 Corinthians 3:12-15. In this passage, Paul speaks of Jesus as the foundation which is laid in the hearts of believers, and adds,

> If any man builds on this foundation using gold, silver, costly stones, wood, hay or straw, his work will be shown for what it is, because the Day will bring it to light. [Paul is speaking here of the Day of Judgment described in Revelation.] It will be revealed with fire, and the fire will test the quality of each man's work. If what he has built survives, he will receive his reward. If it is burned up, he will suffer loss; he himself will be saved, but only as one escaping through the flames.

Thus, the crown of greater opportunity to serve Jesus might be lost. Perhaps the most painful tragedy of all, in the long view of eternity, would be the loss of the opportunity to demonstrate our love and gratitude to Jesus for all He has done for us. Do not let that opportunity slip away, says the Lord. Do not let anybody take that crown away from you.

Pillars in the Temple

The Japanese warlord Hideyoshi who ruled all of Japan in the latter half of the sixteenth century, commissioned a massive statue of Buddha for a shrine in the city of Kyoto. It took five years and thousands of laborers to construct the statue and the great temple which housed it.

In 1596, just a few months after the statue and temple were completed, a powerful earthquake toppled the structure. Great chunks of stone rained down upon the impassive Buddha, grinding the statue into fragments, chips, and dust. As soon as the ground had ceased its rumbling, Hideyoshi ran to the temple and found it in ruins. Enraged, he snatched a bow and arrow from a nearby soldier and shot the arrow at the broken statue. "Curse you!" the warlord screamed to his fallen god. "I spent millions to build you! Couldn't you even look after your own temple?!"

The people of Philadelphia knew what it was like to be shaken by an earthquake. As we discussed at the beginning of this chapter, the city had been leveled by a massive quake in A.D. 17, and the rubble continued to be shaken by severe aftershocks for years afterward. Every time one of these massive aftershocks struck, the people were forced to flee the city and run into the countryside.

But in verse 12, Jesus promises the Philadelphian believers a temple which will not be shaken and from which they will never have to flee. "Him who overcomes," says the Lord, "I will make a pillar in the temple of my God. Never again will he leave it."

A pillar is a symbol of strength and permanence. For example, the great temple of Jerusalem which was destroyed by the Romans in A.D. 70 had two great pillars set in the front of the building. One of those pillars was called Jachin, meaning "established" or "permanent," and the other was called Boaz, meaning "strength." Visit the ruins of an ancient temple in Greece, Italy, or Turkey, and you will notice that often all that remains standing are the pillars. Our Lord promises those who overcome, those who hold on to what they have, a position of strength and permanence in the life to come. They will be pillars of strength in the imperishable, unshakeable temple of God.

This is not the first time Christians have been called "pillars." In Galatians, the apostle Paul refers to fellow apostles Peter, James, and John as "pillars" of the church. The church rested on them, and they supported the church, imparting guidance and knowledge to the early church through the apostolic gift that was given them by the Holy Spirit. In His letter to the believers at Philadelphia, the Lord applied this same symbolism to ordinary believers like you and me. Imagine, Jesus promises that we can become pillars in the everlasting temple of God!

This must have been a profoundly reassuring promise to the believers in Philadelphia, who remembered the terror of earthquake tremors. "When you labor for me," Jesus said in effect, "you will be planted firmly in a stable place, the dwelling place of God, and you will never have to flee from that place." What a picture of security, serenity, and strength!

Unlike the enraged warlord who could only rave and moan over the rubble of his impotent god, we serve a God who lives, who can never be shaken, and who draws us into partnership, fellowship, and intimate communion with Him!

Three New Names

Finally, Jesus promises, "I will write on him the name of my God and the name of the city of my God . . . and I will also write on him my new name." The overcomer will receive the imprint of *three* new names!

The first is "the name of my God." This is a promise that believers will be made *godlike*. How does that statement sound to you? Perhaps you are thinking, "How could I ever be *godlike?*" The average person, hearing the word *godlike,* probably pictures a man with superhuman power, able to hurl thunderbolts, create planets, or reverse the flow of time. But that is not what godlikeness is about at all. That is a description of what it would be like to be Superman, not God.

The Bible instructs us to be *godly,* and *godliness* is merely a shortened form of the word *godlikeness.* The purpose of the Spirit in our lives is to make us godly or godlike—not in terms of God's *power,* but in terms of His *character.* If you are growing and maturing as a Christian, each passing year ought to bring more evidence that you have become a little more like Jesus Christ—a little more patient, compassionate, understanding, and sound in judgment. You should become more godlike, more Christlike.

That is the Lord's promise to the Philadelphian Christians, and to you and me: the name of God, which symbolizes His character, will be written upon our lives. We will be godlike in our spirit and attributes.

Second, Jesus says, "I will write on him . . . the name of the city of my God." We will see a striking description of this fabulous city when we come to the last two chapters of Revelation. It is the New Jerusalem, coming down from heaven "as a bride adorned for her husband." Think back to every wedding you have ever been to and that one magical moment when everyone stands and turns to catch the first glimpse of the bride making her appearance, glorious in her adornment, invoking a collective murmur of wonder throughout the people as she steps down the aisle. That kind of admiring, awestruck wonder is what the New Jerusalem will inspire at its appearance.

The image of the bride also captures the sense of loving sweetness, affection, longing, and intimacy that surrounds a bride and groom. The earth is just a waystation on the road to our *real* home in this beautiful city of God, and we long to be there, in the presence of God, just as a husband longs to be home in the presence of his beautiful bride.

Finally, says Jesus, "I will also write on him my new name." What name is that? The book of Revelation does not tell us. This verse refers to Revelation 19:12, where we are told that when Jesus appears He will have that new name written upon Him, but it is a name that no man knows. However, we do know that when the Lord gives a new name, it is a *descriptive* name, a name which befits the character of the object that is named.

Before Jesus was born in Bethlehem, an angel appeared to Joseph and told him that Mary would bring forth a son, "and you are to give him the name Jesus." Why? "Because he will save his people from their sins."

Jesus is a name which speaks of the Lord's redemptive ministry. It means "Yahweh [the Lord] saves."

At the end of time, when the work of redemption is finished, when we are all home in glory with Him and God's work of saving and redeeming us has been accomplished, Jesus will be given a new work to do. No one knows what it is. No one knows what His new name will be. But whatever this new role, whatever this new name, the church is promised a share in those vast new labors! In the new heaven and the new earth, human redemption will be accomplished—but a new adventure awaits the Lord Jesus and all those who have placed their trust in Him.

The Lord concludes this letter as He concludes all seven letters to the seven churches of Asia. He impresses upon us the fact that these letters spell out our future destiny:

> He who has an ear, let him hear what the Spirit says to the
> churches.

The Philadelphia church was a little church with a little power, a little church that tried, a church against which the Lord had no complaint. Do we hear what the Spirit says to this church? Are we heeding its example? Are we holding on to what we have, obeying the Word of God, remaining faithful to the name of Jesus, guarding our eternal crown?

May it be said of your life and mine that we, like the believers in Philadelphia, are Christians who truly delight our Lord!

Chapter Nine

The Rich/Poor Church

Revelation 3:14-22

 enjamin Disraeli, the flamboyant British prime minister of the nineteenth century, was once the guest of honor at a gala public dinner. Unfortunately, the kitchen was quite a distance from the banquet hall so that by the time the food was set before Disraeli and the other guests, all the "hot" dishes had cooled to an insipid lukewarm condition. After a few bites Disraeli gave up trying to enjoy the unpalatable meal.

Finally the champagne was poured—but instead of being properly chilled, it was the same temperature as the inedible meat and vegetables. Sighing glumly, he turned to the person next to him and held up the glass of champagne. "At last," he said, "they have served me something warm."

There are few things more disagreeable and unappetizing than lukewarm foods. What would you do with a cup of lukewarm coffee? Microwave it! A glass of lukewarm Coca-Cola? "Could I have some ice, please?" An omelette, a filet of sole, a stack of pancakes, a pizza, a châteaubriand with béarnaise sauce that has cooled to a tepid 70 degrees F? Scrape it into the sink disposal or feed it to the dog?

In the seventh and final letter to the churches, the Lord compares the church in the city of Laodicea to a plate of lukewarm food—a disagreeable and unsavory description to say the least. The Lord's message to the

Laodicean Christians is tough and confrontational. Could it be that the Lord was also looking beyond the first-century church in Laodicea? This letter, like the previous six letters, was written to Christians and churches of every century, including our own. The Laodicean letter is meant for all lukewarm Christians—and perhaps its target includes you and me.

Let's take a closer look and find out.

The Bank of America, Macy's, and the Mayo Clinic

The city of Laodicea was located about 100 miles directly east of Ephesus. It was part of a tri-city area, closely associated with Colosse (to which Paul's letter to the Colossians was written) and Hierapolis. Laodicea was famous throughout the Roman province of Asia as a center of wealth, or bustling commercial activity, and of the medical profession. It was the most prosperous of the seven cities of Revelation.

Many large, beautiful homes were built in Laodicea, the ruins of which can still be visited. Some of those expensive homes were probably owned by Christians. A textile and clothing industry flourished in Laodicea. A special breed of black sheep was raised in the area, producing a highly prized, glossy, black wool. The city was also known for its eyesalve, produced by the medical school of Phrygia located there.

As a center of wealth, commerce, and medicine, Laodicea was a kind of first-century Bank of America, Macy's, and Mayo Clinic rolled into one. An understanding of the social and economic setting of the church in Laodicea will help to explain some of the references we find in this letter.

The Amen

As in all the previous letters, our Lord introduces Himself in this letter in words that have deep significance. In His opening lines, the Lord gives the Laodicean believers the key to what they need.

3:14 *"To the angel of the church in Laodicea write:*
These are the words of the Amen, the faithful and true witness, the ruler of God's creation."

The first noteworthy thing the Lord says is that He is the "Amen." This is a familiar word to all Christians, though perhaps it is not so familiar in this particular usage. We are used to hearing or saying Amen at the close of a prayer or when we want to express our agreement with a meaningful statement. It is a word that means "so be it" or "truly."

"Amen" is a word that Jesus used frequently, although we may not be aware of this fact from reading English translations of the four Gospels. If you read through the words of Jesus you will frequently encounter the phrase, "I tell you the truth." Or, if you are more familiar with the King James Version, you find, "Verily, verily, I say unto you." In the original language of the New Testament, what Jesus says is, "Amen, amen, I say unto you." He used this phrase to underscore to His listeners that what He was about to say was extremely important and utterly true. He always highlighted significant truths this way. So when you encounter this phrase in the conversations and discourses of Jesus pay close attention to the important truth He is sharing.

"Amen" is the last word, the mark of trustworthiness, the imprimatur of truth. So it is only fitting that this word applies to Jesus, who is the final Word and who is the embodiment of truth. The book of Hebrews begins by declaring, "In the past God spoke to our forefathers through the prophets at many times and in various ways, but in these last days he has spoken to us by his Son." The word of Jesus is the last word, the reliable truth, the Amen. Anyone who would claim to give revelation beyond the word Jesus has already given is not giving us a new truth but is departing from the final truth, the Amen, that has been spoken to us in the person of Jesus Christ.

God's New Creation

Second, the Lord calls Himself "the faithful and true witness." He has emphasized His truthfulness in previous letters, but here He adds the word "faithful" to stress the fact that He not only tells the truth, but He tells the hard truth. He faithfully, plainly, clearly reveals to the church everything that the church needs to understand. Because of the confrontational nature of this letter, the Lord wants the Laodicean church to be very much aware of the truthful and faithful side of His nature.

The next phrase, "the ruler of God's creation," is in my view a mistranslation. It should actually read "the *beginning* of God's creation." It is the same Greek word we find in John 1:1, which reads, "In the *beginning* was the Word, and the Word was with God, and the Word was God." Two verses later, John amplifies this thought, saying, "Through him all things were made; without him nothing was made that has been made." Jesus is not merely the ruler but the origin, the source, the beginning of God's creation.

Note, too, that the Lord does not use the word "creation" merely to refer to the old creation, the physical universe in which we live, including the great galaxies of space, the planets, the sun, and the earth itself. More than that, Jesus is the source of God's *new* creation as well.

In 2 Corinthians 5:17, Paul writes, "If anyone is in Christ, he is a new creation; the old has gone, the new has come!" We are part of a new world that the Lord is bringing into being. In fact, it has already begun: the old *has* gone, the new *has* already come!

This is a truth the church in Laodicea desperately needed to apprehend. Note that at the end of his letter to the Colossians, Paul adds, "After this letter has been read to you [in Colosse], see that it is also read in the church of the Laodiceans and that you in turn read the letter from Laodicea." So the Laodiceans were to be familiar with Paul's letter to the Colossian believers—the letter in which Paul strongly emphasizes Jesus' link with the beginning of creation. Jesus, says Paul, is the "firstborn over all creation" and the "firstborn from among the dead" through His resurrection. The resurrection, in fact, is the new creation.

The church at Laodicea needed to be told important truth, even painful truth. And the truth they needed to hear was the truth about how to relate to God's new creation.

"I Know Your Deeds"

For the seventh and last time in Revelation, we encounter the phrase "I know your deeds."

3:15–16 *"I know your deeds, that you are neither cold nor hot. I wish you were either one or the other! So, because you are lukewarm—neither hot nor cold—I am about to spit you out of my mouth."*

These are chilling words—especially that opening line, "I know your deeds." Imagine receiving a phone call from an anonymous caller, and his first words to you were, "I know what you did." Would you feel gratified or ashamed to know that someone else knew your deeds?

When the Lord said, "I know your deeds," to the church in Philadelphia, it was cause for rejoicing. But when He said these same words to the church in Laodicea, it was cause for mourning. The Lord had been watching the church in Laodicea, and what He saw was not pleasing. There were two problems in the Laodicean church.

First, there was something tragically lacking in their commitment. "You are . . . neither hot nor cold" says the Lord. Like Disraeli's unappetizing meal, these Christians were tepid and lackluster in their devotion to Christ. The Laodiceans were not like the church at Sardis, which was as cold as death. Nor were they like the church at Philadelphia, which was hot, alive, and vital. They were merely lukewarm.

Archaeologists have discovered an interesting fact about the city of Laodicea. The source of the city's water supply was a hot spring at Hierapolis, about six miles away. The water was carried by aqueduct from this spring, and by the time it reached Laodicea the water was no longer hot, nor was it cold. It was lukewarm. Cold water is refreshing on a hot day, and hot water can be made into a warming, pleasant tea, but lukewarm water is nauseating.

So the Lord used the lukewarm water of Laodicea as an analogy for the lukewarm character of the Laodicean church. And His word to the church is, "I am about to spit you out of my mouth" because of the lukewarm commitment of the people. The word "spit" is a very weak translation. The word should be "vomit." The Lord is not merely saying He finds the works of the Laodicean Christians unappealing, but downright *nauseating*.

How did the Laodicean congregation get into such a state? There can be only one answer: *compromise*.

How do you get lukewarm water out of the tap? You turn on the cold water a little and you turn on the hot water a little. You combine a little of each, and the result is a lukewarm compromise.

Most humans don't like extremes of climate. In fact, some of us are still searching for that mythical corner of the world where the temperature is a constant 72 degrees year-round. What a retirement haven that would be! "Give me my comfort zone!" we say. "Let me just lie in the shade and take it easy."

But Jesus wants to move us out of our comfort zone, just as He wanted to move the Laodiceans out of theirs. What was their comfort zone? What issues were they compromising on?

They were compromising important doctrine. They were compromising truth. They were compromising spirituality for the sake of comfort. They had found that it is much more comfortable to attend a church where nobody takes doctrinal issues too seriously, where discussion of controversial issues is avoided. It is a lot easier to keep the peace if you just tone down the teaching a bit, so that no one gets ruffled or convicted. The Laodicean church had just enough truth to salve the conscience without anyone becoming a fanatic. They had a little truth mixed with enough restraint to keep the truth from affecting their will and launching them into service for Jesus.

The Laodicean church was a comfortable church. You could attend there for years and probably find it very pleasurable. You would never be challenged, rebuked, or corrected. You would never even have your conscience pricked. You would only be encouraged and stroked and flattered, because this was a comfortable, compromising church.

What does Jesus think of such a church?

"I am about to vomit you out of my mouth." Or, to paraphrase, "Yuck! How nauseating! It gags me!" The people may love the lukewarm climate in Laodicea, but Jesus does not. It makes them comfortable, but it makes the Lord sick! And the tragedy of the Laodicean experience is that it is being repeated again and again, in thousands of churches around the world.

Whose Church Is It?

The Laodicean church was symptomatic of an attitude I run into all the time: "The church belongs to the people." I believe this is one of the most dangerous and destructive attitudes a church can have. The idea that the church is owned by the people and that it exists for their benefit is what turns so many churches into what some have called "religious country clubs," operated for the exclusive benefit of the members.

Some years ago a young pastor called me and said, "I need to know what you would do if you were in my place. Last week the chairman of the board of our church called me in and said, 'You've been pastor here for a year, and you're a fine young man. We like you. You're a good Bible teacher. But there are a couple things we want you to understand before we renew your contract as pastor of this church.

"'First, we want you to understand that this is our church, not yours. We were here before you came, and we will be here after you leave. So don't get the idea you're going to make a lot of changes here.

"'Second, understand that we hired you, and we can fire you. If you don't like the way we do things, it's you that will be leaving, not us.'

"That's what they told me," he said. "I have to meet with them again next week. What would you tell them if you were in my shoes?"

I said, "Well, I would say, 'The next time we meet I'd like you all to bring your Bibles, because we're going to have a Bible study.' And when we all sat down together with our Bibles I would say to them, 'I understand that some of you feel this is your church. Now, I want you to show me where the Scriptures say that a church belongs to the people. I've looked and looked, and I can't find it. Instead, I find that Jesus says, "On this rock I will build *my church* and the gates of hell shall not prevail against it." And when Paul speaks to the Ephesian elders, he says, "Tend the flock *of God* which is among you, taking the oversight thereof." I'm willing to stand corrected, but as near as I can tell, there are many passages which say that the church belongs to Christ, and not a single passage which says it belongs to the people.' "

About two weeks later I got a letter from this young man. "I did and said everything you suggested," he wrote, "and you know what? They fired me!"

I admit that I had hoped events would take a different course for this young pastor. But within a few more weeks, I got another letter from him. "Another church has just called me to be their pastor. Before starting a new ministry there, I sat down with the board and we settled all these issues. I think this church and I are going to have a very effective ministry together."

I have followed this young man's ministry in his new church for several years, and I am happy to report that both pastor and congregation love each other, and the work of God is flourishing. I am convinced that a lot of the reason this church is doing so well is that the people in this church remember what the Laodiceans forgot: every church belongs to the Lord, not to the people.

Wretched and Poor

So the Laodiceans were comfortable. Even worse, they had become complacent and smug.

3:17 *"You say, 'I am rich; I have acquired wealth and do not need a thing.' But you do not realize that you are wretched, pitiful, poor, blind and naked."*

How tragic! Notice the big difference between "you say" and "you are." His message is, "*You say* you are rich, but *you are* poor." The faithful and true witness, Jesus Himself, has set the truth before the Laodicean church—the whole truth, even though it hurts. To use a popular expression, the Laodicean church was "fat, dumb, and happy." It was smug, self-sufficient, and complacent. These poor believers had no idea how much trouble they were in!

The Laodicean economy was humming along splendidly. The people had plenty of money, nice homes, plenty to eat. Translated into a twentieth-century cultural context, we would say that they had a beautiful sanctuary with padded mahogany pews, a mighty pipe organ, a golden-throated choir, a dynamic preacher, the wealthiest and most prominent donors, and the respect of the entire community. The Laodicean believers thought they were doing extremely well.

But the Lord, in whose name they were gathered together, looked at their sumptuous, comfortable, complacent church and said, "You are wretched, pitiful, poor, blind and naked." Why are the Laodiceans' self-appraisal and the Lord's appraisal so far apart? Because they are measuring by different standards.

If someone asked you the temperature outside, you might check a thermometer and say, "It's 32 above zero." I might check another thermometer and say, "No, you're wrong. It's actually zero." The truth is that we are both correct. You were looking at a Fahrenheit thermometer, while mine was marked off in centigrade degrees. Zero degrees centigrade equals 32 degrees Fahrenheit. If we measure by different standards, our evaluations will not agree.

Similarly, the Lord and the Laodiceans were measuring the Laodicean church by different standards. The Laodiceans were using the standards of the world. Their church was a pleasant, comfortable, respected body of believers. They thought they were doing splendidly. But Jesus used the standard of what He intended His church to be like.

The church is not a country club, operated for the benefit of its members. The church is not a performing arts center, where one is entertained with dramatic speeches and wonderful music. The church is not a political action group or a protest movement, taking sides on issues in the world's political arena. Elements of these roles may legitimately be expressed in the church from time to time: the church family may gather sometimes for fun and fellowship, or for a special concert, or to take action on important political issues that have strong moral and spiritual implications. But none of these roles constitutes the church's central purpose for existing.

Jesus has already told us what His church is to be like: *salt*. And not just *plain* salt—it must be *salty* salt! He said, "You are the salt of the earth. But if the salt loses its saltiness, how can it be made salty again? It is no longer good for anything, except to be thrown out and trampled by men."[1] A church that is salt should be salty. Like salt which is sprinkled over food, the church should be dispersed throughout its community and its world, flavoring whatever it touches.

The church is to function not only when it gathers together on Sunday, but during the week, as its members go out into the marketplace, the business offices, the shops, the neighborhoods. *There,* in the outside world, is where the real work of the church is done! *There* is where believers are to take the good news of Jesus Christ! *There* is where the church is to be salt, demonstrating before a watching world that Christians respond to opposition, trials, temptations, and joys in a different way than the world does. *There* is where we demonstrate a special attitude toward life, and where we flavor life with a distinct flavor.

The church is also called to be light. "You are the light of the world," said Jesus. "A city on a hill cannot be hidden."2 Light is a symbol of truth. The church is to be a source of truth, literally en*light*ening the world with the gospel, enabling the world to clearly see spiritual reality by the light that it sheds. The church is charged with the task of enabling people to understand the program of God throughout history. The church interprets the events of the day so that men may see not what man intends to do, but what God is already doing and will do in human history. The church declares the truth about humanity's lost condition and the good news that a Savior has come to save us from our sin.

By this standard, the Laodicean church was wretched, pitiful, poor, blind, and naked. It thought itself rich, but it actually had nothing.

The Laodicean Stage of Church History

In this, as in all six previous letters, we must step back and take the long view of church history. Each of the seven churches of Revelation represents a time when the prevailing atmosphere of the worldwide Christian church matched the conditions described in the letter. Looking back across twenty centuries of church history, we can see how accurate each of these prophetic symbols has been.

Now we come to the seventh age of the church, the Laodicean period. It is clear, as both history and prophecy confirm, that Laodicea symbolizes the church of the twentieth century, the last age of the church—

Our own age.

The Laodicean period is characterized by the phenomenon of people dictating what will be taught rather than submitting to the authority of the Word of God. It is significant, I believe, that the name "Laodicea" means "the judgment of the people," or to put it loosely, "people's rights." For isn't that the cry of our times?

Laodicea is where the people tell the ministers what to preach. We see this happening around us today. The apostle Paul predicted in his second letter to Timothy that in the last days, "men will not put up with sound doctrine. Instead, to suit their own desires, they will gather around them a great number of teachers to say what their itching ears want to hear. They will turn their ears away from the truth and turn aside to myths."3 Tragically, this is already taking place around us.

There used to be a time when the church taught that the natural self with which we were born needed to be crucified, denied, kept under careful control. Jesus said, "If anyone would come after me, he must *deny himself* and take up his cross and follow me."4 Yet we live in a day when churches are openly, brazenly advancing the self, teaching that we should assert the self and discover the powers and possibilities of the self, all apart from the necessity of a new birth.

Once the inerrancy of Scripture formed the bedrock of all evangelical churches. You could depend on the fact that the Bible was fully accepted as the inspired Word of God. But now churches, colleges, and seminaries which call themselves evangelical are rethinking the nature of Scripture, denying its inerrancy, and claiming it cannot be fully trusted. Instead of people submitting themselves to the judgment of the Word of God, we have people submitting the Word to their own judgment!

This is the age of compromise within the church. The church of the twentieth century is fast becoming a drifting church, a lukewarm church, a nauseating church in the eyes of the Lord. Once the church exhibited a burning desire to evangelize the world, to save those who were lost. Today, that desire has cooled in many churches, because pastors are telling their congregations that God is too loving to condemn anyone to an eternal separation from Himself. They say that good people who live good lives, even though they live apart from Jesus, will still be saved.

The church in the twentieth century is drifting away from the biblical truth that all have sinned and fall short of the standard of God's perfection, and that no one comes to the Father except through Jesus Christ. Even while the lostness of mankind is made unmistakably plain by the rise of crime, the plague of drug abuse, the failure of morality, the increasing pollution of our planet, compromising Christians in complacent churches continue to preach a feel-good "gospel" that has nothing to do with the authentic good news of salvation by grace through faith in Jesus Christ.

Once it was unheard of that Christians would suggest that the killing of unborn babies should be condoned, or that practicing homosexuals should be ordained to the ministry or married in religious ceremonies. Yet these things are taking place today at an accelerating rate.

Truly, *this* is the age of Laodicea.

"Buy from Me"

The Lord concludes His letter to the Laodicean church with an urgent appeal. This appeal can be divided into three parts. First, verse 18:

3:18 *"I counsel you to buy from me gold refined in the fire, so you can become rich; and white clothes to wear, so you can cover your shameful nakedness; and salve to put on your eyes, so you can see."*

The key to this verse is in those three little words: "buy from me." This is a profound truth that the Lord wants us to grasp: He has *everything* we need to live, to thrive, and to function. He is completely sufficient to supply all our needs, both in the church and as individual believers.

There's nothing wrong with a church having a large building, a great choir, and beautiful music. Nor is there anything intrinsically wrong with a Christian having a big home, a new car, a stereo, a TV, and a VCR. But these are not the things that churches and Christians *need*.

The Lord knows what our truest, deepest needs are: "gold," "white clothing," and "eye salve." These things, of course, are symbols for spiritual realities—realities that we desperately need in our lives. The Lord alone is the source of these spiritual possessions, and He makes them available to us whether we are materially rich and socially respected, or whether we are poor, persecuted, hunted, oppressed, and being put to death.

The first of these spiritual possessions is "gold refined in the fire." Peter tells us that our faith is "of greater worth than gold, which perishes even though refined by fire."5 Faith comes from the Lord Jesus. As we look to Him, our faith is awakened and stirred. We then see how true the Scriptures are and how clearly they fit with and explain our daily experience. The Laodiceans were secure and self-sufficient in their own prosperity, and they had ceased to live by the "refined gold" of faith in Jesus Christ alone.

The second of these spiritual possessions is "white clothes to wear, so you can cover your shameful nakedness." Everyone is morally naked before God. We all have secrets deep within us that no one else knows, that would virtually destroy us if anyone else discovered them. But God knows! He sees us in our nakedness and shame—and He makes us a gracious, compassionate offer: He offers to clothe us in the righteousness of His Son Jesus Christ!

Throughout these letters we have seen that white clothes stand for redemption, for righteousness imparted by Jesus Christ. As Isaiah tells us, our own righteousness is nothing but filthy rags in the sight of God,6 but the righteousness of Christ is perfect and acceptable to God. When we are clothed in the righteousness of Christ Himself, all our shame and sinfulness is removed. As in the words of the hymn,

> Jesus, thy blood and righteousness
> My beauty are, my glorious dress;
> 'Midst flaming worlds, in these arrayed,
> With joy shall I lift up my head.

White clothes stand for the changed character and new position we have received in Christ. They symbolize how God sees the believer who has washed his robes in the blood of the Lamb, which we shall learn more about in Revelation 7.

The third spiritual possession is "eye salve." Notice, first of all, that the Lord used an analogy from the everyday experience of the people He addressed. Speaking to His hungry disciples, He used the analogy of "the bread of life." To the woman at the well, He talked about "living water." In His parables He used everyday analogies from the marketplace, farming, and domestic life to translate deep spiritual truths in terms anyone could understand. In this letter He uses a medical analogy in addressing a community of believers that doubtless contained many physicians on its rolls. Laodicea was a center of medical learning, and it was noted for producing such pharmaceutical products as eye ointment. So He was borrowing from the everyday experience of the Laodiceans to make a spiritual point.

The Lord said that the Laodiceans needed eye salve to enable them to see. We find this same image elsewhere in Scripture—the image of a salve or ointment which opens blind eyes. This symbol refers to the anointing of the Spirit which opens our eyes to understand God's truth. In 1 John 2:27, the apostle says, "The anointing you received from him remains in you, and you do not need anyone to teach you. But as his anointing teaches you about all things and as that anointing is real, not counterfeit—just as it has taught you, remain in him." This does not do away with the need for teaching and preaching, but it does mean that unless the Spirit in you is opening your ears to the meaning of truth, all teaching will fall on deaf ears. When the anointing Spirit of Christ lives within us our eyes are opened to understand the Word of God and we see the Bible in a new, fresh, and penetrating way.

Are you having trouble understanding the Bible? Then ask yourself, "Do I have the Spirit of truth in my life? Or have I not yet come to Jesus and received that anointing salve which will open my eyes to see?" That, truly, is the most momentous and fateful question each of us must answer within our own hearts. And that question brings us to the second part of the Lord's three-part appeal. For in the next few verses, we will encounter one of the most vivid and poignant images in the Bible—the image of Jesus standing at the door of our hearts, knocking, waiting, earnestly desiring to come in and have fellowship with us.

Jesus at the Door

The second division of the Lord's appeal is given in verses 19 to 20, where He tells us how to obtain these spiritual possessions—the "gold," the "white clothes," and the "eye salve."

3:19–20 *"Those whom I love I rebuke and discipline. So be earnest, and repent. Here I am! I stand at the door and knock. If anyone hears my voice and opens the door, I will come in and eat with him, and he with me."*

What a kind and gentle expression of God's love! The Lord approaches this church, with its nauseating smugness, complacency, and failure, and He says, in effect, "I love you! The reason I rebuke you and discipline you is that I care for you!"

If you had loving, nurturing parents, or if you are a loving, nurturing parent, you probably have a deep understanding of the Lord's heart when He says, "Those whom I love I rebuke and discipline." You know that parenting isn't just hugs and bedtime stories and a pat on the head. Sometimes the parent-child love relationship involves pain and tears.

You may remember times when, by your wayward actions, you forced your parents to love you in such a way that "the board of education" was applied to "the seat of knowledge." You went away rubbing your smarting posterior and thinking, "I wish they didn't love me so much!" But in your heart you knew that your parents' rebuke and discipline was a sign of their love for you, and there was a great sense of security in that love.

Jesus wanted the Laodicean Christians to have that same sense of security, knowing that even with all the bluntness of this confrontational message, He loved the church. He loved the Laodicean Christians too much to allow them to go their lukewarm way. He would not let them go.

Verse 20 is, to my mind, the most moving and powerful explanation in the Bible of how to become a Christian. I have used this passage many times in my own witnessing to non-Christians. I have seen hearts melted and lives changed by this beautiful description of Christ standing outside our lives, patiently knocking at the door of our hearts.

The act of receiving Christ takes place in three simple steps. Step one: We *sense* that Jesus stands outside, wanting to come in. This sense often comes upon us when we feel that our lives are empty or meaningless, when we are hurting over the direction our lives have taken, or we feel a sense of guilt and remorse over our sins. At this low point in our lives we hear *good news*: Jesus loves us, He died for us, He has power to forgive our sins and change our lives! Something within us responds. We want Jesus to come in. We long for it. We have awakened to our need and to the Lord's offer to meet our need.

Step two: *We* must open the door. He will not open it. He will not force His way in. He never forces salvation on anyone. There is a famous painting which depicts the Lord standing before the door and knocking. The artist was very spiritually perceptive, for he painted the door without a handle or knob on the outside. This door of the heart can only be opened from the inside, by the occupant himself or herself. Jesus goes only where He is invited.

Read through the Gospels, and you will see several instances where the Lord offered Himself to men and women, then grieved over the fact that they would not receive Him. Remember how Jesus lamented over Jerusalem: "O Jerusalem, Jerusalem, you who kill the prophets and stone those sent to you, how often I have longed to gather your children together, as a hen gathers her chicks under her wings, but you were not willing!"7 In every case, Jesus offers Himself to others but He does not impose Himself on others. When rejected, He is not angry. He is sorrowful.

We must invite Jesus in, saying, "Come, Lord Jesus. Enter my life. Be my Lord. Be my Savior. Deliver me from my sins, and deliver me from my self."

Step three: Jesus enters! He promises that when we invite Him, He comes into our lives. We do not have to have a special feeling, a mystical sensation, an emotional experience (though occasionally people do). We can simply rely on His promise: "If anyone hears my voice and opens the door, I will come in and eat with him, and he with me."

It is a beautiful picture of our relationship with Jesus. He comes in, we have fellowship together, we have communion together, we dwell together in the same place.

The Throne of Jesus

The third division of the Lord's appeal is given in verses 21 to 22.

3:21–22 *"To him who overcomes, I will give the right to sit with me on my throne, just as I overcame and sat down with my Father on his throne. He who has an ear, let him hear what the Spirit says to the churches."*

As we have seen in the Lord's last three letters, Jesus promises that we will share in His reign. The true church will one day reign with Christ. But the Lord makes a very careful distinction in this thought: He distinguishes clearly between *His* throne and *His Father's* throne. The

Father's throne, of course, represents the sovereign government of the universe. God the Father is sovereign over all.

When the Lord completed His work on earth, having endured faithfully to the end, He ascended and sat down on His Father's throne. Both Psalm 110 and the book of Hebrews describe the Messiah as sitting down at the right hand of the throne of God. Thus He is Lord over all the universe right now, exalted on His Father's throne.

But Jesus, too, has a throne. In verse 21, He refers to it as *"my throne."* And Jesus invites the Christian who patiently, faithfully overcomes to reign with Him on His throne. In Scripture, that throne is called the throne of David. When the angel Gabriel appeared to Mary, as recorded in Luke 1, he told her she would have a son, that He would be called the Son of God, and that the Lord God would "give him the throne of his father David, and he will reign over the house of Jacob forever."

The house of Jacob is the nation of Israel. All twelve tribes of Israel are descended from the sons of Jacob. So this is a promise which specifically relates to the future time when Jesus assumes the throne of David and Israel is made the head of the nations. That future time, as we have seen in previous letters, is the Millennium. The promise of these verses is that the resurrected and glorified church will one day share with Jesus in reigning over His millennial kingdom.

This is the same amazing promise the Lord made to His disciples when He said, "I tell you the truth [literally, Amen, Amen], at the renewal of all things, when the Son of Man sits on his glorious throne, you who have followed me will also sit on twelve thrones, judging the twelve tribes of Israel."[8] This promise could not be any plainer.

But the end of the Millennium does not mean the end of the reign of the church alongside Jesus. We shall reign with Christ on into eternity, in the unimaginably sublime realm called the new heaven and the new earth.

In the last verse of Revelation 3, we hear the Lord's refrain for the final time: "He who has an ear, let him hear what the Spirit says to the churches." Are we listening to what the Spirit says to you and me in the church at the end of the twentieth century? The promises and warnings to the seven churches are as relevant to our lives as to the lives of the first-century believers. The seven letters could be summarized as follows:

To Ephesus: "Do not let your love for Jesus grow cold."

To Smyrna: "Do not fear the persecution of the world."

To Pergamum: "Trust the Word of God to keep you strong and faithful."

To Thyatira: "Avoid both sexual and spiritual adultery. Be pure."

To Sardis: "Wake up now! Strengthen what remains and is about to die!"

To Philadelphia: "I will open a door of ministry and witness for you."

To Laodicea: "Don't yield to complacency. Invite me in! Let me revolutionize and transform your life! If you do, you will have a princely position in the age to come!"

Sobered by the knowledge that we live in the lukewarm, Laodicean age of church history, stirred by the confrontational yet comforting message of these seven profound letters to seven churches, we now turn our attention to the next section of the book of Revelation. It is time to see what the world to come will look like.

Chapter Ten

Supreme Headquarters

Revelation 4

he future is big news.

Tune your television to CNN and sit back for a while. Odds are you won't have to watch long before seeing some "expert" give his predictions for the future. First, a scientist is interviewed about future developments in computers, technology, and space. Then a diplomat is asked to pontificate on the future of the Middle East. Next a political pundit speculates on the future of the coming election. Finally, a woman steps in front of a satellite photo to deliver the most dubious prophecy of all—the weather forecast.

The future is also big business.

Despite the fact that we live in the most scientifically sophisticated age in human history, the occult prophecy business is booming. Check the Yellow Pages of any large city directory: You'll find page after page of advertisements for palm readers, tarot readers, astrologers, psychics, and other assorted soothsayers. You can discover your future in the astrology column of your morning newspaper—and if you take three newspapers, you can read three different astrologers, forecasting three completely dissimilar forecasts for your future! You can even have your horoscope read over the phone by dialing a 900 number shown on your TV screen (only $10 for the first minute, $5 for each additional minute).

Our society is fascinated with the future. Indeed, as we approach the year 2000, that fascination seems to be turning into an obsession. People are turning to the occult, to the New Age, to books by Nostradamus and Cayce and Dixon, to supermarket tabloids, to every kooky and irrational source in a frenzied search for certainty about the future.

Ironically, our society has largely bypassed and ignored the best source of information about the future: the book of Revelation.

As we come to Revelation 4, we stand at the brink of the third division of the book. In Revelation 1:19, we learned from the Lord Himself that this book properly divides into three sections. There He told the apostle John, "Write, therefore, [1] what you have seen, [2] what is now, and [3] what will take place later." Part 1 comprised Revelation chapter 1, Part 2, Revelation 2 and 3; and Part 3 begins with Revelation chapter 4 and continues to the end of the book—the part that Jesus calls "what will take place later."

4:1 *After this I looked, and there before me was a door standing open in heaven. And the voice I had first heard speaking to me like a trumpet said, "Come up here, and I will show you what must take place after this."*

Notice that this passage begins and ends with two words, "after this." These words form the hinge of Revelation. In chapters 2 and 3, Jesus addressed the burning issues of the age of the church. But now we reach a transition. The scene shifts abruptly from the church to events that take place "after this." These words signal to us that what John is about to see is a vision of events which come after the church has finished its course, after the church has been removed from the world.

The fact that the remainder of Revelation takes place after the church has been taken up to be with the Lord (the event which has come to be known as the Rapture) is underscored by several details in the opening verses of Revelation 4. Let's examine those details.

John first sees an open door, and through that door he catches his first glimpse of heaven. He is not the first biblical prophet to have the privilege of standing on earth and looking into heaven. The Old Testament prophets Ezekiel, Isaiah, and Daniel also did so. But in John's case, there is an important difference: John, unlike all the other prophets who only looked into heaven, is actually *summoned* into heaven. No prophet in all of Scripture was ever allowed to enter heaven to report what he saw except John.

What is the significance of this fact? I believe it is important in that it symbolizes the point at which the church is removed from the world and taken into heaven, and the point at which a new era of human history begins. From this point on in the book of Revelation there is not a single reference to the church until the very last chapter. There are "saints" referred to throughout the book of Revelation, but the word "church" does not appear again until the Bride of the Lamb appears near the end of Revelation.

Many Bible scholars believe (and I agree) that John the apostle, as he is summoned into heaven, represents the church which will be called out of the world and into heaven at the end of the Laodicean age in which we now live. What John sees during the rest of Revelation is what the church will see from its heavenly vantage point after it is caught away to be with Christ.

This means that as we read on through the book of Revelation, we no longer see events from the standpoint of time but from the standpoint of eternity. In eternity, there is no set yardstick or sequence of events as there is in time. This fact makes the book of Revelation difficult to interpret in many ways, but it also adds to its fascination.

As we examine the rest of Revelation we must be careful not to impose our preconceived notions of time, eternity, and heaven on the events we will witness. Many of us have some rather muddled notions of what heaven will be like. Some people actually think of heaven in the old stereotypical terms of people living on clouds and playing harps. Some of us project our favorite pastimes on heaven, so that a golfer, for example, might picture heaven as an endless golf course where a fellow can hit a ball 500 miles with one swing. In my youth as a cowboy in Montana, we talked about "that great roundup in the sky."

But the reality of heaven transcends all our stereotypes, imaginative notions, and misconceptions. We will have to shed, as much as we are able, the earthbound preconceptions which might blind us to God's truth about eternity as He has revealed it in the book of Revelation.

In God's Revelation, eternal events are not reeled out in a simplistic, linear fashion, all neatly labeled and dated in tidy chronological categories. Events appear here and there, out of sequence. For example, the series of judgments which we will soon examine—the seals of the seven-sealed book, the sounding trumpets, the outpouring of the seven bowls of God's wrath—apparently do not follow one another in chronological order.

The reality of heaven is not that of an ethereal castle floating in the sky or on some other planet. Heaven is a real dimension of existence, and it exists in the here and now. It is a reality of being just beyond the reach of our senses. When John saw the open door into heaven, he was permitted to see into a very real realm, a dimension that is present all the time and from which all the visible affairs of the earth are governed. That is the biblical perspective on heaven, from the book of Genesis to the book of Revelation. To understand what God is revealing to us in this book we must shed our culturally bound, nonbiblical notions of heaven, and learn to see heaven as it is revealed to us in the Word of God.

The Headquarters of Heaven

Shortly after the attack on Pearl Harbor, I took a ship to Hawaii, not as a serviceman, but as a civilian. I vividly remember looking out over the harbor and seeing the dead hulks of America's shattered Pacific fleet, some capsized, some little more than half-submerged piles of twisted wreckage. I was part of a two-man paint crew brought over from the mainland and assigned to repaint the militarily sensitive buildings. Most of the painters in the area were Japanese Hawaiians, and because of the tensions of those times, people of Japanese descent were not permitted into certain areas of the base.

One day my partner and I were brought in to paint the office of Admiral Chester Nimitz, commander in chief of the entire U.S. Pacific Fleet and the chief naval strategist of World War II. I remember the awe I felt as I entered that office. I found myself surrounded by maps and charts of the Pacific islands. *Here in this room*, I thought, *the historic events of this war are being conceived and brought into existence. Within these four walls, the Admiral gathers with his captains and advisers to plan the tactics, advances, and assaults of the greatest conflict in human history.*

But the awe I felt at that moment pales in comparison to what John must have felt in the next scene from the book of Revelation—a scene in which he finds himself in the control center for the entire universe!

4:2–3 *At once I was in the Spirit, and there before me was a throne in heaven with someone sitting on it. And the one who sat there had the appearance of jasper and carnelian. A rainbow, resembling an emerald, encircled the throne.*

Here is the Supreme Headquarters of heaven! The first thing John saw, dominating everything else in this scene, was a great throne and someone seated upon the throne. You might be surprised to find that the *throne* is a central theme of the book of Revelation. Out of 22 chapters in the book, there are only five chapters in which the word "throne" does not appear. This fact impresses us with the truth that the government of

God towers over all human events. Everything that we read about in the newspapers and see on our TV screens, however awesome, saddening, or triumphant, takes place in the shadow of the sovereign throne of God.

Some years ago I was asked to speak at a church conference in England. We met in a Methodist chapel on the road between London and Cambridge. I particularly remember the song service at the beginning of the meeting. The chapel was filled with Christians, singing heartily to the Lord. One of the choruses we sang was the popular "Our God Reigns." I knew the song well so I didn't look carefully at the song sheet as we began singing. But in the midst of the song I happened to glance at the sheet—and I began to smile. For though the words of the song are, "Our God reigns," what was typed on the song sheet was, "Our God *resigns*"!

I was grateful that the people in that room were singing what was in their hearts, not what was on that song sheet. Unfortunately, however, many Christians these days not only sing but *live* as if their God had resigned and was no longer in power. But He has not! Thank God, He reigns! He is on the throne! And that is the theme of the book of Revelation.

The fact that there is a God and that He is on the throne of the universe goes directly against the thinking and spirit of our age. Modern man does not like the idea of a throne, of cosmic Authority, because that means there are absolutes which cannot be changed. Moral and spiritual values are guaranteed by the Authority of the throne.

People of our age want to be their own moral and spiritual authorities. They want the right to choose whatever sexual behavior suits them and to be free of such consequences as AIDS or unwanted pregnancies or to be able to abort unborn babies if those babies happen to be inconvenient. They want to do so without guilt or judgment. They want to be free to make up their own religion, to invent their own gods, or even to become their own gods if it suits them. They want to be free to conduct their business and amass their fortunes without ethical constraints.

But no matter how people may rebel and object, the existence of God's sovereign throne is an inalienable fact of the universe. The operation of His moral law is as certain and irreversible as the operation of such physical laws as the law of gravity. We can no more circumvent the laws of God than we can circumvent the laws of physics. God maintains and enforces those laws, and He is not concerned about man's feeble attempts to repeal the laws that He has issued from His sovereign throne.

"A glorious throne, exalted from the beginning," wrote the prophet Jeremiah amid the tumult and upheaval of his own time, "is the place of our sanctuary."[1] That is the throne that John saw.

The Figure on the Throne

The next observation John records is that there was someone seated upon the throne. As we read his words our expectations are immediately heightened: At last, we think, we shall learn what God looks like! John is permitted to actually see the Lord of the universe on His throne. And how does the apostle describe what he sees?

Colors!

Pure, flashing, jewel-like colors, like the blazing radiance cast off by a prism. There are some Bible scholars who believe the letters of John were written after the book of Revelation. If that is true it might explain why the apostle writes in 1 John 1:5, "God is light; in him there is no darkness at all." Perhaps he penned those words while recalling the rainbow-like cascading colors that reflected the majesty and glory of God upon His throne.

Moses was once told that no man can see the face of God and live. No one, not even John, has ever seen the face of God at any time. All that anyone has ever seen are those manifestations of His Being which tell of His attributes and His glory. John saw a figure seated on the throne of heaven, but the features of that figure were lost in the dazzling nimbus of lights that surrounded the throne.

Compare the vision of John with the vision of the Old Testament prophet Ezekiel. In Ezekiel 1, the prophet describes a vision of God very similar to John's—forms veiled in clouds, scintillating with brilliant lights, giving off lightning-like flashes. Like John, Ezekiel gives us no description of God's features, because God is so much more than a man.

John records that God manifested Himself in spectacularly colored light. These colors are full of rich significance and meaning. From these colors we learn several important things about the figure upon the throne.

First, we learn that it is not merely God the Father whom John sees upon the throne. There are actually three Persons manifested there. The first is signified by the stone jasper, which is really a diamond, the most beautiful and precious of all gems, highly prized for its ability to capture and refract light into a brilliant display of intense colors. The reason "diamonds are a girl's best friend" is that they so beautifully reflect light, enhancing her beauty in a spectacular way. The brilliant crystal John describes here symbolizes the dominant attribute of God the Father: His holy perfection.

The second stone is the carnelian or sardius, which is a beautiful, glowing, blood-red stone. This stone immediately suggests the Son, who gave His blood for us as an atonement for our sins. He is the Lamb of

God, and the precious sacrifice of His blood is suggested by the color of the precious carnelian stone.

The third stone is the emerald. John saw a great rainbow encircling the throne, green as an emerald. Green is the color of nature, the color of creation. A rainbow was first given at the flood of Noah, a sign expressed in nature of God's promise of grace to sinful mankind. "I have set my rainbow in the clouds," God said, "and it will be the sign of the covenant between me and the earth. . . . Never again will the waters become a flood to destroy all life."2

The rainbow in John's vision, brilliant in varying shades of emerald green, circling the throne of heaven, symbolizes the Holy Spirit administering the holiness and redemption of God to all creation. You may wonder, at first, how a rainbow can encircle the throne. Aren't all rainbows arch-shaped?

Actually, all rainbows are circles. When we see a rainbow in the sky we are seeing only part of it. When we stand on the ground and look at a rainbow, half of the refracted image of the rainbow is hidden below the horizon.

The best place to view a rainbow is from an airplane, where the entire circle of it is visible. If you are flying over clouds where a rain shower is taking place and the plane is positioned so that the sun is directly behind you as you watch the rain, you will see the full, brilliant, multicolored circle of the rainbow—and in the very center of the circle will be the shadow of your airplane!

The Twenty-Four Elders

Secondary to the powerful, colorful, scintillating image of God's glory that we have just examined, John then noticed that there were others seated in the Supreme Headquarters of heaven.

4:4 *Surrounding the throne were twenty-four other thrones, and seated on them were twenty-four elders [ancients]. They were dressed in white and had crowns of gold on their heads.*

There has been much debate over what these twenty-four elders or ancients mean. Many Bible scholars consider them to be redeemed saints, both of the Old and New Testaments: twelve elders of Israel, representing the twelve tribes, and twelve apostles. I used to hold this view myself, but one nagging detail of this view always troubled me: If twelve of these elders are the twelve apostles, then one of them would have been John

himself. Does he see himself seated there? Does that make sense? I don't
think so.

Those Bible scholars who see these twenty-four elders as saints point
to their white robes and the golden crowns of victory upon their heads.
The suggestion is that these crowns indicate that they have conquered
evil, and their white robes have been washed in the blood of the Lamb.
But there is another explanation for the crowns and robes, as we shall
soon explore.

I have come to the conclusion that this group of elders is probably
what Daniel and other Old Testament prophets saw when they looked
into heaven. In Daniel 4, the prophet Daniel is called before King
Nebuchadnezzar to interpret the king's dream. In this dream, a great tree
is cut so that only the stump remains. Daniel's interpretation is that the
tree represents Nebuchadnezzar himself, and the dream is a prophecy that
his crown will be taken away from him for a period of seven years.
During those seven years, he will lose his mind and be turned out to eat
grass like a horse or cow. At the end of that time his throne and authority
will be restored to him. This is what Daniel tells the king:

> "The decision is announced by messengers, the holy ones
> declare the verdict, so that the living may know that the Most
> High is sovereign over the kingdoms of men and gives them to
> anyone he wishes and sets over them the lowliest of men."[3]

Clearly there are other inhabitants of the dimension of heaven. They
are associated with God's judgment upon this king and are called "messengers" or "holy ones." In Daniel 7 we find a similar reference. This is
the scene Daniel saw as he looked into heaven:

> As I looked, thrones were set in place, and the Ancient of
> Days took his seat. His clothing was as white as snow; the hair of
> his head was white like wool. His throne was flaming with fire,
> and its wheels were all ablaze. A river of fire was flowing, com-
> ing out from before him. Thousands upon thousands attended
> him; ten thousand times ten thousand stood before him. The court
> was seated, and the books were opened.[4]

So Daniel, like John, saw thrones arrayed about the great throne of
God. Individuals seated upon these thrones took part in the judgments
and decisions which God Himself rendered. We find a similar reference
in Psalm 89:6-7:

For who in the skies above can compare with the LORD?
Who is like the LORD among the heavenly beings?
In the council of the holy ones God is greatly feared;
he is more awesome than all who surround him.

Who, then, are these twenty-four elders in Revelation 4? I believe they are *angels* who have been put in charge of this present age. They are a body of twenty-four intelligent, powerful angels associated with the government of God. They wear crowns because they are victors in their battles with Satan. They wear white robes because they are righteous angels who refused to join the rebellion of the devil.

From Grace to Judgment

As John continued to look, he saw still more symbols—awesome, powerful symbols, both sights and sounds.

4:5–6a *From the throne came flashes of lightning, rumblings and peals of thunder. Before the throne, seven lamps were blazing. These are the seven spirits of God. Also before the throne there was what looked like a sea of glass, clear as crystal.*

Understand that these are symbols which stand for a hidden reality. The real form of the deep things of God is undoubtedly far beyond our ability to comprehend, so He communicates to us through pictures. These pictures are helpful and instructive and tell us all we truly need to understand—but these pictures should not be confused with the deep reality they represent.

Note, first of all, that John relates that "flashes of lightning, rumblings, and peals of thunder" came from the throne. These are sights and sounds associated with the moment God gave the Law to Moses on Mount Sinai. Moses records that the mountain was covered by dark clouds lit by flashes of lightning and that the earth shook constantly with great thundering rumbles. The sight was so awesome that the people of Israel were stunned with fear. These sounds, then, are symbols of the judgment of God.

What we have to understand about the book of Revelation (and what will become abundantly clear the more deeply we explore this book) is that this book describes a time when God's dealings with mankind enter a new phase. At the end of human history God at last turns from grace to judgment. All through the Bible God has demonstrated the gracious dimension of His personality. We have seen Him appealing to people to open their minds and hearts, to listen to His instruction, to receive the truth. He has lovingly, graciously invited all of mankind to join in sweet fellowship with Him.

Now, however, we see at last what results when people reject God and cling to their self-will and sin. Now we see the just and righteous dimension of His personality. We see God in His role as sovereign judge over all people.

My friend Charles Swindoll has said that the first theological statement he ever heard was spoken to him by his mother when he was just a little boy. She said to him, "May God help you if you ever do that again!"

In a way, that is what the book of Revelation is about: For centuries God has warned humankind what sort of judgment their folly would lead to, and now, in Revelation, He carries out that judgment.

The symbols of lightning, rumblings, and thunder are repeated several times throughout the book of Revelation. They are a reference point to which the book returns again and again. When you see these symbols in the book of Revelation—for example, in 8:5, 11:19, and 16:18—you can be certain that they accompany scenes of God's final judgment against the world's evil. Each time there is thunder, lightning, and rumbling, and a further element of judgment is added.

The other symbols which appear in verses 5 and 6 represent the Spirit of God, the instrument of God's judgment. John saw seven burning lamps, blazing with divine vengeance. The lamps represent the Spirit of God.

John also saw a crystalline sea before the throne. As we have already discussed, crystal speaks of purity and holiness. The sea is the Spirit of God in His holy perfection. That is why we call Him the *Holy* Spirit.

Anyone who comes into the presence of God must be holy. As the book of Hebrews tells us, "Make every effort . . . to be holy; without holiness no one will see the Lord."[5] The Spirit of holiness stands before the throne of God like a brilliant, crystalline reflecting pool, mirroring the holy purity of God.

Weird Creatures

Next we are introduced to four weird, wonderful symbolic creatures.

4:6b–8 *In the center, around the throne, were four living creatures, and they were covered with eyes, in front and in back. The first living creature*

was like a lion, the second was like an ox, the third had a face like a man,
the fourth was like a flying eagle. Each of the four living creatures had
six wings and was covered with eyes all around, even under his wings.
Day and night they never stop saying:

> *"Holy, holy, holy*
> *is the Lord God Almighty,*
> *who was, and is, and is to come."*

These are bizarre creatures, unlike anything that has ever existed on
the earth. They are like winged animals, covered with eyes all over their
bodies, even under their wings. Who are these creatures? What do they
represent?

Again, if you turn to the Old Testament book of Ezekiel you will find
a close parallel to the description in the book of Revelation. In Ezekiel 1,
we find very similar creatures, which the prophet calls "cherubim." The
matter of cherubim is yet another area of popular misconception. Many
people think of cherubim (or "cherubs") as pudgy, naked baby angels
who fly about on tiny wings, shooting people with Cupid-like arrows of
love. But cherubim, as Ezekiel describes them, look like this:

> Each of the four had the face of a man, and on the right side
> each had the face of a lion, and on the left the face of an ox; each
> also had the face of an eagle. Such were their faces. Their wings
> were spread out upward; each had two wings, one touching the
> wing of another creature on either side, and two wings covering
> its body.[6]

In Isaiah 6, we find such creatures again, and Isaiah calls them
"seraphim," which means "burning ones." Small details of the descriptions vary from account to account. Sometimes they have six wings,
sometimes only four.

Ezekiel and John both mention the fourfold faces of these creatures—
faces of the lion, the ox, the eagle, and man. Four is always the number
which symbolizes government. These creatures, therefore, are somehow
associated with God's government, both of human affairs and of the created universe.

The many eyes of John's description symbolize discernment and
knowledge. The wings describe soaring strength and rapidity of movement. The faces symbolize the qualities and forces of life in the created
universe. The lion's face speaks of power; the ox of patience; the eagle of

swiftness; the man of intelligence.

What is the function of these four weird yet wonderful creatures of heaven? In Revelation 6 they will summon the four horsemen to action with the command, "Come!" But in this chapter their function is to call all of creation to worship the Creator.

True Worship

Did you know that all of nature worships God? Even inanimate objects—stars, stones, trees, flowers, waters—give Him praise. Nature worships whenever any part of nature fulfills the intention God had in mind for it.

The poet has written,

> Full many a rose was born to blush unseen
> And waste its sweetness on the desert air.

To which I reply: What waste? No rose ever wastes its sweetness! Even if there is no human being within a thousand miles of that rose, God inhales its fragrance and delights in its beauty.

The perfection of nature gives praise and glory to God, its Creator. Examine a flower closely and you can't help marveling at the beauty and complexity of its design, conceived and executed by the power and wisdom of God. All of nature is as amazing as that flower, and the contemplation of nature should lead us to worship and praise Him.

In verses 9 to 11, we see that one of the tasks of these four living creatures is to elicit from the creation—including that part of the creation called *man*—the praise and perfection God intended it to produce.

4:9–11 *Whenever the living creatures give glory, honor and thanks to him who sits on the throne and who lives for ever and ever, the twenty-four elders fall down before him who sits on the throne, and worship him who lives for ever and ever. They lay their crowns before the throne and say:*

> *"You are worthy, our Lord and God,*
> *to receive glory and honor and power,*
> *for you created all things,*
> *and by your will they were created*
> *and have their being."*

This is a powerful, moving song of praise, strongly suggesting to the mind the power of the "Hallelujah Chorus" from Handel's *Messiah*.

These words should not be repeated mechanically or merely skimmed over, because that would be boring. Heaven is anything but boring!

Why does heaven resound with praise to God? Because the inhabitants of heaven continually discover new, exciting, profound aspects of God's wisdom and power! They are continually inspired and re-inspired and re-re-inspired to praise God for the wonderful Creator He is. So should our worship be, for that is *true worship*.

Eugene Peterson has said that true worship accomplishes five specific functions:

1. True worship centers our attention. We are truly worshiping God when we see Him—not our own ego—as the center of everything. True worship means we stop living for ourselves and thinking of ourselves and start living and thinking solely in reference to God and His agenda.

2. True worship gathers people together. As we truly worship, we become part of a family. It is an inclusive, not exclusive, activity.

3. True worship reveals truth. As we truly worship, we begin to understand things we have never seen before. Familiar patterns of life suddenly expand to become new vistas of experience. New realizations dawn. We are uplifted and renewed in mind and spirit.

4. True worship makes us sing. We can't help it. We can't hold it back. Worshiping Christians are always singing. Indeed, Christians can sing even when others weep. As we go through the rest of Revelation we will see that, even in the midst of worldwide travail and judgment, there are many songs being sung, because there is true worship taking place.

5. True worship affirms. As we truly worship, we respond to God's great promises with a resounding "Amen," with thousands of voices united in saying "Yes!" to God.

Peterson beautifully sums up the power of worship as he writes,

> Failure to worship consigns us to a life of spasms and jerks,
> at the mercy of every advertisement, every seduction, every
> siren. Without worship we live manipulated and manipulating
> lives. We move in either frightened panic or deluded lethargy as
> we are, in turn, alarmed by spectres and soothed by placebos. If
> there is no center, there is no circumference. People who do not
> worship are swept into a vast restlessness, epidemic in the world,
> with no steady direction and no sustaining purpose.[7]

Revelation 4 represents far more than just a first glimpse into the realm of heaven and the future. It is a vivid collage of images which focuses our eyes on what worship should be in all times and in all places. What this passage reveals about the condition of our hearts *right now* is at least as important as what it reveals about the future. Can we, with all our hearts, say "Amen!" to the words of this great hymn of true worship?

> Immortal, invisible, God only wise,
> In light inaccessible, hid from our eyes.
> How blessed, how glorious, the Ancient of Days,
> Almighty, Victorious, Thy great name we praise.
>
> Great Father of glory, pure Father of light,
> Thine angels adore Thee, all veiling their sight;
> All praise we would render, O help us to see
> 'Tis only the splendor of light hideth Thee!

For just a moment in our study of Revelation, let's set the future aside and ask ourselves as Christians living in the lukewarm Laodicean age of the 1990s, "Are we, in the here and now, *truly* a worshiping people as God intended us to be?"

Chapter Eleven

The Great Breakthrough

Revelation 5

I n the 1960s the late member of the Beatles, John Lennon (who once claimed his rock-and-roll music was more popular than Jesus Christ), wrote a song called "Imagine" which describes a world made perfect by the elimination of war—and the elimination of religion. This song has been revived in the 1990s as an anthem for a new generation of New Age-influenced young people. They march in the streets, singing "Imagine" or Lennon's other peace anthem, "Give Peace a Chance," while carrying signs demanding peace, demanding plenty, demanding Utopia.

There is nothing new about humanity's longing for Utopia. This wistful desire for a place where there is no war, no poverty, no hunger, no hatred, and no sorrow is the most universal and enduring passion of mankind. Utopian literature can be traced back as far as Plato (around 400 B.C.) and Euhemerus (around 300 B.C.). Some utopian dreamers, such as Thomas More, have placed their hope in human reason as the cure for social evils. Edward Bellamy, in his book *Looking Backward*, suggested that the road to Utopia lay in reforming our economy.

There is, however, only one hope for a utopian society: the Person whose birth was heralded some 2,000 years ago with the words, "On earth peace to men on whom his favor rests." As we come to Revelation chapter 5, we find that we stand at the brink of the realization of mankind's most elusive dream. As we shall see, this dream is destined to be fulfilled—not by economic reforms, human reason, or protest marches, but by the sovereign authority and dominion of the Redeemer, Jesus Christ.

The Ultimate "Mystery Thriller"

In the previous chapter, John the apostle was caught up into heaven, where he saw the throne of God and the court of heaven. Now, in Revelation 5, the scene is still heaven, but the *theme* changes. From a theme of worship of God the Creator, we shift to the theme of worship of the Redeemer, Jesus Christ.

5:1–4 *Then I saw in the right hand of him who sat on the throne a scroll with writing on both sides and sealed with seven seals. And I saw a mighty angel proclaiming in a loud voice, "Who is worthy to break the seals and open the scroll?" But no one in heaven or on earth or under the earth could open the scroll or even look inside it. I wept and wept because no one was found who was worthy to open the scroll or look inside.*

The first questions this passage suggests are, "What does the scroll represent? Why is it sealed?"

Note, first of all, that what John sees is not a book but a scroll, a large rolled strip of paper or parchment, sealed with seven seals on the end so that it cannot be unrolled and read. As we shall see in Revelation 6, the opening of these seals and the unrolling of this scroll will reveal a series of momentous events which will shake the earth to its foundations. In fact, the events described in this scroll will continue to unfurl throughout Revelation 7, 8, 9, and 10.

What does the scroll signify? We are given a clue in Revelation 10:7, where John is told, "But in the days when the seventh angel is about to sound his trumpet, *the mystery of God* will be accomplished, just as he announced to his servants the prophets." The scroll, then, is a "mystery" book. Indeed, you might call it the ultimate "mystery thriller," and its title is *The Mystery of God*. It answers all the great unanswerable questions people have been asking for generations.

Perhaps the most persistent and vexing of these great questions is, "Why can't humankind solve its own problems?" Everyone wants Utopia, but no one knows how to achieve it. Everyone wants an end to war, crime, evil, and prejudice, but no one knows how to end the misery of our humanity. We continue to make such rapid technological and scientific progress that the amount of combined knowledge amassed within the libraries, archives, and data bases of the human race literally doubles every dozen years! One would think humanity, having made such amazing strides, would be on the verge of physical, intellectual, and moral perfection.

Yet the human race has never seen more suffering, nor been in greater peril, than it is right now.

All the greatest, thorniest problems of human society remain as insoluble today as they were thousands of years ago. Why? Why, after all our progress and increased knowledge, can we not solve our most basic human problems?

The scroll of *The Mystery of God* holds the answer.

A Perfect World

The contemporary writer Annie Dillard has posed what she calls "the chief theological question of all time." The question is, "What in the Sam Hill is going on here anyway?"

Have you ever felt that way? Things seem to happen in life that we just can't understand. Unjust, meaningless, random events. In confusion, frustration, and disgust, we say, "What in the Sam Hill is going on here anyway?"

The answer to this "theological question" is in the scroll. God will straighten out the mess that this world has become, and He will fulfill His promise of a golden Utopia where men will live without war, without crime, without hatred. There will be no death, no sorrow, and all tears will be wiped away.

A writer in a popular magazine once described what she thought a perfect world would be like:

No housework.
No drug abuse.
No prejudice.
A relationship that works.
More time with our families.
A decent education for all.
Clean air and water.
A birth control pill for men.
A car really built for families.
Health (no AIDS).
Happiness (no war).
And the pursuit of a family-friendly workplace.[1]

That, according to this writer, would be a perfect world. Clearly, this writer does not expect God to have very much to do with bringing this perfect world about. But isn't that a common attitude in our age? Our image of the perfect world tends to be a mixture of peace on earth and material comfort, with no room for God.

The scroll in Revelation, however, reveals that God has a *different* plan for bringing about true Utopia. That plan is what the book of Revelation is all about, and at the center of it all is Jesus the Redeemer.

At the outset John makes an interesting observation about the scroll. It is, he says, "a scroll with writing on both sides." The ancients hardly ever wrote on both sides of a scroll because, normally, only one side was formed smooth for writing, while the back side was rough and uneven. A scroll with writing on both sides is symbolic of a full and important message. This seems to indicate that the nature of the message will be complex, involved, and lengthy—an indication which chapters 6 through 10 will bear out.

The fact that God's plan was written in the form of a scroll rather than simply being revealed by a voice is also very significant. A written scroll is symbolic of permanent, indelible truth. What God has written, no one can change. As in the famous lines from the *Rubáiyát* of Omar Khayyám,

> The moving finger writes, and having writ
> Moves on; nor all your Piety nor Wit
> Shall lure it back to cancel half a line,
> Nor all your tears wash out a word of it.

Or as Pontius Pilate said of the inscription he ordered hung over the cross of Christ, "What is written is written." The words are indelible. They cannot be changed.

Who Is Worthy?

"Who is worthy?" This question is at the heart of all politics, for it is in the mind of every voter who enters the voting booth. Who is capable of leading us toward the solutions for our problems? Who is smart enough? Moral enough? Strong enough? Who is worthy?

It is also the question that haunts the apostle John in this passage. As he stands looking upon the scroll of God, an angel proclaims an invitation to all the universe: "Who is worthy to break the seals and open the scroll?" The question lingers in the air of heaven like an accusation. No one steps forth.

Throughout human history there have been those who considered themselves worthy to "break the seals," to "open the scroll," to carve out a man-made Utopia on earth. The Babylonian king Nebuchadnezzar boasted of his wisdom and might in building the great empire of Babylon. But his empire soon fell.

Alexander the Great thought he had achieved a Utopian empire. At the age of 32, having extended his rule into Persia, Media, Asia Minor, and India, Alexander wept because he had no more worlds to conquer. Yet within a year Alexander was dead, having gorged and drunk himself to death at an extravagant banquet. Without the force of his will to hold it together, his empire soon disintegrated.

Julius Caesar led his legions across the face of Europe to impose the *Pax Romana*—the Peace of Rome—upon the world by force of arms. But Rome ultimately fell, due to moral corruption within and assault from without by northern barbarians.

The boneyards of history are littered with fallen conquerors and their shattered dreams of a man-made Utopia: Charlemagne and Napoleon, who—each in his own way and his own time—sought to place the world under the banner of France; Germany's Hitler, who envisioned a world-wide Reich that would last a thousand years; Iraq's Saddam Hussein, who vowed to "liberate" the Islamic holy places in Jerusalem and Mecca, and who dreamed of uniting the entire Moslem world, from north Africa to Asia, under his own rule.

Those who considered themselves worthy to "break the seals," to "open the scroll," to subjugate nations and impose their will on the world have usually been narcissistic, egocentric tyrants. Their vision of an earthly "heaven" has usually resulted in an earthly "hell" of wars and suffering. The world regards such figures with a combination of alarm, pity, and loathing.

Yet even the best and most heroic leaders in history have not proven worthy to "break the seals," to "open the scroll," and to bring about a world of peace. George Washington, revered as a man of great leadership and wisdom, could not lead the world into the long-hoped-for golden age. Abraham Lincoln, with his godly heart full of compassion for both the North and South, was unable to resolve the deep social and political problems of his time—some of which continue to haunt us today.

In recent years, a movement was begun to add the likeness of Ronald Reagan alongside the four other faces on Mount Rushmore. But even those who consider President Reagan as standing alongside men like Washington, Jefferson, Theodore Roosevelt, and Lincoln would have to admit that none of these men was able to solve the great problems of history. None was worthy to open the scroll.

No wonder John wept!

He wept and wept, he said, because no one could be found who could unseal the scroll or even look inside. No one knew how to go about it. Among all the leaders of the world there is not one man or woman who has a clue to the solution of the great issues that divide, plague, and imperil the human race.

The Lion and the Lamb

In verse 5, John learns to his amazement that the problem has already been solved! The twenty-four angels of the heavenly council around God's throne know the answer, and one of them discloses the answer to John.

5:5 *Then one of the elders said to me, "Do not weep! See, the Lion of the tribe of Judah, the Root of David, has triumphed. He is able to open the scroll and its seven seals."*

"The Lion of the tribe of Judah" and "the Root of David" are significant Jewish titles. They refer to prophecies from the Old Testament which predict that there would come one from the tribe of Judah and from the family of David who would rule over the earth and put an end to all the earth's pain and sorrows. These two titles refer to the King of the Jews—the same title which Pilate had posted over the cross of Jesus. It is the King of the Jews, the Redeemer Himself, who has gone through death and suffering in order to conquer death and suffering, who is destined to bring about God's kingdom on the earth.

"See, the Lion of the tribe of Judah," says the angel. We, like John, expect to see a great cat-like creature with claws and sharp teeth, shaking its golden mane. But when John turns, he doesn't see a Lion—he sees a Lamb!

5:6 *Then I saw a Lamb, looking as if it had been slain, standing in the center of the throne, encircled by the four living creatures and the elders. He had seven horns and seven eyes, which are the seven spirits of God sent out into all the earth.*

The body of the Lamb is wounded, as if it had been put to death. Without question this Lamb is the slain Redeemer of the world! This moment of John's recognition of his Lord in the symbolic form of a Lamb is echoed in the Fanny Crosby hymn which says,

> I shall know Him, I shall know Him,
> As redeemed by His side I shall stand.
> I shall know Him, I shall know Him,
> By the prints of the nails in His hand.

The marks of the Lord's death are still there, imprinted even in His resurrected body for all eternity. In the uniting of these two symbols—the Lion of Judah and the Lamb that was slain—we see the unity of two themes which pervade both the Old and New Testaments. The lion is a symbol of majesty, power, rule, and authority. The lamb is a symbol of meekness, innocence, and sacrifice. Lions conquer; lambs submit. Lions roar; lambs go to slaughter.

Here, in Revelation 5, the angel announces a Lion, then introduces John to a Lamb. The meaning is clear: Here is the One who conquers by submitting, who is worthy of power and authority by reason of His meekness, innocence, and sacrifice. Here, bound together in a powerful overlapping image, is the lionly Lamb, the fulfillment of God's earthly promises to Israel and His heavenly calling of the church.

It seems odd that many Bible commentators ignore the promises to Israel when considering these verses. The references to the Lion of Judah and the Root of David are clear signs that Israel is coming back to center stage as the end of human history approaches. As the scroll begins to unroll, God is calling Israel to the ultimate fulfillment of promises that were made to it long ago. All of earth's history is moving toward a climax, and the key to it all is the nation of Israel.

Indeed, throughout the entire span of the Bible, Israel has been the key to understanding history. The earth cannot be blessed until the nation of Israel is blessed. Even though the Messiah came to Israel and Israel rejected its Messiah, and even though God has chosen the church as His instrument of ministry to the world from the time of Christ until now, *the time of Israel's full restoration is coming*. The Old Testament prophets predicted it, and John describes it in Revelation: the Messiah, the promised Lion of Judah, the Root of David, is coming to fulfill God's promises to the people of Israel.

The Lion and Lamb theme is the basis for C. S. Lewis's popular fantasy series *The Chronicles of Narnia*. Lewis's great golden lion Aslan, a symbol of Christ, rules in majesty, roars in triumph, and conquers evil— but his real triumph comes only after he submits to being executed by the satanic White Witch. When Aslan is resurrected, the kingdom of Narnia is freed from its bondage to eternal winter. The springtime of the world arrives. The story contains profound symbolic echoes from the book of Revelation.

As the Lion of Judah, Jesus will rule the world with a rod of iron. As the Scriptures prophetically declare in Psalm 2,

> Why do the nations conspire [rage]
> > and the peoples plot in vain?
> The kings of the earth take their stand
> > and the rulers gather together
> against the LORD
> > and against His Anointed One. . . .
> [The Lord says,] "I have installed my King
> > on Zion, my holy hill. . . .
> You will rule them with an iron scepter;
> > you will dash them to pieces like pottery."[2]

Zion is symbolic of the city Jerusalem. In that city, says this prophetic Psalm, Jesus shall reign with a rod of iron and dash to pieces those nations that resist His reign.

But remember, the Lion is also a Lamb. Those who are weak, faltering, helpless, or without hope will find Jesus to be a compassionate, gracious Savior. As the Lamb of God, He is full of mercy and grace.

Those who are rebellious will find Jesus a Lion. Those who are needy will find Him a Lamb.

Notice the special description of the Lamb in John's vision. He has seven horns. In Scripture, an animal's horns speak of power, and seven is the number of fullness. So the Lamb which was slain has full, complete power as a result of His death and resurrection. As the book of Hebrews says, "He is able to save *completely*"—or as the King James Version says, "to the uttermost"—"those who come to God through him."[3] And as Jesus Himself declared following His resurrection, "All power is given unto me in heaven and in earth."[4]

The Lamb also has seven eyes. In Scripture, eyes speak of full intelligence, discernment, and understanding through the Holy Spirit. Again, the number seven indicates that the Lamb's understanding of the events and dynamics of human history is complete and perfect. These seven eyes are the seven spirits of God which, as we have already seen, are a symbol of the Holy Spirit. In John's gospel, we are told that Jesus "did not need man's testimony about man, for he knew what was in a man."[5]

Jesus understands humanity. Thus He is the One who is worthy to take the scroll, to remove the seals, and to disclose and execute God's plan for the final stages of human history.

The Worship of the Lamb

Next, the Lamb who is worthy takes up the scroll—and all of heaven breaks forth into peals of song and praise.

5:7–8 *He came and took the scroll from the right hand of him who sat on the throne. And when he had taken it, the four living creatures and the twenty-four elders fell down before the Lamb. Each one had a harp and they were holding golden bowls full of incense, which are the prayers of the saints.*

The court of heaven understands the meaning of history and the program of God. The realm of heaven rings with worship, and at the center of that worship is the Lamb who was slain. Each of the twenty-four elders has a harp, and there are bowls of fragrant incense, which are the prayers of the saints.

The harp symbolizes the music of inanimate creation. Not only will all human and angelic beings in the universe glorify God, but *all* of creation—the rocks, the trees, the mountains, the hills, the sea—will give praise and worship to God the Father and His Son, Jesus the Redeemer. You see this same image of all creation praising the Creator in Psalm after Psalm. Just as the strings of a harp vibrate in harmony, so the whole of creation will vibrate in harmonious worship of God.

Notice that the elders are depicted as holding the golden bowls of incense. The elders are, in fact, presenting the prayers of the saints to God. There is a profound and exhilarating truth for you and me in this image: *we, the redeemed, actually contribute to the work of redemption through our prayers!*

Of course, we cannot lay the foundation for our redemption. Only Jesus could do that, and He has accomplished that task perfectly. But we do have a role in applying God's redemptive power throughout the earth. As the apostle Paul has written,

> I urge, then, first of all, that requests, prayers, intercession
> and thanksgiving be made for everyone—for kings and all those
> in authority, that we may live peaceful and quiet lives in all godli-
> ness and holiness. This is good, and pleases God our Savior, who

wants all men to be saved and to come to a knowledge of the truth.6

That is what prayer does. When you care about another person and you bring that person before the throne of God in prayer, you become part of the process of applying God's work of redemption to that human heart. You actually become a partner with the God of the universe in changing and redeeming lives! The fact that you and I can become a part of God's eternal program for human redemption should ignite, excite, and transform our prayer life.

A New Song

Some fifty years ago I lived in a tiny room at the North Avenue YMCA in Chicago. One Easter Sunday morning, I rose before dawn and got dressed to attend the great sunrise service in Soldier Field. As I was dressing, I glanced at an open hymn book on my bureau. It was open to the hymn "Beneath the Cross of Jesus." The words of the second verse seemed to jump off the page as I read,

> Upon that cross of Jesus mine eye at times can see
> The very dying form of One who suffered there for me;
> And from my smitten heart with tears two wonders I confess —
> The wonder of redeeming love, and my unworthiness!

I was struck with my own unworthiness, and my heart was melted as I read those words. Yes, I had known before that I was sinful and unworthy, but somehow this was different. The words of the hymn pierced my heart, and the marvel of God's redeeming love swept over me like a completely new emotion. The close walls of that little room faded away, and I seemed to be standing with that great throng in heaven, singing an awestruck song of God's love for mankind, made manifest on the cross.

In the next few verses of this passage, the apostle John hears a song very much like the song that melted my heart one Easter Sunday morning in the 1940s.

5:9–10 *And they sang a new song:*

> *"You are worthy to take the scroll and to open its seals,*
> *because you were slain,*
> > *and with your blood you purchased men for God*
> > *from every tribe and language and people and nation.*
> *You have made them to be a kingdom and priests to serve our God,*
> > *and they will reign on the earth."*

In these verses John hears the four living creatures and the twenty-four elders, their voices joined as a heavenly choir, singing a new song. Why is this song called a new song? Because it is new to the elders and the four living creatures. They have never sung such a song before because, as angels, they have never been redeemed! They have learned about redemption by watching God's grace applied to sinning human beings.

For centuries these angels have observed the human race—willful, rebellious, defiant, sinning men and women like you and me, selfishly seeking our own way while rejecting the patient, forgiving love of God. They have also watched God calling to us, pleading with us, sacrificing His only Son for us, forgiving and redeeming us from our sin. Now, as the end of human history approaches, they join together to sing a song they have never known before, a song they learned from the saints—the song of the redeemed.

There is a grand old song which is rarely heard in churches anymore. I love the words of that song, because they express the yearning of my own heart, and because in just a few lines they express the mood of the heavenly scene in Revelation 5. The chorus of that song says,

> Holy, holy, holy, is what the angels sing,
> And I expect to help them make
>   the courts of heaven ring.
> But when we sing redemption's story
>   they must fold their wings,
> For angels never felt the joy
>   that our salvation brings.

That is why heaven bursts forth in praise and worship: the redeeming sacrifice of Jesus! Yes, we love His teaching and the wonderful life He lived. We marvel at His miracles, His power, and His compassion for sinners. But most of all we praise Him because of the blood He shed on our behalf, and on the behalf of sinners in every age of history.

I never take the cup of communion without thinking of the words of Peter, "For you know that it was not with perishable things such as silver or gold that you were redeemed from the empty way of life handed down to you from your forefathers, but with the precious blood of Christ, a lamb without blemish or defect."[7]

I can't conceive of any thought that is more powerful in melting the human heart than the thought that we who deserve death have been given the gift of eternal life at the cost of the precious blood of Jesus. It is this amazing thought that calls forth the new song of the redeemed.

The old song of the angels is a song of creation. The *new* song is a song of *redemption*.

Worthy Is the Lamb

As John watches, all the universe is caught up in the wonder of God's sacrificial love for mankind. He hears a great, swelling chorus—the voice of millions upon millions of angels!

5:11–14 *Then I looked and heard the voice of many angels, numbering thousands upon thousands, and ten thousand times ten thousand. They encircled the throne and the living creatures and the elders. In a loud voice they sang:*

> *"Worthy is the Lamb, who was slain, to receive power and wealth and wisdom and strength and honor and glory and praise!"*

Then I heard every creature in heaven and on earth and under the earth and on the sea, and all that is in them, singing:

> *"To him who sits on the throne and to the Lamb be praise and honor and glory and power, for ever and ever!"*

The four living creatures said, "Amen," and the elders fell down and worshiped.

If you are familiar with Handel's *Messiah,* then you probably recognize the words of this passage from "Worthy Is the Lamb," which appears near the end of the oratorio. In both its music and its profound theme of redemption it is one of the most beautiful pieces of choral music ever written. At the end, the entire chorus joins in the repeated affirmation, "Amen, Amen, Amen." As you listen to Handel's music it is easy to envision the scenes John describes in this passage of Revelation.

The apostle Paul refers to this same scene in his letter to the Philippians. After encouraging his readers to imitate the humility of Christ—who willingly took the form of a servant, humbled Himself, and died for our sakes—Paul writes,

> Therefore God exalted him to the highest place and gave him the name that is above every name, that at the name of Jesus every knee should bow, in heaven and on earth and under the earth, and every tongue confess that Jesus Christ is Lord, to the glory of God the Father.[8]

Note that the divisions Paul mentions—heaven, earth, and under the earth—are the same divisions John sees in his vision. And in each of those realms, throughout the entire extent of the universe, there is the sound of praise and worship offered to Jesus the Redeemer. The allusion to those "under the earth" refers to those who have already died, including those who die in unbelief and are in hell. So even hell must join with heaven and earth in acknowledging the lordship of Jesus Christ.

Clearly there will be some in eternity who *gladly* confess the lordship of Christ because they have appropriated the sacrifice of Jesus for their own eternal lives. But others will be forced to *reluctantly* confess His lordship. Those who scoff at the Scriptures, who ridicule biblical morality, who mock or persecute godly people will one day be made to see they are wrong and their lives have been wasted. When the illusions and delusions upon which they based their lives have all been stripped away, they will have no choice but to join the rest of creation in openly confessing that Jesus Christ is Lord.

John sees all of this in a vision. It has not yet happened—but it will. When the seven-sealed scroll is finally opened, all of creation will join in acknowledging God and His Son, Jesus. That is the goal toward which all of history is quickly rushing. Every historic event that occurs, and every day that passes, is linked to the moment John witnesses in Revelation 5.

The momentous events that stream across our TV screens and newspaper headlines do not take place in a vacuum. They take place in a grand and cosmic context. They are being woven into an eternal plan. You and I are woven into that plan as well. We have choices to make. We cannot escape the eternal consequences of those choices.

Someday every knee shall bow and every tongue shall confess that Jesus Christ is Lord. There will be no exceptions. You will confess His lordship, and so will I.

The question is: When that moment comes, will our hearts be filled with joy and gladness—or with regret?

It is not a choice for the future, but a choice we must make *today*.

Chapter Twelve

The Riders of Judgment

Revelation 6

I grew up on the Great Plains of Montana. During the summer months we frequently experienced sudden thunderstorms. Often before the storm there would be an eerie calm, a sense of ominous foreboding in the air. Something was coming. We could feel it. It was as though the impending storm hung over our heads, dark and threatening, its pent-up violence waiting to be unleashed.

That is the mood we sense in the affairs of the world today. Even after a period of reduced tensions between the East and West, the breakthrough of freedom in former "Iron Curtain" countries, the rollback of dictatorships in Panama and Nicaragua, and the successful liberation of Kuwait, the world continues to be a very dangerous place. As we approach the end of the second millennium of Christian history, there are many signs of apparent calm around us—yet most of us are still uneasy. We sense there is a storm on the horizon.

The globe bristles with nuclear, chemical, and biological weapons—the arsenals of a worldwide Armageddon. The world still shudders at the very real possibility of economic, ecological, and energy crises. Poverty, hunger, terrorism, AIDS, and crime are just a few of the problems that tear at the fabric of our society today.

You find this mood not only in the writings of Christians but in the secular media as well. To use a different metaphor, it is as if we are floating down the river of time. Somewhere ahead of us we hear a thundering sound. It is growing nearer and louder as we drift downstream. Could it be that this river leads to a roaring cataract—and that we are about to plunge into the abyss?

The Bible has long predicted such a worldwide crisis, and in Revelation 6 we begin to see that crisis take shape.

A "Week" of Years

One of the strongest indicators of the reliability and divine inspiration of the Bible is the fact that all of its various books in both the Old Testament and the New agree and intermesh so closely together. And one of the places in which we find this close correspondence between different parts of the Bible is in the relationship between the Old Testament book of Daniel and the New Testament book of Revelation. Although these two books were written some five hundred years apart, they are so closely interwoven in their themes and prophetic accounts that they could have been produced by the same hand. Unquestionably they were produced by the same Mind, for they both describe the same eternal plan of history.

In Daniel 9, the prophet Daniel describes a great calendar of events, spanning not just centuries but millennia, reaching from his own day on into our own future. Marked out on this calendar is a period of seventy "weeks." These are clearly not seven-day weeks, but rather "weeks" of *years*. In fact, the New International Version, in order to avoid confusion, uses the word "sevens" instead of "weeks." Each "week" is a seven-year period. Seventy "weeks," then, would be 490 years (70 weeks x 7 years = 490 years). The 490-year period that Daniel said would be fulfilled was from the building of the wall of Jerusalem in the days of Nehemiah until the end of the age.

Of those 490 years, 483 years would end on the day the Messiah (or "the Anointed One") would be presented to Israel as King. This timetable was first worked out in the early part of our century by Sir Robert Anderson, who was at one time the head of Britain's Scotland Yard. What Anderson discovered as he was doing his calculations from the book of Daniel was that on the precise day that the 483 years was completed, Jesus rode on the back of a donkey down a dusty road leading from the Mount of Olives into the city of Jerusalem where He was presented to the people of Israel as their King.

That was on the first Palm Sunday. Just a few days later Jesus was rejected and crucified. Again, this is in accordance with the prophecy of Daniel 9, which predicted that "the Anointed One will be cut off and will have nothing"—surely a reference to the crucifixion. Following that, an indeterminate period of time follows, according to the prophecy, and it will be a time of catastrophic upheaval. "The end will come like a flood," the prophecy continues. "War will continue until the end, and desolations have been decreed."[1]

It is during this indeterminate period of time—a time punctuated by war and desolations, culminating in what is ominously referred to as "the end"—that the church comes into being. The era of the church begins on the Day of Pentecost,[2] the day when God began to call out a special people for His name, made up of both Jews and Gentiles. The church that was founded at Pentecost has existed for almost 2,000 years. Its task in the world is nearly completed, but for now it remains on earth, carrying out the work God has given it to do.

The prophet Daniel is then told of other events which are to occur during the last "week" of that 490-year period. These events have not yet happened. Thus many commentators have understood this final "week" to be as yet unfulfilled. These events still lie in our future, and when they occur they will be closely associated with the nation of Israel.

Jesus Himself refers to these events in the final week of Daniel's prophecy in His great prophetic passage in Matthew 24. Before His crucifixion, as He talked with His disciples upon the Mount of Olives, He told them what must come to pass. In that passage He refers several times to what He calls "the end of the age," or more simply (and with echoes of Daniel) "the end." The final seven-year period of Daniel's prophecy is what Jesus refers to when He speaks of "the end of the age." Those seven years will take place when Israel is once again brought center stage in world events.

This seven-year period of Daniel's prophecy and of the Lord's prophecy comprises the fascinating—and sometimes frightening—series of events we will explore in Revelation 6 through 19. If you read the life of Christ in the gospels of Matthew, Mark, Luke, and John, you will notice that fully *one-third* of the story is focused on a single seven-day period: the week leading up to the crucifixion. Similarly, 13 of Revelation's 22 chapters are focused on a single seven-year "week" of time—a period which comprises the end of the history of this age.

This seven-year "week" is characterized by three series of events: (1) the seven seals, (2) the seven trumpets, and (3) the seven bowls of wrath. Each of these series divides four and three—that is, into *four* distinct and recognizable events and *three* revelations of what is occurring behind the scenes, in the hidden realm of the angels, both the Lord's angels and the fallen angels.

The First Seal: A Rider on a White Horse

Revelation 6 begins with the opening of the seven-sealed scroll, held by the Lamb who was slain.

6:1–2 *I watched as the Lamb opened the first of the seven seals. Then I heard one of the four living creatures say in a voice like thunder, "Come!" I looked, and there before me was a white horse! Its rider held a bow, and he was given a crown, and he rode out as a conqueror bent on conquest.*

There has been much disagreement as to who or what this rider on the white horse represents. Some identify him as Jesus, because in Revelation 19 Jesus appears on a white horse, bringing an end to the series of terrible judgments upon the earth. But it is a mistake to identify the rider in Revelation 6 with the rider in Revelation 19. The contexts of the two passages are entirely different, and there are important differences in the way these two riders are described. For example, the rider of Revelation 6 is given a crown, whereas the rider of Revelation 19 appears on the scene wearing "many crowns."

Moreover, the rider of Revelation 6 is summoned by one of the living creatures with the command "Come!" It would be unthinkable for the conquering Christ of Revelation 19 to be summoned by any lesser creature.

However, it is significant that there are similarities between these two riders on white horses. Both are crowned and both are bent on conquest. This suggests that the rider of Revelation 6 may be someone who is *like* Christ in some ways, but is *not* Christ. Who could it be?

I submit that the rider of Revelation 6 is the long-predicted Antichrist, who is spoken of in various places in Scripture, and who is to appear in the last days. The apostle Paul calls him "the man of sin" and "the lawless one," the one who will eventually appear and offer himself as though he were God's Christ.[3]

Jesus Himself said to the Jews of His day, "I have come in my Father's name, and you do not accept me; but if someone else comes in his own name, you will accept him."[4] The rider of Revelation 6 comes like Christ, yet in his own name. As Jesus sadly predicts, many will accept him.

A Powerful Delusion

The rider of Revelation 6 is given a bow, but there is no mention of arrows. This suggests that his conquest is a bloodless one. It pictures the conquest of the world by the Antichrist as taking place by the overpowering of the minds and wills of human beings, without the physical destruction of war. It will take place not by force but by deceit, by lying that misleads people and nations without the shedding of blood.

It is interesting to note that in Matthew 24 the first word Jesus says to His disciples is, "Watch out that no one deceives you." Throughout the rest of that chapter you find reference after reference to the danger of demonic deception in the last days.

As you look around at all the forces of persuasion and deception that surround us today, it is not at all hard to believe that we are indeed approaching the last days. Turn on the television or open a newspaper, and you can read the outrageous propaganda claims of one nation against another—and the more outrageous the lie, the more people seem to believe it!

You may remember that immediately following the liberation of Kuwait by U.N. forces in February 1991, the government of Iraq claimed victory even though its army had been destroyed. Across Iraq and wherever the Jordanian and Palestinian supporters of Saddam Hussein lived, wild rumors sprang up: Four hundred Jews were killed when an Iraqi Scud missile exploded at Israel's Ben Gurion Airport! The Scud missiles were so effective they shot down almost every Patriot missile the Americans launched! Over 100,000 American soldiers were killed by Iraqi forces, but fewer than a hundred deaths were reported by the Western press! Iraq's withdrawal from Kuwait was not a retreat but a tactical redeployment, for Saddam has a secret weapon he will soon use to destroy Israel! Outrageous lies, every one—yet they were believed by hundreds of thousands of Saddam's followers across the Middle East.

In our own society great masses of people are just as willing to be deceived. Millions of people, many of whom are young and many who are certainly old enough to know better, are willingly deceived by the euphoric rush produced by illicit drugs. Millions more are deceived by the false image of sophistication and maturity that cigarette smoking is supposed to impart. Madison Avenue rakes in mountains of money every year by spreading the deception that this perfume or that cosmetic can bring instant romance into a woman's life.

Look at the newsstands and bookstalls. Notice how they bulge with books filled with New Age deception, occultism, and astrology. Notice how eagerly the public laps up claims that we humans can have secret, godlike powers, that we can rule and manipulate others, that we can order the world according to our own wishes. Such deception is continually being fed into our society, and our society hungrily devours the lie.

Clearly, we live in an age of runaway deception.

But in this passage of Revelation, the rider on the white horse appears as a sign that the worst deception is yet on the horizon. As the apostle Paul writes in 2 Thessalonians 2:9-12,

> The coming of the lawless one [the Antichrist] will be in accordance with the work of Satan displayed in all kinds of counterfeit miracles, signs and wonders, and in every sort of evil that deceives those who are perishing. They perish because they refused to love the truth and so be saved. For this reason God sends them a powerful delusion so that they will believe the lie and so that all will be condemned who have not believed the truth but have delighted in wickedness.

How could Paul make it any clearer? The first conquest of evil in the last days is set in motion when God takes all the restraints off of evil and lets deception have its way among men and women until it reaches a climax of mass delusion. The nature of this powerful delusion will become clearer as we proceed through the book of Revelation.

The Second Seal: A Rider on a Red Horse

In verses 3 and 4, the second seal is opened, revealing a new horse and its rider.

6:3–4 *When the Lamb opened the second seal, I heard the second living creature say, "Come!" Then another horse came out, a fiery red one. Its rider was given power to take peace from the earth and to make men slay each other. To him was given a large sword.*

This rider is easy to recognize. It is War, but this form of war is not merely war between opposing armies. It is raw, red slaughter. It is civil anarchy. It is the kind of war that takes place when social order breaks down, when mobs of people take to the streets and begin killing with abandon. We see faint echoes of such war in our own world whenever a mob goes on a killing spree in places like Sri Lanka, Azerbaijan, Zimbabwe, or Korea. We saw it in war-ravaged Iraq in 1991 as rioting and civil war broke out between the government and the Kurdish and Shi'ite populations. We have even seen echoes of this kind of war in the gang wars that have ravaged the ghettos and barrios of Los Angeles, Miami, Washington, D.C., and New York.

But these are only a faint foretaste of the massive destruction to come. In John's day people had no conception of the weapons of mass destruction that are stored up in the world arsenals of the 1990s—the missiles, nuclear warheads, chemical warheads, and biological weapons that threaten to destroy human civilization. The best words John had to describe the destruction he foresaw was the image of a "large sword." This "large sword" is clearly a powerful weapon of destruction. Understandably, many Bible scholars today view this "large sword" as a symbol of the awesome power of the nuclear bomb—a weapon which kills by the tens and hundreds of thousands in a single, all-consuming blast.

If you read Ezekiel 38 and 39, you will find a vivid account of such warfare on a massive scale. There, armies come down out of the north, pour into the Holy Land, and are decimated by what appears to be radiation sickness.

Does the Word of God foresee a monstrous war, fought with the weapons of mass destruction which we now see stockpiled around the world? As we honestly face the prophecies of Ezekiel and Revelation, we have to admit that it is only in our century, with its efficient, high-tech approach to killing, that the fulfillment of these terrible predictions could even come about.

The Third Seal: A Rider on a Black Horse

In verses 5 and 6, the third seal is opened, revealing another horse and rider.

6:5–6 *When the Lamb opened the third seal, I heard the third living creature say, "Come!" I looked, and there before me was a black horse! Its rider was holding a pair of scales in his hand. Then I heard what sounded like a voice among the four living creatures, saying, "A quart of wheat for a day's wages, and three quarts of barley for a day's wages, and do not damage the oil and the wine!"*

Most Bible scholars consider these verses to refer to a period of widespread famine on the earth. They point to the scales as symbolizing food being weighed very carefully, because it is in such short supply that it must be rationed. A day's wages buys only a single quart of wheat or, because it is cheaper, three quarts of barley. This would only be enough food for one person for one day. After a full day's work, you would have enough to feed yourself alone, leaving nothing for your family or anyone else. Luxuries such as oil and wine would be so precious that they could not even be touched.

I do not think, however, that the third seal represents famine. When we examine the fourth seal we will see that famine is specifically listed among the judgments of that seal, along with death by the sword, plague, and wild beasts. Another possible explanation of the third seal is economic upheaval—inflation, recession, panic.

I remember as a boy hearing stories of the economic distress in the post-World War I Weimar Republic of Germany. The Deutsche mark, the German monetary unit, had declined in value so sharply that people would load thousands of bills into a wheelbarrow and haul them to market just to buy one loaf of bread! That is what runaway inflation does: it renders money worthless.

Inflation may well be the justification the Antichrist will use to impose rigid controls over buying and selling, as we shall see in Revelation 13. At that time the whole world will be under such tight economic controls that "no one could buy or sell unless he had the mark, which is the name of the beast or the number of his name."[5]

The Fourth Seal: A Rider on a Pale Horse

In verses 7 and 8, the fourth seal is opened, revealing another horse and rider. Though this horse is called a "pale horse" in the NIV text, the original Greek text uses the word *chloros*, from which we get the word "chlorine." A *chloros* horse is pale green like the color of chlorine.

6:7–8 *When the Lamb opened the fourth seal, I heard the voice of the fourth living creature say, "Come!" I looked, and there before me was a pale horse! Its rider was named Death, and Hades was following close behind him. They were given power over a fourth of the earth to kill by sword, famine and plague, and by the wild beasts of the earth.*

This rider is named Death. Floating along behind Death is a figure identified as Hades (or Hell). Death takes the body and Hades takes the soul.

There are four forms of death referred to in this seal of judgment. First the sword, which refers here not to war but to murder, the deadly assault of one individual human being upon another. Under this seal of judgment, people will take law and vengeance into their own hands and will kill one another without regard to justice.

Second comes famine and widespread starvation. We have all seen pictures of lands that have been ravaged by drought and famine. We have seen the cracked ground, the swollen, distended bellies of little children with spindly legs and hollow eyes. The death that accompanies starvation is one of the most horrible deaths imaginable.

Third comes the devastation of plague. A plague is an epidemic, a rapidly spreading disease. In Matthew 24, Jesus predicted that famines, plagues, and earthquakes would come upon the earth in the last days.

When civilization crumbles, mankind's defenses against disease crumble as well. When there is no sanitation system, no safe drinking water, and not enough food, diseases like cholera, typhoid, and dysentery spread like a consuming fire. Moreover, the plague described in this seal of judgment may be linked to such modern horrors as biological warfare—killing masses of people by unleashing clouds of deadly viruses—or the terrible plague of AIDS.

Fourth, the wild beasts of the earth multiply. Human beings become prey to these predatory creatures. Verse 8 says that a quarter of the earth is given over to these four kinds of attack and devastation. It is difficult to say whether this means that a quarter of the earth's physical geography will be devastated, or whether a quarter of the earth's population will be destroyed. If a quarter of the world's present population were suddenly destroyed, the loss of life would be staggering. If you divide the world's present population—about 5.25 billion—by four, you get a figure of more than 1.3 billion people, or roughly the population of China and the United States *combined*.

Here we have a picture of incomprehensible devastation visited upon the earth as a result of human hatred, barbarity, and sin.

These four seal judgments are references to forces that are already at work in our own society, right now. The only difference between this day and the last days is that these judgments will be carried out to their logical and unprecedented extreme at that time. These four seals confirm God's method, which He has announced many times in Scripture, of forcing men and women to face the truth about themselves. What is that method? He allows evil—the evil that human beings themselves choose to commit—to operate without restraint till people see for themselves its terrible outcome.

Romans 1 declares that God "gave them over" to their own evil passions and allows sin to manifest its consequences in the lives of evil men and women. God confronts us with the unpleasant truth about ourselves *by giving us what we demand*. If men and women choose to believe a lie, then God will send them the "powerful delusion" of the Antichrist that

Paul describes in 2 Thessalonians 2. If men and women seek to kill and destroy, then God will give them the anarchy and mob rule they demand. He may even give them over to nuclear destruction.

If men and women demand more luxury with which to gratify their lusts, then God will give them the economic upheaval and inflation that is the result of greed and immorality. Ultimately their luxuries and money will be worthless, and even the necessities of life will be beyond their reach.

If men and women demand power and control, they will receive the brutal end of unrestrained power: intrigue, murder, disease, and desolation upon the earth. These judgments cannot be halted. They are the inescapable consequences of unrestrained human evil.

The Fifth Seal: The Souls of the Slain

Beginning with the fifth seal, the nature of the judgment changes. The last three seals contain neither horse, nor rider, nor the natural forces of judgment. With the fifth seal comes a different kind of activity—a supernatural activity. Here we see God working, bringing about both favorable and ominous results for the world's people amid the judgments of the four horsemen.

6:9–11 *When he opened the fifth seal, I saw under the altar the souls of those who had been slain because of the word of God and the testimony they had maintained. They called out in a loud voice, "How long, Sovereign Lord, holy and true, until you judge the inhabitants of the earth and avenge our blood?" Then each of them was given a white robe, and they were told to wait a little longer, until the number of their fellow servants and brothers who were to be killed as they had been was completed.*

There is a difficult concept embedded in these verses. How is it that the saints who lived and died over a period of centuries and millennia appear in this passage to be together in heaven at one time? The answer to this question is that this passage gives us a glimpse into the difference between time and eternity. We live in time. The events described in this passage take place in eternity.

In this world, we are born, live, and die in time. But after we die, we enter a great eternal present called eternity. In the realm of eternity, time does not pass, moment by moment. Everything simply *is*. Everyone who died in the past, who will die in the future, or who is dying at this very moment in time emerges together in the same undivided moment called eternity. There is no past or future there. Those concepts belong to time.

Notice the altar which stands over the souls of the slain. This altar has not appeared before in Revelation. But as later references will confirm, this is the altar of the great temple in heaven, the temple which Moses saw when he stood on Mount Sinai. This temple was the model, the pattern which he copied when he built the tabernacle of old. Just as God told him, Moses copied the temple exactly as it was shown to him (see Exodus 34–40).

In the tabernacle which Moses built there were three principle divisions. First, there was the rectangular Outer Court. Just beyond the entrance to the Outer Court was the great brass altar of burnt offering, and just beyond the altar was a brass laver, a washing bowl for the cleansing of the priests. The second division of the tabernacle was the Holy Place, furnished with the table of shewbread, the golden candlestick, and the altar of incense. Separating the second and third divisions of the tabernacle was a veil of fine linen. The third division, which was laid out in a perfect square, was the Holy of Holies, the innermost and most sacred part of the tabernacle. It was the Holy of Holies which housed the Ark of the Covenant.

Elsewhere in the New Testament we learn that the Old Testament temple symbolized the ultimate dwelling place of God: *man himself*! You and I are the ultimate dwelling place of God, as 1 Corinthians 3:16 confirms! When we come to the end of Revelation, we will see this truth fulfilled in history. The temple of God—the original heavenly model which was copied by Moses—is actually symbolic of redeemed human beings, the ultimate dwelling place of God. We humans are made up of three parts—body, soul, and spirit—just as the tabernacle Moses built consisted of three parts—the Outer Court, the Holy Place, and the Holy of Holies.

The Prayer of the Martyrs

The martyrs depicted in these verses—"the souls of those who had been slain because of the word of God and the testimony they had maintained"—are clearly part of the great multitude which appears in Revelation 7:9ff. They form a crowd which no man can number, robed in white, representing every tribe, nation, and language on the earth. They stand before the throne, having been slain because of their unwavering witness for God before a hostile world.

We know that the martyrs of Revelation 6 are a part of that multitude because in this passage they are each given a white robe and told to wait until their brethren would also be martyred. This indicates that those who have already died and those who will later be martyred will constitute a great multitude who all enter eternity together though they leave earth at differing times. This is God's way of expressing the transition from time to eternity, where past and future are eclipsed and only the single, unending moment of the Now exists.

If you have lost a Christian loved one—a father, mother, grandparent, child, or close friend—you probably think of that loved one as waiting in heaven for you to join them. You may have an image of their spirit-forms walking about in heaven, waiting to be rejoined to resurrected bodies, and perhaps looking down from heaven and watching your activities. Such images are merely an accommodation of our limited understanding to the huge mystery that is eternity. Our minds are locked into a time-ordered way of perceiving and experiencing reality, and the reality of a timeless eternity is simply beyond our ability to imagine.[6]

Now notice the prayer these martyrs pray: a call for *vengeance*. This is quite different from the sort of prayer we Christians are normally expected to pray for our enemies. Jesus told us that we should pray for those who mistreat us and persecute us. Our prayer life is to reflect the prayer life of Christ, who prayed, "Father, forgive them, for they do not know what they are doing," even as He hung dying upon the cross.[7]

We see this same attitude in the dying prayer of Stephen, the first martyr, who prayed, "Lord, do not hold this sin against them," as his persecutors stoned him to death.[8] The model of Jesus and the model of Stephen are our examples for how Christians are to pray when others persecute us and mistreat us.

I heard a radio interview of Rachel Saint, the sister of missionary Nate Saint, one of the five brave men who was martyred in Ecuador in 1956 as they attempted to reach the Auca tribe with the gospel. After the murder of her brother Nate, Rachel and several companions went to Ecuador and lived among the same Auca people who had killed her brother. They served and loved those people and taught the gospel to them. Eventually, their love even conquered the heart of the man who had killed Rachel's brother, and he was converted and baptized.

The interviewer asked her, "Why did you go back to this tribe after they killed your brother?"

"In the Auca culture," she replied, "they lived for vengeance. As a Christian, I knew that forgiveness is the only way to live toward those who hurt us."

Most of the Auca tribe was eventually converted to Christ through the faithful, forgiving witness of Rachel Saint and her companions, most of whom were widows of the brave men who were martyred for attempting to bring the gospel to the Aucas. That is the kind of powerful ministry God can accomplish when we allow His forgiving love to flow through us when we suffer mistreatment and persecution.

Why, then, do the martyrs of the fifth seal of Revelation not show this same spirit of forgiveness? Why is theirs a prayer not for God's forgiveness but for God's vengeance? It is because these martyrs no longer live in an age when God patiently endures the injustices of men. The time described in Revelation 6 is a time of judgment, not a time of grace. These are days when wrongdoers are called to account for their crimes. The prayers of these martyrs actually *reflect the mind of God* at this time. Led by the Spirit of God, they are praying for the fulfillment of God's will during the last days.

The Sixth Seal: Nature in Chaos

Verses 12 to 14 reveal the sixth seal of judgment. It is a seal of almost incomprehensible terror and calamity.

6:12–14 *I watched as he opened the sixth seal. There was a great earthquake. The sun turned black like sackcloth made of goat hair, the whole moon turned blood red, and the stars in the sky fell to earth, as late figs drop from a fig tree when shaken by a strong wind. The sky receded like a scroll, rolling up, and every mountain and island was removed from its place.*

This is a vivid and disturbing picture of nature in chaos. The whole natural world goes on a rampage. Compare this description of John's vision with the Lord's description of the same event in Matthew 24:29–30—

> Immediately after the distress of those days "the sun will be darkened, and the moon will not give its light; the stars will fall from the sky, and the heavenly bodies will be shaken."
> At that time the sign of the Son of Man will appear in the sky, and all the nations of the earth will mourn. They will see the Son of Man coming on the clouds of the sky, with power and great glory.

These six seals have carried us almost to the very end of the entire seven-year period of Daniel's seventieth week. These seals represent a telescoped or condensed overview of this very dramatic period in the future of our world and of the human race. After the Great Tribulation, nature itself will be upset by some cataclysmic phenomenon in the cosmos. Perhaps these events will be brought about by the gravitational disturbance of the near approach of some undetected heavenly body.

Whatever the cause, we are told that the effect will be great earthquakes, much more intense than those that have been recorded in recent years in California, Japan, or Soviet Armenia. Volcanoes will rupture and spout deadly flows of lava. There will be aerial phenomena, so that the stars will seem to fall from the sky. The sun and moon will appear darkened, probably as a result of dust and ash. This may well be the effect astronomer Carl Sagan has dubbed "nuclear winter," the darkening of the sun by clouds of dust and ash thrown up by the mass detonation of nuclear weapons.

Jesus' description of these dire events is also recorded in Luke 21:25–27. He says,

> There will be signs in the sun, moon and stars. On the earth, nations will be in anguish and perplexity at the roaring and tossing of the sea. Men will faint from terror, apprehensive of what is coming on the world, for the heavenly bodies will be shaken. At that time they will see the Son of Man coming in a cloud with power and great glory.

It will be a time of terror and inconceivable anguish throughout the earth. What will be the effect of these events on people? John describes the final scene that takes place under the sixth seal.

6:15–17 *Then the kings of the earth, the princes, the generals, the rich, the mighty, and every slave and every free man hid in caves and among the rocks of the mountains. They called to the mountains and the rocks, "Fall on us and hide us from the face of him who sits on the throne and from the wrath of the Lamb! For the great day of their wrath has come, and who can stand?"*

Who can stand? That is the question left hanging at the end of Revelation 6. The answer: No one can stand! It is the end of civilization.

All people who have not yet believed in Christ, who have refused His offer of grace, will be subject to these terrible and catastrophic events. They will cry out in desperate fear, and some will even die of fear, because of the literally heart-stopping cataclysm that will come over all the earth.

Without question John has envisioned for us the scene described by the prophet Isaiah, who wrote, "They will flee to caverns in the rocks and to the overhanging crags from dread of the LORD and the splendor of His majesty, when he rises to shake the earth."9 Isaiah also wrote, "Though grace is shown to the wicked, they do not learn righteousness; even in a land of uprightness they go on doing evil and regard not the majesty of the LORD."10

In that day those who refuse to believe will have reached a stage where they cannot believe. They will not repent and pray to God for salvation. Rather, they will feel a terrible fear and pray to the rocks to fall on them and destroy them.

It is a strange phenomenon, but it is confirmed again and again as true: unbelievers somehow become convinced in their hearts that death is an escape into oblivion! They believe that by death they can escape the terrible consequences of their evil. That is why many people commit suicide as an escape from their sins. They believe they are leaving their problems and their guilt behind and escaping the consequences of their actions in this life. But the Word of God is clear: "Man is destined to die once, and after that to face judgment."11

The Purpose of This Vision

Why does the Lord reveal these terrible scenes to John, and through him, to us? If we belong to the Lord, if we are members of His body, the true church, we will not be a part of this scene. That is the great promise of Revelation, a promise that has been reiterated several times in this book up to this point. The vision containing these cataclysmic scenes has been given specifically to the seven churches of Asia to read and understand. And we have to ask, Why?

The answer, in part, is that God has given us this horrific vision of the future in order to inspire us with the urgency of our witness to the world. Do we want our family, our friends, our neighbors to go through the terrible scenes we have just witnessed? Do we want them to think back on all the conversations we had with them, the opportunities we had to share our faith with them, and to ask, "Why didn't my friend tell me about the Lord? He had the truth, she had the truth! Why did my friend allow me to go through this hell on earth?"

Another part of the answer is that God has given us this revelation so that we can understand where the moral and spiritual forces that now surround us are going to end up. We are told these things so that we can recognize evil, even while it is still cloaked in the alluring disguise of good.

God wants us to be able to judge and discern what is right from those things that merely *seem* right, but which will lead us to our destruction.

One verse in John's gospel tells us the whole story: "Whoever believes in the Son has eternal life, but whoever rejects the Son will not see life, for God's wrath remains on him."[12] Isaiah has put his finger on the reason for these terrible judgments: "The LORD Almighty planned it, to bring low the pride of all glory and to humble all who are renowned on the earth."[13] The pride of man—this terrible lust within us to be in charge, to be in control of our lives and the lives of others, to run everything, to be the center of our own little universe—will some-day be humbled.

God's grace humbles our pride. The sight of God's Son dying in our place forces us to confront the evil in our own hearts. Your sin and mine put Jesus on that cross. If the grace of God, demonstrated on the cross, does not humble us, then God's judgment must humble us. Willingly or not, "every knee shall bow and every tongue confess that Jesus Christ is Lord."

We may prefer to hear about the grace and forgiveness of God. We may prefer to think about that wonderful view of God's throne, with angel choirs gathered around and singing the song of the redeemed. But if we are faithful to the Scriptures we must recognize that a day is coming when the wrath of God will be poured out upon the unrighteousness of the human race. The same God who today extends grace and forgiveness to all men and women must someday judge the sin and rebellion of those who reject His love. That is the scene we have examined in Revelation 6, the first six seals of judgment.

If you and I make sure that we do not have within us a heart of unbelief then we shall never have to fear the shaking of the earth or the darkening of the sky because of God's judgment. In that terrible day when the foundations of the earth crumble, by the grace of God you and I will be able to stand.

Chapter Thirteen

To Jew and Gentile

Revelation 7

n 1936, the mayor of New York City, Fiorello La Guardia, was confronted with a difficult decision. A high-ranking diplomat from Nazi Germany was coming to New York, and the mayor was expected to provide his foreign visitor with protection. Anti-Nazi feeling ran high throughout New York. La Guardia himself found Nazism repulsive and uncivilized. Torn between his revulsion for the Nazis and his sense of duty as mayor, La Guardia was struck by a compromise solution that was sheer inspiration. He hand-selected a contingent of bodyguards from among the New York City Police Department—

And every one of them was *Jewish*.

What a delicious irony: A Nazi who owed his safety and his life to the Jews!

The truth is that every Gentile Christian owes his eternal life to the Jews! As Jesus said to the Samaritan woman at the well, "Salvation is from the Jews."[1] Jesus, the Savior of the world, was a Jew, a descendant of Abraham, Isaac, and Jacob.

From Genesis to Revelation, the Word of God records the past and future history of the world *primarily as it relates to the nation of Israel*. In the Old Testament, of course, Israel is the exclusive focus of events. In the New Testament, a new concept—the concept of a church comprising not only Jews but Gentiles as well—is introduced. Yet, even in the New

Testament, it is Israel that occupies center stage, for the promises we cherish were given originally to and belong to the Jews.

You can see the primacy of Israel in the Gospels, when Jesus sends out His twelve disciples to preach and heal in His name. There He tells them, "Do not go among the Gentiles. . . . Go rather to the lost sheep of Israel."[2]

You can see the primacy of Israel in the Epistles. Indeed, you see it most clearly in Paul's great theological masterpiece, the book of Romans, where he devotes three chapters—the very heart of his argument—to a discussion of the place of Israel in the eternal plan of God. In Romans 9, he shows how God has dealt with Israel in times past. In Romans 10, he outlines the condition of Israel at the present time, existing in a state of unbelief, having rejected the promised Messiah, Jesus Christ. In Romans 11, Paul foretells the time when God will restore Israel to its former prominence among the nations of the earth.

Today Israel again occupies center stage in world events. Ever since its re-establishment as a nation in 1948, the existence of the Jewish state has been the focus of world attention—and world tensions. Even though it is a tiny nation[3] with a population of less than four million people, all eyes—and all TV news cameras—are frequently centered on Israel. Why? There is only one possible explanation for this extraordinary fact: Israel occupies a central place in God's program of human history. God will not let the world forget or ignore the Jewish people.

The central place of Israel in history, in current events, and in God's plan for the future is abundantly clear. Yet as I have studied various commentaries on the book of Revelation and on other books of the Bible, I have been struck by the fact that a surprisingly large number of Bible scholars virtually ignore the important place God has reserved for this great and historic race of people. The same grace which God has shown to His church (to Christians like you and me, and to these Bible scholars) God is still in the process of displaying toward His people, Israel—yet so many Bible scholars seem blithely unaware of God's grace toward Israel.

Across the span of history and throughout the pages of His Word, God has plainly stated His eternal plan for the people of Israel. Now, as we open the pages of Revelation 7, we shall see the culmination of that plan.

A Flashback

The next prophetic event the world will experience is the Rapture, or removal of the church from the world. Not only will the living saints that are in the world at that time be caught up to be with the Lord, but those

Christian saints who have died will also be raised. This event is described in detail by the apostle Paul in 1 Thessalonians 4. It is a stunning event, in which millions of people will simply disappear from the earth, mysteriously, suddenly, and without a trace. Imagine the electrifying effect of this upon all those who are left.

That is how the last days of human history will begin. Immediately after this event, God's program of judgment commences. At the center of this program will be the nation of Israel.

As we saw in Revelation 6, the time of judgment will be a dark and frightening time. Christians do not take pleasure in the cataclysmic suffering of that period, but Christians do look forward to the time of victory, peace, and worldwide blessing that follows the terrible time of judgment. Christians are not pessimists because they foresee a time of judgment to come. Christians are optimists who see even further into the future, beyond the judgment, to a time of peace and restoration. Yet if we are to be true to the Scriptures, we must recognize the reality of God's judgment.

In Revelation 6, we saw the opening of the six seals of judgment. But as we come to Revelation 7, we come to a pause between the first six seals and the seventh and final seal. It is as though God declared an intermission. And after the terrible scenes of judgment in Revelation 6, it's a welcome intermission, isn't it? In this beautiful interlude in Revelation 7, God treats us, the viewers of this astounding vision recorded by the hand of John, to a kind of flashback.

A flashback, of course, is a conventional storytelling device used in books and films to supply an event from a character's past that is significant to the present flow of the story. And that is essentially what we have in Revelation 7—a flashback which supplies a missing piece of the Revelation puzzle. We are taken back to the beginning of the judgments of the seven-year tribulation period to see the working out of God's plan from a different vantage point. What we will see in this flashback is the selection of a special group of Jews who will be given a special mission during the last days.

I call this select group of Jews "Christ's Commandos."

Sealed for God's Service

7:1–3 *After this I saw four angels standing at the four corners of the earth, holding back the four winds of the earth to prevent any wind from blowing on the land or on the sea or on any tree. Then I saw another angel coming up from the east, having the seal of the living God. He* *called out in a loud voice to the four angels who had been given power to harm the land and the sea: "Do not harm the land or the sea or the trees until we put a seal on the foreheads of the servants of our God."*

In the opening chapter of Revelation we were told that much of the truth of this book would be made known to us by symbols. This book is an unusual blend of literal events and symbols, and there are certain symbols to be found in the opening words of Revelation 7.

One such symbol is the phrase "the four corners of the earth." This phrase simply refers to the four compass directions, north, south, east, and west. Some skeptics laugh at this phrase and say the early Christians believed in a square earth with literal corners. Yet people today use this same expression to indicate far-off regions while still acknowledging that the earth is round.

In this passage four angels are depicted as holding back something that is about to come upon the earth. They have been commanded to restrain the four winds, which symbolize the devastating power of natural forces. Anyone who has ever been through a hurricane or a tornado, who has huddled in a basement and listened to the sound of wind approaching like a speeding freight train, who has seen the effect of homes blown off their foundations, or who has seen straws driven like nails through inch-thick boards, has some idea of the raw destructive power of an unleashed wind. That is the kind of power these verses depict as being held back for a time, soon to be released upon the earth.

The land, the sea, and the trees also appear as symbols in this passage. The land or the earth is frequently used as a symbol of Israel throughout the Old Testament. Israel is viewed as a nation with stability and strength because God is its head. Because of the God-based structure, order, and foundation of Israel, it was depicted as "land."

The symbol of the sea is often used throughout Scripture to describe the Gentile nations in general, and the pagan nations in particular. The sea is shifting and unstable, and thus suggests those who are without foundation because they do not recognize the authority of God. The people symbolized by the "sea" worship idols and hold pagan concepts which make them morally and socially unstable.

The symbol of trees frequently speaks of individuals in various places in Scripture. For example, Psalm 1:3 describes a righteous individual as being "like a tree planted by streams of water, which yields its fruit in season and whose leaf does not wither." Trees are symbols of influential men and women, people of authority, who stand out from the crowd like tall trees in a forest.

The four angels who hold back the winds are the first four of the seven angels which sound their trumpets in the following chapters of Revelation. If you carefully compare what takes place under the judgments of the seven angels you will see that the first four of the seven angels control events which affect the land, the sea, and the trees.

In this passage, the four angels are commanded to hold back the winds of destruction until a very important group of people has been sealed by God. The angel which seals this group is described as "coming up from the east," or more literally "from the rising of the sun." This is an allusion to a prophecy of Malachi, the last book in the Old Testament. There the prophet predicts that for those who revere the name of God, "the sun of righteousness will rise with healing in its wings."[4] This is a poetic description of the coming of Jesus Christ in glory and in power. Thus it is in relationship to the coming of Christ that this special group is marked by the angel of the rising sun with the seal of God's ownership.

There is no mystery about what it means when this special group is "sealed" by God. Today, all believers are sealed by God in a special way. That is why Paul tells us, "Having believed, you were marked in him with a seal, the promised Holy Spirit."[5] The presence of the Holy Spirit in us as Christians is the unmistakable mark of God's ownership upon our lives. As Paul declares in Romans, "The Spirit himself testifies with our spirit that we are God's children."[6]

The same Holy Spirit who has sealed us as God's children will also seal this chosen group that is described in Revelation 7. These are thus Spirit-filled, Spirit-led people. The seal is placed upon their foreheads, which indicates that the Spirit rules over their minds, their thoughts, and their will. They are governed by the mind of Christ.

In Philippians Paul writes, "Let this mind be in you, which was also in Christ Jesus."[7] He describes it as the mind of One who, though possessing all rights to infinite glory and honor, willingly lay everything aside and became a servant. That is the mind of Christ. Notice that this select group in Revelation 7 is collectively referred to in verse 3 as "the servants of our God." They serve with that same Christlike willingness to spend themselves, to lay aside their own rights for the cause of God and the sake of others, that Paul describes in Philippians.

Christ's Commandos

The identity of Christ's Commandos is revealed next.

7:4–8 *Then I heard the number of those who were sealed: 144,000 from all the tribes of Israel.*

> *From the tribe of Judah 12,000 were sealed,*
> *from the tribe of Reuben 12,000,*
> *from the tribe of Gad 12,000,*
> *from the tribe of Asher 12,000,*
> *from the tribe of Naphtali 12,000,*
> *from the tribe of Manasseh 12,000,*
> *from the tribe of Simeon 12,000,*
> *from the tribe of Levi 12,000,*
> *from the tribe of Issachar 12,000,*
> *from the tribe of Zebulun 12,000,*
> *from tזthe tribe of Joseph 12,000,*
> *from the tribe of Benjamin 12,000.*

John lists twelve names of twelve tribes, and we must be careful not to gloss over these names too quickly. Let us be sure to emphasize the same things that God emphasized when He gave His inspired Word to us through His servant John. And what God is underscoring in these verses is a significant truth: It is Israel and only Israel that is centerstage in this passage!

These are Christ's Commandos, the 144,000 Jews who are sealed for the service of God by the Holy Spirit.

I once heard a Bible teacher laboriously twist and torture this passage in an attempt to prove that the 144,000 sealed servants listed in this passage are in fact the church. But I can see no way around it. I believe that when God says "Israel" He *means* Israel! This text does not talk about the church; there are other passages in Revelation which talk about the church, and they do so with considerable clarity. But in this passage, God is describing the Jews.

Some years ago, a sect known as Jehovah's Witnesses took this passage of Scripture and applied it to themselves, saying that the servants of Revelation 7 were not Jews but were rather Jehovah's Witnesses. According to this interpretation, only 144,000 souls would be saved, and all of these would be Jehovah's Witnesses. This interpretation seemed to satisfy everyone in the sect—until the membership of the Jehovah's Witnesses grew beyond 144,000! Then they had a problem: What will God do with the leftovers?

So they revised their doctrine and started another category of 144,000. They taught that there was an "earthly band" of 144,000 and a "heavenly band" of 144,000. If you believed the Jehovah's Witnesses' doctrine in the early decades of this century, then you could belong to the "heavenly band." A few more decades passed, and they had another problem: the number of Jehovah's Witnesses had grown larger than 288,000!

So they created a third band of 144,000 called the "servant band." If you join the Jehovah's Witnesses today, you must come in at the servant level. That is just one example of the many ways people can distort Scripture to make it fit a program of human devising.

In this passage, God clearly identifies the 144,000 servants. If you are a student of the Old Testament, you may have noticed that two tribes of Israel—Ephraim and Dan—are not mentioned here. The tribe of Ephraim's brother Manasseh is included, but not Ephraim.

Ephraim and Manasseh were the two sons of Joseph. Because of Joseph's role in preserving the nation of Egypt during the great famine and his role in preserving his own family, including the brothers who sold him into slavery, Joseph's two sons were adopted by Jacob and given an inheritance along with the rest of Joseph's brothers. Simple mental arithmetic tells you that this makes not twelve but *thirteen* tribes of Israel.

What happened to the thirteenth tribe? The thirteenth tribe was Levi. When the land of Israel was divided among the tribes, the tribe of Levi was left out because the Levites were called out especially to be a priestly tribe.

What happened to Ephraim? Ephraim actually appears here under the name of Joseph. Manasseh and Joseph are actually Manasseh and Ephraim, the two sons of Joseph.

What about Dan? The tribe of Dan does not appear in this list, I believe, because they are the tribe which introduced apostasy into the nation of Israel. The closing chapters of Judges give an account of the sordid way the tribe of Dan led Israel into horrible acts and beliefs, including repulsive practices of idol worship and homosexual behavior. The actions of the tribe of Dan actually fulfilled a prediction which Jacob made concerning his twelve sons as he lay on his deathbed: "Dan will be a serpent by the roadside, a viper along the path, that bites the horse's heels so that its rider tumbles backward."[8] This is a poetic depiction of the eventual treachery of Dan in introducing apostasy.[9]

In Matthew 24, there is a statement of Jesus which I believe is often misunderstood and misapplied. I am convinced Jesus is speaking in this passage of the witnessing ministry of the 144,000 Jews when He says, "And this gospel of the kingdom will be preached in the whole world as a testimony to all nations, and then the end will come."[10]

The gospel is always the same in every age. It is the story of God sending His Son as the Savior of lost humanity. It is the story of Jesus, the only human being without sin, who sacrificed Himself for sinful men and women. In Old Testament times this story was told by means of symbols such as animal sacrifices and temple rituals. John the Baptist told the same story when he said, "Whoever believes in the Son has eternal life, but whoever rejects the Son will not see life, for God's wrath remains on him."[11] Jesus told this same story to a Pharisee named Nicodemus when He said, "For God so loved the world that he gave his one and only Son, that whoever believes in him shall not perish but have eternal life."[12] The disciples told the story in the early days of the church, and people who were hungry for life and truth streamed into the church. The body of Christ grew at a phenomenal, exponential rate.

In the last days this same story will be proclaimed to the farthest reaches of the earth, and then the end will come. This has always been a dark and troubled world, full of sin and death, and there has always been just one story that deserves to be called "Good News." It is the story of the death of Jesus, which gives new life to sinners. As the world grows even darker and more troubled in the last days, this story, which will be told by the 144,000 redeemed Jews of Revelation 7, will never have sounded sweeter and more welcome to the human ear.

The Gospel of the Kingdom

Notice, too, that when Jesus says, "And this gospel of the kingdom will be preached in the whole world," He is making a special and often overlooked link between the gospel and what He calls "the kingdom." John the Baptist and Jesus both preached "the gospel of the kingdom" to Israel. They announced that the messianic kingdom, which had long been foretold by the prophets, was at hand, because Jesus the King was in their midst. Of course, the problem for the Jews of that day was that Jesus was not the kind of king they were expecting—a conqueror who would deliver them from Roman oppression.

The kingdom that Jesus came to establish was much greater than a mere political system. Its purpose was to deal with sin, with the terrible heart-condition of man. Israel was expecting a king, but a very different kind of King. It was as if the whole nation was facing west, awaiting the Messiah's coming, as He came riding in from the east. On Palm Sunday, just days before His crucifixion, Jesus deliberately fulfilled the ancient prophecy of Zechariah as He rode a donkey down the side of the Mount of Olives to the cheers and praise of the people of Jerusalem:

Rejoice greatly, O Daughter of Zion!
Shout, Daughter of Jerusalem!

See, your king comes to you,
    righteous and having salvation,
    gentle and riding on a donkey,
    on a colt, the foal of a donkey.[13]

Christ's 144,000 Commandos will fulfill the word of Jesus that this
same "gospel of the kingdom" will be preached in the whole world as a
testimony to all nations—and then the final judgment of God will
descend upon the earth. The 144,000 will proclaim the gospel during the
seven-year period which we call "the last days" of the age or "the
Tribulation." This band of Spirit-filled Jews, converted to Christ after the
church has been taken out of the world, will go throughout the world like
144,000 apostle Pauls, preaching the gospel of the kingdom during the
time of the cataclysmic judgments of the end times.

There is an extraordinary passage in Matthew 10 which confirms the
view that the 144,000 will be the ones who take the gospel of the kingdom to the ends of the earth. In this passage, Jesus sends out His disciples
to preach the gospel in various parts of Israel:

> These twelve Jesus sent out with the following instructions:
> "Do not go among the Gentiles or enter any town of the
> Samaritans. Go rather to the lost sheep of Israel. As you go,
> preach this message: 'The kingdom of heaven is near.' Heal the
> sick, raise the dead, cleanse those who have leprosy, drive out
> demons. Freely you have received, freely give."[14]

Then Jesus goes on to give further instructions to the Twelve, warning them that they will not be welcome everywhere they go. After this
Jesus' words take a startling turn. He abruptly skips over many centuries
of time and begins talking about the last days, when the gospel will once
again be preached in Israel. It is as if the preaching of the gospel of the
kingdom in the last days is merely an extension of the preaching mission
Jesus gave to the Twelve during His earthly ministry. He says,

> Brother will betray brother to death, and a father his child;
> children will rebel against their parents and have them put to
> death. All men will hate you because of me, but he who stands
> firm to the end will be saved. When you are persecuted in one
> place, flee to another. I tell you the truth, you will not finish
> going through the cities of Israel before the Son of Man comes.[15]

What does Jesus mean when He says, "You will not finish going through the cities of Israel before the Son of Man comes"? Certainly there is no record that Jesus ever came to the Twelve when He sent them out to minister to Israel. Rather they came back to Him, reporting to Him on all they had done.

It seems beyond question that as the Lord was charging the Twelve and preparing to send them out, there is a point where He leaps over the entire age in which we are living, to a future time when a group of Jews will be sent out on the same kind of mission the twelve disciples performed under the authority of Jesus in Matthew 10. This future group of Jews will not be just twelve in number but 144,000—that is, twelve squared times ten cubed (12 x 12 x 10 x 10 x 10). Jesus says to His disciples (though He seems to be looking beyond them, to 144,000 as-yet-unborn future disciples), "You will not finish going through the cities of Israel before the Son of Man comes."

From the lips of the Lord Himself, therefore, we have a prediction of the future ministry of Christ's 144,000 Commandos.

The Great Multitude

Now we see what takes place as a result of the preaching ministry of the 144,000.

7:9–14 *After this I looked and there before me was a great multitude that no one could count, from every nation, tribe, people and language, standing before the throne and in front of the Lamb. They were wearing white robes and were holding palm branches in their hands. And they cried out in a loud voice:*

"Salvation belongs to our God,
who sits on the throne,
and to the Lamb."

All the angels were standing around the throne and around the elders and the four living creatures. They fell down on their faces before the throne and worshiped God, saying:

"Amen! Praise and glory and wisdom and thanks and honor and power and strength be to our God for ever and ever. Amen!"

Then one of the elders asked me, "These in white robes—who are they, and where did they come from?"

I answered, "Sir, you know."

And he said, "These are they who have come out of the great tribulation; they have washed their robes and made them white in the blood of the Lamb."

Remember that John is in heaven, and he sees all these things from an eternal point of view. As we have already discussed, there is no chronological sequence, no time limitation, no past, no future in the heavenly orientation. From our earthly standpoint John sees events that are taking place at the close of the seven-year week. He seems to see ahead to the end of the seven-year period, witnessing a great multitude, too great to be counted, that has come through the Great Tribulation. They are not only Jews, but come from every tribe, people, and language. They have washed their robes and made them white in the blood of the Lamb. And take note of this: They have palm branches in their hands.

When was the last time a crowd of people stood with palm branches in their hands, giving praise to Jesus as their King? Palm Sunday, of course. The day Jesus rode on the back of a donkey, down a mountainside and into the city of Jerusalem. In this vision of John, there is a clear prophetic link between the events of Revelation 7 and the entry of Jesus into Jerusalem on Palm Sunday.

On that day long ago, when the road was lined with men, women, and children shouting praise and laying palm branches in His path, Jesus came in fulfillment of Zechariah's ancient prophecy. Israel was given the opportunity to receive her King—but tragically, the leaders of Israel rejected Him.

But a day will come when Jesus is welcomed by a vast, innumerable throng of both Jews and Gentiles, people from across the planet. They will welcome and worship their King with palm branches, just as the throngs that lined the streets of Jerusalem did 2,000 years ago—only this time, the King will not be rejected and crucified. Moreover, this event will be intimately associated with the final restoration of Israel.

Who are these innumerable throngs of people from every race and nation? We know that they are all *martyrs*. They have died for the sake of Christ during the Tribulation, and they now appear before the throne of God as victors over death and hell, joining the angels in worshiping before the throne. Isn't this an exhilarating thought? Just imagine: In the darkest hour of human history yet to come, the greatest harvest of souls the world has ever seen will take place! Millions who have never heard the gospel today will one day be brought into the kingdom of heaven!

I believe that this multitude will consist entirely of those who have never heard the gospel before the Lord's return for the church and the beginning of the seven-year tribulation. For reasons that we will explore later, I am convinced that those who have already heard the gospel *and rejected it* prior to the beginning of the seven-year tribulation will have hardened their hearts against the gospel. This final harvest of a great multitude from around the world will be a harvest of those to whom the gospel is not only good news but *new* news. It will be a gospel they have never heard before.

During those terrible days of judgment, when the witches of war ride their nuclear brooms across the darkening skies of the world's last night, thousands who have never heard before will hear the gospel of the coming kingdom of God—and they will believe! They will turn to Christ in unbelievable masses! And the sad fact is that it will require them to endure great persecution and suffering and will eventually cost them their very lives.

In the coming pages of Revelation, we will discover that the powerful and hateful forces of the Antichrist will hunt down and destroy anyone who does not bear the mark of ownership by the Antichrist, the "mark of the beast." God's followers in those last days will not accept this dreadful mark—and they will pay the ultimate price for bearing witness to their faith in Jesus Christ.

The Fulfillment of a Dream

We will meet these faithful martyrs again when we come to Revelation 20. There we are told that those who were beheaded because of their testimony for Jesus will be raised from the dead to serve the Lord throughout His thousand-year reign. They will be given a spiritual ministry to perform on earth during the Millennium.

The description of the martyrs' ministry is given here.

7:15–17 *"Therefore, they are before the throne of God and serve him day and night in his temple; and he who sits on the throne will spread his tent over them. Never again will they hunger; never again will they thirst. The sun will not beat upon them, nor any scorching heat. For the Lamb at the center of the throne will be their shepherd; he will lead them to springs of living water. And God will wipe away every tear from their eyes."*

Notice the throne and the temple. In fact, we find two thrones mentioned in this passage. First, there is "the throne of God," which is the throne of God the Father, who reigns over all the universe. And second, there are references to "he who sits on the throne" and "the Lamb at the center of the throne," which are references to the throne of Jesus on earth. Remember that in Revelation 3:21, Jesus says to the Laodicean church, "To him who overcomes, I will give the right to sit with me on *my* throne, just as I overcame and sat down with my Father on *his* throne." The throne of Jesus is that throne which was promised in the annunciation to Mary of Jesus' birth: "He will be great and will be called the Son of the Most High. The Lord God will give him the throne of his father David."16

The temple referred to in verse 15 is, I believe, the millennial temple which is yet to be built in Jerusalem, for worship will go on there "day and night." In heaven there is no night. This is the temple described by the prophet Ezekiel in the closing chapters of his book. It is the temple where the nations will come to worship in the days when Jesus Christ rules over the earth for a thousand years. In the prophecy of Micah, there is a beautiful description of this temple from which God's government, justice, and peace will flow out into all the world:

> In the last days the mountain of the LORD's temple will be established as chief among the mountains; it will be raised above the hills, and peoples will stream to it.
>
> Many nations will come and say, "Come, let us go up to the mountain of the LORD, to the house of the God of Jacob. He will teach us his ways, so that we may walk in his paths." The law will go out from Zion, the word of the LORD from Jerusalem. He will judge between many peoples and will settle disputes for strong nations far and wide. They will beat their swords into plowshares and their spears into pruning hooks. Nation will not take up sword against nation, nor will they train for war anymore. Every man will sit under his own vine and under his own fig tree, and no one will make them afraid, for the LORD Almighty has spoken.17

He who sits on the throne of David—the Lord Jesus—will literally spread His tent or tabernacle over them, and they will never again suffer hunger or thirst or the heat of the sun. This is a beautiful description of the blessings of that millennial time to come—blessings like those described by Micah and other prophets.

This is the fulfillment of the utopian dreams of all the prophets of the past: Israel shall blossom as the rose and shall fill the earth with blessing. The nation will be like a beautiful, fruitful vine that runs its branches throughout the earth. Just as Abraham was promised so many centuries ago, all the nations of the earth shall be blessed because of his descendants, the people of Israel. In Isaiah 66, the Lord says that He will gather all nations and tongues to His holy mountain in Jerusalem, to serve in His temple.

All people, both Jews and Gentiles, are under the care of the Great Shepherd of the sheep. We who follow Christ are grateful for the care He gives to us. But we should never forget that the Great Shepherd has more than one fold. As Jesus said in John 10:16, "I have other sheep that are not of this sheep pen. I must bring them also. They too will listen to my voice, and there shall be one flock and one shepherd."

That is what takes place in Revelation 7. The Lord's "other sheep" are brought into the fold, joining the sheep who were saved by grace through faith during all the centuries of Old Testament and New Testament history, prior to the beginning of the Great Tribulation. They have washed their robes and made them white in the blood of the Lamb, just as all other believers of the past and present have done.

As the curtain closes over the scenes of Revelation 7, we see that the Lord will lead His sheep to refreshment and blessing, to cool springs of living water. And God will wipe every tear away from their eyes.

Thus ends the intermission between the first six seals and the final seal of judgment. Now a hush is about to fall over heaven. Great and terrible events are about to commence once more. Angels are returning to center stage of the final drama of human history.

They are the Angels of Doom . . .

▬▬▬▬▬▬▬
▬▬▬▬▬▬▬
▬▬▬▬▬▬▬
▬▬▬▬▬▬▬
▬▬▬▬▬▬▬
▬▬▬▬▬▬▬

Chapter Fourteen

Angels of Doom

Revelation 8

The "Hallelujah Chorus" of Handel's *Messiah* is probably the most powerful and moving musical composition ever written. Music historian Cesar Saerchinger once observed that hearing a performance of the "Hallelujah Chorus" inspires "a spiritual elevation that can never be surpassed."

During the London premiere of the *Messiah* in 1743, King George II was seated in his box as the first rolling strains of "Hallelujah" cascaded forth from the orchestra and chorus. The king was so deeply moved that he spontaneously rose to his feet and stood for the remainder of the performance, his eyes glistening with emotion. The rest of the audience, seeing the king reverently standing as the music swelled, also rose to its feet—a tradition that remains to this day whenever the "Hallelujah Chorus" is performed.

You know this magnificent chorus well. I'm sure you remember that at its climax, wave after wave of *Hallelujahs* sweep over you. It is difficult to experience this music without your heart pounding and your eyes filling with tears. And then—

The orchestra and the chorus suddenly stop!

And there is *silence!*

It is a thundering silence, full of awe and intense anticipation. The echoes of the last *Hallelujah* still reverberate in your ear and in your heart, fading gradually until the silence at last becomes complete. There is a sense of drama, of suspense, of mystery. We know it is not over. The last *Hallelujah* is yet to sound.

Suddenly the silence shatters under the triumphant blow of the final majestic *Hallelujah*. The victory of the Messiah is accomplished.

In the eighth chapter of Revelation, we witness the very moment which is symbolized in the climactic pause of Handel's "Hallelujah Chorus."

8:1–2 *When he opened the seventh seal, there was silence in heaven for about half an hour.*

And I saw the seven angels who stand before God, and to them were given seven trumpets.

The silence described here reminds us of the doxology penned by the prophet Habakkuk: "But the LORD is in his holy temple; let all the earth be silent before him."[1] The half hour of silence in Revelation 8 comes as a dramatic contrast to the shouts of praise and the playing of harps we have heard up to this point. Suddenly, everything—all activity and all sound throughout heaven—ceases with the dramatic opening of the seventh seal. As Earl Palmer observes,

> It is the silence of mystery and intense waiting. . . . There is communicated in a very dramatic way in this quietness the full and awesome authority of God. Everything must wait for his kingly move.[2]

That dramatic, kingly move begins, as this account tells us, with seven angels who are given seven trumpets to sound. These seven trumpets are all part of the consummate event which is the opening of the seventh seal. These seven angels are impressive indeed. We are told that they are the angels who stand before God—a reference which calls to mind the story in Luke 1 of the angel who visited Zechariah to announce the birth of John the Baptist.

After the angel told Zechariah what he and his wife Elizabeth should name the baby, and the special kind of man this child would one day become, Zechariah asked, "How can I be sure of this? I am an old man and my wife is well along in years."

And the angel's reply is significant: "*I am Gabriel. I stand in the presence of God*, and I have been sent to speak to you and to tell you this good news" (emphasis added). It was this same angel Gabriel who announced the coming birth of Jesus to a virgin named Mary.[3]

In Revelation 8 we are introduced to seven angels who stand in the presence of God. They are probably archangels—the highest class of angels—for they are given an extremely important task, the sounding of the seven trumpets. Another of these angels is doubtless the archangel Michael, who appears in the book of Daniel.

There is an ancient apocryphal book that contains an interesting detail. It lists the names of the seven high angels: Uriel, Raphael, Raguel, Michael, Sarakiel, Gabriel, and Phanuel. Notice that their names all end in "el," which is short for Elohim, one of the names of God. These are the seven angels of God, powerful angels who are given apocalyptic trumpets to sound.

Thunder, Lightning, and an Earthquake

Before they blow their trumpets, John records a dramatic scene.

8:3–5 Another angel, who had a golden censer, came and stood at the altar. He was given much incense to offer, with the prayers of all the saints, on the golden altar before the throne. The smoke of the incense, together with the prayers of the saints, went up before God from the angel's hand. Then the angel took the censer, filled it with fire from the altar, and hurled it on the earth; and there came peals of thunder, rumblings, flashes of lightning and an earthquake.

Many Bible scholars identify the angel who holds the golden censer as Jesus Himself. This idea is based on the fact that in the Old Testament, as the people of Israel journeyed through the wilderness, they were led by a great angel called "the Angel of Jehovah [YHWH or Yahweh]." Most evangelical scholars feel this was an appearance of the pre-incarnate Christ—the Son of God Himself leading His people through the wilderness.

In Revelation the nation of Israel is once again at the forefront of events. So it makes sense that this same "Angel of the Lord" would appear again in connection with the nation of Israel—and that this "Angel" may in fact be Jesus Himself.

What is the meaning of the golden censer? A censer is a container in which incense is burned, and it is a symbol of a priestly function. We are told throughout the book of Hebrews and in many other New Testament passages that Jesus is our High Priest. For example, Paul tells us that Jesus, our High Priest, "is at the right hand of God and is also interceding for us."[4]

Clearly that is the function we see this angel performing. He takes fire from the altar of brass, adds to it the incense of the prayers of the saints, and offers them on the golden altar of incense before God. It is a beautiful and revealing portrayal of the function of prayer.

Sometimes we feel that our prayers to God go unanswered—and even unheard. But in this passage we see that the prayers of the saints—especially the intercessory prayers we pray for one another—are like a fragrance in the nostrils of God. Our prayers delight God, reminding Him of the prayers and the character of Jesus, who prayed His high priestly prayer for others in John 17, just hours before offering Himself as a sacrifice for our sake.

The prayers of the saints are mingled with the incense of the priestly prayers of the great angel himself—an angel which may actually represent the Lord Jesus Christ Himself. If the burning incense of this passage is symbolic of the prayers of the saints imploring God to act, then the image of the angel hurling that fiery censer to earth is a symbol of *answered* prayer. The time has come for God to *act*.

And just look at the result of God's action:

Thunder! Rumblings! Flashes of lightning! A great earthquake! These are the sights and sounds which mark the close of the age of mankind upon the earth. But they also mark the beginning of God's kingdom upon the earth.

You may recall that when we examined Revelation 4:5 we listened with John to these same cataclysmic sounds: "From the throne came flashes of lightning, rumblings and peals of thunder." In these present verses, an earthquake is added as well.

Later, in Revelation 11, the seventh angel will sound the seventh trumpet and these same sounds will be heard again. At that time the angel will proclaim, "The kingdom of the world has become the kingdom of our Lord and of his Christ, and he will reign for ever and ever."[5] With that, the scroll will be fully unrolled.

These sounds of global upheaval and the violence of nature accompany the end of each of the series of seven—the seven seals, the seven trumpets, and the seven bowls of the wrath of God. At the opening of the seventh seal, we learn that when the great Angel casts the fire of God upon the earth, the moment has come when God fully and finally answers the prayers of His people.

The Prayer of the Ages

There is one prayer that the people of God have been praying throughout the ages of history which has not yet been answered. I believe

Adam must have prayed this prayer even as he was forced to leave the Garden of Eden. Perhaps Noah prayed this prayer as he came out of the ark and set foot upon a world washed clean by the waters of the flood. Abraham must have prayed this prayer as he looked for a City yet to come. We know that King David prayed this prayer, for we find it in many forms embedded in the Psalms. We know that all the apostles, including Paul, prayed this prayer, for it permeates the New Testament.

This prayer was taught by Jesus to His disciples, and many churches pray this prayer at some point during every worship service. The words of this prayer are, "Thy kingdom come, thy will be done on earth as it is in heaven." From the beginning of human history right up to this very moment as I write these words, this is a prayer that has not been answered. We do not now see God's kingdom visibly on the earth.

Yes, the kingdom is present in invisible form in the church. We see its influence over the affairs of men, and we recognize that God, as King and Creator of the universe, is sovereign over all events in heaven and on the earth. Yet we know that on this earth there are other wills at work than the will of God alone. All around us are the constant reminders of the operation of sinful human wills—and also of sinful demonic wills.

But when we come at last to the end of these three series of judgments that are depicted in the book of Revelation, the long centuries of human yearning, our prayers for God's kingdom to come in visible power and authority over the earth will be fulfilled.

The Zenith of Judgment

The seventh trumpet appears to usher in what Jesus calls "the great tribulation" in His Olivet discourse of Matthew 24. There He says, "For then there will be great distress [or tribulation] unequaled from the beginning of the world until now—and never to be equaled again."[6] Jesus is describing what we are about to see—the very zenith of God's judgment against sin upon the earth.

In Revelation 8:6, we come to one of the most difficult sections of the book to interpret.

8:6 Then the seven angels who had the seven trumpets prepared to sound them.

The sevenfold judgment is about to commence. Bible scholars are divided as to whether the seven judgments of the seven trumpets are literal physical judgments or symbols of something else (and perhaps something worse than what is pictured).

My own view, however, is that these seven judgments are *both* literal and symbolic. This is how God frequently works. He pictures something which is invisible and can't be imagined by means of a literal event.

For instance, the sun is a literal object. It is a great shining star which warms our earth and keeps the entire solar system working. But the sun is also a potent symbol, and is used as such throughout Scripture. We refer to the sun in everyday life as a symbol of light, of knowledge, and of truth.

Fire, too, is a literal phenomenon. You can warm yourself by it or burn yourself with it. Yet in Scripture fire often appears as a symbol of torment and judgment.

The Old Testament prophecy of Joel opens with a vivid description of a literal plague of locusts that comes upon the land and devours every green thing. But as you continue reading in Joel, this literal and dramatic description of a plague of locusts soon becomes a symbolic prophecy of a military invasion by a vast Babylonian army.

So scriptural events often merge the literal and symbolic into a single profound image. I believe that is the nature of the trumpet judgments which begin in Revelation 8. Throughout its history Israel has used literal trumpets as a blaring public warning of an imminent emergency or event. So, in this series of seven trumpets we hear God's public announcement of imminent judgment.

But there is nothing new or historically unprecedented in God's judgment of mankind through the events of human experience. There are calamitous events going on all around us right at this moment, and these events trumpet the judgment of God against human sin. He is speaking to us, even shouting to us—but the human race has turned a deaf ear to God's warning.

One such event is the plague of drug abuse that is ruining millions of lives, particularly young lives, not only in America but around the world. Drugs destroy the mind, burn out the body, drain the economy, and transform human beings into something worse than animals. What is this scourge saying to us as individuals and as a society?

Clearly, the plague of drugs is a literal catastrophe, the consequence of a philosophy of sinful self-indulgence, the lust for pleasure without any consideration of the moral or social or physical implications of the act. It is a consequence of self-centeredness and irresponsibility. Though God did not send the plague of drugs, He is attempting to speak to us through it. He is saying to us, "See the destructive results of sin and selfishness!" Yet our society continues along the same path, willfully blind to the warning God is shouting to us.

Jesus once rebuked the Pharisees because they could interpret the literal signs of approaching bad weather, yet they refused to interpret the signs of the times. As we look at the devastation that drug abuse has brought upon our society, we have to ask ourselves if we are any more discerning than the Pharisees.

The AIDS epidemic is another literal and frightening event taking place in our society. It has already consumed many thousands of lives in many countries worldwide, and it will inevitably swallow many more lives in the years to come. A friend of mine who is a missionary doctor tells me that half of the women and nearly a third of the men in Uganda, a country in central Africa, are afflicted with AIDS. The country faces almost total annihilation because of this incurable and loathsome plague. Though not nearly so widespread in North America, it is nonetheless a fast-spreading epidemic.

The AIDS epidemic is clearly a literal and ongoing event—but does it also have a symbolic dimension? I am convinced that it does, and that God is attempting to speak to our society through the means of the AIDS epidemic.

Just as AIDS robs people of their immunity against other infections, so does indulgence in sexual promiscuity rob us of our defense against moral and spiritual errors, according to the Word of God. Many people today are easy targets for strange cults and New Age philosophies because their moral and spiritual defenses have been stripped away by their desire for a sexually promiscuous lifestyle. That is why Paul writes, "No immoral, impure or greedy person—such a man is an idolater—has any inheritance in the kingdom of Christ and of God. Let no one deceive you with empty words, for because of such things God's wrath comes on those who are disobedient."[7]

The epidemic of abortion in our society is also a literal and ongoing phenomenon in our society. In America, it means the murder of 1.6 million innocent, unborn lives every year—and the vast majority (approximately 98 percent) of these abortions take place not because of rape or incest or a threat to the mother's health, but simply because the conception was unplanned and a baby would be inconvenient. A struggle which has the makings of a virtual civil war is taking place in our nation at this very hour, and the pain and anguish of this crisis should be sending us a message—but are we listening?

What does it say to an entire generation of young people when the law of the land permits the destruction of human life for the sake of convenience and so-called "choice"? What lesson are the children of many of our states learning when their teachers are *required by law* to tell them, as early as the sixth grade, how to go about obtaining an abortion without their parents' knowledge or consent? What are we teaching them about the value of human life?

You can see the answer in the vacancy of their eyes. We are losing the souls of an entire generation. Like the ancient people of apostate Israel, we are tossing our children into the fiery maw of the demon-god Molech, deliberately sacrificing them to our own selfishness. The plague of abortion is the visible expression of our sin and willful brutishness as a society. How can we expect God not to judge the perpetrators of such a monumental social injustice?

The First Angel

Let us now see what the trumpets of the angels signify.

8:7 *The first angel sounded his trumpet, and there came hail and fire mixed with blood, and it was hurled down upon the earth. A third of the earth was burned up, a third of the trees were burned up, and all the green grass was burned up.*

This description is reminiscent of the seventh plague that befell Egypt during Moses' confrontation with Pharaoh, when hail and lightning came upon the whole land. In Revelation 8 we see hail and lightning mingled with blood. This is not a new phenomenon. Scientists and historians have recorded other times when red rain fell from the sky.

Camille Flammarion's book *The Atmosphere*, published in the nineteenth century, documents a number of such occurrences in Europe and elsewhere, such as the red rain which fell on San Pier d'Arena, near Genoa, Italy, in 1744. Flammarion observed that this red rain terrified the people very much because of a bitter war that was then raging in the region. What actually causes red rains? The book concludes that what many witnesses "call a shower of blood is generally a mere fall of vapors tinted with vermilion or red chalk. But when blood actually does fall, which it would be difficult to deny takes place, it is a miracle due to the will of God."[8]

Similar events have been documented in our own century. Though scientists have never explained how a blood-red rain could fall from the sky, such rains have left great puddles of grisly looking water on the ground. Revelation 8 foresees a time when hail and fire, mingled with blood, will descend not on some isolated region of the earth, but over great portions of the land. It will devastate much of our natural world.

Notice that the plagues of the first four trumpets all fall on creation, causing massive environmental damage. It is as though the Lord were saying, "You have taken the natural world for granted, abused it, and plundered it. You want a devastated world? Very well, then. You shall have it." As always, the worst judgment God can mete out to sinful humanity is to give humanity what it demands.

But the destruction that is depicted here doesn't just have a literal dimension. It is also powerfully symbolic. It is designed to teach us a truth of God that is invisible to the eyes of men at that time. As we have already observed, the earth is used in Scripture as a picture of Israel, which God intended as an example to the world of a nation governed by God. I believe this passage depicts a judgment that is directed not only against the natural world and the environment, but upon Israel—both its leaders (symbolized by the trees) and its people (symbolized by the grass).

Old Testament prophets pointed to a future time when God would judge His people Israel. For example, Zephaniah records the word of the Lord, who says,

> At that time I will search Jerusalem with lamps and punish those who are complacent, who are like wine left on its dregs, who think, "The LORD will do nothing, either good or bad." Their wealth will be plundered, their houses demolished. They will build houses but not live in them; they will plant vineyards but not drink the wine.9

The prophet Jeremiah calls this "the time of Jacob's trouble."

The Second Angel

Next, John describes the judgment brought about by the second angel and the second trumpet:

8:8–9 *The second angel sounded his trumpet, and something like a huge mountain, all ablaze, was thrown into the sea. A third of the sea turned into blood, a third of the living creatures in the sea died, and a third of the ships were destroyed.*

The first trumpet judgment assaulted the earth. The second attacks the sea. A great blazing mountain-like object falls into the sea. This could be the result of an unimaginably violent volcanic eruption—some vulcanologists believe that Sicily's Mount Etna is primed to explode much like Washington state's Mount Saint Helens did in 1980. Or it could be a massive meteor falling out of space and flaming through the atmosphere, landing at last in the sea.

Whatever this mountain-like object is, it will cause the sea to become blood-red. Again, the phenomena called "red tides" have occurred before, caused by tiny red marine organisms that multiply rapidly, giving the water a bloodlike color. What would cause the "red tide" of Revelation 8 to occur in the aftermath of the fall of the blazing object? We don't know. We only know that the resulting havoc will leave a third of all marine life dead and a third of all shipping destroyed.

If these are literal events, there is also a symbolic dimension to them. The image of the great mountain, blazing with fire and tumbling into the sea, symbolizes a great kingdom aflame with revolution. The prophet Jeremiah, for example, records some strikingly similar imagery when he conveys the Lord's judgment against Babylon:

> "I am against you, O destroying mountain, you who destroy the whole earth," declares the LORD. "I will stretch out my hand against you, roll you off the cliffs, and make you a burned-out mountain."10

As we can gather by comparing this passage with other passages of Scripture, the symbol of the mountain-like object falling into the sea probably symbolizes the influence of what is popularly called "the revived Roman Empire," the ten-kingdom coalition of Western European and Western allied nations that will be prominent, under the leadership of the Antichrist, during the Tribulation period. And as we have discussed before, the sea is frequently used in Scripture as a symbol of the Gentile nations of the earth. So the symbolic image of these verses suggests a time when the Antichrist-led coalition will fall upon the Gentiles of the world like a flaming, destroying mountain, conquering the Gentile nations while destroying many Gentile lives.

As happened in the first trumpet judgment, and as will happen again and again throughout these seven judgments, we see the repetitive use of the term "a third." Under the seals of judgment, the losses were limited to "a fourth," but here we see losses of "a third," again and again. What is the difference between the judgments of the seven seals and the judgments of the seven trumpets?

Four is the number of human government. Under the seal judgments God was indicating that He uses human government to limit the onslaught of the four terrible horsemen of Revelation 6. Human government will still retain some vestige of restraining power during those days.

But in Revelation 8, even that limited amount of restraint has been removed. Under the trumpet judgments, God alone restrains. Three is the divine number, the symbol of God's attributes. By the repeated phrase "a third" God is indicating that only His mercy and grace limits these terrible apocalyptic judgments to one-third of the earth.

The Third Angel

Now John describes the judgment brought about by the third angel and the third trumpet.

8:10–11 *The third angel sounded his trumpet, and a great star, blazing like a torch, fell from the sky on a third of the rivers and on the springs of water—the name of the star is Wormwood. A third of the waters turned bitter, and many people died from the waters that had become bitter.*

This great star which falls into the rivers and the fountains of the earth is very likely a comet or comet-like object which breaks up when it enters the atmosphere and scatters itself throughout the earth, falling into the rivers and springs and poisoning them. It is interesting to speculate that the form of poisoning described in these verses might actually be a form of radiation. In fact, we may have already witnessed a foregleam of such an event when a nuclear reactor experienced a catastrophic meltdown at the Chernobyl nuclear power plant in the Soviet Union. I suspect that it is no mere coincidence that the word *Chernobyl* is actually Russian for "Wormwood"! I believe God was desperately trying to warn us during that terrible nuclear accident—but, as usual, humankind refuses to listen.

Again, I believe the destruction depicted has a symbolic as well as a literal dimension. It is designed to teach us God's truth about the invisible realm of man's internal being. Rivers, of course, symbolize great masses of people moving together in one direction—entire populations caught up in one idea, one mindset, moving predictably and inexorably like a river toward a single destination. The springs symbolize the sources of moral or philosophical leadership. The star symbolizes a prominent leader.

It appears from these symbols that some great person, widely recognized as a leader, will suddenly reverse his policy. He will, in essence, *fall*. Many people will be embittered by the turnabout of this influential leader. In the mass struggle that ensues, many will experience moral and spiritual death.

This is exactly the scene that is described for us later in Revelation under the rule of the Beast that comes from the earth. Moreover, in Revelation 9, we will see a similar "star" when we witness the fifth and sixth trumpets of judgment. A more complete discussion of the symbol of the star will appear in the following chapter.

The Fourth Angel

Next, John describes the judgment brought about by the fourth angel and the fourth trumpet.

8:12 *The fourth angel sounded his trumpet, and a third of the sun was struck, a third of the moon, and a third of the stars, so that a third of them turned dark. A third of the day was without light, and also a third of the night.*

Now compare this verse with the words of the Lord Jesus from His Sermon on the Mount in Luke 21. Jesus says,

> There will be signs in the sun, moon and stars. On the earth, nations will be in anguish and perplexity at the roaring and toss-ing of the sea. Men will faint from terror, apprehensive of what is coming on the world, for the heavenly bodies will be shaken.[11]

There is no question that Jesus here describes the same event that John relates as the judgment of the fourth trumpet. But not only is this a literal event in which the sun, moon, and stars are darkened or fail for a time to give their light, this is also a powerfully symbolic event.

The sun, moon, and stars are used in various places in Scripture to symbolize earthly authorities. The highest such authorities—kings, prime ministers, dictators, and presidents—would be portrayed as the sun. Lesser authorities would be portrayed as the moon and stars. Thus, we see depicted here a hierarchy of civil authority—authority which some-how is eclipsed under the judgment of the fourth trumpet.

What does the darkening of these heavenly bodies mean in a symbol-ic sense? It means that these authorities will be morally darkened. The light of truth and reason will be withdrawn from them. Instead of display-ing sound moral judgment, their judgment will be darkened and evil. They will display no ethical restraint, no compassion, no justice. People under their government will experience only deceit, cruelty, treachery, oppression, and merciless exploitation.

By the grace of God, this darkening will still be limited to a third. Some restraint of evil will still be possible in those evil times, but only by the sovereign grace of a sovereign God!

The Warning of the Eagle

In verse 13, an eagle appears with a message of warning and lament. If you study Revelation in the King James Version, you will find the word "angel" instead of "eagle," but the more authoritative and reliable Greek manuscripts use the Greek word for "eagle."

8:13 *As I watched, I heard an eagle that was flying in midair call out in a loud voice: "Woe! Woe! Woe to the inhabitants of the earth, because of the trumpet blasts about to be sounded by the other three angels!"*

After the woes that have already befallen the earth, it is difficult to imagine what could follow in the next three trumpet blasts that could be any worse—yet as we shall see, the eagle's threefold cry of "Woe!" is well-deserved.

As we examine this passage, we should note that there is a mistranslation in the text. The phrase "Woe to the inhabitants of the earth" would be better translated "Woe to those who make their home on earth." This may seem a small difference at first, but it is actually an extremely important distinction. During the days of the Great Tribulation there will be many new converts, redeemed followers of Christ, who are inhabitants of the earth but who do not make their home on earth. They will live and act as though their citizenship is in heaven.

Those "who make their home on earth" are a moral and spiritual class of people who live only for the present life and care nothing for the things of God and the life to come. Someone has well described such people with a bit of doggerel that reads,

> Into this world to eat and to sleep,
> And to know no reason why he was born,
> Save to consume the corn,
> Devour the cattle, flock and fish,
> And leave behind an empty dish!

I'm sure you know people like that. They care only about the present, about their own immediate and self-centered needs, their own pleasures, their own will. They give no thought to others. They give no thought to the purpose of life or the meaning of their own existence. They give no thought to God.

The warning of the eagle is that a terrible doom is coming upon all those who live for the moment, who live for self, who have no larger framework for their lives than today's pleasures. This is the kind of moral decay that will exist in that day. The first four trumpets, which should have been "loud" enough to awaken anyone with ears to hear, appear to have fallen on deaf ears among those "who make their home on earth." The next three trumpets—two of which we will examine in the following chapter—shall bring unimaginable woe upon those who live only for the moment and for self.

From Bad to Worse to Worst

There is a clear sense of progression in the judgments we have witnessed thus far in Revelation. We have seen that each series of seven judgments is divided into four and three. In the judgments of the seven seals, the first four seals were represented by the four horsemen. The next three seals then gave us insight into what was going on behind the scenes of judgment.

In this series of trumpet judgments, we first hear the sounding of the first four trumpets, followed by a soaring eagle who announces that even more profound woes await the final three trumpet judgments.

In the seven bowls of wrath we will again see the same division—a group of four judgments followed by a group of three.

This pattern seems to suggest the degrees of comparison with which even kindergarten-age children are familiar. If you are comparing size, you can talk about objects being "small," "smaller," and "smallest," or "big," "bigger," "biggest." If you are comparing evil, you can say that this is "bad," that is "worse," and something else is the "worst." That is the pattern we see in the judgments of Revelation—a steadily crescendo-ing series of judgments, inexorably progressing toward a fearsome climax: the bowls of God's wrath, the worst judgments of all.

How do you feel about the judgment of God? Does the idea of God's wrath make you uncomfortable? It does most people, including many pastors and Bible teachers.

We like the idea of God's love and grace and forgiveness, but we often try to skirt the issue of His justice and holiness. It is part of our fallen nature that we do not want to squarely, honestly face the fact that sin has consequences—terrible consequences—and that righteousness and justice are not matters to be taken lightly. Our sin cost Jesus a trial of suffering and death upon the cross, plus the unimaginable torment of separation from God the Father. The triumph of the Resurrection overshadows but can never erase the horror of those hours upon the cross. In the same way, the triumph of God at the end of Revelation does not erase the horror that will come upon the human race during God's climactic judgment of sin at the end of history.

Because we are bent by sin, our nature is to tolerate and indulge sin. But our God is a holy God. If He were to allow the ever-increasing sin of the world to go unchecked, His holiness would be open to question.

The judgments that we see in Revelation are only unprecedented in degree, not in kind. God has been sending such judgments to the earth throughout the history of mankind. There have been disasters, signs in the heavens, red rain from the skies, poisoned waters, plagues, and horrors too numerous and terrible to recount since the earliest days of the human race. In Revelation, however, these judgments come to an apocalyptic climax. Our task is to seek to understand these judgments and learn the lessons God would teach us through them. It is for our eternal good that God has made us witnesses of these events.

God judges nations and societies and cultures. But God also judges individuals. Sometimes He uses hardships and sufferings to chasten and correct us. This is not to say that everyone who undergoes suffering is being judged by God. There are many reasons why suffering comes into our lives, and into the lives of the most godly and devout saints. But the fact is that some people do experience hardships as a result of God's judgment. So we should learn to understand the role of God's corrective judgment in our lives so that we can become the people He wants us to be.

First, *judgment frightens us*. It's supposed to. Judgment chills our blood. It alarms us and scares the living daylights out of us—but it also arrests our attention. Like children watching a horror movie, we are fascinated by the horror of judgment even while we want to hide our eyes from it. The first effect of judgment is to arouse our fear.

Second, *judgment sobers us*. It forces us to reassess the way we have been living our lives. It changes our priorities. As C. S. Lewis has said, fear and pain and judgment are "God's megaphone for reaching a deaf world."

Third, *judgment corrects us*. It forces us to face the unpleasant truth about ourselves. We don't like that. We don't want to hear about our imperfection and our sinfulness. But judgment is like a mirror: it strips away our illusion and restores us to a realistic view of ourselves. It enables us to see clearly, to reason accurately, to plan carefully, to live thoughtfully, and to think the thoughts of God after Him.

Fourth, *judgment humbles us*. Judgment forces us to recognize that we are not in control of our circumstances. We are not equipped to run our own lives. We are not masters of our own fates, captains of our own souls. We are not autonomous. Stripped of our own delusions of self-godhood, we are able at last to seek God's control and guidance over our lives. We become willing to seek the wisdom of the Word of God rather than leaning on our own limited understanding.

Finally, *judgment reassures us*. It is one of the beautiful paradoxes of God's Word that judgment actually comforts us. It answers the great prayer of Habakkuk, "LORD . . . in wrath remember mercy."[12] The fact is, God does not relish the idea of judgment anymore than you or I. The prophet Isaiah makes a fascinating statement about God's judgment, saying "The LORD will rise up . . . to do his work, his strange work, and perform his task, his alien task."[13]

Clearly, judgment is not something that God enjoys. He considers it "strange work," an "alien task." You can see that in the way God always gives ample warning before He sends judgment. He sends reminders and attention-getters long before He sends destruction, because He is a *loving* God, slow to anger and rich in mercy. Just as He gave the evil city of Nineveh an opportunity to change its ways in the days of the prophet Jonah, so He gives you and me and the entire world the chance to wake up, pay attention, and act before our sin gets out of hand.

People who have only a nodding acquaintance with the Bible are fond of saying, "I believe in a loving God. The God I worship is not judgmental." That's a well-intentioned yet fatally flawed point of view. The fact is that it is the very *love* of God that makes Him a judge! God loves His creation and He loves human beings. He hates sin because sin destroys both us and His creation. God *must* judge sin to eliminate evil once and for all and to bring about the world of universal blessing which human beings have longed for since the first couple was cast out of Eden.

Thank God we worship a God of both love and judgment! *Thank God* that even in the severity of His judgments, He remembers mercy! How thankful we are for a God who protects us and watches over us, even when we would rebelliously and ungratefully wish to go our own way.

And how especially thankful are we who have ears to hear, who have listened and learned from what the Spirit says to us through the book of Revelation. We have heard the eagle's cry, "Woe! Woe! Woe to those who make their home on earth!" And we have taken refuge in the Rock of our salvation, where the judgment that is coming upon the rest of the world can't harm us.

Now we await the trumpet blasts of the last three angels.

Chapter Fifteen

All Hell Breaks Loose

Revelation 9

We have seen echoes of it before: an entire nation of peace-loving people of all walks of life—students, shopkeepers, farmers, teachers, machinists, bankers—is whipped into an emotional fervor by the harangues of a demagogue, induced to take up gun and uniform and march blindly into the fires of all-out war. The thirteenth-century Mongols followed Genghis Khan throughout China, India, the Middle East, and Europe, leaving more than 40 million dead. The French followed Napoleon on a binge of conquest that killed 5 million and kept Europe in turmoil for two decades.

In our own century, the German people followed a strange little man with a Charlie Chaplin mustache to unimaginable depths of butchery and inhumanity. Today, when you look at faded newsreel footage of Adolf Hitler giving one of his frenzied speeches before the German throngs, it is hard to imagine that anyone would truly believe what he said and follow his deluded dreams of conquest.

Yet it seems the fate of people to forever allow such wicked leaders to goad them into destroying millions of lives while themselves marching into the blast-furnace of history. And the worst that humanity is capable of has not yet been seen. All of the bloody wars of history are just a foregleam of the final conflict to come.

A day is coming when a great leader will rise up and draw millions to a fiery doom. This leader will be the crowning desecration in a long line of bloody conquerors—more terrible by far than Khan or Napoleon or Hitler or Hussein. The doom that was prophesied by the eagle's scream—"Woe to those who make their home on earth!"—will at last fall upon the human race.

And all hell will break loose.

The Fifth Angel

In chapter 9, we arrive at the judgment of the fifth angel and the fifth trumpet.

9:1–6 The fifth angel sounded his trumpet, and I saw a star that had fallen from the sky to the earth. The star was given the key to the shaft of the Abyss. When he opened the Abyss, smoke rose from it like the smoke from a gigantic furnace. The sun and sky were darkened by the smoke from the Abyss. And out of the smoke locusts came down upon the earth and were given power like that of scorpions of the earth. They were told not to harm the grass of the earth or any plant or tree, but only those people who did not have the seal of God on their foreheads. They were not given power to kill them, but only to torture them for five months. And the agony they suffered was like that of the sting of a scorpion when it strikes a man. During those days men will seek death, but will not find it; they will long to die, but death will elude them.

In the judgment of the third angel with the third trumpet we saw a great star fall into the sea. In this remarkable passage another star falls—but this time onto the earth. Here, as in previous depictions of judgment, we are probably witnessing a literal event—perhaps the fall of a brilliant meteor from the skies. There have been many times in history that meteors have fallen to earth and created havoc for human beings.

The text makes it clear, however, that this is also a symbolic event. The star represents an individual who is given a key by which he opens up the gateway of hell, which is called here the Abyss.

In Luke 8, when Jesus cast the host of demons named Legion out of a man by the Sea of Galilee, the demons "begged him repeatedly not to order them to go into the Abyss."[1] The same Greek word for Abyss is used in this passage as in Revelation 9. In this account, Jesus allows the demons to enter into a herd of swine rather than be cast into the Abyss. The swine then run over the edge of a cliff and perish in the water below. This is a strange story and one which raises many interesting questions, yet one thing is clear: demonic beings have an intense dread of being cast into the great Abyss.

By examining other passages of Scripture we can see that demons have already been imprisoned in the Abyss. Jude 6 tells us there are angels which are "kept in darkness, bound with everlasting chains for judgment on the great Day." It seems apparent that in these scenes in Revelation 9 we come to that "great Day" referred to in the book of Jude, for in this passage the "star" which falls to earth becomes a being who takes the key to the Abyss and opens it. Out of the Abyss come great clouds of billowing smoke, darkening the daytime sky. Then out of the inky clouds come hordes of locusts, so thick and numerous that they have the appearance of clouds—yet another image laden with both literal and figurative meaning.

I vividly remember one summer from my boyhood in Minnesota when the land was visited by a plague of locusts. The remembered image remains vivid in my mind, and it echoes the image John relates in this passage: millions and millions of locusts, swarming like billowing clouds, darkening the daytime sky. They descended onto the fields of standing grain with the sound of a hailstorm. As they munched on the vegetation, they sounded like a rushing river. They destroyed everything in their path, leaving nothing behind but bare earth, stubble, and disillu-sionment. As horrible as those midwestern locust plagues were, they were just a foreshadowing of what John witnesses when the angel sounds the fifth trumpet of judgment.

At the same time that we see a literal plague of locusts unleashed, we also see the release of demons—invisible spirit beings from the pit of hell. The demons are released to go out across the earth like a plague of locusts.

What sort of being is this that falls to earth like a star or a meteor and that is given the power to unleash the destructive powers of hell? There is a clear connection between this judgment and that of the third trumpet, the falling of the other great star into the sea. We identified that first star as a powerful political leader who, after a period of enjoying enthusiastic popularity, would abruptly change his policy and embitter entire classes of people.

As we shall see as we continue to explore this passage, the person represented by this second star is a Jewish religious leader who turns apostate and unleashes demonic forces, like clouds of deadly locusts, upon the earth. I believe this leader is Jewish because of the clues given in the passage.

The locusts/demons were told not to harm "the grass of the earth or any plant or tree, but only those people who did not have the seal of God on their foreheads." Clearly grass, trees, and plants represent people, as we have already seen in Revelation 7. More specifically, they represent Israel. Yet there is a certain group of them—the 144,000 who have been sealed by God—who are guarded and protected from demonic influence and control by the Spirit of God. Those unbelievers upon whom the locusts/demons are unleashed are not destroyed, but are instead tormented for a period of five months.

The being represented by the second star, then, is that person the apostle Paul refers to in 2 Thessalonians as "the Man of Sin," a crucially important individual who arises in the last days. This man sits in the temple of God and claims the worship of Israel and of the entire earth. He is well known, even among casual students of the Bible and biblical prophecy. He is sometimes called the Antichrist.

The Scorpion's Sting

It was a hot, steamy afternoon in Vietnam, 1960. I was in the country to speak to pastors of the Tribal Churches. That afternoon I settled back on a cot in a little wooden building, planning to take a brief nap. Then out of the corner of my eye, I caught a glimpse of something scurrying across the top of the doorframe. I jumped off the cot to get a closer look. As I moved closer, it ran down the side of the doorframe, and out onto the floor. It stopped, facing me.

It was a scorpion.

I had seen scorpions before, but I had never seen one like this. It was black and it was *big*—fully six inches long. It actually reared itself up on its hind legs, defiantly staring me in the face with its tiny bead-like eyes. Its segmented, stinger-tipped tail was curled far forward in my direction, ready to strike. Clearly, this was not the kind of scorpion you kill with your shoe. It was the kind that could only be dispatched with a bazooka.

I hastily scanned the room for something with which to smash it—preferably something with a very long handle—when it darted off and disappeared behind a desk. I never saw that scorpion again—but I was never comfortable in that room after that.

I later asked my Vietnamese friends what would have happened to me if the scorpion had stung me. They said that the scorpion's venom causes indescribable anguish for about 24 hours—not just at the site of the wound but throughout the body. There is nothing you can take to relieve the pain. In fact, a pain killer would only exacerbate the effect of the venom, making the pain worse. The pain, often accompanied by temporary paralysis and fever, must simply be endured.

That is what the sting of a scorpion is like, and that is the metaphor which appears in Revelation 9:3 and 5, where John writes that the locusts/demons "were given power like that of scorpions of the earth"—power not to kill the unbelievers on the earth, but rather "to torture them for five months. And the agony they suffered was like that of the sting of a scorpion when it strikes a man." The Antichrist has loosed a horde of demons upon the earth, and these demons afflict the human race with their agonizing "sting." This "sting" is the demonic propaganda of the Antichrist, the hellish lies he uses to ensnare the minds and hearts of those who are naked to demonic attack because they have not been sealed by the Holy Spirit. The metaphor of a scorpion's sting speaks of the lies which the Antichrist inflicts, deceiving and mentally tormenting the world on a massive scale.

A number of years ago, I led a home Bible class in Palo Alto, California. One of our members was a young woman who had recently moved to California from Alaska. The winter nights are very long in Alaska, so to while away the time, she and a friend began amusing themselves with a Ouija board. To them it was nothing but harmless entertainment, an innocent game. They gave no thought to the fact that when they asked questions of the Ouija board, they were actually seeking contact with demonic intelligences. Their "harmless entertainment" soon led them into involvement with horoscopes and astrology.

The first inkling this woman had that she was involved in something wrong came when she was awakened one night by voices in her head. The voices insisted that she get out of bed and write obscene words on a piece of paper. She resisted, but the voices told her she would get no relief, no sleep, until she did as she was told. So she arose, took pen and paper, and filled the sheet of paper with obscenities. Then she went back to bed and fell asleep.

This happened again the following night, and the night after that. The oppression of her spirit grew night by night, and the voices insisted that she write more and more obscenities for longer and longer periods of time. Eventually she found herself sitting up for hours at night, writing and writing, like a secretary taking demonic dictation. Her anguish and her fear became unendurable.

Her nightly sessions continued to worsen after she moved to California. Finally, she brought this problem to me and asked for help. We searched the Scriptures together, particularly those passages which deal with the occult and demonic activity, and we prayed together. I counseled and prayed with her several times, and God delivered her from this terrible obsession. I have had the chance to visit with her since that time, and the problem has never recurred.

The point is that the forces this young woman trifled with are real and deadly. I don't want to contemplate what might have happened to her if she had continued without getting help. Clearly she opened herself to the scorpion's sting of demonic torment. In the last days, the Antichrist will unleash a torrent of occult and demonic ideas, lures, lies, and delusions, and virtually the entire human race will writhe under the spiritual torment of the scorpion's sting.

The Angel of the Abyss

In verses 7 through 11 John goes on to describe, in metaphoric terms, the locusts/demons from the Abyss and the horrible delusion they bring upon the earth.

9:7–11 *The locusts looked like horses prepared for battle. On their heads they wore something like crowns of gold, and their faces resembled human faces. Their hair was like women's hair, and their teeth were like lions' teeth. They had breastplates like breastplates of iron, and the sound of their wings was like the thundering of many horses and chariots rushing into battle. They had tails and stings like scorpions, and in their tails they had power to torment people for five months. They had as king over them the angel of the Abyss, whose name in Hebrew is Abaddon, and in Greek, Apollyon.*

In symbolic terms, John relates to us the nature of the propaganda which the Antichrist will unleash upon the earth—and the effect of that propaganda upon the human race. At first glance, the symbols in this passage may seem difficult to understand, but they are really not difficult to interpret. They are consistent with symbols used elsewhere in Revelation and other prophetic books of Scripture.

The locusts take on the appearance of war-horses wearing something like crowns of gold, which speak of authority. As people hear the teachings and claims of this magnetic leader, he gives the impression of speaking with authority and power. The locusts wear human-like faces, which suggests intelligence. The teaching of the Antichrist will appear reasoned and appealing to the mind. Hair like women's hair suggests that which is alluring and attractive, which the Antichrist's propaganda will be.

But his propaganda will also be like lions' teeth—penetrating, cruel, and frightening. When it is too late, many will find his teachings to be a deadly, devouring force from which there is no escape. Iron breastplates speak of hardness and callousness of heart, for the demonic forces behind the Antichrist's power are the most pitiless, merciless beings in the universe. Once their torment begins, there is no relief and no escape.

The sound of the locusts' wings is like the thundering of many horses and chariots rushing into battle. The Antichrist's message will appear as an overpowering sound, symbolizing the fact that it will come forcefully and overpoweringly. This speaks of the fact that it will be irresistible to the masses, so that the Antichrist himself will become widely popular.

The stings in the locusts' tails, like the stings of scorpions, speak of the terrible aftermath of the Antichrist's influence: mental, emotional, and spiritual torment inflicted by demonic powers upon all those who opened themselves up to their oppression.

All of this will take place under the leadership of an invisible demonic king, the very angel of the Abyss. And who else could this be but Satan himself! Here we see the terrible infusion of demonic forces that will take place upon the earth in the terrible last days of human history—and it will all take place under the leadership of Satan himself.

These terrible events, including the delusion of the entire human race into following after satanic leadership, has been foretold elsewhere in Scripture. As Paul warns his spiritual son Timothy, "The Spirit clearly says that in later times some will abandon the faith and follow deceiving spirits and things taught by demons."[2]

We have already seen in our own culture the warning shocks of the satanic earthquake that will someday shake the world. In the 1960s we saw a massive outpouring of evil into the world: self-styled messiahs and gurus, bizarre religious cults, UFO cults, drug cults, satanic "churches" and witches' covens, and even mass-murder cults such as the Manson family. Respect for traditions, authority, and moral standards crumbled. Revolutionary movements and terrorists—from American radical groups such as the Symbionese Liberation Army (Patricia Hearst's kidnappers) and the Weathermen to West Germany's Baader-Meinhof gang and the Japanese Red Army—came to bloody, explosive prominence during those years.

The present New Age movement, which has its attractive and alluring side as well as its overtly demonic practices, had its early stirrings in the decade of the '60s. The leaders, gurus, and channelers of the New Age tell us that ancient spirit-masters of past ages are able to bring hidden wisdom to us in the twentieth century. I know of many people who have given themselves over to New Age delusion and have ended up in a state of mental torment and despair.

As potent as these demonic powers appeared in the decade of the '60s and the flowering of the New Age in our own time, they are severely limited and restrained compared with what will come upon the world in the last days. The forces from the Abyss are clearly trying to break through into our own world—and they are enjoying some limited success, as the continuing spiritual turmoil in our world demonstrates. But a day will come when *all* restraints are removed, and the horror of that day will exceed all human imagining.

The Sixth Angel

In verses 12 to 16 we hear the sounding of the sixth trumpet by the sixth angel.

9:12–16 *The first woe is past; two other woes are yet to come.*

The sixth angel sounded his trumpet, and I heard a voice coming from the horns of the golden altar that is before God. It said to the sixth angel who had the trumpet, "Release the four angels who are bound at the great river Euphrates." And the four angels who had been kept ready for this very hour and day and month and year were released to kill a third of mankind. The number of the mounted troops was two hundred million. I heard their number.

John now hears a voice that comes from the horns of the golden altar. We have already seen this altar in Revelation 8—the altar of incense on which was offered before God the prayers of the saints who were then living on the earth. In that passage an angel took fire from the altar and threw it down upon the earth—and judgment followed.

Here, in the terrible events of the sixth angel and the sixth trumpet, the prayers of the saints in Revelation 6 are finally answered. Do you remember their prayer? "How long, Sovereign Lord, holy and true, until you judge the inhabitants of the earth and avenge our blood?" This second woe, the sixth trumpet judgment, is God's specific answer to their prayer.

Notice that God's answer takes the form of releasing four powerful fallen angels who have been bound for centuries at the great river Euphrates. But these evil beings have not been given free reign in the earth. God's control over them is sovereign, and His timing of this event is surgically precise. These fallen angels are released at the "very hour and day and month and year" God had long ago predetermined. No power, human or demonic, could change the timing of that event by as much as a second.

Notice that these events are all linked with the Euphrates River, the ancient boundary between the East and the West. The Euphrates flows

out of the mountains of Armenia, down through the present-day lands of
Iraq and Iran, and into the Persian Gulf. In the ancient world it formed
the eastern boundary of the Roman Empire. The Romans lived in constant fear of the warlike Parthians who lived on the other side of the river.
Israel, too, once feared invasion from across the Euphrates, for the great
warrior nations of Assyria and Babylonia had previously ventured down
from the north, across the river and into Israel.

In our own era, the Euphrates River was strategically important during the 1991 Gulf War which liberated Kuwait. During the 100-hour
ground campaign of that war, the U.S. Army's 24th Mechanized and
101st Airborne Divisions trapped the elite Republican Guard of Iraq with
its back pinned against the Euphrates River. Unable to escape, the Iraqi
forces were decimated in one of the most lopsided military victories in
recorded history.

It is at this ancient and historic river that four evil beings are somehow bound at this very moment, awaiting the very hour and day and
month and year that God has foreordained for their release.

The 200-million-man army described in verse 16 has been subject to
various interpretations. Many Bible commentators have claimed that this
army is composed entirely of soldiers taken from the vast populations of
Asian nations such as China, India, Japan, and Indochina. It is certainly
true that the reference to the Euphrates River suggests that a barrier has
been removed so that armies from the East can cross into the West.

But note the *number* of angels released at the Euphrates: *four.* Four is
the number of worldwide human government. It symbolizes the four
directions of the compass—north, south, east, and west. This fact strongly suggests that the 200 million soldiers will come not from any one
country or even any one direction, but from *all* directions.

It would be virtually impossible for any one nation—or even a coalition of nations such as NATO—to field such a vast army. Using the 1991
Gulf War as a yardstick of comparison, the armies of the thirty-nation
U.N. coalition and the opposing army of Iraq added up to a combined total
of about one million men and women in uniform—one-half of one percent
of the 200-million-man army described in Revelation 9. The largest army
in the world is that of the Soviet Union with a little over 3 million men,
followed by China with 2.3 million and India with 1.1 million. For one
nation to field an army of 200 million would be logistically impossible.

The only logical conclusion is that the soldiers described in this passage come not only from the East, but from all directions. And they
gather in one place. We find the name of that place in Revelation 16, and
it is a name which has become associated with the end of the world:

Armageddon.

Armageddon—the Hebrew word for the Mount of Megiddo—is a place in northern Israel, less than 20 miles southeast of the modern port city of Haifa. Revelation 9 gives us our first glimpse of the terrible forces of death and destruction that will gather in the plain of Megiddo. There the great armies of the earth will assemble from every point of the compass to fight the last and bloodiest war of all of human history.

Monstrous Slaughter

A fascinating mystery surrounds the additional description of this gathering of armies in verses 17 through 19. John recounts the vividly colorful symbols and images of his vision of the final conflict.

9:17–19 *The horses and riders I saw in my vision looked like this: Their breastplates were fiery red, dark blue, and yellow as sulfur. The heads of the horses resembled the heads of lions, and out of their mouths came fire, smoke and sulfur. A third of mankind was killed by the three plagues of fire, smoke and sulfur that came out of their mouths. The power of the horses was in their mouths and in their tails; for their tails were like snakes, having heads with which they inflict injury.*

What does this description mean? It hardly seems possible that John himself understood what he was looking at. All he could do was record his impressions of future warriors, armor, and weaponry far beyond his ability to imagine. In fact, the events described in this ancient book of prophecy are still in our own future, and thus may be beyond our ability to imagine as well.

Yet it seems clear that what John envisions for us is the machinery of modern (or future) military destruction translated into the military terminology of his own day. Breastplates of various colors seem to suggest armored chariots—that is, tanks, troop carriers, missile launchers, rocket batteries, artillery pieces, and aircraft of various countries bearing the identifying colors of their nations of origin. Since there are so many nations gathered, it would be necessary that each nation's war material be clearly identified.

The lions' mouths which spouted fire and smoke suggest cannons, mortars, rocket launchers, and even missiles killing great masses of people with fire, radiation, and poison gases. The fact that one-third of the human race is destroyed in this conflict strongly suggests that weapons of mass destruction, including nuclear weapons, will be used.

Another intriguing image is that of the horses' tails, described as being like snakes, having heads that inflict injury. These words could apply to various kinds of modern armament—helicopter gunships with rotors mounted on their long tail assemblies, or perhaps missiles which leave a snake-like trail of smoke in their wake and inflict injury with their warheads. Perhaps it is a description of weapons that are yet to be invented.

Regardless of what the details of these future images mean, the overall picture is clear—and frightening. This last and greatest of all military campaigns will result in monstrous slaughter on an unbelievable scale. This scene will become still clearer as future chapters of Revelation return to this horrific scene and fill in additional nuances and details of the total picture.

The Unrepentant Human Race

The final scene under the sixth trumpet judgment is the reaction of mankind to these events of unprecedented calamity and horror.

9:20–21 *The rest of mankind that were not killed by these plagues still did not repent of the work of their hands; they did not stop worshiping demons, and idols of gold, silver, bronze, stone and wood—idols that cannot see or hear or walk. Nor did they repent of their murders, their magic arts, their sexual immorality or their thefts.*

Even after all the catastrophes and upheavals that have occurred, both natural and man-made, the human race remains unrepentant and hard-hearted. Notice that the first and foremost sin mentioned by John is that of demon worship. This one sin explains all the rest, as well as mankind's irrational and self-destructive unwillingness to repent.

These people have willingly and completely enwrapped themselves in a satanic delusion. Indeed, they have fallen under the spell of the "powerful delusion" Paul mentions in 2 Thessalonians 2:11. By their own willfulness, they have rendered themselves incapable of repentance, even as the fire of holy judgment begins to rain down all about them. And the ultimate source of their willfulness is the worship of demons. Some, perhaps, began to dabble in demonic things without any real understanding of the consequences, just as my friend from Alaska fooled with a Ouija board and astrology, and just as so many people today flirt with occult rituals or the New Age. Yet, even though they began naively, they paid the ultimate sacrifice for their sin: their eternal souls.

I suspect that few people set out to worship demons *knowing* they are demons. They may seek the advice of a "spirit being" which speaks through a "channeler" or "medium." They may keep a medal, amulet, or figurine as a "good luck charm." They may seek "spiritual power" from a crystal that they keep on their desks or wear around their necks. But the practice is idolatrous nonetheless—and the source of the power of such practices is hell itself.

There is a note of sarcasm in John's words when he talks about "idols that cannot see or hear or walk." The superstitious submission of oneself to an idol made of wood or stone or crystal is the ultimate in human folly! How can we, who are created in the likeness of God, make ourselves grovel and pray before inert lumps of dead matter? Yet it is not unusual anymore to encounter well-educated, successful, intelligent men and women in our own culture harboring beliefs and practicing rituals that are scarcely a step removed from pagan tribal rituals of a prior age.

John tells us that the hardened, unrepentant unbelievers of the last days will continue their murders—possibly including the killing of the very young through abortion and infanticide and the killing of the very old and infirm through involuntary euthanasia. Abortion is already practiced worldwide with few restrictions, and increasing numbers of legally-sanctioned infanticide and euthanasia cases are already taking place.[3]

John goes on to say that the people in the last days will not repent of their magic arts. The original Greek word for "magic arts" is *pharmakeia,* from which we get such words as pharmaceutical and pharmacy. This is in fact a reference to the use of illicit mind-altering and mood-altering drugs—a practice which is clearly an epidemic in our own culture. Drug abuse is such an obviously self-destructive and irrational form of behavior that it's a wonder people engage in it. It's clear that, once started, a drug habit is hard to stop—but why do people start? Because drugs have the "magical" power to alter the way people perceive and experience reality. It is one of the sorceries of our age—and the problem will grow worse, not better, as we near the end of this age.

The people of that time will also engage in sexual immorality and theft. Certainly there is no lack of sexual immorality or thievery in our own era, but as the end nears, the extent and the brazenness of such sins will greatly increase. All of these things will take place in the shadow of an unprecedented holocaust in which one-third of the human race is obliterated. On the brink of judgment, human beings will not only refuse to repent, they will actually accelerate the pace of their sinning. It is as though people insisted on carrying on their idolatry, their murders, their drug and sex orgies, and their robberies while the mushroom clouds of nuclear war bloomed all around the horizon. It can only be described as spiritual mass insanity.

Why Judgment?

In the face of humanity's obdurate refusal to turn away from its sin we must ask, "Why judgment? What is judgment for if it is totally ineffectual in producing a change of heart and a change of life?"

Remember, however, that the book of Revelation has already told us that *millions will repent*. Let us not forget that "great multitude which no man can number," people of every tribe and nation and language who have washed their robes and made them white in the blood of the Lamb. They have come out of the Great Tribulation, and they are before the throne of God. They have learned the lesson of the judgments. They have believed. They have received the grace of God.

Here we witness the harshest, most chastening, most all-encompassing judgment ever unleashed upon the earth. Yet the human race is so perverted by its bent to sin, selfishness, and idolatry that millions of people remain completely unaffected. Their hearts are hardened. They have trampled the grace of God underfoot.

God never expected to convert the world through judgment. His plan is to save mankind through grace. But His judgment has the effect of causing us to think soberly and seriously. It causes us to listen to grace. It makes us attentive to the way of escape God has offered. In a time of judgment we see the power, the majesty, and the utter inescapability of God. It forces us to ask, "What can I do to be saved? Is there no way out? What can I do?"

And for those who respond to His judgment, God provides a message of hope and grace. He shows us the suffering love with which He loves us, exemplified by the cross. He shows us His compassionate heart—the divine heart that wants nothing more than to bear our pain and our sorrow. The positive effect of judgment is that it melts our pride, silences our excuses, and prepares our hearts to humbly receive His grace.

"How shall we escape if we ignore such a great salvation?"[4] asks the writer of Hebrews. How indeed? How can any of us escape if we ignore the gift of God's grace. For if we ignore the grace of God while He is speaking to us—and even *shouting* to us—through both His blessings and His chastening, then our end is clear. "Today, if you hear his voice," the writer of Hebrews concludes, "do not harden your hearts."[5]

God does not want to judge the people He has created, the people for whom He has given His only Son to die. But for those who reject the way of escape which God has supplied in His love and His mercy, all that is left is judgment.

You have heard the phrase, "Stop the world, I want to get off!" Many of us feel that way, especially if we read our newspapers alongside the open book of Revelation. It is clear that the world is lumbering inexorably toward global judgment. No one wants to be here when the axe of divine judgment finally falls.

The good news is that we don't have to undergo the judgment that is coming upon the rest of mankind. If we lay hold of the great salvation God freely offers us by His grace, we will be safe in the presence of Jesus when all hell breaks loose on earth.

The End of Mystery

Revelation 10

n 1955 the Rev. Billy Graham was in his mid-thirties and just gaining an international reputation as an evangelist. He was in London conducting one of his evangelistic crusades at Wembley Stadium when he received an invitation to No. 10 Downing Street, the residence of the prime minister of England. Upon his arrival, Graham was introduced to a weary-looking but keen-eyed Sir Winston Churchill. As it later turned out, this was to be Churchill's final year as prime minister after a long and illustrious career in public service.

Chomping an unlit cigar, Churchill appraised young Graham with a penetrating eye. "Young man," he said, "I've heard a great deal about these crusades you are having up at Wembley. Now, I want to ask you a question. You know the troubled shape the world is in. Personally I don't think the world has much longer to go." He paused hesitantly. "Can you give an old man any hope?"

It seemed to Graham that Churchill was seeking hope not merely for a troubled world, but for an aging and troubled man. So he took out the pocket New Testament he always had with him and showed the prime minister that the Bible offers not only hope for the world in the ultimate triumph of Jesus Christ, but hope for individual human beings in the plan of salvation.

If Churchill ever made a decision to commit his life to Jesus Christ, Graham never learned about it. But the question Churchill asked the young Billy Graham is the same question millions struggle with today. Evil is on the rise. The world is becoming an increasingly more perilous place. We are fouling our own nests with toxic pollutants, destroying the delicate ozone layer above our world, building weapons of mass destruction at a frenzied pace.

Everywhere you go people are wondering, "With the troubled shape the world is in, do we have much longer to go? Can anyone offer the human race any hope? Why doesn't God intervene in human affairs? Is He really in control? Or is the world taking an uncontrolled plunge to destruction?"

These are the questions we confront in Revelation 10.

In Revelation 8 and 9, we caught a horrifying glimpse of the cataclysmic future of our world. But beginning with Revelation 10 and continuing into part of chapter 11, we find a kind of intermission, a parenthetical interlude that divides the sixth and seventh trumpet judgments. As we have already observed, in each series of judgments—the seals, the trumpets, and the bowls of wrath—there is always a break between the sixth and seventh judgments.

The First Mystery

Revelation 10 presents us with three intriguing mysteries: (1) the mystery of the mighty angel; (2) the mystery of God which the angel proclaims; and (3) the mystery of the little scroll which is held in the angel's hand. The first mystery is introduced to us in the first four verses of Revelation 10.

10:1–4 *Then I saw another mighty angel coming down from heaven. He was robed in a cloud, with a rainbow above his head; his face was like the sun, and his legs were like fiery pillars. He was holding a little scroll, which lay open in his hand. He planted his right foot on the sea and his left foot on the land, and he gave a loud shout like the roar of a lion. When he shouted, the voices of the seven thunders spoke. And when the seven thunders spoke, I was about to write; but I heard a voice from heaven say, "Seal up what the seven thunders have said and do not write it down."*

Here, then, is the first mystery: What is the identity of this mighty angel? As with any good mystery, the solution lies in carefully interpreting the clues.

There are clues given in Revelation which identify this angel as "the Angel of the Lord" or "the Angel of Yahweh," the great angel who accompanied the people of Israel as they wandered through the wilderness in the days of Moses. In the Old Testament this Angel often appeared to Israel at key intersections of Israel's history. Here, in Revelation, Israel again occupies center stage of God's program, and again this Angel makes a prominent appearance.

The Angel comes robed in a cloud, which is symbolic of the divine being. When the people of Israel marched in the desert following their captivity in Egypt, they were preceded by a pillar of cloud by day and a pillar of fire by night. This pillar of fire was, of course, this self-same pillar of cloud, yet lit from within by brilliant light or glory that gave it a fiery appearance against the contrasting background of night. Later, when the tabernacle was completed, and still later when the great temple was built, this cloud filled with fiery glory came down and filled the Holy of Holies, the most sacred domain of the house of worship. Once resident in the Holy of Holies, it was called the Shekinah, the cloud of glory, and it represented the presence of God among the people of Israel.

Here, in the very first descriptive phrase regarding this Angel, we find our first clue which identifies the Angel as the Lord Himself—Jesus, God the Son, appearing in His pre-incarnate form as the Angel of Jehovah.

The next clue is that of the rainbow above the Angel's head. The last time we saw the symbol of the rainbow was in Revelation 4, where a rainbow encircled the throne of God. This rainbow appears as a crowning adornment. Its association with the throne and its appearance as a crown suggests that the rainbow symbolizes kingly, divine glory.

The Angel's face has the shining appearance of the sun, and his legs appear as fiery pillars. These details of the vision recall John's initial glimpse of Jesus as He stood amid the churches in Revelation 1. Here, as John watches, the Angel plants one foot upon the sea and the other upon the land. He stands astride the earth like a giant colossus—a vivid image that symbolizes the Lord's ownership of and authority over the entire earth.

The last clue is the Angel's shout, which John likens to the roar of a lion. This echoes a detail from Revelation 5, where we saw the slain Lamb who was also the Lion of the tribe of Judah. He roars in triumph over the earth. Here is yet another indication that Israel is returned to prominence in God's eternal program during the last days. Clearly God intends to use His chosen people in a special way throughout the period of judgment and on into the time of the establishment of the kingdom after the ultimate revelation of Jesus Christ.

Imagine what an encouragement this scene must have been to the apostle John. It is also an encouragement to us in this Laodicean age of church history, for it enables us to see that all the cosmic and cataclysmic events that have their stirrings in our own time and their culmination in the last days are continually and firmly controlled by the Angel of God. He is working out history's events according to His own inescapable timetable.

Moreover, this image should forever erase from our minds the false stereotype of angels that has arisen over the years—dreamy, effeminate creatures who sit on clouds languidly plucking on harps. That is not how angels are pictured in Scripture. I like the way Eugene Peterson describes them: "Vast, fiery, sea-striding creatures with hell in their nostrils and heaven in their eyes." That's more like it!

The Thundering Reply

To the roar of this Angel comes a booming reply: seven great peals of thunder. The thunder did not come in the form of random, chaotic crashes of sound, but as a resoundingly momentous message. John heard and understood the message and, with pen poised over paper, was about to write it down. Suddenly a voice came from heaven saying, "Seal up what the seven thunders have said and do not write it down." This is the only portion of John's vision which is sealed from our view. The rest has been revealed and disclosed for our edification, just as the name Revelation implies.

Wouldn't you like to know what the seven thunders said? Well, so would I! I have studied commentary after commentary on Revelation, and I have not found one Bible scholar who can tell us what John heard by the seven thunders. This one portion of the vision may have been given to John for his own understanding and enlightenment, or there may have been some deeper and unknowable reason for the sealing of the message. John gives us no reason, and it is possible he himself did not know. He simply did as he was told by God.

The only thing we can know about the sealed message of the seven thunders is that in Scripture thunder always symbolizes the judgment of God. Thus, the sealed message certainly has something to do with God's judgment.

This, then, is one mystery of Revelation 10 which has no certain solution. But there is one possible clue. I refer you to Psalm 29 where the psalmist makes *seven* separate references to the voice of the Lord *thundering* over the earth in judgment. Is this psalm related to the sealed message given to John in the seven thunders of Revelation? I invite you to read the psalm for yourself and draw your own conclusion. If the message of the seven thunders itself remains sealed to this day, then I will add no imperfect conclusions of my own to the matter.

In 2 Corinthians 12, the apostle Paul tells of a time when he (like John) was caught up into heaven, where he saw and heard "things that man is not permitted to tell." There are truths which God has revealed to a select few of His faithful followers which He chooses not to disclose to the rest of us. I believe that in the proper season God will reveal these truths to us—but not yet. "The secret things belong to the LORD our God," we read in the Old Testament, "but the things revealed belong to us and to our children forever."[1]

As serious inquirers into the truth of Scripture, we have a more important task than speculating on the things God has hidden, and that is to diligently study the things He has already plainly revealed in His Word.

The Second Mystery

Now we approach the second mystery—the mystery of God Himself.

10:5–7 *Then the angel I had seen standing on the sea and on the land raised his right hand to heaven. And he swore by him who lives for ever and ever, who created the heavens and all that is in them, the earth and all that is in it, and the sea and all that is in it, and said, "There will be no more delay! But in the days when the seventh angel is about to sound his trumpet, the mystery of God will be accomplished, just as he announced to his servants the prophets."*

Here is a glimpse of what lies in store for us in coming chapters of Revelation. The end of the Ultimate Mystery is at hand. The mystery of God is about to be revealed.

In this scene the mighty Angel begins by raising his right hand to heaven. Is this gesture familiar to you? It is part of the ritual that is observed whenever a witness takes an oath in court to tell "the truth, the whole truth, and nothing but the truth." This traditional courtroom ritual originated here, in these very words of Scripture. The raising of the right hand signifies that a solemn oath is being given, an important truth is about to be disclosed.

The Angel swears in this scene by God, the Maker of the heavens, the earth, the sea, and everything in them. You may wonder, if this Angel is indeed Christ the Creator Himself, why He would swear by Himself. I would remind you that in the book of Hebrews, when God swore an oath to Abraham to keep His promises, He swore by Himself because there was no one and no thing greater by which to swear.[2] That is what Jesus, in the form of this mighty Angel, is doing in these verses. He is swearing by the triune God—Father, Son, and Holy Spirit—that the long delay is at last over and the mystery of God is about to be revealed.

The question which has preoccupied the thoughts and hopes of believers for centuries is about to be answered.

The Long Wait Is Over

Every generation of Christians has expected the imminent return of the Lord Jesus. We read in Acts that the Christians of the first century A.D. expected His return in their own lifetime. Read the letters of Paul, and you can see that he expected the Lord's return in his own lifetime.

Nearly 2,000 years later, the Lord has not returned.

Our generation of believers like every other before it continues to expect the Lord's return. I believe His return could easily take place before the end of this century—yet it may not. The Lord alone knows, and at this particular moment as I write these words, the mystery of God remains unresolved.

But another moment is approaching when the Angel will say, "No more delay! The mystery of God will be accomplished!" What now appears to be a strange, silent, mysterious reluctance on God's part to carry out His promise will at that time be revealed and fully understood by us all. It is that moment that we look forward to. It is that moment upon which we have pinned all our hopes for the future. For at that moment, God will begin His reign on earth.

It may surprise you to know that in the entire span of time from Creation until now, God has never reigned on earth. Yes, He is the sovereign King over all of the universe, over both heaven and earth. He has ruled, overruled, and intervened on earth. He governs all human events, yet He does so for now in a way that appears remote and incomplete. He has never used His absolute power to bring about an end to demonic evil, human rebellion, and global injustice and suffering. He does not receive the worship and honor that is His due as the sovereign King. He has authority that He chooses for now not to exercise.

God is sovereign and He rules over the universe, but He does not reign on earth. When He finally establishes His reign, all sin and all suffering will cease. That is our eternal hope for which we pray whenever we repeat the words, "Thy Kingdom come, thy will be done on earth as it is in heaven."

We will see the actual inauguration of that reign in Revelation 11:17, when the twenty-four elders praise God, saying, "We give thanks to you, Lord God Almighty, the One who is and who was, because you have taken your great power and have begun to reign." That will be the moment of fulfillment for the prayers of all the centuries of saints, and for the predictions of all the millennia of prophets.

One such prophet was Ezekiel, who described the beginning of God's reign on earth in Ezekiel 36. In that passage the prophet says that God will call the nation of Israel back into prominence. He will take out of them the evil heart of flesh and put His Spirit within them and He will forgive all their sins. You find parallel prophecies in many other Old Testament books.

The apostle Paul, in Romans 11, underscores the importance of the hope of God's future reign on earth. He warns, first of all, that Gentile believers should be careful not to take a boastful or judgmental attitude against Israel for its present unbelief. "If you do," he says, "consider this: You do not support the root, but the root supports you."[3] Israel, he says, is the root, and all Gentile believers are the branches that have been grafted onto that root by the grace of God. But the promises and the primacy in the plan of God still belong to Israel the root, and Gentile Christians — the ingrafted branches — dare not forget that.

Tragically, many modern Christians *have* forgotten that. Some Christian teachers today, in violation of Paul's stern warning in Romans 11, teach that Israel has no future, that all the promises that were given to Israel in the Old Testament have now been transferred to the church. Nothing could be further from the truth! As Paul concludes,

> I do not want you to be ignorant of this mystery, brothers, so that you may not be conceited: Israel has experienced a hardening in part until the full number of the Gentiles has come in. And so all Israel will be saved, as it is written:

> "The deliverer will come from Zion; he will turn godlessness away from Jacob. And this is my covenant with them when I take away their sins."[4]

Not only does Israel have a future, it is in fact the *focal point* of God's plan for the future. All of us who consider ourselves biblical Christians should therefore cultivate a love and respect for the nation and people of Israel.

Often ignored by politicians and historians, Israel has always been close to the center of human events, even during the most recent Diaspora

(Dispersion) of the Jews from the destruction of Jerusalem in A.D. 70 to the re-founding of the Jewish state in 1948. Many times Satan has attempted to destroy these people in order to thwart God's plan. The Holocaust of World War II was only the bloodiest and most monstrous of many past attempts to eradicate God's chosen people from the earth. To this day, Israel and its neighbors continue to be the focus of the world's deepest concerns, tensions, and fears.

There will come a day, and I do not believe it is far off, when Israel will again be revealed as the centerpiece of God's plan for human history. Satan understands this quite well, and he will not rest until he has either been conquered himself or has succeeded in destroying Israel. But Satan will not succeed. In dozens of Old Testament passages, God has promised to restore the people of Israel to their land, to restore their status as the people of God, and to accomplish the promises that have awaited fulfillment for several thousand years.

One ancient promise which still awaits the fulfillment that will be accomplished when the Lord begins His reign on earth is this beautiful promise from Isaiah 35:

> Strengthen the feeble hands,
>> steady the knees that give way;
> say to those with fearful hearts,
>> "Be strong, do not fear;
> your God will come,
>> he will come with vengeance;
> with divine retribution
>> he will come to save you."
>
> Then will the eyes of the blind be opened
>> and the ears of the deaf unstopped.
> Then will the lame leap like a deer,
>> and the mute tongue shout for joy.
> Water will gush forth in the wilderness
>> and streams in the desert.
> The burning sand will become a pool,
>> the thirsty ground bubbling springs.
> In the haunts where jackals once lay,
>> grass and reeds and papyrus will grow.[5]

Beautiful, reassuring, inspiring words of hope for a future age! No wonder the announcement of the Angel that the long delay is over, the mystery of God is accomplished, had such a powerful effect upon the emotions of the apostle John.

The Third Mystery

Menelik II was emperor of the African nation of Ethiopia from 1889 until his death in 1913. Historians credit him with having brought Ethiopia into the twentieth century by introducing public education, telephone and telegraph service, and railroads to his country. However, this forward-thinking monarch had one rather backward and superstitious eccentricity. He believed that whenever he felt ill, all he needed to do to feel better was to eat a few pages from the Bible.

Menelik practiced this form of self-medication for years, and it did him no apparent harm. Then, during the last few years of his life, he suffered a series of strokes that left him partially paralyzed. After one such stroke in December 1913, he was feeling very weak and ill. He asked his aides to tear the entire book of 1 Kings out of the Bible and feed it to him, page by page. It was later reported that he died about the time he was consuming the story of King Solomon and the Queen of Sheba.

In verses 8 to 11, we encounter the third mystery, the mystery of the scroll. In this passage, the Angel gives the apostle John a book to eat. Unlike the book that Menelik consumed, the little scroll the Angel gives John neither heals him nor kills him—but it does give him a sour stomach.

10:8–11 *Then the voice that I had heard from heaven spoke to me once more: "Go, take the scroll that lies open in the hand of the angel who is standing on the sea and on the land."*

So I went to the angel and asked him to give me the little scroll. He said to me, "Take it and eat it. It will turn your stomach sour, but in your mouth it will be as sweet as honey." I took the little scroll from the angel's hand and ate it. It tasted as sweet as honey in my mouth, but when I had eaten it, my stomach turned sour. Then I was told, "You must prophesy again about many peoples, nations, languages and kings."

The symbolism of eating the Word is a way of indicating that the truth written on the scroll becomes personal. It is not merely read but it is actually assimilated. That is what happens when we eat food, is it not? There is a lot of truth to the old saying, "You are what you eat." The food you eat becomes *you!*

When corned beef and cabbage eaten on Saturday night becomes a part of your flesh and bone by Sunday afternoon, doctors call it *metabolism*. They don't know exactly how it works, but it's a convenient label. The food we eat becomes, in a very short time, the body we wear—often to our dismay if we have a problem with weight control. And John experiences in his vision the symbolic act of *metabolizing* and *assimilating* the Word of the Lord. He is taking the Word of the Lord internally, becoming personally involved in it, becoming changed by it, and ultimately allowing it to become a part of his own makeup.

We find this same imagery in the prophecy of Ezekiel, where he writes:

> Then I looked, and I saw a hand stretched out to me. In it was a scroll, which he unrolled before me. On both sides of it were written words of lament and mourning and woe.
>
> And he said to me, "Son of man, eat what is before you, eat this scroll; then go and speak to the house of Israel." So I opened my mouth, and he gave me the scroll to eat.
>
> Then he said to me, "Son of man, eat this scroll I am giving you and fill your stomach with it." So I ate it, and it tasted as sweet as honey in my mouth.6

Then Ezekiel was sent to deliver a message to Israel. Later in the chapter, Ezekiel says,

> The Spirit then lifted me up and took me away, and I went in bitterness and in the anger of my spirit with the strong hand of the LORD upon me.7

Note the striking similarity between what Ezekiel experienced when he ate the scroll and what John experienced in Revelation 10. In both cases the prophecy that is received and consumed tastes sweet at first, but leaves an unpleasant sensation in the stomach.

The little scroll that John receives from the Angel contains the methods of God in working out His purposes on the earth. Certainly there is an element of sweetness in the plan of God, when John first bites into it. But as he assimilates the truth of God, as he becomes more and more deeply and personally involved with it, a sour sensation arises within him. This symbolizes the fact that God's truth has a painful and unpleasant dimension to it when we really apply it to our own lives.

The truth of God tastes sweet as long as it is "out there," in the realm of promise and hope and future glory. But once the truth of God trespasses "in here," in the realm of conviction and judgment and the exposure of our sinfulness and nakedness before God, it becomes a sour and unpleasant experience.

Has the Word of God ever dealt with you like that? Perhaps you read a passage about the eternal destiny of the believer, the promise of heaven, the hope of a new heaven and new earth under the Kingship of God, and you felt eager and excited about the promises of God. Yet, upon further reading and reflection, a realization sinks in: Before you can experience that bright future, God will have to *change* you. He will have to reshape your thinking and your attitudes and your bigotries. You will have to forsake some bad habits. You will have to, as Jesus said, "pluck out your eye" and "cut off your hand" in order to obey God's truth for your life.

There is pain in change. There is anguish in true obedience. There is a price to be paid for the glorious future God has promised us. This is all part of God's program for us, both the sour and the sweet.

The judgment of God touches us all. God is already loose in the world, and He will find us right where we live. He will invade our lives whether we like it or not. If our hearts are really resonating in tune with the heart of God we will not treat His judgment lightly. His Word will touch us personally and pierce our souls and sour our stomachs and force us to realize that *we* are part of the problem. It is not just others "out there" who must change their ways. *We* must be changed as well. The secret places of our hearts must be illuminated, searched, and cleaned out. This is not a pleasant truth, but it *is* the truth.

You Are the One!

I'm sure you remember that one sordid episode which mars the biography of King David. He had committed adultery with Bathsheba, then—to cover his first sin—arranged for the murder of her husband Uriah, one of his own most loyal soldiers. Afterwards, thinking he had gotten away with his crimes, certain that no one else suspected, David continued on with his life as usual.

But God knew. God spoke to the prophet Nathan and sent him to David, instructing Nathan to tell a story to the king. Obediently, Nathan told David the story of an injustice that had been committed in David's own realm. It was the story of a rich man who owned a large flock of sheep. This man wanted to entertain some friends, so he looked next door and saw the one little lamb his poor neighbor cherished as a household pet. Instead of taking a sheep from his own large flock to feed his guests, the rich man stole and slaughtered the only lamb of his poor neighbor.

David was indignant upon hearing this tale of injustice. Angrily he growled, "The one who did this deserves to die! I'll see that he repays the poor man four times over!"

Nathan fixed the king with an accusing stare. *"You* are the one!" he said. "You could have had as many wives as you chose"—and David already had several wives—"but instead you stole another man's wife and had him killed."

In that moment David was confronted by the fact that God's judgment was not "out there," it was "in here." Even the king was subject to the burning touch of God's fiery judgment.

God's truth has that effect on us. It had that effect on John. When he ate the scroll, it was sweet in his mouth, but turned his stomach sour.

But afterwards John was given a new assignment. "Then I was told," he relates in verse 11, " 'You must prophesy again about many peoples, nations, languages and kings.' "[8] There is an instructive principle here: After you have personally entered into the painful yet cleansing experience of God's judgment in your life, you are then prepared to speak to someone else about the program of God. John has been given the privilege of ministering *again* to nations, peoples, languages, and kings. This is a new ministry, and it is described for us in Revelation 11 through 14.

From this point onward in Revelation, we will find a pronounced change of scene and perspective. In a sense, John is being sent back over the terrible scenes of judgment to bring us detailed, magnified, zoomed-in highlights of the judgments of the last days. These scenes will involve "many peoples, nations, languages and kings."

All of this will unfold in the next few chapters of Revelation. John is qualified to reveal to us the judgments of God because he himself has allowed God to enter into his own soul and search it with the light of truth.

Have you and I made the same commitment before God? Have we exposed our inner secrets to the light of God's Word, His truth, and His judgment? The words of the great hymn "May the Mind of Christ My Savior" are certainly the message that confronts us in Revelation 10:

> May His beauty rest upon me,
> As I seek the lost to win.
> And may they forget the channel,
> Seeing only Him.

The beauty of God that rests upon us as we seek to win the lost for Him is the beauty of a life that has been opened, searched, cleansed, and made new by the transforming truth of God. When He has tried us, then we are prepared to go out into the world, armed with the convicting Word of His gospel, ready to impact other lives for God.

Chapter Seventeen

The Last Warning

Revelation 11

W hile in college I had the somewhat torturous experience of being required to read Victor Hugo's novel *Les Misérables* in the original French. Years later, I could only remember two impressions from my encounter with that book: (1) a rather sketchy sense of the general plot of the book, and (2) the fact that the French do not care what you do so long as you pronounce their language properly!

Some time ago I had the opportunity of seeing *Les Misérables* produced on the San Francisco stage. What a contrast between that stage production and my unfortunate encounter with Monsieur Hugo in my college days! The drama, the costumes, the staging, and the music made it all so *real*. The characters took on real flesh and blood. It was like being magically transported to those rousing days following the French Revolution.

The events that are presented in Revelation 4 through 10 are vivid and vast in scope: seals are opened, trumpets blast, and terrible judgments are poured out on a global scale. Yet the very scope of these events is so large as to seem almost impersonal.

As we come to Revelation 11, I find myself experiencing a similar sensation to the one I felt watching the stage production of *Les Misérables*. Here, Revelation inaugurates a new format. Instead of pulling back from the events of the last days with a wide-angle lens, as in chapters 4 through 10, this section of Revelation pulls in for a tight close-up of the personalities of the final drama of the human race. Just as I experienced during the stage production of *Les Misérables,* we now see the characters of Revelation taking on real flesh and blood. The drama intensifies as we learn how the program of God is going to be carried out in the last days—and through whom it will be performed.

When John ate the scroll given him by the Angel, an important change came over the narrative. From this point forward John is no longer a mere observer viewing the last days of mankind on earth as if watching a news broadcast. For the rest of this compelling story John himself becomes a part of the action.

The Measure of the Temple

In the first two verses of chapter 11 John is given a symbolic task to perform.

11:1–2 *I was given a reed like a measuring rod and was told, "Go and measure the temple of God and the altar, and count the worshipers there. But exclude the outer court; do not measure it, because it has been given to the Gentiles. They will trample on the holy city for 42 months."*

The act of measuring a given area is clearly a symbolic action, and we have seen it before in the Old Testament prophecies of Ezekiel and Zechariah. We will see it once again later in Revelation. These measurements symbolize God's ownership. By instructing John to measure the temple and the altar and to count the worshipers, God is staking His claim of ownership upon them. They are His to use, either for blessing or for judgment.

We use measurements in the same way today. If you have a dispute with your neighbor over a property line (or if you just want to avoid future disputes when you purchase a piece of property), you hire a surveyor who measures the property, sets monuments in the ground, establishes the boundaries, and prepares a written document that certifies your ownership. In a similar way, God has given His servant John a measuring rod and instructed him to measure the temple and altar, and to count the worshipers there—but John is to exclude the outer court of the temple.

Clearly the temple John is to measure is an *earthly* temple as contrasted with the *heavenly* temple we first glimpsed in Revelation 6. There is, you will recall, a temple in heaven, the same temple Moses saw when he was on Mount Sinai. Moses was instructed to make an exact copy of that heavenly temple when he built the tabernacle in the wilderness. It is important to understand, however, that the heavenly temple is itself merely a symbol of the *true* dwelling place of God. That true dwelling place of God—as will be unmistakably revealed in the final chapters of Revelation—*is man himself*!

You and I, as believers in the risen Christ, *are* the temple of the living God of the universe! Paul wrote to the Corinthian believers, "Do you not know that your body is a temple of the Holy Spirit, who is in you, whom you have received from God?"[1] The heavenly temple symbolizes the profound dignity and honor that God confers upon our race in choosing us to be His ultimate dwelling place for all eternity.

Yet that heavenly temple, which symbolizes our humanity, is also pictured in the design of the earthly temple. It is clear from the mention of "the holy city" in these verses that the earthly temple John is told to measure is located in Jerusalem. As I write these words, however, there is no temple standing in Jerusalem.

The Once and Future Temple

The last Jerusalem temple was destroyed by Roman forces under the command of General Titus, son of the Roman Emperor Vespasian. Titus led the campaign to quell the Jewish uprising against Roman rule which began in A.D. 66, engulfing the entire region of Judea, and ended only after Titus's troops laid siege to Jerusalem in A.D. 70. Across Judea, over a million Jews died by Roman swords, and the siege of Jerusalem led to such cruel privation and starvation that the people of the city ate their own children in order to survive.

When the Romans finally breached the defenses of Jerusalem they leveled the city and demolished the temple that stood upon the Temple Mount (also called Mount Moriah), fulfilling Christ's prophecy that "the time will come when not one stone will be left on another; every one of them will be thrown down."[2] From A.D. 70 until this day, there has been no Jewish temple on that site.

Today on the Temple Mount, the site of the original temple of Solomon and of the temple destroyed by Titus, two non-Jewish structures stand. These structures are sacred to Muslims. One is the al-Aqsa Mosque. The other and far more prominent structure is the Dome of the Rock, which was built between 685 and 691 by the Arab caliph 'Abd al-Malik. The Dome of the Rock is a beautiful *mashhad* or pilgrimage shrine, constructed of bright blue walls richly ornamented with marble and mosaic. Its shining golden dome dominates the skyline of Jerusalem.

For decades the Israeli people—particularly those of the Orthodox Jewish faith—have wanted to rebuild the temple on the site of the original Temple of Solomon. The Dome of the Rock and the al-Aqsa Mosque, however, pose a problem to rebuilding the temple. Even after 1967, when the Jews recaptured the old city of Jerusalem, only Muslims have been allowed to worship on the Temple Mount, the third most sacred site of the Islamic faith. Neither Jews nor Christians are allowed to worship there, even though the site is deeply significant to all three religions. Islam regards the site of the Dome to be the place where the Prophet Muhammad ascended into heaven.

Some time ago I visited the Temple Mount in the company of a Jewish friend. There in the shadow of the Dome of the Rock, on the very ground where Solomon had built his magnificent Temple for the Lord and where Jesus walked with His disciples, my friend and I took out our Bibles and began to read and pray. Within a few minutes we were noticed by some Islamic guards who told us we could not worship there, that the Temple Mount had been consigned to Islamic authority by the Israeli government.

The strong Islamic passion for its holy places on the Temple Mount poses a formidable obstacle to any effort to construct a new Jewish temple on the site. In fact, most Israeli Jews I have talked to—as well as a large number of non-Israeli Jews—seem to favor tearing down the Dome of the Rock so that a new temple can be constructed in its place.

In recent years, however, Asher Kauffman, a godly Jewish engineer, has done exhaustive work locating the exact site of the original ancient temple. He is convinced, and is in turn convincing many others, that the temple was not built on the same place where the Dome of the Rock now stands, but slightly north of the Dome. In fact, the site he has fixed as the ancient temple site is still an area of open ground upon which a single small shrine, the Dome of the Spirits, now stands. If he is correct it would then be possible for the Jewish temple to be reconstructed on its original site without disturbing the Dome of the Rock.

This raises an interesting possibility relative to the task John has been given to measure the earthly temple. If the new temple is built north of the Dome of the Rock, as Asher Kauffman suggests it should be, the outer court of the temple would encompass the Dome of the Rock. Some Bible commentators suggest that Revelation 11:2 (where John is told not to measure the outer court because it has been given to the Gentiles for 42 months) is a reference to the area where the Dome of the Rock now stands. I would not dogmatically assert this to be true, but it is an interesting possibility. Regardless of how this will specifically come to pass, we do know that the temple will be rebuilt, and there will be some non-Jewish control of a portion of the Temple Mount for 42 months.

Some quick mental arithmetic will quickly show you the significance of those 42 months. Divide 42 months by 12 and you get a figure of 3 1/2 years—exactly half of the seven-year period we have already learned will be the interval of the Great Tribulation. Thus, the Gentiles—non-Jewish people—will control part of the Temple Mount during half of the Tribulation. But which half? The first or the second?

Clues given us in Revelation suggest that it is the first half of the seven-year "week." This period of time would allow for the construction of a restored Jewish temple on the top of Mount Moriah. The fascinating thing is that the preparations for the fulfillment of this prophecy of Revelation have already begun.

At this very moment there are several organizations in Israel which have zealously dedicated themselves to reconstructing the temple on Mount Moriah. I have met and talked with some of these people, and have visited some of the preparations they have made for the temple's restoration.

One organization is training a great host of young men to be priests in the temple. These men are learning the ancient levitical rituals. Priestly garments have been created for them to wear, patterned after what is known of the garb of the Old Testament priesthood. I have seen some of these garments with my own eyes. Without question, there are Jews in the Holy Land making full-scale preparations to put a functioning temple back on the holy mount.

Whether the new temple of Jerusalem will be built before the church is removed from the world or not, no one can say. But imagine the consternation in the Arab world when construction of the temple begins! And imagine the international crisis that will ensue if Muslim holy places are torn down to make way for the temple! No wonder the eyes of the world are constantly focused upon the Temple Mount in Jerusalem.

Certainly the eyes of God are set upon the Temple Mount. These first few verses in Revelation 11 make that clear. He is saying to the world, "My servant has surveyed and measured this site. It is mine. I intend to use it." It is a sign of God's ownership of this holy place in the last days.

Two Witnesses

From verses 3 to 14, the lens of John's narrative zooms in for a close view of two important characters in the ultimate drama of the human race. Without announcement or fanfare they come out of the wings and onto the stage of Revelation.

11:3–6 *"And I will give power to my two witnesses, and they will proph-esy for 1,260 days, clothed in sackcloth." These are the two olive trees and the two lampstands that stand before the Lord of the earth. If anyone tries to harm them, fire comes from their mouths and devours their ene-mies. This is how anyone who wants to harm them must die. These men have power to shut up the sky so that it will not rain during the time they are prophesying; and they have power to turn the waters into blood and to strike the earth with every kind of plague as often as they want.*

In one of Paul's great speeches, recorded in the book of Acts, he makes the statement that God never leaves Himself without a witness. John's narrative bears out Paul's words. Here, in the midst of the worst period of apostasy in human history, God still preserves witnesses who testify about Him before the world.

The witnesses of Revelation 11 are two men in sackcloth (that is, burlap). It was the traditional garb of the prophet when he was sent to warn of impending judgment. These two witnesses appear dressed in sackcloth because their ministry is to strip away the delusions, lies, and satanic propaganda which the Man of Sin, the Antichrist, promulgates as "truth" in that day.

It's fascinating to see how the picture of the last days as revealed in Revelation intermeshes with the prophecies of Jesus. He, too, spoke about this temple and the Man of Sin. He said that the sign of the last days would be when the abomination that causes desolation stands in the holy place. The holy place is the temple of Jerusalem, and the abomina-tion of desolation, which was also predicted by the prophet Daniel, is a description of the actions and person of the Man of Sin, the Antichrist.

Paul, too, prophesies regarding the Man of Sin. He writes,

> Don't let anyone deceive you in any way, for that day will not
> come until the rebellion occurs and the man of lawlessness is
> revealed, the man doomed to destruction. He will oppose and will
> exalt himself over everything that is called God or is worshiped,
> so that he sets himself up in God's temple, proclaiming himself to
> be God.[3]

So the Lord and the apostles agree that a temple will be built on Mount Moriah and will be occupied by the one whom John calls "the Antichrist" in 1 John 2:18. We shall meet him again when we come to Revelation 13, for he is the beast that rises from the earth as recorded in that chapter.

All of this is set against the dramatic background of the Man of Sin, defiling the temple, claiming the worship of the world for his own, claiming indeed to be God. In the humanistic, New Age, and self-fulfillment movements of our own age, we see stirrings of this spirit—a spirit which says that we are gods, that we can invent any reality we wish with the power of our own thoughts. We see it in the bestselling pop-religious writings of Shirley Maclaine and other New Age gurus, some of whom claim to be God themselves. The Man of Sin will raise this philosophy to the nth degree and demand that the world bow to *him*—and the world will eagerly submit!

But even in that day of abomination, the Lord God will have a witness.

For a period of 1,260 days, God's two witnesses will testify of God before a world that has sold its allegiance to Satan and Satan's Antichrist. Again, some quick mental arithmetic reveals a pattern: 1,260 days equals 42 months equals 3 1/2 years equals one-half of the seven-year "week" of the Great Tribulation.

I believe there is significance in the fact that the two 3 1/2-year periods are described in different designations: 42 months versus 1,260 days. Why would John express precisely equivalent time periods in different designations? I believe he did so in order to show that they are *not* the same 3 1/2-year period. Rather, they are two different halves of one seven-year "week."

If the first 42-month period mentioned here, the time when the Gentile nations trample the holy city, is the *first* half of that seven-year period (and I believe it is), then this second period of 1,260 days most likely represents the *second* half of the Tribulation. So these two witnesses will appear during the last half of the seven-year "week."

The Lord Jesus told us that there is coming a time of trouble such as has never been on the earth before. Even the Nazi Holocaust cannot compare to it. That time of ultimate calamity and misery for the human race is the last 3 1/2-year period of the seven-year "week." The appearance of these two witnesses on the stage of Revelation inaugurates the period of the Great Tribulation.

Who are these two witnesses? We are given certain clues as to their identity. First we are told they are "the two olive trees and the two lampstands that stand before the Lord of the earth." It is easy to recognize these symbols because we also find them in the Old Testament prophecies of Zechariah. In Zechariah 4, he writes of two olive trees that drip their oil into two lampstands as a witness to Israel in Zechariah's own day. It is in the context of this passage that the oft-quoted words appear, "'Not by might nor by power, but by my Spirit,' says the LORD Almighty."[4]

In Revelation 11 we have two men who are symbolized as lampstands giving light in the midst of the darkness of the earth. The olive oil represents the Spirit of God. Thus, as the lampstands are fed by oil dripping from the olive trees, these witnesses are fed by the Spirit of God Himself, and their witness cannot be extinguished. These two men cannot be eliminated from the earth until their work is done. They are especially protected by God—a fact that is attested by their description as human flamethrowers. If anyone tries to destroy them, fire comes out of their mouths.

There are several clues here and throughout Scripture that strongly suggest that one of these two witnesses is the prophet Elijah. In 2 Samuel, there are two separate occasions in the life of Elijah when the king sends a company of fifty soldiers to capture Elijah, and each time fire comes down from heaven and destroys the soldiers. In the last book of the Old Testament, the prophet Malachi predicts the reappearance of Elijah: "See, I will send you the prophet Elijah before that great and dreadful day of the LORD comes."[5]

In Matthew's account of the transfiguration of Jesus, Moses and Elijah meet with Jesus in the presence of three of His disciples, Peter, James, and John. Afterwards, these disciples walk down the mountain with their Lord and ask, "Why . . . do the teachers of the law say that Elijah must come first?" Jesus' reply is intriguing: "To be sure, Elijah comes and will restore all things. But I tell you, Elijah has already come, and they did not recognize him, but have done to him everything they wished. In the same way the Son of Man is going to suffer at their hands."[6]

Jesus was saying that, yes, Elijah will come at some future time and restore all things—and yet a prophet had *already* come to Israel in the spirit and power of Elijah, and had been martyred. Matthew records that when Jesus said this, "the disciples understood that he was talking to them about John the Baptist." Jesus was making a double-edged statement: a prophecy affirming Malachi's words that God will send "the prophet Elijah before that great and dreadful day of the LORD comes," and a pronouncement upon the hardened hearts of those contemporary Jews who had resisted and killed John the Baptist.

So it seems clear from the evidence of both the Old and New Testaments that one of these two witnesses must be Elijah. But who is the other? There are yet more clues.

We learn, first, that these two witnesses are given power to suspend all rain upon the earth. This, of course, reminds us of Elijah, who had authority from God to withhold the rain from the land. For 3 1/2 years it did not rain in Israel until he prayed and asked God to restore the rain again.

Second, the two witnesses also have the power to turn the waters into blood and to bring plagues among the people. This is a clear echo of the ministry of Moses when he sought to free his people from the cruel grasp of the Egyptian pharaoh. Moses turned the waters into blood and called various plagues down upon the Egyptians. That is why many Bible expositors see these two witnesses as Moses and Elijah reappearing in the flesh during the last days.

Other Bible scholars suggest that the two witnesses must be Elijah and Enoch, for they are the only two men in the Old Testament who did not suffer physical death. Both were caught up into heaven without dying. In some of the earliest Christian writings there are references to Enoch and Elijah as the two witnesses of Revelation 11.

So there is room for speculation as to the identity of the other witness who appears alongside Elijah in the last days. For me, however, the matter is settled when I recall that it was Moses and Elijah who appeared together on the Mount of Transfiguration with Jesus. Peter tells us that the transfiguration event was a picture of the coming again of Jesus.[7] In light of the fact that the appearance of the two witnesses comes in close conjunction with the coming of the Lord, I think it likely that the two witnesses are Moses and Elijah.

An Attack from the Abyss

The ministry of the two witnesses is explained next.

11:7–10 *Now when they have finished their testimony, the beast that comes up from the Abyss will attack them, and overpower and kill them. Their bodies will lie in the street of the great city, which is figuratively called Sodom and Egypt, where also their Lord was crucified. For three and a half days men from every people, tribe, language and nation will gaze on their bodies and refuse them burial. The inhabitants of the earth will gloat over them and will celebrate by sending each other gifts, because these two prophets had tormented those who live on the earth.*

Notice in this passage the words "when they have finished their testimony." No one can interfere until their work is done. But once their work is done, the beast from the Abyss launches an attack, overpowering and killing God's two witnesses.

The phrase "the beast that comes up from the Abyss" takes us back to Revelation 9:11, where we saw the star that fell from heaven take the form of a living being. This star-being was given a key with which it opened the Abyss and let loose a swarming plague of symbolic locusts. Their king, we are told, was from the Abyss and his name was Abaddon (Hebrew for "destruction") and Apollyon (Greek for "destroyer"). This demonic king, as we saw, was Satan himself.

The Man of Sin, as the apostle Paul tells us, will be possessed by Satan.[8] Just as Satan entered into Judas before the betrayal of the Lord, so Satan will enter into the Antichrist to control and direct his actions. It is Satan, through the person of the Antichrist, who attacks these two witnesses and puts them to death. They have been a constant irritant, a thorn in his side. They keep telling the truth to people who want only to embrace their delusions. They keep blunting the Antichrist's carefully concocted propaganda. All the world is under the control of the Man of Sin except these two men—so he at last has them killed.

The vile and godless society of the world under the Antichrist takes the death of the two witnesses as a cause for global celebration. One is reminded of a saying that was common among ancient Roman generals, "The corpse of an enemy always smells sweet!" The entire civilization of the last days seems to take that same kind of ghoulish delight in the death of these witnesses. In the wake of the deaths of its two godly enemies, an evil world displays a shockingly gruesome, vindictive glee.

The unbelievers of that time will celebrate the death of their enemies in the only way they know how: a big blowout of a party! Even today, when unbelievers have an occasion to celebrate, a victory to commemorate, some bad news to forget, or even if they just have some time to kill, their cry is, "Let's party!" It hardly seems coincidental that this party involves the same practice Christians use to celebrate the birth of Christ: the giving of gifts. So this party seems made to order by the Antichrist, whose name means "opposite of Christ." The Antichrist's celebration takes a custom associated with Christian celebration and inverts it for a vile purpose: gloating over the death of godly men.

Instead of burying the bodies of the two witnesses, the Antichrist has their bodies put on display for the world to see and gloat over. The statement that "the inhabitants of the earth will gloat over them and will celebrate" seems to anticipate today's technology of satellite television. TV is already an indispensable feature of even the poorest Third World cultures today, and one network, CNN, is watched via satellite in virtually every nation on earth.

The bodies will be displayed in a city that is called "Sodom and Egypt"—"Sodom" because of its corruption and "Egypt" because of its persecution. The city is also identified as the place "where also their Lord was crucified." Without question, the center of corruption and persecution of godliness in the last days of the human race will be none other than the holiest city of the Holy Land, Jerusalem itself.

The Second Woe

The party won't last long. God always has the last word, and in verses 11–14 He states the last word in a loud voice from heaven.

11:11–14 *But after the three and a half days a breath of life from God entered them, and they stood on their feet, and terror struck those who saw them. Then they heard a loud voice from heaven saying to them, "Come up here." And they went up to heaven in a cloud, while their enemies looked on.*

At that very hour there was a severe earthquake and a tenth of the city collapsed. Seven thousand people were killed in the earthquake, and the survivors were terrified and gave glory to the God of heaven.

The second woe has passed; the third woe is coming soon.

These two witnesses are privileged to pass through the same experience their Lord went through, and in the same city of Jerusalem. Like Jesus, they are cruelly killed for the "crime" of bearing witness to the truth of God. Then they are resurrected 3 1/2 days later and ascend into heaven before the eyes of a startled crowd.

And look at the reaction of the crowds who witness the resurrection of the two witnesses! Twice we are told of the terror that pulsates through the people who see this resurrection take place. When they see God's resurrection power unleashed, they feel the chill dread of their own doom and defeat. *Who can oppose such power?* they wonder. Jesus once said that the worst anyone can do to you is to put you to death—for after that, what more harm can anyone do to you? But the resurrection of these two witnesses reveals that *not even death* can defeat God's servants and hinder the inexorable advance of God's program!

The triumphant truth contained in these verses should seize our imaginations and thrill us to the heart: The destiny of these two witnesses is the same that every believer in Jesus will certainly experience. Yes, we shall all die—except those who are caught up when the church is removed at the end of this church age, and even they shall be changed in the twinkling of an eye. If we die, we shall be resurrected. We shall ascend to be with the Lord forever in heaven.

We need not be surprised at the resurrection of the two witnesses, for this is how God takes loving care of all of His own, all those who trust in

Jesus Christ. Nor is it surprising that "those who live on the earth" in that time, having seen the resurrection take place before their eyes, cry out, Who is able to defeat the God of resurrection?

This scene of resurrection reminds me of the splendid lines of John Donne:

> Death be not proud, though some have called thee
> Mighty and dreadful, for thou art not so,
> For those whom thou think'st thou dost overthrow,
> Die not, poor death, nor yet canst thou kill me . . .
> . . . death, thou shalt die.[9]

Your hope and mine, the hope of all believers throughout the ages, is that death cannot ultimately claim us. Death itself must die in the lake of fire to come.

The resurrection and ascension of the two witnesses precipitates the momentous events which signal the end of man's reign upon the earth—and the beginning of God's reign. A massive earthquake strikes, just as occurred during the crucifixion of Jesus and again at His resurrection. The earthquake is centered in Jerusalem, and a tenth of the city collapses, killing 7,000 people.

There are also Old Testament references to this earthquake. In Zechariah 14, the prophet announces that the Messiah will stand upon the Mount of Olives, and when His feet touch the mountain it will separate in half. Half will move to the north and half to the south, creating a great valley between. One can easily imagine what a massive earthquake would do to modern Jerusalem, with its population of nearly a million people.

I have no doubt that what is described in this passage is a literal earthquake, because the largest fault line on earth runs just east of Jerusalem, down the valley of the River Jordan. Called the Great Rift Valley, this fault extends under the Dead Sea and down into Africa. It is the valley where the great African lakes, Lake Victoria and Lake Nyansa, are found. It is the great geological fracture that divides the African continent from Asia.

You may be familiar with the theory of continental drift and the movement of the vast subterranean tectonic plates upon which our continents rest. If so, you have some understanding of how fragile—in a long-term, geological sense—the internal structures of our land masses are, and how prone they are to stress, cracking, and movement. These are the forces which produce earthquakes, and these forces are a major concern in the region of the Holy Land. The geological forces that will one day produce the earthquake John describes in Revelation 11 are building up even now beneath the ground in Israel and beyond—and have been for hundreds of years.

The Seventh Angel and the Seventh Trumpet

In Revelation 11:15-19, the seventh angel sounds the seventh trumpet, the final blast of the trumpet series of judgments. This close-up view of the Great Tribulation draws to a close, and a new phase of God's program comes into view.

11:15–19 *The seventh angel sounded his trumpet, and there were loud voices in heaven, which said:*

"The kingdom of the world has become the kingdom of our Lord and of his Christ, and he will reign for ever and ever."

And the twenty-four elders, who were seated on their thrones before God, fell on their faces and worshiped God, saying:

"We give thanks to you, Lord God Almighty, the One who is and who was,[10] *because you have taken your great power and have begun to reign. The nations were angry; and your wrath has come. The time has come for judging the dead, and for rewarding your servants the prophets and your saints and those who reverence your name, both small and great—and for destroying those who destroy the earth."*

Then God's temple in heaven was opened, and within his temple was seen the ark of his covenant. And there came flashes of lightning, rumbling, peals of thunder, an earthquake and a great hailstorm.

We have seen these sights and sounds twice before. They mark the end of the Tribulation period and the beginning of the Millennium, the Lord's thousand-year reign upon the earth. The voices of the twenty-four angelic elders proclaim the advent of His kingdom. They worship Him because He has taken His great power and begun to wield it as the King over all the earth.

In Revelation 20 we will gain a much clearer view of the Millennium, and what follows the Millennium. We will see the brief satanic rebellion at the end of the thousand-year reign of Christ, followed by the new heaven and the new earth, where Jesus will continue His reign for ever and ever, as this passage declares.

Revelation 11:18 gives us a condensed review of the entire Tribulation period and the entire millennial period. It begins with the anger and rebellion of the nations: "The nations were angry; and your wrath has come." These words look back to the seventieth week of Daniel [for a discussion of the 70 weeks of Daniel, see chapter 12]. They also echo the words of Psalm 2:

> Why do the nations conspire
> > and the peoples plot in vain?
> The kings of the earth take their stand
> > and the rulers gather together
> against the LORD
> > and against his Anointed One.
> "Let us break their chains," they say,
> > "and throw off their fetters."

This prophetic psalm describes the great rebellion of the last days, which the twenty-four elders of Revelation 11 also describe when they say, "The nations were angry. . . ." And how will God answer the anger and rebellion of the nations? The elders go on to say, ". . . and your wrath has come." And with God's wrath against the rebelling nations comes the judging of the dead and the rewarding of His servants and the saints, both small and great, who honor the Lord.

By comparing this passage with other passages of Scripture, we learn that the dead are raised at the beginning of the Tribulation period. Paul describes it in 1 Thessalonians 4, where he describes the "Rapture" or removal of the church.

Then, at the end of the thousand-year reign of Christ during the Millennium, there is another raising of the dead—the wicked dead who stand before the Great White Throne judgment. We will come to that event later in the book of Revelation.

The Millennium will be a time when the servants of God are rewarded. "The time has come for judging the dead," says verse 18, "and for rewarding your servants the prophets and your saints and those who reverence your name, both small and great." At this point in Revelation, we must take a picture out of the book of Matthew and insert it into the design of Revelation like a piece of a jigsaw puzzle. It is the picture of Jesus in Matthew 25 saying to His disciples,

> When the Son of Man comes in his glory, and all the angels
> with him, he will sit on his throne in heavenly glory. All the

nations will be gathered before him, and he will separate the people one from another as a shepherd separates the sheep from the goats. He will put the sheep on his right and the goats on his left.[11]

What does Jesus mean when He talks about separating the "sheep" from the "goats"? He is prophesying about a coming judgment of all those who claim to be believers and followers of Christ. Some, the "sheep," are genuine in their profession of Christ. Others, the "goats," have made a profession with their mouths that has not been matched by the life they have led and the inner condition of their hearts. What will the basis of that judgment be? Jesus goes on to state the criteria in Matthew 25:

> Then the King will say to those on his right, "Come, you who are blessed by my Father; take your inheritance, the kingdom prepared for you since the creation of the world. For I was hungry and you gave me something to eat, I was thirsty and you gave me something to drink, I was a stranger and you invited me in, I needed clothes and you clothed me, I was sick and you looked after me, I was in prison and you came to visit me."
> Then the righteous will answer him, "Lord, when did we see you hungry and feed you, or thirsty and give you something to drink? When did we see you a stranger and invite you in, or needing clothes and clothe you? When did we see you sick or in prison and go to visit you?"
> The King will reply, "I tell you the truth, whatever you did for one of the least of these brothers of mine, you did for me."[12]

Our lives as professing followers of Christ will be judged according to how we react to the needs of the helpless, the hopeless, and the homeless. In this passage Jesus goes on to say that those who did *nothing* for the needs of "the least of these brothers of mine" will be told, "Depart from me, you who are cursed," and they will be sent away to eternal punishment. These are the "goats" that are separated from the sheep of God's flock.

This judgment of professing believers occurs at the beginning of the Millennium. It is a judgment of the living who survive the Tribulation. Yet again we see how John's prophetic vision of the future has powerful applicability in our own lives today. The way we live our lives right now reveals the true state of our hearts.

On that day some will be found among the sheep and some among the goats. Their deeds will tell the story.

The Return of the Lost Ark

Finally, in this passage we are told that God's temple in heaven is opened and the ark of the covenant is revealed within it. But don't expect to see Indiana Jones anywhere nearby! The motion picture *Raiders of the Lost Ark*, in which the swashbuckling archeologist Indiana Jones searched for the lost ark of the covenant, had an unfortunate tendency to distort and invent facts about the ark. Here is how the Bible describes the ark and its history:

The ark was a chest made of acacia wood, overlaid with pure gold. It was not large—less than 4 feet long and just over 2 feet high and 2 feet wide. It contained the original tablets of the Ten Commandments which God gave to Moses on Mount Sinai, along with a pot of manna and the staff of Aaron. It was ornamented with golden statues of two angels on either side of the mercy seat of God—thus joining in one object symbols of both the law of God and His mercy. The ark was carried by the Jews during their forty years of wandering in the wilderness, and it occupied the Holy of Holies in the tent-tabernacle, and later in the tabernacle of David and the great Temple of Solomon. The ark disappeared into the mists of history during the destruction of Jerusalem by Nebuchadnezzar of Babylon around 600 B.C.

But the ark of gold which occupied the Holy of Holies in the time of Moses, David, and Solomon was a copy, a representation of the true ark that stood in heaven as a sign of God's promise to Israel, the ark which John now sees in Revelation 11. The earthly ark was sometimes captured by enemies such as the Philistines and was eventually taken away and probably destroyed by the Babylonians, along with the other temple treasures. But the heavenly ark has endured, standing outside the reach of time and Israel's enemies, a guarantee that God will never forget His people, Israel.

In Revelation 12 through 14, we will again see Israel come into prominence. Once again the vision of John will shift to another perspective, a different "camera angle" on the same events we have already witnessed in the seven seals of judgment and the seven trumpets of judgment. It is important to remember that Revelation does not present us with a sequential chronology of events labeled A, B, C, D, and so forth. The vision that John records is subtle, non-sequential, and non-linear in its presentation, filled with shifts of perspective, flashbacks, and Old Testament allusions.

For the third time in our exploration of Revelation, we shall retrace the last 3 1/2 years of the Tribulation period until we come to Revelation 15 and 16, which is a reprise of the scene we have just encountered at the close of Revelation 11 — a scene of lightning, thunder, a great earthquake, and a storm of hail. In this passage, the cataclysmic disturbances in the earth and the sky signal the close of the seventh trumpet judgment. In Revelation 15 and 16, they will signal the close of the judgments of the seven bowls of wrath. Yet the seven seals, the seven trumpets, and the seven bowls are in reality three different views of the same events.

The Certainty of Glory

What a privilege God has given us in the pages of Revelation. He has allowed us a glimpse into the last chapters of human history. We can watch the news broadcasts and read our newspapers and not have to wonder what it all means, where it's all going, because God has already shown us the conclusion of the trends and events which already surround us.

In Revelation we see that a time is coming when Jesus will reign over all the earth. Unlike the days we live in, those times will be characterized by righteousness and peace. In that day, all drug traffic will cease. There will be neither brushfire wars nor nuclear terrors. Abortion mills will no longer exist. Divorce, domestic violence, and child abuse will be unheard of. Crime statistics will drop to zero. Sex scandals will be unknown. Truth and love for God shall be reinstated in the school curricula.

In the words of the Scriptures, "the earth will be filled with the knowledge of the glory of the LORD, as the waters cover the sea"![13] So let us not lose hope. Let us encourage one another with the certainty of the glory to come.

Chapter Eighteen

The Woman and the Serpent

Revelation 12

"Sometimes we see a cloud that's dragonish," said Antony in Shakespeare's *Antony and Cleopatra*.[1] As we come to Revelation 12, we find that a dragonish cloud looms over human history. It is a thundercloud, a cloud that betokens war on a scale beyond human imagining—not merely war on earth, army against army, but war in heaven, Dragon against Angel. And shining radiantly against the dragonish shadow of these ominous events we see a poignant symbol of virtue and vulnerability: a mother and her newborn child.

What do these vivid symbols mean? What is this "dragonish cloud" that John sees in his vision, and which even now hangs over our heads?

12:1–6 *A great and wondrous sign appeared in heaven: a woman clothed with the sun, with the moon under her feet and a crown of twelve stars on her head. She was pregnant and cried out in pain as she was about to give birth. Then another sign appeared in heaven: an enormous red dragon with seven heads and ten horns and seven crowns on his heads. His tail swept a third of the stars out of the sky and flung them to the earth. The dragon stood in front of the woman who was about to give birth, so that he might devour her child the moment it was born. She gave birth to a son, a male child, who will rule all the nations with an iron scepter. And her child was snatched up to God and to his throne. The woman fled into*

*the desert to a place prepared for her by God, where she might be taken
care of for 1,260 days.*

There is rich and powerful symbolism in this passage. Our task is to
interpret it and understand the reality behind the symbols of John. What
do they mean? What or whom do they symbolize?

Two of these symbols are relatively easy to identify: the dragon and
the male child. Once we find out who they are, the third symbol—the
woman—becomes unmistakable.

There is no mystery to the dragon's identity, for John will disclose
that to us in verse 9: "that ancient serpent called the devil, or Satan, who
leads the whole world astray." In the opening verse of chapter 12, the
devil is symbolized as a great red dragon with seven heads and ten horns
and seven crowns upon his heads. But he is also "that ancient serpent"—
the very one who appeared in the Garden of Eden to the first woman,
Eve, deceiving her and introducing sin into the human race.

Dragons, of course, symbolize satanic worship in many cultures
around the world. As John says in verse 9, the career of the devil has
been devoted to deceiving the entire human race and leading human
beings astray.

An Iron Scepter

The male child who is born to the woman is the next easiest to identify because verse 5 says that He is the one "who will rule all the nations
with an iron scepter." This is one of four references in Revelation to
Psalm 2. In verse 9 of that prophetic, messianic psalm we read, "You will
rule them with an iron scepter."

Though the book of Revelation is truly rooted in the *entire* Old
Testament, it would be a valid analogy to compare Revelation to an oak
tree that grows and expands out of the acorn of Psalm 2. In this psalm we
read that the One enthroned in heaven says, "I have installed my King on
Zion, my holy hill,"[2] and that this King will rule the nations with an iron
scepter. Clearly this is a reference to the thousand-year reign of Jesus
Christ during the Millennium, as is pictured for us in the book of
Revelation.

The reference to an iron scepter (in Psalm 2 and Revelation 12:5)
always indicates a millennial scene. The iron scepter speaks of strict justice. The Millennium will be a time of worldwide blessing and prosperity
when the curse of sin will be at least partly removed from the natural
world. But sin will still manifest itself to some degree—hence the iron

scepter of Christ. As we shall see in Revelation 20, righteousness will reign on earth during the Millennium, but it will have to be enforced.

After the Millennium the new heaven and the new earth will appear. At that time Christ will no longer reign with a scepter of iron. Nothing evil can enter into the new heaven and the new earth. When sin is finally extinguished forever, the defining characteristic of Christ will no longer be His iron reign but tender, shepherdlike love as He ministers personally and kindly to His redeemed people.

A Woman of Mystery

That brings us to the mystery of the woman. Why is she clothed in the sun? Why is the moon under her feet? Why are twelve stars arranged in a crown over her head? There are several theories as to whom or what this symbolic woman represents.

Roman Catholic scholars have concluded that she is Mary, the mother of Jesus. Having understood that the child who will rule the nations with an iron scepter is Jesus, it certainly makes sense that the mother of that child would be Mary. The problem with this theory, however, is that there is no way you can fit Mary into verse 6 where we read that she "fled into the desert to a place prepared for her by God, where she might be taken care of for 1,260 days." That never happened to Mary, and it never will. The woman in Revelation 12 does not represent a single individual but rather a community of people.

Some Bible scholars say she symbolizes the church. Certainly there is some substantiation for this view, in that the church is pictured at the close of Revelation as a woman, the bride of Christ. But as with the previous theory this view has an insurmountable problem: It is impossible for the woman to represent the church because she is depicted as giving birth to Jesus. The church did not produce Jesus; Jesus produced the church! The church was "born" out of the wounded side of Jesus.

What, then, is the true identity of this woman of mystery? Let's examine the clues one by one and see where they lead.

The clues are significant: The woman is clothed with the sun, the moon is under her feet, and a crown of twelve stars is on her head. There is only one other place in Scripture where you find all these symbols clustered together in one place: Genesis 37, the story of Joseph the boy-dreamer. He dreamed one night that the sun, the moon, and eleven stars bowed down before him. The sun, moon, and stars represented his father, mother, and eleven brothers, respectively. Eventually this dream would come true—but not until after those eleven brothers sold Joseph into slavery, not until after Joseph overcame trials of false accusation and unjust imprisonment, not until after Joseph became second in command over all of Egypt.

The symbols of the sun, moon, and stars make it clear: The woman represents the people of Israel, all of whom are descendants of Joseph's father Jacob. Joseph himself would be the twelfth star. In Romans 9:5 Paul said of the people of Israel, "from them is traced the human ancestry of Christ." That is why Jesus told the Samaritan woman at the well, "Salvation is from the Jews."[3] Even the salvation of the Gentiles comes by way of the Jews, because it is the Jewish race that produced Jesus Christ.

So here again, in the symbolism of the woman clothed in the sun with the stars at her head and the moon at her feet, we have a picture of Israel coming again into prominence in the last days.

The Great Snatch

To understand the vivid images and symbols of Revelation 12 we should remember that we are viewing earthly scenes from heaven's point of view. In Revelation 4 we saw that John was caught up into heaven and shown all the things that follow in Revelation 4 through 19. When you look at earthly events from heaven's standpoint, time is never a factor. This vision does not present a sequence or an ordered chronology. It presents occurrences arranged according to their meaning and importance from a heavenly, eternal perspective. Events that may be widely separated in time may be clustered together in eternity's view. From heaven's perspective we are shown *what* happens, not *when* it happens. If we approach this chapter—and indeed all of Revelation—with this point of view, symbols that once seemed murky and obscure will pop into focus.

With this outlook in mind, let's take another look at the great red dragon of this passage. With its seven heads, ten horns, and seven crowns, it sounds like something out of a monster movie. But there is a concrete reality behind these grotesque symbols—a reality we will explore in greater depth when this dragon reappears in a somewhat altered form in Revelation 13. For now it is enough to understand the dramatic significance of these images as they are presented in Revelation 12.

What we have in Revelation 12 is a kind of tableau, like a scene in a wax museum, of three-dimensional figures frozen in place at the climactic moment of a dramatic event. Satan, the great dragon, is crouched

with its fangs bared and its eyes smoldering, watching Israel as she prepares to give birth to her long-promised Son. Israel is pregnant and crying out in her labor pains. The dragon's intention is clear: it seeks to
devour Jesus as soon as He emerges from the womb of Israel and makes
His appearance upon the earth. What is the historical reality represented
by this grim and symbol-laden tableau?

This scene takes us back to the historical birth of Jesus, to the days
of the Roman Empire and its subjugation of Israel. It takes us back to the
time of King Herod the Great and the demonic malice and enmity that
filled his heart when he learned of the birth of Jesus. It is easy to see the
events of that time in the symbolic tableau of Revelation 12:1-4.

Also in verse 4 we are told that the dragon swept a third of the stars
from the sky with his tail. Elsewhere in Revelation and in other parts of
Scripture we learn that stars frequently symbolize prominent human
leaders. In this context they specifically symbolize the leaders of the
nation of Israel. In one of the great prophetic passages of the Old
Testament, Isaiah specifically states, "The prophets who teach lies are
the tail." In other words, Satan accomplishes his deceptive, destructive
work through false, lying prophets.

In Revelation 12:4, where the dragon's tail sweeps a third of the
stars out of the sky and casts them to earth, we are given a symbol of the
leaders (stars) of Israel being deceived and brought down from their
moral position before God, and the dragon's tail (the lying prophets) are
the means Satan uses to deceive them.

The dragon of world power in Jesus' day was the Roman Empire,
which in the Jewish land of Judea was represented by the person of
Rome's puppet king Herod the Great. Though in his early career Herod
had been a comparatively progressive and benevolent despot, his notori-
ous cruel streak and murderous paranoia were already in full evidence
by the time Christ was born. In a fit of jealous rage Herod murdered his
favorite among his eight wives, as well as several of her family members. He later murdered his own firstborn son Antipas. So his attempt to
kill the newborn Son of God by slaughtering the infants of Bethlehem
was true to form for this brutal and unfeeling man. Like a dragon, he lay
in wait for the child to be born—then *pounced*, beastlike, spilling blood
as if it were water.

But God intervened, sparing the infant Jesus from the maw of the
dragon. Warned by the appearance of an angel in a dream, Joseph and
Mary took Jesus on a secret journey to Egypt beyond the reach of Herod.

This brings us to verse 5. It is at this point in the symbolic allegory
of the dragon, the woman, and the child that we come upon a startling

statement. John writes, "She gave birth to a son, a male child, who will rule all the nations with an iron scepter. And her child was snatched up to God and to his throne." Completely ignoring any chronology or sequence of historical events, this symbolic scene takes a sudden jump from the birth of Jesus to His ascension some 30 years later, skipping over His life, ministry, death, and resurrection in a single breath. In this image, John is shown only the birth and ascension into heaven of Jesus. This symbol encompasses both the beginning and the ending of His earthly ministry.

But a problem of interpretation arises at this point. The problem is this: The clear implication of Revelation 12:5 is that Jesus was "snatched up to God" in order to deliver Him from harm, from the reach of the dragon. Yet we know from reading the gospels and the book of Acts that Jesus' ascension was by no means an escape from harm. Rather it was a triumphal exit following His victory over death. The resurrected Lord was completely beyond the reach of His enemies, and there was no harm anyone could do to Him. Why, then, does this tableau in Revelation 12 depict Jesus as having been "snatched up to God" as a child is snatched out of the path of an onrushing car?

Here is where the interpretation of Revelation becomes sensitive, because of the non-linear, non-chronological nature of the vision. The interpretation is this: There *is* an aspect of our Lord Jesus Christ which does find deliverance from danger, from the rage of the red dragon, by being snatched away into heaven. By this I mean the *body* of Christ that is on the earth today — that is, the *church*.

Throughout the New Testament, the Lord and His church are regarded as one. When Saul (later the apostle Paul) was confronted by an appearance of Christ on the Damascus Road, Jesus said to him, "Saul, Saul, why are you persecuting me?" Saul had never even met Jesus — but he was persecuting the church. When Jesus spoke to Saul of His church He identified completely with that church. If Saul was persecuting the Lord's church, Saul was persecuting *Him,* because they were one.

Paul later wrote to the Corinthians, "Now you are the body of Christ, and each one of you is a part of it."[4] The church, he said, is a body, and "the body is a unit, though it is made up of many parts; and though all its parts are many, they form one body. So it is with Christ."[5] The church and the Lord *together* are the body of Christ. So when we come to Revelation 12 and see that the child, representing Christ, was "snatched up to God and to his throne," it becomes clear that this is a reference to *the removal of the church* from the world and from the threatening presence of the dragon.

During the late 1960s, the heady times of the Jesus People and Body Life, the young "street" Christians used to refer to the "Rapture" or removal of the church as the Great Snatch. Perhaps it's only coincidental, but that's the same word the NIV translators used in Revelation 12:5—"her child was snatched up to God and to his throne." Deeply embedded in this verse is yet another promise that God will one day rescue every true Christian from the great dragonish cloud of persecution that is coming upon the world.

As if to confirm our interpretation of verse 5 as a promise of the Great Snatch of the church out of the world, verse 6 carries us on into the Tribulation period. In leaping immediately from the birth of Christ to the removal of the church and the beginning of the Tribulation, these verses in Revelation 12 completely eclipse all the centuries of the church age in which we now live.

In verse 6, the woman (representing the people of Israel) flees into the desert to a place prepared for her by God. There she is taken care of for a period of 1,260 days—a significant time period, as we learned in the previous chapter. In Revelation 11, we saw that the two witnesses will prophesy for a period of 1,260 days—the last 3 1/2 years of the seven-year Tribulation period. So it would be reasonable and consistent to conclude that the desert exile of the believing Jewish people (represented by the woman) would also take place during the same 3 1/2-year period in which the two witnesses prophesy against the Antichrist.

Notice, too, that a subtle shift has taken place in the symbolism represented by the woman. In verses 1 through 4 the woman represented the Jewish nation which was to bring forth Jesus, the Son of God. In verse 5 the child is born and is snatched up to God's throne. In verse 6 the woman flees into the desert to escape the persecution of the Antichrist and the Tribulation. The *fleeing* woman, then, represents not the Jewish people as a whole—for many Jews will be deceived by the Antichrist— but the *believing* remnant of the Jews, those who have trusted in the Messiah and have refused to submit to the rule of the Antichrist.

War in Heaven

At verse 7 we come to an abrupt change of scene. The perspective changes. Instead of looking at earthly scenes from a heavenly perspective, we now become spectators to a scene which takes place in heaven itself. It is a scene of conflict, invisible to the people of earth, yet profoundly affecting the life of every man, woman, and child who ever lived.

12:7–9 *And there was war in heaven. Michael and his angels fought against the dragon, and the dragon and his angels fought back. But he was not strong enough, and they lost their place in heaven. The great dragon was hurled down—that ancient serpent called the devil [which means "the Accuser"], or Satan [which means "the Adversary"], who leads the whole world astray. He was hurled to the earth, and his angels with him.*

Here we have the first reference in Revelation to Michael. Who is Michael? We can tell who Michael is by what he is doing in this passage: he is leading the battle against the great red dragon, Satan.

We first meet Michael in the Old Testament prophecy of Daniel. He is called "the great prince who protects your people"—that is, the people of Daniel, the Jews. The return of Michael in Revelation 12 is yet another signal that Israel is at the forefront of the events of this book.

From this scene in Revelation, as well as other scenes throughout the Scriptures, we can conclude that for millennia past, for the present, and for some time in the future, up until the last days, Satan has been given access to heaven. In the book of Job, Satan appears before God and requests permission to torment the life of Job. In Zechariah, Satan is pictured as accusing the saints before God in heaven.

And Paul tells us in Ephesians 6 that we do not wrestle against flesh and blood, that other people are not really our problem. Our real opponent is the devil and his army of wicked spirits who manipulate people and events. And where are the devil and his allies? These "spiritual forces of evil," Paul tells us, are "in the heavenly realms."[6] Throughout this age, right at this very moment, Satan still has access to heaven.

But Revelation 12:7-9 depicts a time during the last days, during the seventieth week of Daniel, when God has had enough of the presence of Satan in heaven. He sends Michael, the great archangel, along with a great force of angels, to drive Satan and his army of evil spirits out of heaven, hurling them to earth. We have already seen this same event depicted previously in Revelation 9:1, where we saw a great star fall from heaven onto the earth. This star was given the key to the Abyss, and it opened the Abyss and loosed a horde of evil spirits upon the earth.

Other accounts of the fall of Satan out of heaven are found in Ezekiel 28 and Isaiah 14.

How To Slay a Dragon

In verses 10 through 12, we learn that the final victory over Satan and his forces is drawing near.

12:10–12 *Then I heard a loud voice in heaven say:*
"Now have come the salvation and the
*   power and the kingdom of our God,*
*   and the authority of his Christ,*
For the accuser of our brothers,
*   who accuses them before our God day and night,*
*   has been hurled down.*
They overcame him
*   by the blood of the Lamb*
*   and by the word of their testimony;*
they did not love their lives so much
*   as to shrink from death.*
Therefore rejoice, you heavens
*   and you who dwell in them!*
But woe to the earth and the sea,
*   because the devil has gone down to you!*
He is filled with fury,
*   because he knows that his time is short."*

This loud voice that the apostle John hears seems to come from the martyrs of Revelation 6 who were given white robes, and who are seen under the altar calling out to God, "How long, Sovereign Lord, holy and true, until you . . . avenge our blood?" In this scene, these same martyrs now rejoice that the devil has been cast out of heaven.

These martyrs speak of "the accuser of our brothers, who accuses them before our God day and night." The "brothers" here are the believing Jews, the remnant of Israel who remain on the earth during those days. The white-robed saints in heaven announce that the time has come for the Lord to reign over the kingdom long ago promised to Israel.

Verse 11 is an especially important verse for you and me, because its truth is applicable in the here and now. It tells how the saints of any age can overcome the evil purposes of the devil as he attempts to deceive us, neutralize our effectiveness for God, and immobilize us with the poisonous emotion of guilt. In this verse we find a three-step plan for defeating the attacks and accusations of Satan:

Step 1: Trust in the blood of Christ. Have you ever heard the devil accusing you in your conscience and emotions? Has an inner voice ever demanded of you, "What right do you have to call yourself a Christian? Look at all your sins and failures! Look at the mess your life is in! How could God ever love a sinner like you?" How do you handle such accusations when they come to mind?

John records these words: "They overcame him [Satan] by the blood of the Lamb." And so should we. We must begin by honestly admitting that the accusation of Satan is *true:* We are sinners! Our lives are a mess! We lie, we thoughtlessly hurt other people, we act selfishly, we have impure thoughts, we act angrily and maliciously. It's all true. So let's admit it to ourselves, to God, and to that insistent, accusing voice.

Then, let's remind Satan that we are covered by the blood of the Lamb. Our sins have all been nailed to the cross of Christ. Jesus took our sins on Himself, so we are no longer to be judged or accused before God. That is why the apostle Paul says, "Therefore, there is now no condemnation for those who are in Christ Jesus."[7]

A dear, godly woman I know once wrote a poem that describes the experience of one who has faced and defeated the accusation of Satan by taking refuge in the blood of the Lamb. She writes,

> I sinned, and straightway, posthaste, Satan flew
> Before the presence of the Most High God,
> And made a railing accusation there.
> He said, "This soul, this thing of clay and sod,
> Has sinned. 'Tis true that he has named thy Name,
> But I demand his death, for Thou hast said,
> 'The soul that sinneth, it shall die.' Shall not
> Thy sentence be fulfilled? Is Justice dead?
> Send now this wretched sinner to his doom.
> What other thing can righteous ruler do?"
> And thus he did accuse me day and night.
> And every word he spoke, O God, was true!
>
> Then quickly One rose up from God's right hand
> Before whose glory angels veiled their eyes.
> He spoke, "Each jot and tittle of the Law
> Must be fulfilled; the guilty sinner dies!
> But wait! Suppose his guilt were all transferred
> To Me, and that I paid his penalty.
> Behold, my hands, my side, my feet! One day
> I was made sin for him, and died that he
> Might be presented faultless at Thy throne."
> And Satan flew away. Full well he knew
> That he could not prevail against such love,
> For every word my dear Lord spoke was true!

That is the meaning of the blood of the Lamb. There is no way to defend ourselves against Satan's accusations, no way to avoid the guilt and shame of our sinfulness, without complete reliance upon the work of the cross and the blood of the Lamb. When Jesus covers you with His righteousness and makes a new creature out of you, Satan has nothing left with which to accuse you. The sins of the past are dead and gone.

Step 2: Share your testimony. All around us—in our offices, our neighborhoods, our schools, even in our own families—there are people who struggle under the heavy burden of sin and guilt and the devil's accusation. Their lives are lonely, empty, and fear-ridden. Shame lurks in the hidden chambers of their hearts. But *you* can help them. How? By the word of your testimony.

John records that those who overcame Satan did so "by the word of their testimony." It is not only our duty but our *joy* to share with others the freedom we have received through Jesus Christ. Perhaps the message of that freedom first entered your life through the testimony of a friend, a neighbor, a co-worker who cared enough about you to share his or her testimony with you. Are you in turn sharing that message with others—or have you bottled up that tremendous good news inside you? Are you overcoming Satan by the word of your testimony?

Step 3: Put everything you are and have on the altar of Jesus Christ. Satan was overcome, as John records, because "they did not love their lives so much as to shrink from death." In other words, they loved Jesus more than everything, even more than their own lives. They would give up anything for Jesus—reputation, status, possessions, even life itself! They would rather die than bring shame to their Lord and His name. That is the third and final way to overcome Satan.

Step 1, reliance upon Jesus and His shed blood, means that we have exercised *faith*. Step 2, sharing the word of our testimony, means we are exercising *love* toward others who are bound by Satan's lies. And Step 3, sacrificing all that we are and have for the sake of Christ, means that we have laid hold of the *hope* of the Christian faith—the hope that the loss of possessions, honor, and life itself means nothing compared to the promised inheritance of eternal life with Jesus. These three steps represent the three great values of the Christian life: *faith, hope*, and *love!*

As Paul wrote to the Corinthians, "Now these three remain: faith, hope and love." These are the three steps to overcoming our enemy. These are the weapons with which frail, weak human beings like you and me can go forth and slay a dragon!

His Time Is Short

The victory over the dragon brings great rejoicing to heaven—but intensified horror and suffering on the earth. The devil is enraged by the resistance of those who remain faithful to God. He knows that his time is short. In just 3 1/2 years he will be bound and consigned to the Abyss. So he moves quickly, and cataclysmic events of the last days increase in severity and violence.

12:13–17 *When the dragon saw that he had been hurled to the earth, he pursued the woman who had given birth to the male child. The woman was given the two wings of a great eagle, so that she might fly to the place prepared for her in the desert, where she would be taken care of for a time, times and half a time [meaning one year, plus two years, plus half a year, or a total of 3 1/2 years], out of the serpent's reach. Then from his mouth the serpent spewed water like a river, to overtake the woman and sweep her away with the torrent. But the earth helped the woman by opening its mouth and swallowing the river that the dragon had spewed out of his mouth. Then the dragon was enraged at the woman and went off to make war against the rest of her offspring—those who obey God's commandments and hold to the testimony of Jesus.*

This woman, you recall, represents not all Jews of the last days but only the believing remnant. Those Jews who have not believed are suffering under the judgments that are foretold in the Old Testament prophecies. This is "the time of Jacob's trouble," when apostate Jews are cruelly eliminated by the dragon and the faithful remnant is pursued and persecuted. The remnant escapes to the desert, and the swiftness of their flight from danger is symbolized by the eagle's wings.

Many Bible scholars believe the faithful Jews of the last days will flee to the city of Petra, south of the Dead Sea—a strangely beautiful city hewn out of the rock of the earth that is presently an attraction for tourists and archeologists in the Holy Land. Perhaps this is true, but no one can say with certainty.

What is important in these verses is that God will care for this believing remnant in a supernatural way. They will be borne out of danger on the metaphorical wings of an eagle. I am sure it is no coincidence that this is the very same metaphor God used when the nation of Israel was led out of Egypt by Moses. "You yourselves have seen what I did to Egypt," God said to Israel through His servant Moses, "and how I carried you on eagles' wings and brought you to myself."[8] This is a picture of God's loving protection and care for the people who are His faithful remnant in that day.

The symbolism of the river of water which the serpent spews in an effort to overtake the woman is likely an image of a vast host of soldiers sent by the Antichrist to overtake and destroy the faithful of Israel in the last days. But God will protect His faithful remnant, probably by means of a natural cataclysm—perhaps an earthquake—that causes the destruction of the Antichrist's armies and the frustration of his plans.

The Antichrist will be diverted from attacking the faithful Jews of Israel (symbolized by the woman), and will instead turn his attention to "the rest of her offspring" and make war against them. Who is John describing in this phrase? Most likely "the rest of her offspring" refers to "Christ's commandos," the 144,000 Jews we first met in Revelation 7 and will meet again in Revelation 14. They are the special band of believing Jews who move out into the four corners of the world, preaching the gospel of the kingdom to all the nations. The devil gives his final attention to destroying this group because of their powerful and effective witness to the world.

The rage of the devil is increasing as he grows more and more desperate, knowing that his time is short. Like any wild and dangerous beast, the devil becomes more deadly and ferocious as he is backed into a corner.

In the next chapter of Revelation we shall see the terrible and climactic unleashing of Satan's power upon the earth. I'm sure you can feel it: the pace of events in the book of Revelation is quickening. God's plan in human history is crescendoing toward its culmination.

But for just a moment let's pull back from this examination of future events and look at the world around us. What sort of events are you hearing about on your radio, or watching on your television, or reading about in your newspaper? I'm sure you can feel it all around you: the pace of events in the world is quickening, too. The crescendoing drumbeat of God's plan can be felt in the world around you as surely as you can feel it in the book of Revelation.

Don't you sometimes feel as though you are moving on a river that is approaching a waterfall? Don't you feel the current growing swifter as you draw nearer to that sudden vertical cataract that lies ahead of the human race? With each passing day, it becomes easier and easier for me to believe that we must be coming close to the time that is described in these chapters of Revelation.

If that is true, then there is an urgent question staring us in the face right now. It won't go away, it won't even wait. We must answer this question *today,* because the time is growing too short to put off the decision. The question is:

How are you doing in your personal battle with Satan? In your battle with the Accuser, amid the decline and pressure and steadily worsening moral condition of this world, how are you doing? Are you relying daily upon Jesus and His blood as the source of your righteousness? Are you sharing the word of your testimony with others? Have you placed all you have on the altar of Jesus Christ?

How is your faith? How is your hope? How is your love?

Every day that goes by brings the dragon closer to his ultimate defeat—and he knows it. Armed with weapons of faith, hope, and love, we are part of God's army, sharing in His victory over the dragon, marching in triumph toward a future day when the accusing voice of the dragon will be silenced forever.

I believe God's triumph over Satan is coming in the not-too-distant future. The battle is raging even now. You and I are a part of it. Let's fight to win!

Chapter Nineteen

When Men Become Beasts

Revelation 13

t has to be the most famous number in the world. If you are issued a license plate or a credit card with this sequence of digits it sends a shiver of unreasoning fear down your spine. Books have been written and movies based on the mystery of this sinister number:

> **666**

Some friends of mine once owned a house with 666 as the street address. These three baleful digits were emblazoned on the wall of their home, inscribed on their mailbox, and painted on their curb. They petitioned the city planning commission to change their house number—and after much discussion and head-scratching the city agreed.

Is the fixation that so many people have with the number 666 a mere superstitious obsession, like being afraid of the number 13? Does this number have some sort of occult significance? Does it pose a spiritual threat to you and me today?

In Revelation 13 we will learn the secret and the significance of this strange number—and of the even stranger beasts associated with it.

In Revelation 12 the apostle John saw a great red dragon with seven heads, ten horns, and seven crowns. This dragon was clearly a symbolic representation of Satan. In the first four verses of Revelation 13 John sees a further manifestation of this same ominous beast.

13:1–4 *And the dragon stood on the shore of the sea.*

And I saw a beast coming out of the sea. He had ten horns and seven heads, with ten crowns on his horns, and on each head a blasphemous name. The beast I saw resembled a leopard, but had feet like those of a bear and a mouth like that of a lion. The dragon gave the beast his power and his throne and great authority. One of the heads of the beast seemed to have had a fatal wound; but the fatal wound had been healed. The whole world was astonished and followed the beast. Men worshiped the dragon because he had given authority to the beast, and they also worshiped the beast and asked, "Who is like the beast? Who can make war against him?"

John saw this beast rising out of the sea. The sea, as we have seen several times before in Revelation, is a symbol of the Gentile nations of the world. This appearance is another manifestation of Satan as a world-wide evil power on the earth. In Revelation 12 the beast represented the Roman Empire of the first century and was the instrument used by the devil in his failed attempt to destroy the male child born to the woman, Jesus the Son of God. In Revelation 13 we see the same beast arising at a different time in history—the last days.

If you read Daniel 7, you will find many parallels to the events of Revelation 13. Daniel, too, saw beasts rising up out of the sea. He saw four beasts: a beast like a lion, another like a bear, a third like a leopard, and a fourth which was unique in that it was a fantastic creature with ten horns. In many ways it is indistinguishable from the beast which John sees in Revelation 13.

We learn in Daniel that the beasts he saw represented four great world empires of his day and following. The first beast, which was lion-like, represented Babylon. The second, like a bear, represented Medo-Persia. The third, like a four-headed leopard, represented Greece. These same images are incorporated in the beast from the sea which appears in John's vision.

The fourth beast, with its ten horns and seven heads, is identifiable as the Roman Empire. In this one strange beast all the powers of the previous beasts have been combined: the lion-like ferocity of Babylon, the bear-like Medo-Persian power to crush and dismember, the leopard-like swiftness of the Greeks.

The Woman on the Beast

To fully interpret the meaning of the beast of Revelation 13 we will need to look ahead a bit to Revelation 17 where this many-headed, many-horned beast appears again. We will examine Revelation 17 more thoroughly in due course, so at this time we will only extract a few of the salient features of that chapter that will shed some additional light on Revelation 13. In chapter 17, John sees a woman riding on a red beast — a beast with seven heads and ten horns. An angel explains to John what these symbols mean. In Revelation 17:7 and 8 John writes:

> Then the angel said to me: "Why are you astonished? I will explain to you the mystery of the woman and of the beast she rides, which has the seven heads and ten horns. The beast, which you saw, once was, now is not, and will come up out of the Abyss and go to his destruction. The inhabitants of the earth whose names have not been written in the book of life from the creation of the world will be astonished when they see the beast, because he once was, now is not, and yet will come."

This passage clearly identifies the beast of Revelation 17 with the beast of Revelation 13, for we find these two parallel passages:

From Revelation 13:3	*From Revelation 17:8*
The whole world was astonished and followed the beast.	The inhabitants of the earth . . . will be astonished when they see the beast. . . .

The phrase in chapter 17, "the beast . . . once was, now is not, and yet will come," seems to refer to a line in Revelation 13:3 which reads, "One of the heads of the beast seemed to have had a fatal wound, but the fatal wound had been healed." If the beast of Revelation 13 and 17 represents the same Roman Empire that John saw in symbolic form in Revelation 12, then the clear implication is that there will be a revived form of the Roman Empire in the final seven-year period of the history of civilization.

This point is made very clear in the next words of the angel in Revelation 17:9 —

> This calls for a mind with wisdom. The seven heads are seven hills on which the woman sits.

Later in Revelation 17 the image of the woman is explained as symbolizing a great city. What city is famous for being built upon seven hills? The answer is obvious: Rome.

Why the World Is Astonished

In Revelation 17:9-11, the angel goes on to further explain the meaning of the beast:

> They [the seven heads of the beast] are also seven kings [or kingdoms]. Five have fallen, one is, the other has not yet come; but when he does come, he must remain for a little while. The beast who once was, and now is not, is an eighth king. He belongs to the seven and is going to his destruction.

Is that clear to you? Clear as mud, most likely! Yet there are some things we can identify in this portion of John's revelation. Concerning these seven kings we are told, "five have fallen, one is, the other has not yet come."

The Roman historian Livy (born around 60 B.C., died A.D. 17) wrote that there had been five forms of Roman government up to his time. Rome originally began as a loosely connected cluster of city-states, each governed by its own king. This confederation soon fragmented, and in place of kings the city-states elected consuls. The consuls were succeeded by dictators who rose up and took over the government by force. These were later overthrown and replaced by a council of ten rulers called decemvirs. When that form of government failed, tribunes were elected by the people. Those were the five forms of government that had ruled Rome, then fallen.

But then John is told "one is." That would be the imperial form of government, the emperors of Rome, beginning with Julius Caesar (born 100 B.C., died 44 B.C.) and continuing well into the fifth century A.D. And, the angel adds, a seventh is yet to come, "but when he does come, he must remain for a little while." Then the beast will appear.

The beast is one of the seven kings, but will be revived and will thus become an eighth king. Something very strange will happen to the beast: once dead, it will be called back into existence. Its deadly wound is healed, and it makes its reappearance in history. No wonder the whole world is astonished at the revival of the beast.

When we return to Revelation 17 we will learn some very startling things about the imperial form of Roman government. But for now let's read just one more verse from chapter 17. In verse 12 the angel says:

> The ten horns you saw are ten kings who have not yet received a kingdom, but who for one hour will receive authority as kings along with the beast.

Bible scholars sometimes talk about a revived Roman Empire to be made up of ten nations which will give their authority and allegiance to a single leader. This satanically controlled man will rule in the geographic area of the old Roman Empire. That's why many Christians have followed the rapidly evolving situation in Europe with such interest—not only the breakdown of Eastern European communism, but the rise of the Western European trade bloc, the European Community (EC). We have seen a fascinating change taking place as nations which were once fiercely nationalistic and individualistic have begun to unite together into a kind of "United States of Europe."

For a while the EC comprised ten member nations, which created quite a stir among Christians looking for the rise of a ten-nation revived Roman Empire. Then the EC grew to eleven, twelve, and thirteen nations, casting doubts on whether this was indeed the prophesied community of ten kingdoms. The EC may indeed be some sort of forerunner for the revived Roman Empire—or it may not. What we do know from John's prophecy is that some sort of coalition of European nations will arise, and time will tell exactly what form that coalition will take.

Proud Words and Blasphemies

Let us return now to Revelation 13 and witness the actions of this grotesque beast—and the effect his actions have upon the world.

13:5–6 *The beast was given a mouth to utter proud words and blasphemies and to exercise his authority for forty-two months. He opened his mouth to blaspheme God, and to slander his name and his dwelling place and those who live in heaven.*

What sort of activity is John describing? What does he mean by "proud words and blasphemies"?

We must understand that *blasphemy,* as the term is used in Scripture, does not mean "cursing." When you hear someone rip off a round oath, that is cursing, not blasphemy. To blaspheme is to claim godlike powers, to claim oneself to be God, or to identify God with lesser persons or objects. Idolatry is blasphemy, for example, because when a person worships an idol he is reducing God to the same level as that idol.

Claiming to have godlike powers is blasphemy—a sin which many leaders in the New Age and self-fulfillment movements are guilty of—because this act places God and human beings on the same level.

Those who ridicule and slander people who believe in God also commit a form of blasphemy. When John speaks in this passage of "those who live in heaven" (and a more precise translation would be "those who tabernacle in heaven"), he is not speaking of those who have died and gone to heaven, but of saints who live on the earth yet whose lives are governed by heavenly realities. They "tabernacle in heaven" because they believe in the unseen spiritual realm of heaven and their thinking is guided by the Word of God. As Christians, we are strangers and sojourners on the earth, and our citizenship (as the apostle Paul says) is in heaven.[1]

Beyond Space and Time

In verses 7 and 8 we learn more about this world leader whom the book of Revelation calls the beast, and of the power he wields throughout the world.

13:7–8 *He was given power to make war against the saints and to conquer them. And he was given authority over every tribe, people, language and nation. All inhabitants of the earth will worship the beast—all whose names have not been written in the book of life belonging to the Lamb that was slain from the creation of the world.*

The beast, the leader of the revived Roman Empire, is given enormous power—including the power of life and death over every nation and culture in the world. The beast will have achieved the dream of every conquering tyrant in history, from Alexander the Great and Genghis Khan to Napoleon and Hitler: complete domination over all the world.

This does not mean that he will directly rule every nation on earth, but his rule and influence will be so vast and far-reaching that every other government will bend to his will. If he sneezes in Rome, they'll say "Gesundheit!" in Beijing, Moscow, and New York—metaphorically speaking. You can get some sense of the influence this leader will have when you picture the influence wielded by a superpower such as the United States—only in his case there will be no other superpower to oppose him or restrain his actions.

All around the world, people will die by the thousands at his command. Among those who die will be many believers, martyred for Christ in the last days of human history. These will be the martyrs we saw in Revelation 7, that great multitude of martyrs which no man could number, coming out of the Tribulation from all nations, languages, tribes, and peoples. These are the ones who have washed their robes in the blood of the Lamb and made them white—and they will pay the ultimate price for opposing the leader of the revived Roman Empire.

In verse 8 there is a reference to "All inhabitants of the earth." This sentence in verse 8 should actually read, "All the earth dwellers will worship the beast." We have seen this term before in Revelation, and it is a reference not to those who live on planet Earth, but to those who live only for this world, the materialists and humanists who have no use for heavenly things, no heavenly citizenship, no life except the so-called "good life" here on earth.

In contrast to these materialistic "earth dwellers" are "those who tabernacle in heaven," whose names are "written in the book of life belonging to the Lamb that was slain from the creation of the world." This is an amazing statement, and we will learn more about the book of life later in Revelation. But for now let's focus on one implication of this statement: the timeless, eternal dimension of the cross of Christ.

Notice that phrase: "the Lamb that was slain from the creation of the world." This statement confirms again that time is not a factor in eternity. The death of the Lamb actually took place in time, on earth, at a specific date on the calendar—yet it is reckoned here as an eternal event which has meaning for people who have lived ever since the beginning of time. That is why an Old Testament saint such as Abraham could be born again by grace through faith just like a New Testament saint—even though the tree which would be hewn into the cross of Christ had not even been planted as a seed in Abraham's time!

The death of Jesus Christ was an event that can be fixed at a particular set of coordinates in space and time—yet it is also the summit of God's eternal program, utterly *transcending* both space and time. Thus the cross casts its shadow over all of creation.

The Law of Consequences

John now picks up the refrain which Jesus used repeatedly throughout His ministry and in His seven letters to the seven churches of Asia: "He who has an ear, let him hear." In other words, "Listen up! Important message coming!"

13:9–10 *He who has an ear, let him hear.*
   If anyone is to go into captivity,
      into captivity he will go.

> *If anyone is to be killed with the sword,*
> *with the sword he will be killed.*
> *This calls for patient endurance and faithfulness on the part of the saints.*

Every now and then I must correct what I consider to be mistranslations in the New International Version, which we are using as our study text. At times it is simply not a good reflection of the meaning of the original text. In fact, the NIV translation of verses 9 and 10 is virtually meaningless, since the phrase "If anyone is to go into captivity, into captivity he will go" is a tautology, a statement that restates itself. Here is how those verses *should* read:

> He who has an ear, let him hear.
> If anyone leads [others] into captivity,
>   into captivity he will go.
> If anyone kills with the sword,
>   with the sword he will be killed.
> This calls for patient endurance and faithfulness on the part of
> the saints.

There is a big difference in these translations, is there not? Now these words have a sharp edge of meaning to them. They are words of encouragement to the saints of the last days. All over the earth faithful people are being imprisoned and killed, but God doesn't want the faithful to be discouraged. He is saying, "Judgment is coming soon, and those who have persecuted you will receive the consequences of their sin. Don't let the injustice and the slaughter of these days hinder your faith. Hang in there! Endure for my sake! Keep the faith!"

These verses tell us that the law of consequences cannot be suspended forever. God has not forgotten any injustice committed against His children. He cannot be mocked—and neither can we. Even though it looks like evil has triumphed for now, judgment is on the way. Sooner or later the one who kills with the sword dies by the sword. The one who takes hostages must someday be taken into captivity. So God calls His people to wait, to endure, and to remain faithful, as in the lines of James Russell Lowell:

> Though the cause of evil prosper,
>   Yet 'tis truth alone that's strong.
> Truth, forever on the scaffold,
>   Wrong, forever on the throne,

Yet that scaffold sways the future,
And behind the dim unknown,
Standeth God within the shadows
Keeping watch above His own!

A Second Beast

John sees another beast—this time rising out of the earth.

13:11–12 *Then I saw another beast, coming out of the earth. He had two horns like a lamb, but he spoke like a dragon. He exercised all the authority of the first beast on his behalf, and made the earth and its inhabitants worship the first beast, whose fatal wound had been healed.*

Throughout the book of Revelation, the earth appears as a symbol of Israel. Since this beast arises out of the earth most biblical scholars believe that this beast represents a leader among the Jews. He comes from Israel and has "two horns like a lamb" yet he speaks "like a dragon." He is a dangerous fraud—a dragon in sheep's clothing! This is the Antichrist, the one who comes instead of Christ, the one who blasphemously offers himself *as though he were Christ*! It is for this reason that I believe the term *Antichrist* should properly be applied to this *second* beast, although *both* beasts are anti-Christian in character.

Notice that this beast has "two horns like a lamb." Horns symbolize power, so this man has two lamb-like powers. They are two of the same powers Jesus has: the power of a priest and the power of a prophet. This second beast—the Antichrist—acts as both priest and prophet, thus usurping the role of Jesus. Just as Jesus is our High Priest, leading us toward true worship of the Father, the Antichrist will lead the world toward worship of the first beast.

Many Bible scholars have noted that at this point in Revelation we have the unveiling of an unholy trinity. The first beast corresponds to the Father, the second beast corresponds to the Son, and the dragon—Satan himself—plays the role of the invisible Holy Spirit. This is Satan's imitation of the true God.

The second beast—the Antichrist or false prophet-priest—accomplishes his aim of seducing the world into worship of the first beast in a powerfully graphic way.

13:13–15 *And he performed great and miraculous signs, even causing fire to come down from heaven to earth in full view of men. Because of the* *signs he was given power to do on behalf of the first beast, he deceived the inhabitants of the earth [again, this phrase is better rendered "those who dwell on the earth"]. He ordered them to set up an image in honor of the beast who was wounded by the sword and yet lived. He was given power to give breath to the image of the first beast, so that it could speak and cause all who refused to worship the image to be killed.*

Here we see the second beast performing his satanic parody of an Old Testament prophet. The prophets of old acted as channels for God's miraculous power in order to establish their authority to speak for God. The Lord worked fabulous miracles through His servants Moses and Elijah. His two witnesses in the last days (who, as I stated earlier, are probably Moses and Elijah returned to the earth) will also do fabulous miracles, including calling down fire from heaven.

Paul tells us that the devil has power to produce miracles as well.[2] So we must not trust every miracle, assuming it has been done by God. It may be the work of the Enemy, Satan himself. That is exactly the kind of miracle the second beast performs in Revelation 13 where he draws upon demonic powers to call down fire from the sky in imitation of the miracles of God's true prophets. By this blasphemous demonstration of satanic power, the false prophet deceives the world.

Many Bible scholars have concluded that since the Antichrist/false prophet is a Jew, he has his headquarters in Jerusalem. I tend to agree. I believe he is the one whom the prophet Daniel identifies as making a covenant with the Jews for one "week"—that is, for seven years. With this covenant, he will seemingly resolve the centuries-old riddle of the Middle East: the ancient hatreds between the Arabs and Jews whose roots are co-mingled in the soil of Palestine.

As a result of this covenant, the way will be cleared for the rebuilding of the Jewish temple on Mount Moriah, probably alongside rather than replacing the ancient shrines of Islam, as we saw in Revelation 11 (see chapter 17). During this seven-year period the Jews will be led to believe that the reconstructed temple is for the worship of the one true God, Jehovah. But Daniel predicts that this "prince who will come" shall break the covenant in the middle of the "week"—that is, after only 3 1/2 years—and he will enter the temple himself, exalt himself as God, and receive the worship of the world. This same prediction is made by the apostle Paul in his second letter to the Thessalonians.[3]

Notice that the *political* leader of the European coalition is in Rome. The *religious* leader, meanwhile, is headquartered in Jerusalem. There he causes an image of the Roman leader to be erected in the temple for the worship of the world. Moreover, John says that the Antichrist "was given power to give breath to the image of the first beast, so that it could speak and cause all who refused to worship the image to be killed." How does the second beast give life to the image of the first beast?

If you have been to Disneyland or Walt Disney World, you have seen so-called "audio-animatronic" figures—for example, Abraham Lincoln in the Hall of Presidents exhibit. These amazingly lifelike figures are the result of a robotic technology that was first developed in the 1960s and which continues to be improved year by year. They move and speak and gesture with near-human ease. They nearly convince you they are alive.

Technological trickery is only one form of "magic" we humans are susceptible to. The master illusionist David Copperfield has made elephants float in the air and once convinced a live audience (as well as a TV audience of millions) that he had caused the Statue of Liberty to disappear.

Will the false prophet employ some Disneyesque technology to "give breath to the image of the first beast"? Or will he create an illusion in the style of David Copperfield? Or will he employ out-and-out demonic magic?

It hardly matters. As science writer Arthur C. Clarke once said, "Any sufficiently advanced technology is indistinguishable from magic." By whatever means he chooses to employ, the false prophet will create an idol in the temple that will be so impressive, so awe-inspiring, so lifelike and convincing that he will be able to claim godlike powers for both himself and the first beast—and the world will *rush* to give him the worship and obedience he demands.

The Number of the Beast

In verses 16 through 18 we see the power that this second beast, the Antichrist, wields over the world's economic system.

13:16–18 *He also forced everyone, small and great, rich and poor, free and slave, to receive a mark on his right hand or on his forehead, so that no one could buy or sell unless he had the mark, which is the name of the beast or the number of his name.*

This calls for wisdom. If anyone has insight, let him calculate the number of the beast, for it is man's number. His number is 666.

This passage indicates that worldwide commerce will be rigidly controlled from a central headquarters. The technology to accomplish this is already in place. It's called a credit card. A person's entire credit profile can be encoded on that little magnetic strip on the back of the credit card so that any merchant will instantly know if you are credit-worthy—or a dead-beat. Thanks to the credit card, we are rapidly becoming a cashless society.

It used to be that all transactions were carried out with legal tender—what we think of as "real money," coins and dollar bills. The ability to write checks made it possible to keep better track of our spending while freeing us from having to carry so much cash on our person. Banks and merchants report that from the mid-1980s to the beginning of the 1990s the use of checks as purchasing instruments has declined by about 50 percent, while credit card use has skyrocketed! We have become a plastic society!

What's the next step? The technology already exists that would enable us to miniaturize a person's credit profile to such a degree that it would fit on a tiny disk implanted on a person's skin—say, on the back of the hand or on the forehead. A person's identification and credit profile could be read by simply having his or her disk implant read by a scanning device, like the bar code readers in supermarkets. This would be a likely solution to the growing problem of lost or stolen credit cards.

As we compare the book of Revelation to the rapidly changing world around us, we detect an almost science-fictional quality to the vision of John. Many of the predictions found in Revelation could never have taken place in his own era because the *technology* did not exist. When he described the entire world witnessing the deaths and exhibited bodies of the two witnesses in Revelation 11, John seemed to anticipate today's technology of satellite TV. Here in Revelation 13 he seems to foresee our present trend toward a completely electronic economy. This is yet another sign that the events described in Revelation may be drawing very near.

Though Satan seems incapable of creating anything new or good, he appears obsessed with producing hellishly distorted imitations of the real things of God. In this same vein, the mark John describes as imprinted on the right hand or forehead of the people of the last days can only be Satan's imitation of God's seal on His own people.

In Revelation 7 we learned that 144,000 people from the tribes of Israel were sealed on their foreheads by God. This seal indicates God's ownership of these people. They belong to Him. Moreover, the apostle Paul says that Christians are sealed today by the Holy Spirit. God's Spirit comes to dwell in us and He will never leave us. It is the sign that we belong to God. "You are not your own," says Paul, "you were bought at a price."[4]

Christians in the first century often had to make a public choice once a year. They had to choose between declaring "Caesar is Lord" or "Jesus is Lord." Many died because they would not say "Caesar is Lord." In the last days this kind of persecution will be revived. Believers will again be required to make a public choice. Inspired by Satan, these two leaders will force people to declare the condition of their ownership. They will be required to say either, "The beast is Lord" or "Jesus is Lord." There will be no middle ground.

The mark that John describes is said to be either the name of the beast or the number of his name. This is a reference to the first, not the second, beast. Later in Revelation, the second beast will be called "the false prophet" and the first beast will simply be called "the beast." The mark, then, is the name or number of the first beast. His name is not given, but the number is: 666.

I would hasten to add that I believe there is no more foolish waste of time than trying to identify some person living today as the beast of Revelation, using the number 666 as a secret code of some sort. People have spent hours and hours on such attempts and have even written entire books on the subject. Those efforts are doomed to failure—and for several very good reasons.

The theory goes that if you substitute numbers for letters you can arrive at a numerical value that will add up to 666 and that will give you the name of the beast. Many ancient languages used letters for numbers. In Roman numerals, for example, I = 1, V = 5, X = 10, L = 50, C = 100, and so on. The Greek language also had alpha-numerical equivalents. The obvious fallacy so many seem to ignore is that they are trying to solve this riddle using the English alphabet! This makes as much sense as a first-century Greek trying to work the crossword puzzle in today's *New York Times!*

The list of individuals who have been identified as the beast by number-crunching Bible scholars down through the years is as long as your arm. Let me list just a few of the lucky candidates who have made the list:

Caligula, the mad despot of Rome, was one of the first. His name has been calculated to add up to 666. Interestingly, civil unrest in Palestine in the winter of A.D. 39 led Caligula to issue an order that his statue be erected in the Temple of Jerusalem—an order he later withdrew.

Nero was another. A few years after the death of Caligula, Nero became ruler of Rome. "No one has known all that a prince could do," he announced, and proceeded to proclaim himself God over all the many cultures then under Roman rule—including the culture of the Jews. By means of tortuous calculations, his name also was made to add up to 666.

With a little manipulation the name of one of Nero's successors, Domitian, also was calculated as equaling 666. As was the name of Muhammad. And Oliver Cromwell, John Knox, and Martin Luther. A varied assortment of Roman Catholic popes made the list. In our own century, the list has included such mixed company as Adolf Hitler, John F. Kennedy, Henry Kissinger, Pope John Paul II, and Mikhail Gorbachev. By one inventive method or another, the name of each one of these individuals was somehow calculated to equal 666. Obviously they can't all be the beast!

We need to remember what John says in verse 18: "This calls for wisdom." The method that most people employ to figure out the identity of the beast is simply ridiculous. It requires no wisdom—just a cheap pocket calculator. "If anyone has insight," says John, "let him calculate the number of the beast." As the above list of "suspects" makes abundantly clear, on this subject we seem to have a shortage of insight—but no shortage of imagination!

Of all the flawed thinking that has been employed by people trying to unmask the beast, perhaps the most fatuous error of all is the simple misreading of Revelation 13:18. Look at the text again:

> This calls for wisdom. If anyone has insight, let him calculate the number of the beast, for it is man's number. His number is 666.

The clue is in the line, "for it is man's number." It doesn't say, "for it is *a* man's number." It is *man's* number. There's a big difference. The number of the beast is not a number associated with a particular individual. This number is a symbol that reveals the *character* of the beast. It reflects the claims and actions and lifestyle of the beast.

If you see someone who demands worship and adulation as if he were God; if you hear him make claims of unusual powers and grandiose prerogatives; if he makes himself out to be a master of heavenly mysteries and a teacher of hidden knowledge; if he commands your loyalty and obedience and faith—then you are listening to a man who reflects the mind and spirit of 666. That is man's number.

As often happens, people have taken the number of the beast and twisted it into a more complicated and convoluted (not to mention ludicrous!) mystery than God ever intended. Playing puzzle games with numerological formulae is an occult practice—not sound Christian doctrine. As Eugene Peterson very wisely observes, the current obsession with treating the number of the beast as a religious guessing game "is not divine mystery, but a confidence man's patter; it is religion that makes a show, religion that vaunts itself, religion that takes our eyes off of the poor and suffering and holy Christ. In the language of numbers, 666 is a triple failure to be a 777, the three-times perfect, whole, divine number."[5]

Rightly and wisely understood, there is a two-pronged message of genuine assurance in Revelation 13:9–18, beginning with the clarion call, "He who has an ear, let him hear." It is a message of practical, meaningful counsel for those who are called upon to endure opposition, persecution, and the testing of their faith, both in the last days and in our own day. Following are the two prongs of this message:

First, John is encouraging those who suffer under persecution and oppression to endure faithfully. God is sovereign, and He will not allow injustice to win in the end. Sooner or later, the human instruments of Satan's plan will hang themselves, just as Judas did.

But in his attempt to control the world and destroy God's people, Satan will influence the governments of the world to become totalitarian and barbaric in their control over every aspect of their citizens' lives. Those governments, under the domination of the devil, will attempt to control not only the behavior but the beliefs of their people. They will use violence, torture, and intimidation to maintain that control. That is why John says,

> He who has an ear, let him hear.
> If anyone leads [others] into captivity,
>   into captivity he will go.
> If anyone kills with the sword,
>   with the sword he will be killed.
> This calls for patient endurance and faithfulness on the part
> of the saints.

The second prong of John's message is this: Be on guard, be discerning, "test the spirits" (as John says in his epistles) to see whether they are of God or of Satan.[6] And John goes on to tell us the warning signs to watch for: When anyone ascribes godlike prerogatives to himself, makes pretentious claims, demands obedience, professes to possess supernatural powers and an inside connection with higher realms, that is not God talking. It is just man—fallen, limited, sinful, proud, arrogant, ridiculous man! He claims to be the Lamb, but he is just a goat! He claims to be 777, but he is only 666!

So refuse to be deceived by him. Refuse to follow him. Even laugh at him—but remember that he is also dangerous. He may persecute you. He may take your possessions, your freedom, your family, and even your life away from you. Be prepared to hold out even unto death.

This is the two-pronged message of both encouragement and warning in Revelation 13. It is a message that is gaining new urgency and new relevance with each passing day. The pace of world events is quickening. We are approaching the great cataract of human history.

He who has an ear, let him hear—and be prepared.

Chapter Twenty

The Time of Harvest

Revelation 14

My generation will always remember comedian Jimmy Durante for his big heart, his generous nose, his felt hat, and of course that *voice*—a voice like a road-grader rasping on coarse gravel. In the 1950s, Durante hosted a television show, an episode of which featured a guest appearance by the great opera singer Helen Traubel.

During the show, Durante and Traubel sang a duet called "The Song's Gotta Come from the Heart." The unlikely pairing of "the Schnozzola" and the opera diva was such a hit with the audience that Durante and Traubel later recorded the song. The record was an extraordinary success.

Madame Traubel later observed, "It's a pleasure to record with a great *artiste* whose voice sounds just as good on a phonograph with a bad needle."

How is *your* singing voice? Is it a "scratchy-needle voice" like Durante's, an operatic voice like Madame Traubel's, or somewhere in between? Can you imagine being called upon to sing before an audience of 144,000 people?

As we approach Revelation 14, we find that this is exactly what is in store for us. Durante and Traubel sang, "The Song's Gotta Come from the Heart," and if ever there was a song that came straight from the heart, it is the song sung by the heavenly choir of the redeemed.

14:1–5 *Then I looked, and there before me was the Lamb, standing on Mount Zion, and with him 144,000 who had his name and his Father's name written on their foreheads. And I heard a sound from heaven like the roar of rushing waters and like a loud peal of thunder. The sound I heard was like that of harpists playing their harps. And they sang a new song before the throne and before the four living creatures and the elders. No one could learn the song except the 144,000 who had been redeemed from the earth. These are those who did not defile themselves with women, for they kept themselves pure. They follow the Lamb wherever he goes. They were purchased from among men and offered as firstfruits to God and the Lamb. No lie was found in their mouths; they are blameless.*

Here is a reappearance of the 144,000 chosen out of all the tribes of Israel, last seen in Revelation 7. John Wesley once said, "Give me a hundred men who love nothing but God and hate nothing but sin, and I will shake the whole world for Christ." In Revelation 14, we see that Jesus will choose not twelve, not even Wesley's hundred, but *144,000 men!* And, they will indeed *shake* the whole world right to its foundations in the closing days of this age.

Notice, first of all, the *location* of the 144,000 and the Lamb. The opening sentence tells us they are "standing on Mount Zion," that is, the Temple Mount in Jerusalem. The setting of this passage, clearly, is here on earth, in the city of Jerusalem in Israel—not heaven. The 144,000 are "Christ's Commandos," believing Jewish men chosen out of the twelve tribes of Israel and sealed by the Spirit of God for a special task: the evangelization of the world in the last days. In Revelation 14 we see them standing alongside the Lamb, Jesus Himself, upon the Temple Mount.

Heaven on Earth

Because of the non-chronological way John's vision is unfolding, you may be wondering just where Revelation 14 fits into the sequence of events of the last days. So let's tie up some loose ends. At this point in history, the "Rapture" or departure of the church has already taken place. The believers of our own age—the church age—have been removed in the event Paul refers to in 1 Thessalonians 4, where he describes Christ's coming to remove His church from the world. Paul concludes the fourth chapter of his first letter to the Thessalonians with the words, "so we ever will be with the Lord forever."

So at the time the 144,000 servants of the Lord stand on Mount Zion with Jesus, the earth is undergoing the throes of the Tribulation and the church has been removed to heaven. But please understand this: even though the church is "in heaven," it is still "on the earth." The church is in the heavenly realm, the heavenly dimension—but it is, as Paul said, "with the Lord," and the Lord is on the Temple Mount with the 144,000 faithful men of Israel. If this seems confusing to you, it is probably because of a common misconception many people have about heaven.

The problem is that when people think of heaven, they picture a place up in the clouds or far off in outer space. This is the same mistake Soviet cosmonaut Gherman Titov made when he returned from an orbital space-flight in 1961 and reported, "In my travels around the earth, I looked around and I didn't see God or angels or heaven." Like that Soviet space-man, we are mentally bound to stereotypes of heaven as being "in the sky." We have trouble picturing heaven as occupying not only all of space but all of earth as well.

Heaven, as it is pictured in the Bible, is actually another dimension of existence, just beyond the reach of our five senses. You can be in heaven at the same time you are on earth. As I read these prophetic passages of Scripture, I become more and more convinced that this is clearly the case: the church *is* with the Lord—but the *Lord* is on the *earth* throughout those seven turbulent years! The church is with the Lord, but it is invisible to the rest of the world, ministering to this select group of 144,000 Jews. During this time, Jesus will periodically appear to these living Jews, standing with them and empowering them for their mission.

If this is true, then Jesus will be in exactly the same condition with them as He was with the eleven disciples after His resurrection, when for a period of 40 days He appeared to them from time to time. As you examine the gospel accounts of the time between the Lord's resurrection and ascension, you find He was often with them in various times, various places, and suddenly He would not be with them. It was as if He would step back into the realm of invisibility after appearing for a while in their midst.

Now, in Revelation 14, we have pictured for us a similar set of appearances by the risen Christ—only instead of appearing to twelve disciples, He appears to *12 times 12 times 1,000*, all men of Israel chosen for a special mission during the last days.

What does Scripture tell us about these 144,000 men?

A New Song

First, *these men learn a new song which they hear from heaven*. They hear a great choir of voices singing the song of the redeemed.

Who is in this choir? Rather than stating the answer to this question plainly, the passage gives us some tantalizing (and, I think, definitive) clues. Verse 3 simply describes this choir with a pronoun: "And *they* sang a new song. . . ." And the sound of that song was like "the roar of rushing waters and like a loud peal of thunder." But it was also a sweet sound, "like that of harpists playing their harps."

Surely, what the 144,000 hear is the church, which is "with the Lord," singing the song of the redeemed! You and I will be in the choir. Even if we have "scratchy-needle voices," we will be there, belting out the greatest song ever sung. The sound of it will be as powerful as the sound of rushing water and the clap of thunder, yet the beauty of it will be like a symphony of harps!

That song will ring in the ears of the 144,000 living, mortal men of Israel, all followers of the risen Messiah, as they stand on the Temple Mount. These men will be like those described by Henry David Thoreau, who said, "If a man does not keep pace with his companions, perhaps it is because he hears a different drummer." The 144,000 will be out of step with the rest of the world, because they will be committed men, hearing the beat of a different drum, the melody of a different reality, the music of heaven itself.

The 144,000 will learn the song of the redeemed because it will reverberate in their souls. They will know by their own experience what redemption truly means.

Celibates, Not Chauvinists

The second thing we learn from Scripture about the 144,000 is that *they have kept themselves for the Lord alone*. They are separated unto Jesus. "These are those," says the passage, "who did not defile themselves with women, for they kept themselves pure."

Understand that this passage is not an insult to women, to marriage, or to sex. These men are not chauvinists. They are celibates. Marriage is not pictured here as wrong for everyone, but marriage would be outside of God's will for these 144,000 specially dedicated men.

The apostle Paul once explained that the reason he himself was unmarried was to devote his life totally to the Lord. A married person has concerns and responsibilities that have to do with maintaining a good marriage relationship and managing the affairs of the household. This is as it should be. But an unmarried person is free to do things a married person cannot. An unmarried person is even free to undertake risks and demanding tasks, if need be, in order to serve Jesus. That is the special condition of these 144,000 redeemed men of Israel.

Followers of the Lamb

The third thing we learn about these men is that *they were committed to following the Lamb* wherever He would lead them, anywhere on the earth. I believe these 144,000 are the "brothers" the Lord refers to in Matthew 25, when He says that when He comes again as the Son of Man, He will sit on His throne and will judge the nations according to how they have treated "the least of these brothers of mine." Those who hate and persecute the 144,000 chosen men of Israel will have much to answer for in the day of worldwide judgment.

Firstfruits of the Harvest

The fourth thing we learn about the 144,000 is that *they are called the "firstfruits" of the harvest* during the Tribulation period. We have seen that when these men go out to preach to the world, a great multitude, beyond human ability to number, will respond to their message— people from every tribe and nation and people and language. We will see another aspect of this harvest in Revelation 20:14-15.

Transformed Men

The fifth thing we learn about them is that *they are transformed men.* They are born again. They have been cleansed and changed by God's grace in a miraculous way. "No lie was found in their mouths," says the passage. "They are blameless." These redeemed Jews recognize their crucified Messiah, and they have committed their lives to Him. As Jude's epistle tells us, all those who truly believe in Jesus Christ will be presented to God "without fault and with great joy."[1]

The First Angel and the Gospel of Creation

Suddenly the scene of the vision changes, and John describes what he sees: three angels flying through the heavens. Each in turn makes a significant announcement.

14:6–7 *Then I saw another angel flying in midair, and he had the eternal gospel to proclaim to those who live on the earth—to every nation, tribe, language and people. He said in a loud voice, "Fear God and give him glory, because the hour of his judgment has come. Worship him who made the heavens, the earth, the sea and the springs of water."*

Notice that John refers to the gospel which this angel proclaims as the "eternal gospel," the gospel that lasts for ever and ever. We learn from the angel's words that this gospel is the gospel of creation. That is, it is a testimony to the creative power and love of God which we find all around us in nature. The angel tells everyone living on the earth to worship God who made the heavens and the earth.

This is one of several references in Scripture to the fact that the universe itself is a witness to the reality of God. "The heavens declare the glory of God," says Psalm 19, "the skies proclaim the work of his hands." And in Romans 1, the apostle Paul writes, "For since the creation of the world God's invisible qualities—his eternal power and divine nature—have been clearly seen, being understood from what has been made. . . ."

Many years ago, before the present state of conflict that exists between science and religion, scientists used to view the created order as irrefutable evidence of God. For example, the German astronomer Johannes Kepler (1571–1630) saw God as a "Divine Mathematician" whose mind could be discovered in the precise mechanics of the universe. And Sir Isaac Newton (1643–1727) saw God as the "Divine Presence" who set the universe in motion. "This most beautiful system of the Sun, planet and comets," wrote Newton, "could only proceed from the counsel and dominion of an intelligent and powerful Being."

You and I are a part of the created order, too. Our very being—the miracle of our self-aware souls and our "fearfully and wonderfully made" bodies—bears witness to the existence and glory of God. We breathe because God has put the breath of life in us. We think because God made us in His image—intelligent, feeling creatures patterned after One who thinks and feels. As Paul said to the Athenians, "In him we live and move and have our being." This is the fundamental cry of nature: "Your existence, and the existence of all that is, bears witness to the existence of God. You cannot live without Him. Therefore, worship Him!"

In the great faith chapter of the New Testament the writer to the Hebrews says, "Anyone who comes to him must believe that he exists, and that he rewards those who earnestly seek him."[2] That is the basis for God's judgment of mankind. In that day He will, in effect, ask mankind, "You knew I was essential to your very existence. Did you worship me?"

The Second Angel and the Cry against "Babylon"

14:8 *A second angel followed and said, "Fallen! Fallen is Babylon the Great, which made all the nations drink the maddening wine of her adulteries."*

This is the first mention in Revelation of "Babylon the Great." In chapters 17 and 18, "Babylon" will move onto center stage, symbolized by a woman who rides the beast mentioned in the previous chapter. We will explore the meaning of "Babylon" more fully in the next chapter, but for now it is enough to note that "Babylon" is a reference to the false church—the church which professes to be Christian but which really is not. It is this false church, "Babylon," which is destined to go through the great Tribulation after the true church is removed.

Before it even appears in the text, God wants us to know that this false church, "Babylon," is treacherous and adulterous—and doomed to fall.

The Third Angel and the Warning against the Beast

14:9–11 *A third angel followed them and said in a loud voice: "If anyone worships the beast and his image and receives his mark on the forehead or on the hand, he, too, will drink of the wine of God's fury, which has been poured full strength into the cup of his wrath. He will be tormented with burning sulfur in the presence of the holy angels and of the Lamb. And the smoke of their torment rises for ever and ever. There is no rest day or night for those who worship the beast and his image, or for anyone who receives the mark of his name."*

In Revelation 13, we saw that the Antichrist will exert total economic control over the whole world. No one will be able to buy or sell without the mark of the beast imprinted upon the back of the hand or the forehead. Now in the words of the third angel we see that to accept that mark is to make a fatal choice. Anyone who receives that mark will experience the fury of God's wrath to the dregs.

Do you find this troubling? I suspect any grace-oriented Christian would be shocked by this "fire and brimstone" passage of the Bible. Some Christians may go so far as to find this depiction of wrath contrary to the gospel of love that is found elsewhere in the New Testament.

Yet I submit to you that there is no contradiction in the Scriptures or in God's character in the matter of wrath and grace. Throughout the Bible, we see that God's love is freely available to men and women everywhere, and at all times, over and over, we see God *pleading* with mankind to accept the escape from judgment that He has made available by the sacrifice of His Son.

"Do not allow yourself to come to such an end," is the continual urging of God. "I love you and I can provide everything you need. Love me, and find the fulfillment your heart longs for." Yet many men and women respond, "No, God, I do not want to love you. I will take the life you give me and all the good things you provide, but I do not want you. I will run my own life, serve my own ends, rule my own kingdom." God has three choices in the face of such human rebellion.

One: He can indulge it and allow it to go on forever. But in that case all the cruelty, injustice, hatred, pain, and death that now prevails on the earth will go on forever, too. God does not want that—and neither does man.

Two: God can *force* man to obey and control the human race as if it were a race of robots. But to take away our free will would be to take away our capacity to give our love to God freely. Love cannot be forced.

Three: This is God's only *real* choice. He must withdraw Himself from those who refuse His love. He must let them have their way forever. Since God is necessary to our existence, the decision to reject God is a decision to plunge ourselves into the most terrible sense of loneliness and isolation a human being can know.

Ultimately, it is *we* who choose whether God will judge us. It is *we* who decide either to accept or refuse His grace, love, and forgiveness. It is *we* who choose everlasting life—or everlasting death.

A Resurrection Promise

Again, light breaks through to brighten a bleak scene as John records a message of encouragement for the faithful saints of that day.

14:12–13 *This calls for patient endurance on the part of the saints who obey God's commandments and remain faithful to Jesus.*

Then I heard a voice from heaven say, "Write: Blessed are the dead who die in the Lord from now on."

"Yes," says the Spirit, "they will rest from their labor, for their deeds will follow them."

While the earth is filled with violence and hate, while the smoke of the torment of the beast's followers billows into the sky, the calling of the faithful is to wait with patience and perseverance. To those who die under the persecution of this period, Jesus makes a promise: "Blessed are the dead who die in the Lord from now on."

Notice especially that last phrase, "from now on." Why does the Lord add this phrase? Certainly, all who have ever died in the Lord are blessed, aren't they? As a pastor, I have stood by many a graveside and have repeated the words, "Blessed are the dead who die in the Lord. They shall rest from their labor and their deeds will follow them."

But there is a special reason why John, under the direction of the Lord Jesus, adds the words, "from now on." The Lord wants to give a special word of reassurance to these saints in the last days because, living in such a hostile and evil world, they will feel that they have missed the resurrection! The church has already been taken out of the world, and the dead in Christ have already been raised. Many of these latter-day faithful will begin to wonder, "If I die now, after the departure of the church and the resurrection of the dead, will I also be resurrected—or have I forever missed my opportunity?" This is the same sort of doubt Paul addressed when he wrote,

> Brothers, we do not want you to be ignorant about those who
> fall asleep, or to grieve like the rest of men, who have no hope.
> We believe that Jesus died and rose again and so we believe that
> God will bring with Jesus those who have fallen asleep in him.[3]

So the Lord says, in effect, "Blessed are the dead who die in the Lord *from now on.* Be encouraged and emboldened. Your resurrection is still to come. You will rest from your labor, your deeds will follow you." What a tremendous promise for all those who are faithful to the Lord, both in that future time of tribulation and right now. We have a promise of *rest* after a lifetime of trial and labor.

Rest is something we all long for. God, by His grace, has promised us rest from the labor and sorrow of this life, and a reward for the deeds we have done out of love for Him.

The Harvest

Now we come to another change of scene. We come to the time of harvest.

We have seen that the 144,000 redeemed from the tribes of Israel are the "firstfruits" of the harvest of the last days. If they were the firstfruits, the rest of the harvest cannot be far behind.

14:14–16 *I looked, and there before me was a white cloud, and seated on the cloud was one "like a son of man" with a crown of gold on his head and a sharp sickle in his hand. Then another angel came out of the temple and called in a loud voice to him who was sitting on the cloud, "Take* *your sickle and reap, because the time to reap has come, for the harvest of the earth is ripe." So he who was seated on the cloud swung his sickle over the earth, and the earth was harvested.*

Who is the one seated on the cloud "like a son of man," wearing a victor's crown and holding a sickle in His hand? There can be no doubt. It is the Lord Jesus.

Remember that in Matthew 13 Jesus gave the disciples a parable of wheat and weeds growing in a single field. In the parable the servants asked their master, "Do you want us to go and pull them up?" But the master replied, ". . . No, let both grow together until the harvest. At that time I will tell the harvesters: First collect the weeds and tie them in bundles to be burned; then gather the wheat and bring it into my barn." Then Jesus interpreted that parable to the disciples, saying, "The harvest is the end of the age [i.e. the seven-year Tribulation period to which we have come in the book of Revelation] and the harvesters are angels."

Here is how Jesus describes that end-time harvest in Matthew 13:

> The Son of Man will send out his angels, and they will weed out of his kingdom everything that causes sin and all who do evil. They will throw them into the fiery furnace, where there will be weeping and gnashing of teeth. Then the righteous will shine like the sun in the kingdom of their Father. He who has ears, let him hear.

These are plain and clear words from the lips of Jesus Himself. But there is still *another* scene of harvest.

14:17–20 *Another angel came out of the temple in heaven, and he too had a sharp sickle. Still another angel, who had charge of the fire, came from the altar and called in a loud voice to him who had the sharp sickle, "Take your sharp sickle and gather the clusters of grapes from the earth's vine, because its grapes are ripe." The angel swung his sickle on the earth, gathered its grapes and threw them into the great winepress of God's wrath. They were trampled in the winepress outside the city, and blood flowed out of the press, rising as high as the horses' bridles for a distance of 1,600 stadia [about 180 miles or 300 kilometers].*

In Revelation 14:14–16 and 17–20 we have two accounts of two harvests. Are these merely two views of the *same* harvest? Or do these two harvests actually symbolize two *different* events in the eternal plan of God?

Close examination reveals that there are several significant differences between these two harvests. Notice that the *first* harvest described in verses 14-16 is a harvest of *wheat*. It is cut with a sickle and is a separation of the true wheat from the "false wheat," or *darnel* (a weed that closely resembles true wheat). As we have seen, the angels will separate the true wheat from the false.

But what is pictured for us in verses 17–20 is a harvest of grapes, not wheat. In Scripture the vine is frequently a symbol of Israel. Both Isaiah 5 and Psalm 80, for example, describe Israel as a vine brought out of Egypt and planted by God in a new land.

What, then, does the harvest of grapes and the "winepressing" in verses 17-20 signify? It is the judgment of the apostate (unbelieving) Israel—that part of the Jewish nation which (in contrast to the 144,000 redeemed of Israel) has rejected its own Messiah.

It is a strange irony that most of the present nation of Israel does not believe its own Scriptures. Many Jews are atheists, denying the God of the Old Testament and the relevance of the Scriptures to the Jews as a specially chosen people. The "winepressing" then is a judgment for this apostasy, a judgment which Jeremiah 30 calls "the time of Jacob's trouble" and which is also described in other Old Testament passages.

The "winepressing" is a time of warfare against Israel, beginning with an invasion of the nation by great armies from the north. It is a time when Palestine will be overrun. It is at this time that the woman we saw in Revelation 12—a symbol of true, faithful Israel—will flee into the desert to hide. But apostate Israel will be destroyed, and Jerusalem itself will be sacked and partially destroyed, as described in Zechariah 14.

In Joel 3, we find this vivid prophetic description of the "winepressing" judgment:

> Let the nations be roused;
>> let them advance into the Valley of Jehoshaphat,
>> for there I will sit
>> to judge all the nations on every side.
> Swing the sickle,
>> for the harvest is ripe.
> Come, trample the grapes,
>> for the winepress is full
>> and the vats overflow—
>> so great is their wickedness!

In Revelation 14:20 we find a sudden and dramatic shift from symbolism to grim, literal reality. Grapes are thrown into the winepress (that is a symbol), but what pours out? Not symbolic wine, but literal *blood*—reminiscent of the symbolic equivalence we find in the Lord's Supper, where wine stands for the blood of Jesus Christ. In this verse, symbolism is exchanged for unadorned documentary-style reporting—the reporting of war and carnage on an unimaginable scale. In this passage we see that human history ends much as it has always been conducted—with senseless mass bloodletting.

Our earliest recorded history is largely a history of war and atrocity. For example, Shalmanesar III of Assyria, who ruled from his capital city of Nineveh, boasted in his court records, "With the blood of the enemy soldiers, I dyed the mountain as if it were wool."

In recent years, we have learned more sophisticated and efficient ways of killing than the spears and swords of ancient Assyria. When the atomic bomb was dropped on Hiroshima in 1945, 70,000 lives were extinguished in a single flash. And yet, so horrifying is the threat of nuclear war that we easily forget that atomic weapons were never necessary to produce mass slaughter.

The death toll at Hiroshima pales before the 125,000 killed by firearms and bayonets in the invasion of Iwo Jima in 1945. We also tend to forget the days of the Civil War, when our own soil was bathed in the blood of American men—a bloodletting so vast and terrible that it consumed more American lives than World Wars I and II, Korea, and Vietnam *combined*. All this bloodletting was accomplished entirely with bayonets, firearms, and cannonballs.

In Revelation 14, we see the ultimate in raw human slaughter, a slaughter so intense that all previous wars seem tame by comparison. There will be blood flowing out of the "winepress," splashing as high as a horse's bridle, covering the land for 180 miles, stretching the entire length of Israel. It is a terrible scene of judgment—and it is not a scene of nuclear devastation, but of the epidemic madness of battlefield slaughter.

Before this book is over, we will look beyond these scenes of judgment, beyond the slaughter, beyond the misery that is to come upon the earth. There is a new day coming after the judgment, after the day of the "winepress." When "Jacob's trouble" is finally over, Israel will blossom and spread its branches throughout the whole earth like a vine, and Israel's Messiah will reign. It will be the long dreamed-of Utopia.

But before that morning dawns, the long night of the human race will grow darker.

Much darker.

Chapter Twenty-One

Earth's Last Trial

Revelation 15 and 16

On Tuesday, January 29, 1991, radio listeners in St. Louis, Missouri, were startled to hear that the end of the world was just moments away. Regular radio programming was interrupted by the jarring attention signal of the Emergency Broadcast System, followed by the voice of an announcer who said, "Your attention, please! This is not a test! The United States is under nuclear attack! I repeat, this is not a test!"

Scores of people who heard the news on their car radios raced home to be with family members when the missiles begin to fall. Some made frantic phone calls to loved ones: "Get to a basement or a shelter now! . . . Yes, of course it's true! The radio said it was not a test!" Others flipped the radio dial or turned on their televisions to get confirmation of the horrible news.

Soon they discovered that only one radio station, KSHE, was carrying the alert. Everywhere else across the radio and TV dials, life went on as usual. An hour after the initial panic, radio station personnel went on the air with an announcement that the "alert" was a fake broadcast, completely unauthorized by the station management. The station apologized for the actions of disc jockey John Ulett who was attempting, in his words, "to jolt people and make people think about the horrors of nuclear war."

It jolted people, all right. But it was a stupid and irresponsible stunt, and the ensuing panic could have resulted in property damage, injury, or death for Ulett's listeners. Fortunately no one was hurt.

But for a few very long minutes, a lot of people in St. Louis got just a faint foretaste of what the earth's last trial will be like—a trial of fear, horror, death, and destruction unlike anything the world has ever known before.

In Revelation 15 and 16 we come to the final series of God's judgment, the seven bowls of wrath. At this time the great cry of the oppressed of all ages of human history will finally be answered—the cry: "How long, O Lord, how long?" After centuries of patient waiting, of putting up with man's might-means-right arrogance, greed, and murder, God finally calls a halt to the whole horrid business of human sin. As Eugene Peterson so eloquently puts it, "Surely, after all these centuries it is time to . . . call the perpetrators of these cruelties on the carpet and wipe the condescending smiles off their faces with a once-for-all judgment."

Victors over the Beast

The third and final series of judgments is about to begin. The seven bowls are poised to tip over, ready to spill out a torrent of white-hot wrath upon the rebellious human race.

15:1–4 *I saw in heaven another great and marvelous sign: seven angels with the seven last plagues—last, because with them God's wrath is completed. And I saw what looked like a sea of glass mixed with fire and, standing beside the sea, those who had been victorious over the beast and his image and over the number of his name. They held harps given them by God and sang the song of Moses the servant of God and the song of the Lamb:*

> *"Great and marvelous are your deeds,*
>   *Lord God Almighty.*
> *Just and true are your ways,*
>   *King of the ages.*
> *Who will not fear you, O Lord,*
>   *and bring glory to your name?*
> *For you alone are holy.*
>   *All nations will come*
>   *and worship before you,*
>   *for your righteous acts have been revealed."*

Notice, first of all, that this passage contains a promise from God that this is the last of the series of judgments. With these seven last plagues, writes John, "God's wrath is completed." This final set of judgments is the turning point, the historical pivot upon which God's plan now turns. At the conclusion of the seven bowls of wrath, God will begin to set up His kingdom on the earth. The book of the history of mankind will be closed. A new book will be opened, and the opening lines of the history of the kingdom of God will be written on its pages.

In this scene, John describes a great host of martyrs, men and women who have given their lives for the cause of Christ during the Antichrist's reign of terror. In his vision, John sees them standing *upon* a sea of glass or crystal (not "beside" it, as the NIV translates).

We first saw this sea of glass in Revelation 4 (see Chapter 10: "Supreme Headquarters"), and there we interpreted this symbol as representing the Holy Spirit. In particular, the sea of glass speaks of the holiness and the purity that the Spirit imparts to us when we give our lives to Jesus Christ. It is only God's purity, given to us as a gift, that enables us to stand—as these martyrs now stand—in the holy presence of God. We do not dare stand in His presence unless we are standing on the crystalline-pure support of His righteousness.

Next we notice that the sea of glass is "mixed with fire," because the holiness of the Spirit has been manifested in the lives of these martyrs amid the fire of persecution. These martyrs, John adds, "had been victorious over the beast." In the world's eyes, they were "losers." They were captured, imprisoned, reviled, hated. Some were even tortured. Then they were put to death—all for the "crime" of confessing Jesus as Lord! They were powerless, stripped of everything, even life itself. Yet upon their arrival in heaven, they are crowned as victors!

This image is a beautiful and insightful revelation of how God confounds the plans, the schemes, and the viewpoint of man. He takes defeat and stands it on its head. He transforms human evil into eternal good.

Perhaps the most pervasive defect we have as human beings is our stubborn insistence that our perceptions, our illusions should be taken for objective reality. No matter how hopelessly wrong we are, we always insist we are right. The Antichrist is the supreme example of this disordered thinking.

He imprisons, tortures, and murders the followers of Christ under the illusion that he is demonstrating his absolute power and ridding himself of his enemies. In reality, all he is doing is running a shuttle service to heaven! The Antichrist expects the world to worship him—yet he is nothing but an elevator boy in God's service, taking saints by the carload up to glory! In the Old Testament, we find that God can even speak through a donkey to accomplish His purpose.[1] Here at the end of the New Testament we see that God can even use the Antichrist to accomplish the purposes He has ordained.

The host of martyrs upon the glassy sea have two songs to sing, the Song of Moses—found in Exodus 15, the song the Israelites sang as they came out of Egypt and crossed the Red Sea—and the song of the Lamb, which is recorded here in Revelation 15:3–4. These are the first and last songs recorded in Scripture, and both are songs of God's deliverance of His people by divine power, by the blood of redemption.

When Moses and the Israelites sang the Song of Moses they were looking back to the blood of a lamb. This blood was put over the lintels of the doorposts to keep the Israelites safe when the Angel of Death passed over the land of Egypt. Any house that was not marked by the blood of the lamb would be visited by death.

In Revelation 15 the martyrs also look back to the blood of a Lamb. They praise God for delivering them by His power from the wrath of the Antichrist—a deliverance that was accomplished by the blood of redemption shed by the Lamb of God.

Notice that in the Song of the Lamb there is not one word about the martyrs' own achievements. They never say, "O Lord, how faithful we have been to you! How true we have been to your word! How patiently we have endured!" The only pronouns in this song are pronouns which refer to God:

> "Great and marvelous are *your* deeds,
>   Lord God Almighty.
> Just and true are *your* ways,
>   King of the ages.
> Who will not fear *you*, O Lord,
>   and bring glory to *your* name?
> For *you* alone are holy.
>   All nations will come
>   and worship before *you*,
>   for *your* righteous acts have been revealed."

That is the song that will be on our hearts when we too stand in the presence of God. We will certainly not feel that we have done anything. We will simply marvel in awestruck gratitude at all that God has done for us!

The Seven Last Plagues

From verse 5 to the end of chapter 15 we see the stage being set for the final judgment upon mankind. Seven angels bearing the bowls containing the seven last plagues step forth. The ultimate drama of the human race is drawing to a climax.

15:5–8 *After this I looked and in heaven the temple, that is, the tabernacle of the Testimony, was opened. Out of the temple came the seven angels with the seven plagues. They were dressed in clean, shining linen and wore golden sashes around their chests. Then one of the four living creatures gave to the seven angels seven golden bowls filled with the wrath of God, who lives for ever and ever. And the temple was filled with smoke from the glory of God and from his power, and no one could enter the temple until the seven plagues of the seven angels were completed.*

Just picture the images that John witnessed in his vision—the opening of the temple, the emergence of the angels clad in shining white and gold, the entire scene wreathed in billowing smoke that was given off by the power and glory of the living God! This awesome scene reminds us of the vision Isaiah describes in chapter 6 of his prophecy:

> In the year that King Uzziah died, I saw the Lord seated on a throne, high and exalted, and the train of his robe filled the temple. Above him were seraphs, each with six wings. . . . And they were calling to one another:
>
> "Holy, holy, holy is the LORD Almighty;
> the whole earth is full of his glory."
>
> At the sound of their voices the doorposts and thresholds shook and the temple was filled with smoke.[2]

The sight that Isaiah describes is the most awesome sight imaginable—but no more awesome than the sight John sees as the great temple of heaven opens and the seven angels file out of the Holy of Holies bearing the seven bowls of God's final wrath!

John tells us that this smoke symbolizes the powerful glory of God—and perhaps this is the origin of the old expression, "Holy smoke!" The holy smoke of God's glory fills the temple so that no one can enter it until the awesome and awful work of the angels has been accomplished.

Why can no one enter the temple? There can only be one answer—and I'm afraid it is a grim and traumatic answer indeed. I'm convinced that the fact that the temple has become impassable means that the time has come when repentance is finally no longer possible. For thousands of years God has been patient with mankind—but no longer. Once this scene of judgment begins, it will be played out to the fullest. It is then too late to pray.

The First Bowl of Judgment

Final judgment commences in Revelation 16. The seven angels pour out their bowls in rapid succession. The world has never seen such horror and suffering as this period of judgment brings. No wonder the Old Testament prophets have called this time "the great and terrible day of the Lord." This is the period Jesus described when He said, "If those days had not been cut short, no one would survive."[3]

The seven-bowls judgment represents a brief but incalculably intense period at the close of the last 3 1/2 years of the Great Tribulation. As we examine the seven bowls of wrath you will notice that each corresponds to one of the trumpet judgments. In other words, the seven bowls represent an *intensification* of the trumpet judgments we have already seen.

In Revelation 16:1-2, the first angel pours out the first bowl of wrath upon the earth.

16:1–2 *Then I heard a loud voice from the temple saying to the seven angels, "Go, pour out the seven bowls of God's wrath on the earth."*

The first angel went and poured out his bowl on the land, and ugly and painful sores broke out on the people who had the mark of the beast and worshiped his image.

As we saw in the trumpet judgments of Revelation 8 and 9, these seven bowl judgments will be both *literal* and *symbolic*. The judgments will actually occur as John describes them, but they have a symbolic meaning as well. They reveal a truth that otherwise would be unknown.

We have previously seen that the earth is a symbol for Israel. So the judgment of the first bowl being poured out upon the earth represents a judgment within the land of Israel. In a literal sense, this judgment will fall upon the whole world. In a symbolic sense, this judgment will fall with special force and horror upon apostate Jews who follow the beast, who are deceived by his lying propaganda and who accept the Antichrist rather than Jesus Christ as their Messiah.

The corruption, pain, and ugliness that will afflict the flesh of men and women in the days of the first bowl of wrath are an outward symbol of the inner corruption, pain, and ugliness of sin. This judgment is in the form of sores—painful and ugly lesions that break out over the whole body. If you have ever experienced an outbreak of boils—painful, inflamed, pus-filled swellings on the skin—you have just the barest beginning of an idea of the suffering this judgment entails.

Or you might compare this plague of sores to our present-day plague of AIDS—an epidemic that has come suddenly upon our world, a disease that was unknown just a few years ago, a disease which unleashes a host of other diseases in the body, including cancers, inflammations of the skin, and viral infections. Presently this virus can only be transmitted by an exchange of body fluids, through sexual activity, or through a drug-user's needle. But imagine what would happen if the fast-mutating AIDS virus were to change to a form that could be transmitted as easily as the common cold is now. Such an altered virus could spell the end of civilization. And someday it may.

Behaviorally transmitted diseases such as AIDS are forms of judgment on society—not in the sense that God looks down upon individual AIDS victims with the intent to destroy them, but in the sense that God has warned that certain forms of behavior carry consequences. AIDS is that kind of consequence. It is a form of God's judgment, calling us to look at ourselves and take seriously what is happening in our society.

The Second Bowl of Judgment

Here we are introduced to the second angel and the second bowl of wrath.

16:3 *The second angel poured out his bowl on the sea, and it turned into blood like that of a dead man, and every living thing in the sea died.*

The sea, as we have seen previously, represents the Gentile nations, especially those around the Mediterranean Sea within the old Roman Empire. Under this judgment the sea literally becomes blood-red. We have already seen foreshadows of this phenomenon in the so-called "red tide" which scientists have occasionally observed in the Caribbean and other seas sheltered by land masses. There is a microorganism which, given the right set of conditions, multiplies precipitously, turning the water a deep scarlet. All sea life in the affected area dies. It is a scene of horror.

Does Revelation 16:3 describe such a "red tide" of microorganism-infected seas which causes all the fish to float dead upon the surface as if on an ocean of blood? Would it occur on every ocean across the world? Surely that would be such a catastrophic event as to make life impossible on the globe.

Perhaps the "red tide" would infect only the Mediterranean. This would still be a horrible event to contemplate. If the Exxon Valdez oil spill in Alaska and the Persian Gulf spills unleashed by the Iraqis in 1991 can create such havoc, what would it be like if the entire Mediterranean "turned into blood like that of a dead man, and every living thing in the sea died"?

One can only speculate.

The Third Bowl of Judgment

We are introduced next to the third angel and the third bowl of wrath.

16:4–7 *The third angel poured out his bowl on the rivers and springs of water, and they became blood. Then I heard the angel in charge of the waters say:*
"You are just in these judgments,
you who are and who were, the Holy One,
because you have so judged;
for they have shed the blood of your saints
and prophets,
and you have given them blood to drink
as they deserve."
And I heard the altar respond:
"Yes, Lord God Almighty,
true and just are your judgments."

This judgment falls on the rivers and the springs, just as we saw in the trumpet judgment. The fresh water of the rivers becomes polluted by the same blood-like phenomenon that poisoned the saltwater seas. The literal dimension of this judgment probably takes place within the limits of the Roman world.

Symbolically, however, this judgment speaks of the pollution of the fountains of wisdom and refreshment in society—that is, the leaders of thought, the politicians, the philosophers, the writers, the scientists of our age. They are the shapers—or benders!—of minds. They are the ones to whom people look for refreshment of ideas and leadership in philosophy.

We already are witnessing the growing pollution of the fountains of wisdom and refreshment in our own society, particularly with the poisonous idea that man is his own God and has absolute sovereignty over his own destiny. The pollution of the mood and mind of our culture is growing steadily worse as we approach the day of judgment.

After this third bowl of judgment is poured out, John hears the voice of the third angel. The angel affirms that God's judgment is right and just. It is based on the principle we hear so often these days: "What goes around, comes around." What you dish out, you will someday have to take. Those who shed the blood of the prophets and the saints of God will have to drink what they have spilled: a torrent of blood.

Then something amazing takes place: the altar speaks! The altar is the symbol of redemption, of the *substitute* sacrifice, of the shedding of *innocent* blood that removes the penalty of sin from the *guilty*. In the day of judgment when it is too late to pray, even the altar, the symbol of God's mercy and grace, will declare that God is just in meting out consequences and judgment to those who have earned it.

The Fourth Bowl of Judgment

In verses 8 and 9 we are introduced to the fourth angel and the fourth bowl of wrath—and the earth turning on its axis begins to resemble a pig roasting on a spit.

16:8–9 *The fourth angel poured out his bowl on the sun, and the sun was given power to scorch people with fire. They were seared by the intense heat and they cursed the name of God, who had control over these plagues, but they refused to repent and glorify him.*

For a brief time the sun's heat is suddenly increased. Scientists are familiar with this phenomenon. Every now and then great flares of nuclear fire burst outward from the surface of the sun, interacting with the earth's magnetic field and causing disruption in radio communication. Apparently a solar flare of immense magnitude creates intense heat upon the earth. Given the reported depletion of protective ozone that is now taking place in the earth's upper atmosphere, this heat may be accompanied by an increase in ultraviolet radiation from the sun which would produce severe sunburns. The result will be widespread anguish and suffering all over the earth.

Amazingly, John's account indicates that the human race is aware that this terrible heat is the direct result of God's judgment—yet they persist in their rebellion! They know that God has done this because only God can control the sun, yet the folly of unbelief so grips their thoughts and emotions that the people of the world have lost the capacity for repentance. Their hearts are so hardened that they cannot even be melted by the torch of a solar flare.

As Albert Einstein once observed, "It is easier to denature plutonium than to denature the evil spirit of man."

The Fifth Bowl of Judgment

John now introduces us to the fifth angel and the fifth bowl of wrath.

16:10–11 *The fifth angel poured out his bowl on the throne of the beast, and his kingdom was plunged into darkness. Men gnawed their tongues in agony and cursed the God of heaven because of their pains and their sores, but they refused to repent of what they had done.*

The scope of this bowl of judgment is limited, focused upon the kingdom of the beast—that is, the revived Roman Empire of Western Europe. This judgment encompasses a great area of the earth, causing a sudden and unexplainable darkness to fall.

This is not the first time such a phenomenon has occurred. In the middle of the day on May 19, 1780, the entire region of New England was covered by darkness—a day which has become fixed in New England history as The Dark Day. The mysterious blackout lasted for several hours.

In the early afternoon of March 19, 1886, a similar zone of darkness moved across central Wisconsin, causing the sky to turn from a bright cloud-dappled blue to midnight black in the space of about a minute. This darkness blanketed several villages and towns to the west of Lake Winnebago and lasted about ten minutes. Similar unexplained occurrences of sudden darkness have occurred in Memphis, Tennessee (December 1904), Louisville, Kentucky (March 1911), and other places and times in the United States and around the world. All of these events have two things in common: (1) no one was ever able to explain these events in terms of a known phenomenon such as an eclipse, and (2) most of the people who experienced these events were filled with terror, believing the end of the world had come.

The events in the sky or beyond the sky which caused these midday nightfalls might have been the same as that which caused three hours of darkness during the crucifixion of Christ. When this event occurs again at the time of the fifth bowl judgment, it will not be a predictable, explainable event such as an eclipse of the sun. It will be strange, unforeseen, inexplicable—and therefore it will be *terrifying* to those who experience it. It will be a literal event, but it will also have a symbolic dimension.

The unexplained darkness upon the earth symbolizes the removal of moral light—the light of God's truth and righteousness—from the world. The darkness that envelops the kingdom of the beast foreshadows the terrible "outer darkness" into which Jesus says unrepentant sinners will one day be cast.[4]

The Sixth Bowl of Judgment

The judgment of the sixth bowl of wrath follows quickly after the judgment of darkness.

16:12–14 *The sixth angel poured out his bowl on the great river Euphrates, and its water was dried up to prepare the way for the kings from the East. Then I saw three evil spirits that looked like frogs; they came out of the mouth of the dragon, out of the mouth of the beast and out of the mouth of the false prophet. They are spirits of demons performing miraculous signs, and they go out to the kings of the whole world, to gather them for the battle on the great day of God Almighty.*

In the midst of this description of judgment comes an interjection. A voice seems to come out of heaven itself. It is the voice of Jesus.

16:15 *"Behold, I come like a thief! Blessed is he who stays awake and keeps his clothes with him, so that he may not go naked and be shamefully exposed."*

Then, following this interjection, the description of judgment continues, concluding with one of the most chilling words in our language, *Armageddon.*

16:16 *Then they gathered the kings together to the place that in Hebrew is called Armageddon.*

The sixth bowl judgment falls upon the Euphrates River. This river, you may recall, was mentioned also in the context of the trumpet judgments. In Revelation 9:14, at the time of the sixth trumpet judgment, four angels were released which had been bound at the Euphrates River, unleashing a war that would kill a third of the human race.

In the judgment of the sixth bowl of wrath, the judgment upon the Euphrates is again depicted as a prelude to ultimate war. As the bowl is poured out, the river dries up, preparing the way for invading armies of the "kings from the East"—that is, from nations which possibly include China, India, Japan, and other Asian countries.

We have seen in recent years that some of these countries have risen to great prosperity and military power. The transformation of Japan from a humiliated and devastated nation in 1945 to one of the most powerful economic forces of the late twentieth century is nothing less than amazing. The transformation of China from a backward agrarian economy to near-superpower status is equally amazing. We can be virtually certain that these historical changes have been in preparation for the day of judgment that is coming at the end of this age.

People are fond of quoting Rudyard Kipling's line, "East is East, and West is West, and never the twain shall meet." But that's not the entire quotation:

Oh, East is East, and West is West, and never the twain shall meet.
Till Earth and Sky stand presently at God's great Judgment Seat.[5]

Kipling knew! There is a time coming when East and West *shall* come together. It will happen in a place called Armageddon!

The Euphrates River will be dried up, and the barrier to invasion from the East will be removed. You may remember from news reports of the 1991 Gulf War how the Euphrates River formed an impassable barrier to the armies of Saddam Hussein as they attempted to retreat from U.N. forces. They were bottled up with the armies of 30 countries before them and the Euphrates at their backs. But in the day of the sixth bowl of judgment, invading armies will roll across the cracked, dry riverbed of the Euphrates—right into the jaws of World War III!

Here we are given insight into the way nations are moved by unseen forces. Leaders of nations think that they control events, when it is actually *they* who are controlled by events—and by unseen spiritual forces. In this passage we see three evil spirits in the appearance of frogs which proceed out of the mouths of the satanic trinity—the red dragon, the scarlet beast, and the false prophet. With demonic miracles they deceive the nations, manipulating and maneuvering them into launching the final war of human history.

It is a time of terror and unparalleled destruction. All the nuclear arsenals of the world will be unleashed. The armies of the world—200 million warriors—will gather into Palestine to bathe the Holy Land in blood.

At first their war will be with one another. Then in utter desperation they will turn and make war against the Lamb of God Himself!

As in each of the previous series of seven judgments, we find in this series a parenthesis, an interlude, between the sixth and seventh judgment in the series. In the seven-bowls-of-wrath series the parenthesis is only a verse long—verse 15. Here Jesus speaks, saying, "Behold, I come like a thief!" This reference to the Lord's thief-like coming resonates with Paul's words of assurance to the Thessalonians:

> Now, brothers, about times and dates we do not need to write
> to you, for you know very well that the day of the Lord will come
> like a thief in the night. While people are saying, "Peace and
> safety," destruction will come on them suddenly, as labor pains
> on a pregnant woman, and they will not escape.[6]

Paul seems to refer to the same events John records for us here. The Lord Jesus came for His church at the beginning of the seven-year Tribulation period. He and the church remain on earth—invisible and behind the scenes. But at the end of the seven years, at the very climax of history, Jesus will suddenly appear to all the world.

The purpose of the Lord's coming, as announced here, is to strip off the garments of hypocrisy with which the human race has clothed itself. We have all seen what it looks like when a person is stripped of his hypocrisy. We have seen it when a politician has had to publicly confess corruption, or when a sports figure has had to confess an addiction to drugs or gambling, or when a religious leader has had to confess to a lack of honesty and integrity before his Lord and his followers. It is always God's work to remove the facades, to expose the shams, to bring out the truth. That is why Jesus says, "Blessed is he who stays awake and keeps his clothes with him, so that he may not go naked and be shamefully exposed."

The only garments that can never be taken away from us are the garments of righteousness we have received by grace through faith in Jesus Christ. Those who are dressed in the garments of *His* righteousness in that day will be blessed indeed.

The Seventh Bowl of Judgment

Some two hundred years ago Napoleon Bonaparte stood upon a high promontory in northern Israel, looking out over the plain of Esdraelon which stretches eastward from the foot of the Mountain of Megiddo. He was silent, even brooding, as he contemplated the vast, bare expanse of land that lay at his feet. Then he said, "Here indeed all the armies of the earth may gather for battle." The plain that stretched before him is the place the Bible calls Armageddon.

World War I was once given the optimistic title of "The War to End All Wars." Clearly it was a name that couldn't stick. But the war that takes place on the plain of Esdraelon will undoubtedly be "The War to End All Wars," "The Mother of All Battles," and any other superlative you would care to add. It will precipitate the final bowl of judgment, the seventh bowl. It will ring down the final curtain on the human drama.

It will signal The End.

In verses 17 to 21 of Revelation 16, the seventh angel acts.

16:17–21 *The seventh angel poured out his bowl into the air, and out of the temple came a loud voice from the throne, saying, "It is done!" Then there came flashes of lightning, rumblings, peals of thunder and a severe earthquake. No earthquake like it has ever occurred since man has been on earth, so tremendous was the quake. The great city split into three parts, and the cities of the nations collapsed. God remembered Babylon the Great and gave her the cup filled with the wine of the fury of his wrath. Every island fled away and the mountains could not be found. From the sky huge hailstones of about a hundred pounds each fell upon men. And they cursed God on account of the plague of hail, because the plague was so terrible.*

The seventh bowl of wrath is poured out upon the air, upon the atmosphere of the earth. This brings to mind Paul's description of Satan as "the ruler of the kingdom of the air."[7] This judgment—particularly coming as it does on the heels of the Battle of Armageddon—probably describes the effect of nuclear warfare, which would release vast clouds of poisonous radiation upon the earth. The disastrous nuclear accident at the Chernobyl power plant in the Soviet Union, which poisoned the atmosphere for miles around, was just a faint glimpse of what would happen to the air we breathe in the event of an all-out nuclear exchange.

So it may well be that the final bowl of God's judgment is tipped by the finger of man himself—a finger that is even at this moment poised over the nuclear button. In our high-speed, high-tech, ballistic age, humankind is never more than a few minutes away from potential doom.

In these verses we see that God replies to the poisoning of the atmosphere with a great shaking of the earth—in fact, the greatest quake the world has ever known. John does not supply the Richter scale reading in these verses, but it undoubtedly shoots clear off the scale! As a result, Jerusalem is split into three parts by the derangement of the earth.

As we noted when we viewed this earthquake from the vantage point of Revelation 11:13, there is a parallel description of this event in Zechariah 14, where the prophet tells us that the Mount of Olives will be split in half, part moving to the north, part to the south, creating a great valley between. From other passages of Scripture we learn that the topography of the entire land of Israel will be altered by this event.

At this time, God will also judge Babylon the Great, the city which represents the false church. We will see that judgment in the next two chapters of Revelation.

The earthquake that splits the city of Jerusalem is also accompanied by a terrible storm of hail. Great chunks of ice weighing over a hundred pounds will fall from the sky, killing and destroying with random, indiscriminate force. Again, this is an example of a catastrophe of seemingly outlandish proportions—yet there is precedent for such phenomena in our own recorded history.

For almost as long as I have been a student of Revelation, I have been clipping accounts of apocalypse-like phenomena from the back pages of newspapers. Sometimes people say, "These plagues and judgments in Revelation are simply beyond belief! How could such things happen?" In reply I can simply open a file folder and pull out eyewitness accounts from newspapers. The fact is, there have been accounts of hailstones (or should we call them hail*boulders*?) weighing as much as *300 pounds* each that have fallen on different parts of the world.

What is the natural phenomenon that produces such mammoth weapons of natural destruction? No one knows. But we do know that the events of the last days will be so cataclysmic that the forces of nature will be in complete upheaval. Further descriptions of these times can be found in Ezekiel 39. It will be a time when, as Jesus says, "Men will faint from terror, apprehensive of what is coming on the world."[8]

The End

But there is *good* news! This is The End—not the end of Revelation, certainly, but of the terrible judgments that will come upon the earth. There is one event out of the seven-bowls-of-wrath judgment that John will magnify and detail for us in the next two chapters of Revelation: the destruction of Babylon the Great. But after that, Jesus will reveal Himself in power and glory. He will be seen by all the world, just as the Scriptures have predicted for so long.

After that, a new chapter will begin for both heaven and the earth.

As we close this chapter of Revelation, I believe there is a very practical, contemporary lesson God wants us to take from this passage and apply to our lives. The book of Revelation was written for the seven churches of Asia, and these seven churches represent the entire church upon the earth today. This prophetic vision was given to us to apply not tomorrow or a thousand years from now. It was given to us in order *to change our lives right now.*

And the message of this moment that comes out of this timeless vision is one which is repeated several times in Revelation 16: *judgment does not produce repentance.* We have just seen how judgment after judgment rained down upon the earth, yet the people of the last days remained rebellious and hardened in their hearts.

Judgment cannot produce repentance. It was never intended to. In fact, as we have seen in this passage, judgment often seems to make people even more stubborn and resistant to the truth. How, then, does God change the hearts and lives of people? By the demonstration of His grace and mercy! That is what Paul tells us when he says, "Do you show contempt for the riches of his kindness, tolerance and patience, not realizing that God's kindness leads you toward repentance?"9 It is grace that changes and melts the human heart. It is grace that changes minds. It is grace that changes lives.

So let us be grateful for the grace of God in our lives. Let us be thankful that God presently restrains the evil of man from having full reign upon the earth. Someday that evil will be unleashed, and in these past few chapters we have seen the result of unrestrained human evil. But for the time being, as wicked and perilous as this sorry old world often is, it is still an ordered and peaceful world compared with the horror and chaos of the coming time of tribulation. There is anarchy and bloodshed on the horizon, but it belongs to another day, after you and I are removed from this earth. Today we live in an age of God's kindness and grace.

It is the grace of God, not His judgment, that has brought us from death into life. It is His grace that invites us to a personal relationship with Jesus Christ. It is grace that changes us and makes us into new creatures. And ultimately it is grace that teaches us how to live in a world gone mad.

The world is plunging toward its last and most terrifying trial. Yet even though the world is falling out of control, you and I can stand firm upon the grace and righteousness of God.

Chapter Twenty-Two

The Dragon Lady

Revelation 17:1–19:5

Out of all the many questions Christians ask about the vivid and symbol-laden book of Revelation, the most often asked question is certainly this: "Will the church go through the Great Tribulation?" The feeling behind this question is certainly understandable in view of the upheaval, the persecution, and the judgments that will take place during that time. We have journeyed through the Tribulation period as mere witnesses. Who in his right mind would want to live in the middle of such a swirl of events?

So Christians are invariably relieved as they take a close look at Revelation and find that the answer to the question is a very clear *No*.

Or is it?

Actually, the answer is *No*—and *Yes*.

The true church of Jesus Christ—all those individual believers who truly know the Lord and are alive when the Tribulation period begins—will be caught up with Jesus when He comes for His church. Only after the departure of the true church will the Tribulation period begin.

But the true, believing church of Jesus Christ is not all of the church, not all of what we know as Christendom today. There *is* a church that will go through the Great Tribulation. That church exists today, and it will *continue* to function through the seven years of tribulation, even after the Lord comes and removes *His* true church from the world.

It is this *other* church to which we now come, and to which John devotes more than two entire chapters of Revelation. We had a hint of this other church in Revelation 2, the letter to the church at Thyatira, where the Lord says,

> You tolerate that woman Jezebel, who calls herself a prophetess. By her teaching she misleads my servants into sexual immorality and the eating of food sacrificed to idols. I have given her time to repent of her immorality, but she is unwilling. So I will cast her on a bed of suffering, and I will make those who commit adultery with her suffer intensely, unless they repent of her ways. I will strike her children dead. Then all the churches will know that I am he who searches hearts and minds, and I will repay each of you according to your deeds.[1]

The "Jezebel" of this passage is a forerunner of all the thousands of deceivers and false teachers who would infect and seduce later generations of the church, on down to our own generation and beyond. Her "children" are the false Christians whom she spawned in the Thyatiran church—and in a metaphorical sense, those later Jezebel-like deceivers who continue to lead people astray in our own age. "Jezebel" and her "children," says the Lord, will be cast into great tribulation, suffering, and destruction. That is the fate of the false church which John now details for us in Revelation 17:1 through 19:5.

The Mother of Prostitutes

The present passage is a detailed account of what John touches on only briefly during his description of the seventh bowl of judgment, Revelation 16:19, where he writes, "God remembered Babylon the Great and gave her the cup filled with the wine of the fury of his wrath." Now, beginning with Revelation 17:1-6, we will look deeply into that cup and fathom the dreadful wine of God's wrath against the counterfeit, apostate church which He calls Babylon the Great.

17:1–6 *One of the seven angels who had the seven bowls came and said to me, "Come, I will show you the punishment of the great prostitute, who sits on many waters. With her the kings of the earth committed adultery and the inhabitants of the earth were intoxicated with the wine of her adulteries."*

Then the angel carried me away in the Spirit into a desert. There I saw a woman sitting on a scarlet beast that was covered with blasphemous names and had seven heads and ten horns. The woman was dressed in purple and scarlet, and was glittering with gold, precious stones and pearls. She held a golden cup in her hand, filled with abominable things and the filth of her adulteries. This title was written on her forehead:

MYSTERY
BABYLON THE GREAT
THE MOTHER OF PROSTITUTES
AND OF THE ABOMINATIONS OF THE EARTH.

I saw that the woman was drunk with the blood of the saints, the blood of those who bore testimony to Jesus.

When I saw her, I was greatly astonished.

The beast, as we have already seen, represents the political leader of the coalition of nations of Western Europe, the revived Roman Empire. It is he who will dominate the world economy in the last days. In this passage we see a woman sitting astride the beast.

The apostle John focuses our attention on this woman, giving us ten specific clues as to what she symbolically represents. In the entire book of Revelation, which is so richly saturated in symbols and metaphors, the symbol of this woman receives more attention than any other in the book. In fact, the symbol of the woman on the beast is surrounded by more identifying clues than any other symbol in Revelation. Obviously she is extremely important to the overall meaning of John's vision.

Here are the ten clues.

Clue No. 1: A Prostitute

The first clue is that this woman is a prostitute. The use of a symbol with sexual overtones indicates gross, obvious, physical wrongdoing. Prostitution is the ultimate in promiscuous, unfaithful behavior, so this woman depicts unfaithfulness to God on the part of someone who claims to honor God. Just as a prostitute offers momentary sexual gratification but without love or faithfulness, so the prostitute in this passage points to some organization or entity which claims to worship God but is actually unfaithful to Him.

Clue No. 2: Universal Influence

The second clue is that this woman has universal influence. She is "the great prostitute, who sits on many waters." Later, in verse 15, the meaning of "many waters" is unmistakably explained: "Then the angel said to me, 'The waters you saw, where the prostitute sits, are peoples, multitudes, nations and languages.'" People all over the world are influenced by the teaching of this prostitute.

Moreover, verse 2 makes it plain that the organization or entity which the prostitute represents exercises great power over the political systems of the world: "With her the kings of the earth committed adultery." The prostitute also misleads great populations of the earth with the teaching she spreads: "the inhabitants of the earth were intoxicated with the wine of her adulteries."

Clue No. 3: She Is Seated upon the Beast

The third clue is that she is seated upon the beast. This indicates a relationship between the prostitute and the beast. It is clear from this imagery that the woman dominates and steers the beast, as a rider would dominate and control the direction of a horse—but only for a time. As verses 16 and 17 tell us,

> The beast and the ten horns you saw will hate the prostitute. They will bring her to ruin and leave her naked; they will eat her flesh and burn her with fire. For God has put it into their hearts to accomplish his purpose by agreeing to give the beast their power to rule, until God's words are fulfilled.

Throughout the book of Revelation we find reminder after reminder that God is ultimately in control. He allows many things to happen, but even the worst events work together to accomplish His purposes.

Clue No. 4: Purple, Scarlet, Gold, and Jewels

The fourth clue is that the woman is obviously very wealthy and expensively adorned. She wears fabric dyed in purple and scarlet—the most costly cloth available in the ancient world—as well as jewelry of gold, precious stones, and pearls. These are symbols of precious spiritual truths which are only used as an outer adornment to make the woman outwardly attractive to the beholder.

Clue No. 5: The Golden Cup

The golden cup in her hand is the fifth clue. Outwardly it is precious, shining, pleasing to the eye. Gold is a symbol of divine activity in

Scripture, so this golden cup gives every appearance of being a utensil of God's service. Yet it is filled with false religious concepts, with "abominable things," with spiritual adulteries and filthiness.

Many Bible commentators have pointed out that this cup appears to be a counterfeit of the communion cup of the New Testament—the cup of the Lord which is associated with the truth of God. On the outside the cup in the prostitute's hand gives the appearance of precious truth; on the inside it is vile and nauseating.

Clue No. 6: Mystery, Babylon the Great

The sixth clue is in the inscription upon the prostitute's forehead: "Mystery, Babylon the Great." The word "Mystery" indicates there is something deeper here than appears on the surface.

The historical Babylon was the fabled capital city of the mighty Babylonian empire, which dominated the ancient world. It was located on the Euphrates River, about 50 miles south of Baghdad in what is now the country of Iraq. The founding of Babylon is recorded in Genesis— where it was called Babel when it was established by Nimrod, the hunter of human souls. It became the focus of idolatry for all of the ancient world.

But the Babylon that appears in John's vision is not the literal Babylon that stood on the River Euphrates. The title "Mystery" indicates that there is a deeper symbolism to be discerned. The Babylon which the woman symbolizes is *spiritually* identified with ancient Babylon—that is, with the practice of idolatry and spiritual adultery.

The use of the label "Babylon" as a symbol of idolatry is similar to Revelation 11:8, where Jerusalem is referred to as "Sodom" and "Egypt" because that city had become a source of false teaching and corruption.

Clue No. 7: The Mother of Prostitutes

The seventh clue is that the woman is called "the mother of prostitutes." She is not alone in her adulteries. She has spiritual offspring who also practice her idolatries and spread her false teachings.

Clue No. 8: Persecutor of Christians

The eighth clue is that the woman is a persecutor of the true believers in Jesus Christ: "I saw that the woman was drunk with the blood of the saints, the blood of those who bore testimony to Jesus." Here is a repulsive image indeed: a woman who becomes intoxicated—and euphorically so!—by drinking the blood of the righteous!

Clearly, this is an image of a group or entity which cannot tolerate opposition from those who would bear witness against her falsehoods and adulteries. To those who preach the truth she responds with death and violence—and she revels drunkenly in the slaughter!

Clue No. 9: Seven Hills

The next clue to the identity of the woman is given in verse 9, where John writes,

> This calls for a mind with wisdom. The seven heads [of the beast] are seven hills on which the woman sits.

That first line is important: Identifying the reality behind the symbol of the woman requires wisdom. It is not a matter that is immediately obvious. It requires thought and study.

There is one city that was famous in ancient times, as it is today, for being built on seven hills—the Aventine, Caelian, Capitoline, Esquiline, Palatine, Quirinal, and Viminal. That city is Rome. But before we jump to any conclusions (remember, "this calls for a mind with wisdom"), let's look at one more clue.

Clue No. 10: The Great City

The final clue is found in verse 18, the last verse in the chapter. John writes:

> The woman you saw is the great city that rules over the kings of the earth.

In John's day that could only be one city: Rome. Where could one find a greater city in all the world than the capital of the empire that had *conquered* the known world? Truly, the city of Rome literally ruled over the kings of the earth.

Now we must carefully piece all these clues together into one composite picture of the truth behind the symbol of the woman. This entity which is symbolized by the woman has prostituted itself and been unfaithful to God; it has global influence; it is outwardly adorned with the garments and jewelry of precious spiritual truths, but is inwardly filled with false religious concepts and spiritual adulteries. Plainly, the woman represents an institutional religious body which outwardly professes to be Christian, which adorns itself with Christian truths, yet is corrupt and abominable within.

The fact that this institution is unquestionably identified with Rome makes it impossible to avoid the conclusion that the woman is a symbol for the Roman Catholic Church. Historically, the Catholic Church has had a powerful position in world affairs—in times past, popes have actually exercised power over kings! Even in our own secular age when the pope no longer has the power to make a king grovel at his feet, the Vatican still has vast international influence, the status of a separate, sovereign nation within the city of Rome, and its own diplomatic embassies in the capitals of many nations.

Given a history which includes the atrocities of the Inquisition and the wielding (often in a corrupt way) of political power in the international sphere, it is not beyond the reach of imagination to foresee a future Roman Church persecuting true Christians for heresy; forming an alliance with (and temporary dominance over) the beast, the world political ruler of the last days; and engaging in Babylon-like idolatry and spiritual prostitution (which, after all, were the very abuses and excesses that led Luther and the other Reformers to begin the Protestant Reformation). The imagery of the prostitute astride the beast seems to suggest that the Roman Catholic Church, which arose during the present church age, shall achieve its greatest power in the last seven years of human history, during the Tribulation.

Remember the last line in verse 6: "When I saw her, I was greatly astonished." Why was John so astonished? At the time John recorded his vision the church in Rome was the church of the catacombs. It was a persecuted and suffering church, having no earthly power and no worldly influence. Undoubtedly it came as a great surprise to John to see that the suffering church he knew in Rome would one day become a great and powerful force, dominating the kings of the earth while prostituting its own truths.

I hasten to add that by taking this view we are *not* engaging in "Catholic-bashing." As we interpret this passage, we recognize that, while the Roman Catholic Church is an *institution,* Roman Catholics are *people.* The Catholic Church itself makes just such a distinction, teaching that it is the *clergy*—the pope and the hierarchy—which constitute the Church, not the people. There are believing and non-believing people in the Catholic Church, just as there are believing and non-believing people in Orthodox churches, Anglican churches, mainline Protestant churches, evangelical churches, fundamentalist churches, charismatic churches, independent churches, and neighborhood Bible studies. Moreover, there have been many godly popes, bishops, priests, and nuns through the centuries. I've met and known many godly Catholics, both clergy and laypeople, over the years.

You may wonder how Roman Catholic scholars interpret the symbol of the prostitute who sits upon the seven hills. They cannot question that verses 9 and 18 are clear references to Rome—but they claim they are references to *pagan* Rome, the capital of the Roman Empire. But there is a problem with that view. John would not have been at all astonished to witness pagan Rome persecuting the saints. But to see *the church itself* persecuting the saints of God is an astonishing thing indeed!

It would be simplistic to say that the woman in this passage represents *only* the Roman Catholic Church. What John symbolically describes for us in this passage is not so much one specific religious organization but a body of religious thought and behavior which is strongly typified by Roman Catholic tradition, but which can also be found in other traditions and denominations—and which might well be called "Babylonianism." Babylonian Christianity would be that kind of religion which takes extra-biblical teachings from pagan sources and brings them together under the guise of Christianity. It involves using religious authority in order to gain earthly power or status. Just as the founders of Babylon said when they erected the Tower of Babel, the goal of "Babylonianism" is, "We will make a name for ourselves."

Clearly there are many denominations, churches, and individual Christians who reflect the error of Babylonian Christianity. Eugene Peterson makes the observation that just as prostitution is commercialized sex, so worship under the auspices of the prostitute of Revelation 17—that is, Babylonian Christianity—is "the commercialization of our great need and deep desire for meaning, love and salvation. . . . It is the diabolical inversion of 'You are bought with a price,' to, 'I can get it for you wholesale.' "[2]

To anyone who might be offended at the identification of the prostitute of Revelation 17 as the Roman Catholic Church, let me add this: Remember that the woman wears an inscription on her forehead which reads in part, "The mother of prostitutes." Many Christian denominations, organizations, movements, churches, groups, and subgroups that exist today can trace their lineage back to the so-called mother of all churches, the Roman Catholic Church.

After the Lord comes to take His true church out of the world, all these various institutions will still be on the earth. Some will be missing a few members, some will be reduced by half, some will lose virtually their entire membership! But it should neither surprise nor offend us to think that the Roman Catholic institution that remains when the true church is removed should become a corrupt and prostituted body, nor that its "children"—the Presbyterian or Baptist or Pentecostal churches of the Tribulation—should be any less corrupt!

Man looks on the outward structure of an institution and calls it a "church"; Jesus Christ knows His true church because He can see into every individual human heart.

The End of the Beast

In verses 7 through 14, as John stands gazing in astonishment at the woman sitting upon the scarlet beast, one of the seven angels of judgment explains to John the meaning of the woman and the beast and shows him the ultimate destruction and defeat of the beast in battle against the Lamb of God.

17:7–14 *Then the angel said to me: "Why are you astonished? I will explain to you the mystery of the woman and of the beast she rides, which has the seven heads and ten horns. The beast, which you saw, once was, now is not, and will come up out of the Abyss and go to his destruction. The inhabitants of the earth whose names have not been written in the book of life from the creation of the world will be astonished when they see the beast, because he once was, now is not, and yet will come.*

"This calls for a mind with wisdom. The seven heads are seven hills on which the woman sits. They are also seven kings. Five have fallen, one is, the other has not yet come; but when he does come, he must remain for a little while. The beast who once was, and now is not, is an eighth king. He belongs to the seven and is going to his destruction.

"The ten horns you saw are ten kings who have not yet received a kingdom, but who for one hour will receive authority as kings along with the beast. They have one purpose and will give their power and authority to the beast. They will make war against the Lamb, but the Lamb will overcome them because he is Lord of lords and King of kings—and with him will be his called, chosen and faithful followers."

We already examined the interpretation of the beast when we delved into Revelation 13. There we saw that the beast represents a revived form of the Roman Empire—ten nations which hand over their sovereignty to one political leader. In this passage, the angel describes seven "kings" or forms of government. Five had passed into history, one was dominant in John's day, and another would remain for a little while, and then an eighth "king"—the beast—would come into being.

What many people do not realize is that the sixth form of government, the one that dominated John's era and which the angel described when he said, "one is," is the longest-enduring form of government in human history: the imperial form. The Roman imperial line began with Julius Caesar (born 100 B.C., died 44 B.C.), who turned the Caesar surname of his Julian family into a title that became synonymous with "emperor." The imperial line continued virtually until the fall of the Western Empire in A.D. 476.

Yet, even though the line of the Italian caesars came to an end many centuries ago, the imperial/caesarian form of government continued to hold power until 1918! In that one year *both* of the last two "caesars"—the German Kaiser and the Russian czar—were overthrown. The word *caesar* in German is "Kaiser"; in Russian it is "czar." Thus the Imperial form of government has existed for some 1900 years, from the time of Julius Caesar until our own century.

Following the sixth, or imperial, form of government, the angel told John that a seventh was yet to come and would "remain for a little while." Then would follow the eighth, which is the beast.

The end of the beast is described in verses 13 and 14, where John writes that the ten nations "will give their power and authority to the beast. They will make war against the Lamb, but the Lamb will overcome them because he is Lord of lords and King of kings—and with him will be his called, chosen and faithful followers." Notice that when the Lamb appears the church is already with Him—further proof that the church has already been gathered up to be with Jesus *before* the seven-year Tribulation begins.

The Destruction of Mystery Babylon

Then the angel describes to John the destruction of the prostitute at the hands of the beast which she once dominated. Verses 15 through 18 serve as a prelude to Revelation 18, in which John gives us a more detailed impression of the destruction of the prostitute, Babylon the Great.

17:15–18 *Then the angel said to me, "The waters you saw, where the prostitute sits, are peoples, multitudes, nations and languages. The beast and the ten horns you saw will hate the prostitute. They will bring her to*

ruin and leave her naked; they will eat her flesh and burn her with fire.
For God has put it into their hearts to accomplish his purpose by agree-
ing to give the beast their power to rule, until God's words are fulfilled.
The woman you saw is the great city that rules over the kings of the
earth."

For a while the prostitute—the false church—dominates the beast.
But the beast apparently resents her domineering ways—and the beast
turns. It rends and destroys the woman, consuming her with its teeth and
with fire. This is a more detailed exposition of God's judgment against
"Babylon," which we first encounter during the seventh bowl of wrath in
Revelation 16:19—"God remembered Babylon the Great and gave her
the cup filled with the wine of the fury of his wrath."

In Revelation 18 we return for a third and still more detailed exposition of the judgment of the prostitute, the false church.

18:1–3 *After this I saw another angel coming down from heaven. He had*
great authority, and the earth was illuminated by his splendor. With a
mighty voice he shouted:
  "Fallen! Fallen is Babylon the Great!
  She has become a home for demons
and a haunt for every evil spirit,
  a haunt for every unclean and
    detestable bird.
For all the nations have drunk
  the maddening wine of her adulteries.
The kings of the earth committed adultery
  with her,
and the merchants of the earth grew rich
  from her excessive luxuries."

Three reasons are given for the overthrow of the prostitute: First, she
has become demonic, a haunt for evil spirits. Even today, during the
church age, we see demonic teachings and ideas infiltrating various quarters of the church. During the Tribulation, after all church structures and
institutions have been swept free of true followers of Christ, there will be
no restraint upon the religiously motivated evil that remains. Places
which are now sanctuaries of worship shall become haunts of evil in the
last days.

Second, Mystery Babylon is overthrown because kings have committed adultery with her. She has lusted after earthly power and has been

spiritually unfaithful in her flirtations and intrigues with the power-brokers of this world.

Third, Mystery Babylon is overthrown because the merchants of the earth have grown rich from her excessive luxuries. In a world of human need and tremendous poverty the false church has lavished riches and excessive luxuries upon itself.

The Kings and Merchants Mourn

Remember that there will be many people who will turn to Jesus Christ for salvation during the terrible cataclysm of the last days. As decadent and depraved as the false church has become, there is still a thin, fading veneer of the grand old truths clinging to her crumbling walls — enough truth that some people are actually able to find in that church the way to God.

To any of these true saints who are within the church during the last days, God issues a warning call, a plea to come out of the false church before it goes down to its destruction.

18:4–5 *Then I heard another voice from heaven say:*
"Come out of her, my people,
so that you will not share in her sins,
so that you will not receive any of her plagues;
for her sins are piled up to heaven,
and God has remembered her crimes."

Then God gives further reasons for His judgment against the prostitute, the false church:

18:6 *"Give back to her as she has given;*
pay her back double for what she has done.
Mix her a double portion from her own cup."

This is simply the law of retribution at work. "What goes around comes around," and often in multiplied force. In verses 7 and 8 God continues to detail the prostitute's sin — and her fate.

18:7–8 *"Give her as much torture and grief*
as the glory and luxury she gave herself.
In her heart she boasts,
'I sit as queen; I am not a widow,
and I will never mourn.'

Therefore in one day her plagues will overtake her:
    death, mourning and famine.
She will be consumed by fire,
    for mighty is the Lord God who judges her."

Here we learn that the false church is judged for her arrogant, self-indulgent pride. She has queenly pretensions—and queenly tastes in luxuries. But in the midst of her glory and luxury, judgment falls upon her—a judgment of torture, grief, famine, and death. The beast and the ten horns (the ten nations) turn against her and destroy her with fire. But even beyond these horrors inflicted on her by her former allies comes a further judgment from God.

18:9–10 *"When the kings of the earth who committed adultery with her and shared her luxury see the smoke of her burning, they will weep and mourn over her. Terrified at her torment, they will stand far off and cry:*

" 'Woe! Woe, O great city,
O Babylon, city of power!
In one hour your doom has come!' "

Here is a scene of sudden judgment from God—so sudden that the kings of the earth look upon the smoking ruin of Mystery Babylon and cry out, "In one hour your doom has come!" Remember that, in the context of Revelation 16, God's judgment against Babylon was announced at the moment of the great earthquake which split the city of Jerusalem. The kings who committed adultery with her, who then turned on her and destroyed her, are now terrified by the sudden and total end that has come upon her. They are mourning, of course, not for the prostitute herself but for their own loss.

18:11–13 *"The merchants of the earth will weep and mourn over her because no one buys their cargoes any more—cargoes of gold, silver, precious stones and pearls; fine linen, purple, silk and scarlet cloth; every sort of citron wood, and articles of every kind made of ivory, costly wood, bronze, iron and marble; cargoes of cinnamon and spice, of incense, myrrh and frankincense, of wine and olive oil, of fine flour and wheat; cattle and sheep; horses and carriages; and bodies and souls of men."*

They mourn because their *business* has been ruined by the destruction of Mystery Babylon. False religion has been good for business—but now it's all gone. Notice that at the end of the long list of merchandise that was once sold by Babylon come the words, "and bodies and souls of men." Slaves! Fine young people who once served Babylon without pay, without laying claim to their rights and freedom, and who devote themselves to lifelong poverty and chastity, all because of a mistaken devotion to a false religious system.

The lament of the peoples of the earth continues.

18:14–19 *"They will say, 'The fruit you longed for is gone from you. All your riches and splendor have vanished, never to be recovered.' The merchants who sold these things and gained their wealth from her will stand far off, terrified at her torment. They will weep and mourn and cry out:*

"'Woe! Woe, O great city,
dressed in fine linen, purple and scarlet,
and glittering with gold, precious
stones and pearls!
In one hour such great wealth has been
brought to ruin!'

"Every sea captain, and all who travel by ship, the sailors, and all who earn their living from the sea, will stand far off. When they see the smoke of her burning, they will exclaim, 'Was there ever a city like this great city?' They will throw dust on their heads, and with weeping and mourning cry out:

"'Woe! Woe, O great city,
where all who had ships on the sea
became rich through her wealth!
In one hour she has been brought to ruin!'"

The merchants and seamen are terrified and amazed at the sudden judgment that has befallen this great city. Notice how many times the phrase "one hour" occurs. Clearly the destruction that befalls Mystery Babylon is incomprehensibly swift and sudden. It seems to be a fiery judgment from God and suggests the possibility of volcanic activity.

Geologists have long known that the entire western edge of the Apennine Mountains—from the region of Rome on the central coast all the way south to Mount Etna on the island of Sicily—is subject to earthquakes and potential volcanic activity. The Apennines are among the youngest mountains in Europe, and the geologic stresses beneath those mountains are such that they cause the entire range to rise at a rate of a fraction of an inch per year. So it may well be that tremendous volcanic destruction will befall Rome in the final days of Daniel's seventieth week.

Heaven Rejoices

In contrast to the mourning over Babylon that takes place upon the earth, there is rejoicing in heaven.

18:20 *" 'Rejoice over her, O heaven!*
Rejoice, saints and apostles and
prophets!
God has judged her for the way she
treated you.' "

Note that the cruel treatment by Mystery Babylon goes back to the time of the apostles. Whenever religious error opposes the truth, the frontline defenders of the truth—the prophets, apostles, and saints—are made to suffer for it. But God does not let these attacks go unanswered. In the end Mystery Babylon must pay the price of judgment for its mistreatment of God's spokespeople and servants.

18:21–24 *Then a mighty angel picked up a boulder the size of a large millstone and threw it into the sea, and said:*

"With such violence
the great city of Babylon will be
thrown down,
never to be found again.
The music of harpists and musicians,
flute players and trumpeters,
will never be heard in you again.
No workman of any trade
will ever be found in you again.
The sound of a millstone
will never be heard in you again.
The light of a lamp
will never shine in you again.
The voice of bridegroom and bride
will never be heard in you again.
Your merchants were the world's great men.

By your magic spell all the nations
   were led astray.
In her was found the blood of prophets
   and of the saints,
   and of all who have been killed
      on the earth."

To such solemn words as these any additional commentary would be superfluous. So let us simply append the first five verses of Revelation 19 — verses which complete the flow of chapter 18.

19:1–5 *After this I heard what sounded like the roar of a great multitude in heaven shouting:*
"Hallelujah!
Salvation and glory and power belong to our God,
   for true and just are his judgments.
He has condemned the great prostitute
   who corrupted the earth by her adulteries.
He has avenged on her the blood of his servants."

And again they shouted:
"Hallelujah!
The smoke from her goes up for ever and ever."

The twenty-four elders and the four living creatures fell down and worshiped God, who was seated on the throne. And they cried:
"Amen, Hallelujah!"

Then a voice came from the throne, saying:
"Praise our God,
   all you his servants,
you who fear him,
   both small and great!"

You may be surprised to learn that this chapter marks the first appearance of the word *Hallelujah* — not only in the book of Revelation but in the entire New Testament! There are many Hallelujahs in the Psalms and throughout the Old Testament, but this exhilarating shout of praise does not appear in the New Testament until the last few chapters.

But at this point in Revelation, the shouts of Hallelujah become thunderous, resounding, even deafening. The final and utter destruction of Mystery Babylon precipitates a Hallelujah Chorus in heaven that brings the entire heavenly host to its feet in a standing ovation of praise.

Gone is the adulterous institution that wrapped up God's truth in a tissue of demonic lies, that set deadly snares for unwary believers, that introduced error and abomination into the world in the name of God. Verse 3 confirms that the destruction of Babylon is not merely an earthly catastrophe but God's holy judgment upon an evil society of human beings. "The smoke from her goes up for ever and ever," a statement which demonstrates that it is not merely an event in time that we are witnessing, but an event in *eternity,* in the realm of "ever and ever."

"Babylonianism" Here and Now

Let us now leave that solemn and sobering picture. The lesson to us is clear: God will not tolerate Babylonianism wherever it may be found—not in the Roman Catholic Church, in your church or mine, or even in your *life* or mine. And we know what the error of Babylonian Christianity is: using religion and God's name to glorify ourselves; using God's truth as a means of enriching ourselves; and mingling error with God's truth.

You and I as saints are called to separate ourselves from Babylonian error, from the lust for earthly glory and position obtained by religious devotion. Whenever an individual Christian puts on a pious act while his heart runs after status and material gain, he is being seduced by the silken spirit of Babylon. Whenever a church seeks to gain influence by impressing others with outward splendor, you have the seeds of Babylonianism. Beware that those seeds don't take root in your church and your life!

In the book of Acts, we saw Babylonianism take root in the lives of two church members named Ananias and Sapphira. Outwardly they seemed godly and devout, but what they really sought was not the glory of God but the glorification of self. They used a seemingly selfless and charitable act—selling a piece of land and donating a portion of the proceeds to the church—as a way of gaining false status as people of piety and devotion. God's judgment against their hypocrisy was as sudden as His judgment against Mystery Babylon.

All through the book of Revelation God has shown us the shape of things to come—and the more we see in Revelation, the more it becomes clear that the future has its roots in the present. There are trends taking shape all around us that will have their ultimate and cataclysmic effect in the last days.

The book of Revelation may at times convey the feeling of a science fiction movie filled with futuristic imagery and incredible special effects. But this book was not given to entertain us with strange images of a future age. It was given to us *to change our lives in the here and now.*

Babylonianism is with us today. It has infected many denominations, many churches, and many individual lives. Has it infected you? Has it infected me? God has given us these sobering visions of the fate of the Babylonian church so that we would examine ourselves honestly and earnestly. For if we continually search our own hearts and ruthlessly examine our own lives, we need never fear the judgment of God.

Chapter Twenty-Three

The Rider on the White Horse

Revelation 19:6-21

 n 47 B.C., the Roman army under Julius Caesar soundly defeated the forces of King Pharnaces, who fought the Romans for control of the kingdom of Pontus in Asia Minor. After his victory Caesar returned to Rome and made the famous announcement, *"Veni, vidi, vici,"* or, "I came, I saw, I conquered."

Some 1700 years later a Polish military strategist, King John III Sobieski, led a brilliant campaign to drive the Ottoman invaders out of central Europe. Leading a force of 25,000 men, he came to the aid of the German emperor Leopold I and beat the invaders back from the walls of Vienna, saving the city and the emperor. The Polish king was given an audience before Pope Innocent XI, who congratulated him on his victory.

King John's reply was: "I came, I saw, *God* conquered."

So shall it be in the last battle in the last days. God will destroy the prostituted "Babylonian church" just before the triumphal return of Jesus. The Lord will come, the world will see, and God will conquer.

Christ and His Bride

In the previous chapter we viewed the destruction of the woman, Mystery Babylon, who had polluted herself and the world with her spiritual adultery. At her destruction the depraved kings and merchants of the world mourned—but a shout of Hallelujah went up in heaven.

Now in Revelation 19:6–8 we hear the heavenly chorus of Hallelujahs rising to a mighty crescendo as a woman of virtue (in vivid contrast to the abominable woman of Revelation 17 and 18) steps forward to take her place as the true bride of Christ.

19:6–8 *Then I heard what sounded like a great multitude, like the roar of rushing waters and like loud peals of thunder, shouting:*

"Hallelujah!
  For our Lord God Almighty reigns.
Let us rejoice and be glad
  and give him glory!
For the wedding of the Lamb has come,
  and his bride has made herself ready.
Fine linen, bright and clean,
  was given her to wear."
(Fine linen stands for the righteous acts of the saints.)

We have come at last to the wedding of the Lamb. Here the Lord claims His bride for Himself. We will meet the symbol of the bride again in Revelation 21 and 22 when a great city which is figuratively described as "the bride, the wife of the Lamb," comes down from heaven. But it is here in Revelation 19 where the wedding of Jesus and His bride takes place.

Most Bible commentators identify the bride as the church, in view of Paul's statement in Ephesians:

Husbands, love your wives, just as Christ loved the church and gave himself up for her to make her holy, cleansing her by the washing with water through the word, and to present her to him-self as a radiant church, without stain or wrinkle or any other blemish, but holy and blameless.[1]

Though the word "bride" does not appear in this passage from Ephesians, the imagery Paul uses clearly suggests our Lord's bridegroom relationship with the church. It dovetails precisely with the imagery of Revelation 19:6-8.

Other passages of Scripture lead me to believe that the bride in this text *includes* the church, but also extends beyond the church to include all the redeemed saints of all the ages. Jesus speaks of this wedding supper of the Lamb when he says, ". . . many will come from the east and the west, and will take their places at the feast with Abraham, Isaac and Jacob in the kingdom of heaven."[2] Thus Old Testament saints are part of the bride as well.

In Revelation 21 and 22, when the New Jerusalem, the Holy City, comes down out of heaven "prepared as a bride beautifully dressed for her husband," it will have twelve gates named for the twelve tribes of Israel and twelve foundations named for the twelve apostles. In that imagery we see the combining of the Old Testament and New Testament saints in the symbol of the bride of the Lamb.

The statement in verse 7, "his bride has made herself ready," seems to imply that the judgment seat of Christ has already taken place. This judgment, which is unlike the fiery and destructive judgments we have seen in Revelation, is a judgment of believers. Paul speaks of this judgment when he writes,

> We must all appear before the judgment seat of Christ, that each
> one may receive what is due him for the things done while in the
> body, whether good or bad.[3]

The judgment seat of Christ will be a time of evaluation, not punishment. Its purpose is not to settle destiny but to determine the degree of reward. It is a time when our service to the Lord while we were in our earthly bodies will be appraised. Those things done for self-glorification or self-gratification and those things done in the energy of the flesh rather than the Spirit will be destroyed. As Paul writes,

> If any man builds on this foundation [Christ] using gold, silver,
> costly stones, wood, hay or straw, his work will be shown for
> what it is, because the Day will bring it to light. It will be
> revealed with fire, and the fire will test the quality of each man's
> work. If what he has built survives, he will receive his reward. If
> it is burned up, he will suffer loss; he himself will be saved, but
> only as one escaping through the flames.[4]

All that will be left after our deeds have been tested at the judgment seat of Christ will be those that were not burned up. If our deeds have been made of gold, silver, or costly stones, they will survive along with us. If they were made of wood, hay, or straw, they will be consumed by fire. When we, as individual members of the bride of Christ, appear before Him, arrayed in bright and clean fine linen, John says, in verse 8, that our linen garment will be those righteous acts that we have done, and that have survived the test of the judgment seat of Christ.

The Wedding Feast of the Lamb

In verses 9 and 10 all heaven celebrates the wedding of the Lamb and His bride.

19:9–10 *Then the angel said to me, "Write: 'Blessed are those who are invited to the wedding supper of the Lamb!'" And he added, "These are the true words of God."*

At this I fell at his feet to worship him. But he said to me, "Do not do it! I am a fellow servant with you and with your brothers who hold to the testimony of Jesus. Worship God! For the testimony of Jesus is the spirit of prophecy."

It is a great honor to be invited to this wedding feast. It is a feast to which the entire human race is invited—but only a fraction of the human race will attend. The invitation is the gospel, and the gospel has gone out to all men and women everywhere, in every age of history. Some accept the invitation. Some reject it.

In Matthew 22 Jesus tells the story of a great king who sends out invitations to a wedding banquet in honor of his son. The people he invites refuse his invitation, so he sends a second invitation, this time listing the lavish menu and pleading with the people to attend. Still they ignore the invitation. Some just go about their business—but some actually mistreat and murder the servants who carry the invitation!

This part of the story appears to be a reference to the leaders of Israel. When Jesus presented Himself to Israel on Palm Sunday, riding on a donkey as Zechariah had predicted, the common people of Israel rejoiced and received Him, but the leadership rejected Him and crucified Him. In a metaphoric sense, they thus refused to come to the banquet hall.

Then, said Jesus, the king sent his messengers out into all the highways and byways with instructions to invite *anyone*—no matter how poor, disreputable, or shabby—to come to the wedding feast. When the guests arrived, the king noticed one man who had no wedding clothes on. When the king asked how he got into the banquet hall without wedding clothes, the man was speechless—he had no explanation. The king ordered him bound and cast into outer darkness.

Clearly this is a picture of the wedding feast of the Lamb. Only those who are suitably attired in the righteousness of God may attend. Those who have rejected the invitation and those who have tried to enter through the back door, clad in their own filthy rags, are barred from the festivities.

The Spirit of God has been calling men and women throughout the centuries, from Old Testament times through our own New Testament era and on into the future, even in the Tribulation period. The invitation goes out to everyone: "Come to the marriage feast of the Lamb!" What a privilege that will be, to see the Bridegroom face to face, to be a member of His beloved bride, to share in the intimacy of fellowship with the Lord Jesus!

I am reminded of the lines of the great Scottish saint of the eighteenth century, Samuel Rutherford:

> The Bride eyes not her garments,
> But her dear Bridegroom's face.
> And I will not gaze at glory,
> But on my King of Grace.
> Not at the crown he giveth,
> But on His pierced hands,
> The Lamb is all the glory
> Of Emmanuel's land.

It is almost impossible to adequately describe the beauty of this scene and the reality of the joy that awaits us. So incredible is the grace of God in extending His invitation to the human race that the angel adds, "These are the true words of God." But to experience the joy of the Lamb's wedding feast, we must first accept the invitation!

The Spirit of Prophecy

John is so moved by the vision of the marriage supper of the Lamb, a vision presented by an angel of the Lord, that he falls down to worship the angel. The angel immediately rebukes him. "No, don't do that!" the angel says in effect. "I am merely another servant of the King, just like you, just like all those who bear the testimony of Jesus. Don't worship me, worship God!"

Then the angel adds an interesting statement: "For the testimony of Jesus is the spirit of prophecy." All prophecy points only to Jesus, and all testimony to the power of Jesus is prophetic!

Some people think that the purpose of prophecy is to open a window on the future. But no, the spirit and essence of prophecy is *to bear witness to Jesus*. He is the central figure of all Scripture—and of all history. We are not to focus our attention on future events but on the One who will bring them to pass. Our focus of worship is the Lord.

The Climax of History

In verses 11 through 16 we come to the great climax of history. This is the divine event that has been expected not just for centuries but for millennia. All human events since the fall of man have been moving toward this moment—the unveiling of the presence of Jesus in power and great glory. It is the most often prophesied event in the Bible.

Three times in the book of Revelation, at the conclusion of each series of seven judgments—the seals, trumpets, and bowls of wrath—we have been brought to the very brink of this event. And each time the Spirit of Truth has brought us back again to see in a more intense and vivid way what the Lord is doing in the last days.

But here, at last, we come to the event itself!

This is what Paul calls "the splendor of his coming," or more literally from the original Greek, "the outshining of his presence." Jesus came as a thief for His church at the beginning of the Tribulation period, the last "week" of Daniel. He took the church away suddenly and unexpectedly, just as a thief steals treasure out of a house. Since then He has been invisibly present with the church behind the scenes of the last days of history, sovereignly directing events.

From time to time the book has shown Jesus to us—meeting with the 144,000 on Mount Zion and directing various activities taking place upon the earth. But suddenly He breaks through from the invisible realm to the startlingly visible! All eyes see Him! The supreme moment of human history has arrived! This is how Jesus Himself described that event:

At that time the sign of the Son of Man will appear in the sky, and all the nations of the earth will mourn. They will see the Son of Man coming on the clouds of the sky, with power and great glory.[5]

In the first chapter of Revelation, John also describes this event:

Look, he is coming with the clouds, and every eye will see him.

The Names of the Rider

Here John gives us another view of this event, a view that is rich in symbolism and detail.

19:11–16 *I saw heaven standing open and there before me was a white horse, whose rider is called Faithful and True. With justice he judges and makes war. His eyes are like blazing fire, and on his head are many crowns. He has a name written on him that no one knows but he himself. He is dressed in a robe dipped in blood, and his name is the Word of God. The armies of heaven were following him, riding on white horses and dressed in fine linen, white and clean. Out of his mouth comes a sharp sword with which to strike down the nations. "He will rule them with an iron scepter." He treads the winepress of the fury of the wrath of God Almighty. On his robe and on his thigh he has this name written:*

KING OF KINGS AND LORD OF LORDS.

This Rider on a white horse is not the Lone Ranger—though like the Lone Ranger He arrives on the scene just in the nick of time! He is identified for us by four different names:

1. "Faithful and True"

In verse 11 He is called "Faithful and True." It is in this capacity that He "judges and makes war"—and His judgments and His warfare are just. He is not an aggressor but a Holy Avenger. He sets wrongs to right. He exposes hidden corruption and injustice. He eliminates crime and hatred. He prosecutes the guilty and comforts the innocent.

2. An unknown name

In verse 12 there is another name for this Rider: "His eyes are like blazing fire, and on his head are many crowns. *He has a name written on him that no one knows but he himself.*" There is a clear connection between the blazing eyes and the crowns (or diadems) on His head. Blazing eyes speak of full discernment, of penetrating knowledge. Many diadems speak of full authority. The two together complete a picture of omniscience and omnipotence —but omniscience and omnipotence vested in a *man*. That is the crucial point of this passage.

The wonder of Jesus is that He is a man who manifests the fullness of God. That is what is revealed by His unknown name. What this suggests is that no one knows the full extent of the mysterious union of God and man in Jesus Christ. I suspect that new aspects of the amazing enigma that God has become a man will be revealed to us throughout eternity. That is why heaven continually breaks out with new shouts and hymns of praise: the wonder of the Lord's nature keeps manifesting itself in new ways!

3. *"The Word of God"*

In verse 13 there is still another name: "He is dressed in a robe dipped in blood, and his name is the Word of God." The Word of God is associated with the robe dipped in blood, with the armies of heaven who follow Him, and with the sword that comes out of His mouth. Some commentators refer to the "robe dipped in blood" as a reference to the cross. I have a different view.

I believe that the "robe dipped in blood" refers to a remarkable dialogue found in Isaiah 63. The dialogue is between the prophet Isaiah and the Warrior-Messiah. As Isaiah is shown the coming of Christ, it is as though he is standing in Jerusalem looking south toward Edom. There he witnesses the approach of a great warrior with crimson-stained garments, and this conversation takes place:

ISAIAH:
Who is this coming from Edom,
    from Bozrah, with his garments stained crimson?
Who is this, robed in splendor,
    striding forward in the greatness of his strength?

WARRIOR-MESSIAH:
"It is I, speaking in righteousness,
    mighty to save."

ISAIAH:
Why are your garments red,
    like those of one treading the winepress?

WARRIOR-MESSIAH:
"I have trodden the winepress alone;
    from the nations no one was with me.
I trampled them in my anger
    and trod them down in my wrath;
their blood spattered my garments,
    and I stained all my clothing.
For the day of vengeance was in my heart,
    and the year of my redemption has come."

This is surely a parallel passage to Revelation 19:13, which says that the Rider's robe was dipped in blood. The blood on the Rider's robe was not His own blood, shed for the redemption of sinners, but the blood of the wicked, pressed in the terrible winepress of judgment. Yes, Jesus did shed His blood as an atonement for sin, but the day of repentance and receiving grace has passed by the time the Rider appears on the scene. The blood that stains His garment is not the blood of atonement. It is the blood of God's vengeance.

The sharp sword which appears in the mouth of the Rider is the Word of God. In the opening vision of Revelation, John saw the Lord Jesus with a double-edged sword proceeding out of His mouth. It is a symbol of the power of the Word—the power to smite nations, and even destroy them if necessary.

Have you ever been smitten by the Word of God? Have you ever experienced the feeling of being pierced by some truth from the Bible? Sometimes it happens when you are seriously studying and meditating in the Word. At other times it may happen when you just hear a word of Scripture on the radio or in a conversation or in a letter from a friend. But God's Word has that kind of power—power to seize our attention and awaken our slumbering conscience. Suddenly we feel not merely naked but *transparent* before God, and we become aware that He sees more deeply into us than we see into ourselves.

On the day of Pentecost, the Jews who listened to the preaching of Peter "were cut to the heart," according to Acts 2:37. They were smitten by the Word of God. The story in Acts 5 of Ananias and Sapphira, who lied to the Holy Spirit, is another case in point. When Peter, speaking by the Spirit, exposed their lies, they dropped dead instantly. They were killed by the sword of the Word that comes from the mouth of the Lord.

Note, too, that when the Word of God comes in the visible personification of Jesus in verse 13 and following, He leads an army of saints and angels. The book of Jude quotes the prophet Enoch as saying, "See, the Lord is coming with thousands upon thousands of his holy ones to judge everyone, and to convict all the ungodly of all the ungodly acts they have done in the ungodly way, and of all the harsh words ungodly sinners have spoken against him."[6] Similarly, we have seen that Revelation 17:14 promises that the Lord's "called, chosen and faithful followers" will be with Him at His return. All those who return with Jesus, both saints and angels, will wield the sword of the Spirit, the Word of God, just as their Commander, Jesus, does.

4. "KING OF KINGS AND LORD OF LORDS"

In verse 16 is the fourth name: "KING OF KINGS AND LORD OF LORDS." This name is linked to the statement in verse 15, "He will rule them with an iron scepter." This is an echo—in fact, the third such echo in

Revelation—from Psalm 2. The iron scepter is a symbol of stern and righteous justice. It is the standard of God's morality—a standard which cannot be bent, diminished, or turned aside. When our Lord returns in triumph He will destroy the evil nations and rule over the rest.

This rule will be the millennial rule. Even though sin and sinners will still exist, righteousness will reign over all the earth. Sin will not be able to interfere with God's justice and peace because sinners will immediately be restrained by the Lord's iron scepter.

The Last Battle

Now we come to the last and most terrible battle of human history. It is not the first time we have visited this scene of war. We caught our first glimpse of this event in Revelation 9; then were given a view from another aspect in Revelation 16. Now, in Revelation 19:17-21, we gain still more insight into the terrible man-made, sin-inspired cataclysm called Armageddon. Here we will see the winepress of God's wrath at work.

19:17–18 *And I saw an angel standing in the sun, who cried in a loud voice to all the birds flying in midair, "Come, gather together for the great supper of God, so that you may eat the flesh of kings, generals, and mighty men, of horses and their riders, and the flesh of all people, free and slave, small and great."*

The call to slaughter has been sounded. The Battle of Armageddon has begun. As we have seen in previous descriptions of these events, 200,000,000 soldiers from all the armies of the earth are gathered into the land of Palestine.

There are other prophetic accounts of this battle elsewhere in Scripture. Ezekiel 38 and 39 records it in great detail. Joel 2, Daniel 11, and Isaiah 24 provide additional detail to this prophetic vision of a war that still lies in mankind's future—a war in which the king of the north comes down into the Holy Land and is met by a king of the south (the army of Egypt). Ezekiel 38:15-16 predicts that the armies of many nations "will advance against my people Israel like a cloud that covers the land." The slaughter that ensues will be unlike anything else in the history of man.

This is the event John describes as "the winepress of the fury of the wrath of God Almighty." The killing will continue—mindlessly, senselessly, relentlessly—until Jesus suddenly appears to impose divine justice on the world.

A Fiery Fate

John describes the fate of the anti-Christian enemies of the Lord.

19:19–21 *Then I saw the beast and the kings of the earth and their armies gathered together to make war against the rider on the horse and his army. But the beast was captured, and with him the false prophet who had performed the miraculous signs on his behalf. With these signs he had deluded those who had received the mark of the beast and worshiped his image. The two of them were thrown alive into the fiery lake of burning sulfur. The rest of them were killed with the sword that came out of the mouth of the rider on the horse, and all the birds gorged themselves on their flesh.*

When Jesus reveals Himself and every eye sees Him, it would seem that the only logical thing for the nations to do is to lay down their weapons, fall down and worship Him. Incredibly, the anti-Christian leaders actually turn on the Lord and launch an *assault* against Him!

But it is an unequal contest. The beast and the false prophet are immediately captured and thrown into the lake of fire, which in Revelation 21 and 22 is called "the second death." Fire: it is the ultimate symbol of eternal torment —an inward torment that burns on and on and never ends.

One Little Word

After the beast and the false prophet are dispatched into eternal torment, the rest of God's enemies are destroyed—not by a physical weapon of mass destruction, but by God's *Word* alone. "The rest of them were killed with the sword that came out of the mouth of the rider on the horse"—a sword which symbolizes the Word of God. Just as the universe was created by the Word of God, so His enemies can be destroyed by His Word.

We have seen the power of the "sword" from the mouth of Jesus before. When Jesus was in the Garden of Gethsemane, soldiers approached Him to take Him away. "Who is it you want?" Jesus asked.

"Jesus of Nazareth," the soldiers replied.

"I am he," the Lord said, using precisely the same "I AM" statement God used when He said to Moses, "I AM WHO I AM. This is what you are to say to the Israelites: 'I AM has sent me to you.' "[7] Hearing those same words—"I AM"—from the mouth of Jesus, the soldiers fell backwards to the ground. That is the power of the "sword"—the Word of God—in the mouth of Jesus.

The Lord could have walked out of the garden a free man had He chosen to do so. No force on earth could have resisted His Word. But He gave Himself into their hands. He sacrificed Himself through the eternal Spirit.8 It will be a different story when He comes again in power and triumph. The enemies of God will be overthrown by a mere word from His lips.

There is a savor of this truth in Martin Luther's great hymn "A Mighty Fortress Is Our God." It's the line that says that when the Lord confronts the devil, "one little word shall fell him." And Satan *shall* be felled—just like a tree that is cut down for firewood. The next chapter will see the felling of Satan.

But in the meantime, a question arises from Revelation 19—a question every person reading these words must confront: What do you do with Jesus?

The return of Christ is the fulcrum of history. All hope for this broken, dying world flows from the fact that He is coming again. How do you and I live our lives in light of that fact?

The record of the life of Jesus is unassailable: He came, He lived, He taught, He died, He rose again. Someday He will return and He will conquer. Jesus is the great issue of life. Our existence finds meaning only in Him.

How has the coming of Jesus Christ to a little Jewish town 2,000 years ago affected your life? How do you think His coming to a war-torn globe in the murky, uncertain future affects your life? What do you do with Jesus?

And what will He do with you?

Chapter Twenty-Four

One Thousand Years of Peace

Revelation 20

ver a hundred years ago, the French novelist Victor Hugo wrote,

> In the twentieth century war will be dead. The scaffold will be dead. Hatred will be dead. Frontier boundaries will be dead. Dogmas will be dead. But man will live. He will possess something higher than all these: a great country, the whole earth, a great hope, the whole heaven.

Someone once said, "The future isn't what it used to be." If Monsieur Hugo could see how his prediction turned out, I'm sure he would agree: the future—our present—is a far cry from what Hugo thought it would be.

The art of war is alive and well. The scaffold may be dead, but only because it has been replaced by the electric chair, the gas chamber, and the lethal injection. Hugo would be grieved indeed by the incidence and ferocity of crime in our society. Nations still struggle with each other. The world is high on dope, low on hope, divided, polluted, deluded, and sick with fear.

What has happened to the cherished dreams of Utopia? Where is the golden age man has longed for since the beginning of time? Where is the peace and prosperity we have sought for so long? The dream seems further beyond our grasp today than at any other time in history. And yet—

And yet the realization of that dream could be just around the next corner—only a few years away! We know that from our study of the book of Revelation. We know that the climax of human history lies ahead of us: the Second Coming of Jesus in visible power and glory. Jesus will reclaim the earth from Satan and his fallen angels, He will end the dominion of evil among men, and He will fulfill the promise of an earthly kingdom which was made to Abraham and again to David many centuries ago.

It is important to understand that there should be no break between chapters 19 and 20. There is nothing inspired about the present system of biblical chapter divisions, which were devised by Stephen Langton, Archbishop of Canterbury in the early thirteenth century. Much less is there anything inspired about a chapter division such as this one, which breaks the flow of the events of John's vision. In the original Greek text (which has no chapter or verse divisions), this account moves seamlessly to those events which follow the return of the Lord.

In the flow of the original text we see the events of chapter 19—the appearance of the Rider on a white horse, along with His heavenly armies.

20:1–3 *And I saw an angel coming down out of heaven, having the key to the Abyss and holding in his hand a great chain. He seized the dragon, that ancient serpent, who is the devil, or Satan, and bound him for a thousand years. He threw him into the Abyss, and locked and sealed it over him, to keep him from deceiving the nations anymore until the thousand years were ended. After that, he must be set free for a short time.*

Twice in that passage we see the phrase "a thousand years." It occurs a total of six times in Revelation 20. The word "millennium" comes from two Latin words, *mille annum*, meaning "a thousand years." It is this passage that teaches clearly and unambiguously about the Millennium of peace that lies in our future, beyond the seven years of tribulation, beyond the great final Battle of Armageddon.

A Doctrinal Battleground

This passage is one of the great doctrinal battlefields of Scripture. Two contrasting views of future events clash head-on in this chapter: *premillennialism* and *amillennialism*. If you're like me, you probably get tongue-tied just looking at those words on the page, much less saying them aloud. So, for simplicity's sake, we will simply call the advocates of these two views "pre-mills" and "a-mills."

Pre-mills, such as myself, take this passage literally and believe that Christ will set up His kingdom for a thousand years upon the earth. Such an event would be the fulfillment of many Old Testament prophecies concerning the reign of the Messiah upon the earth.

The a-mills or non-millennialists believe that the Millennium is taking place right now (the "a-" prefix in amillennialism means no or none). The a-mills say there will be no thousand-year reign of Christ in the future. Instead, they say the Millennium pictured in Revelation 20 is a picture of the present age of the church and is being fulfilled in a figurative or metaphorical way. They say the binding of Satan described in verse 2 took place when Jesus defeated Satan upon the cross. Satan, they say, has been bound ever since, throughout the entire history of the church.

A quick glance at the headlines is enough to make you scratch your head over this claim. As someone once remarked, "If Satan is bound today, it must be with a very long chain!"

Now, it is true in one sense that Jesus overpowered and bound Satan at the cross. As Paul writes, "And having disarmed the powers and authorities, he made a public spectacle of them, triumphing over them by the cross."[1]

Jesus likened Satan to a strong man, fully armed, who guards his own house and possessions. Those "possessions" represent the human race. Both a-mills and pre-mills believe Satan is in control and possession of the human race. Paul affirms this fact, calling Satan "the god of this age."[2] But Jesus said that He Himself was the stronger one who "attacks and overpowers" Satan, disarms Satan, and divides up Satan's possessions.[3]

The a-mills, who believe that the Millennium is now being fulfilled, say that Revelation 20 gives us a symbolic depiction of Christ's work on the cross. The scene where Satan is bound and consigned to the Abyss for a thousand years is actually a "flashback" to the crucifixion.

But pre-mills like myself believe the Millennium of Revelation 20 still lies ahead of the human race—and we point to several key passages of Scripture to support this belief. Scripture indicates that the binding or restraint of Satan that took place at the cross was valid only to those who believe in Jesus Christ.

"The god of this age," says Paul of Satan, "has blinded the minds of *unbelievers,* so that they cannot see the light of the gospel of the glory of Christ, who is the image of God."[4] Satan has a power to blind unbelievers, but he is restrained in his power over those who believe. That is why Peter, writing to Christians, says, "Your enemy the devil prowls around like a roaring lion looking for someone to devour. Resist him, standing firm in the faith. . . ."5 Even Christians need to believe, to exercise their faith, in order to oppose the devil.

So Satan is bound—yet in a *limited* way. He is restrained from attacking and controlling those who are protected by faith in Christ and His sacrifice on the cross. Satan is still the god of this world. He is still the strong man who counts among his possessions the majority of the human race. He is still the prince of the power of the air. During this present age, Satan is on a very long chain indeed!

Into the Abyss

But there are profound differences between the manner in which Satan was bound at the cross and the way he is bound in this passage in Revelation. Notice first that the binding of Satan in Revelation 20 makes no reference to the cross, but instead follows immediately on the heels of the Second Coming of Christ. Keeping in mind the fact that there were no chapter divisions in the original manuscripts, the events of Revelation 20 are clearly related to the events of Revelation 19. In context, we see the visible appearance of Christ in His glory and triumph, followed in the very next breath by the binding of Satan and his consignment to the Abyss.

Second, notice that the binding of Satan is not done by Jesus. It is done by a great angel—possibly the archangel Michael. The angel first binds Satan with a great chain. The chain is a metaphor, symbolizing a restraint upon Satan. You could not bind a spiritual being such as Satan with a literal, physical chain, but the chain stands for a spiritual reality: the limiting of Satan's power and ability to function.

But the angel doesn't simply restrain Satan with a chain. He also *throws Satan into the Abyss*, then locks and seals the door! This clearly indicates that Satan is totally removed from the earth for a thousand years.

In Revelation 9 we saw a star fall from the sky to the earth. The star was given the key to the Abyss, which it opened, releasing billows of smoke and a locust-like swarm of demonic powers upon the earth. Clearly the Abyss that is pictured here is separate from the earth. When Satan is thrown back into the Abyss, we get a picture of his total removal from this planet during the Millennium.

Third, the angel shuts and locks the door to the Abyss. It cannot be opened from the inside. It is a sealed prison. Even a demon on a very long chain could not escape from it to work his mischief in the world.

Fourth, the angel seals the door of the Abyss so that it cannot even be opened from the *outside*. No power—not even a power standing outside of the Abyss—may open it and release Satan during his thousand-year imprisonment. He has been arrested and jailed without possibility of parole.

And what about demons, the rest of Satan's army, the ones Paul calls "wicked spirits in heavenly places"? Where will they be during the Millennium? John's vision doesn't say, but the question is answered for us in Isaiah 24, a chapter that is often called "The Little Apocalypse." The prophet writes:

> In that day the LORD will punish
> the powers in the heavens above
> and the kings on the earth below.[6]

We have already seen the punishment of the kings on the earth. This was accomplished in Revelation 19:17-21 when the Lord and His armies arrived and destroyed them. Isaiah continues:

> They will be herded together
> like prisoners bound in a dungeon;
> they will be shut up in prison
> and be punished after many days.
> The moon will be abashed, the sun ashamed;
> for the LORD Almighty will reign
> on Mount Zion and in Jerusalem,
> and before its elders, gloriously.[7]

There seems to be little question that these are parallel passages. Isaiah indicates that Satan *and his angels* are removed from activity on the earth. It is a complete exile from which there is no escape for a thousand years. Demons will be banned from the face of the earth for a full thousand years.

Our amillennial friends will say that the thousand-year period is not to be taken literally. It is merely a metaphor, they say, for an indefinite period—or perhaps a way of saying that Satan is shut up completely and forever. But the answer to this argument comes from the last phrase in verse 3: "After that, he [Satan] must be set free *for a short time*." The word "time" is *chronos* in the Greek, from which we get "chronology." It is clearly a reference to a specific period of time—which means that the thousand years must be a specific period of time as well.

The words "a thousand years" appear six times in this chapter. Elsewhere in Scripture, if God wants to indicate an indefinite or eternal period of time He simply states it as such. It is hard to imagine why God should repeatedly say "a thousand years" in this one chapter of Scripture if He did not mean a literal thousand years. In fact, He says it so plainly and repetitiously that it is almost as if He wanted to head off any disputes over the matter!

Another argument of the a-mills is that Revelation 20 is the only biblical passage that teaches about a future Millennium. But while it is only in this passage that the thousand-year duration of the Millennium is given, the Bible is generously sprinkled with references to the earthly kingdom of the Messiah, when the throne of David will be restored over the nations. These passages are found in both the Old and New Testaments. In fact, the Bible is drenched with the good news of the coming kingdom—and in Revelation 20, God tells us that His kingdom will last for a thousand years.

Moreover, God even tells us *why* Satan is shut up in the Abyss for a thousand years: "to keep him from deceiving the nations anymore until the thousand years were ended." Today, the lies of Satan hold the nations spellbound. The world is captivated by drugs, by the wrongful use of sexuality, by the lust for power, by the lust for money, by the lust for status and fame. These lies have been poured into human ears from unseen powers since the first man and the first woman walked the earth. The record of human history is a record of the deceitfulness of Satan.

But when Satan is bundled off into the Abyss, all of his deceptions will cease for a thousand years. He will be locked in and sealed over. For the first time in thousands of years, the world will rest easy. The human race will at last be free of the "bedevilment" of satanic influence.

The Reign of the Saints

Next John gives us an exhilarating view of one of the most sublime aspects of the Millennium for you and me: as saints, *we will reign with Christ.*

20:4–6 *I saw thrones on which were seated those who had been given authority to judge. And I saw the souls of those who had been beheaded because of their testimony for Jesus and because of the word of God. They had not worshiped the beast or his image and had not received his*

mark on their foreheads or their hands. They came to life and reigned
with Christ a thousand years. (The rest of the dead did not come to life
until the thousand years were ended.) This is the first resurrection.
Blessed and holy are those who have part in the first resurrection. The
second death has no power over them, but they will be priests of God and
of Christ and will reign with him for a thousand years.

Notice the three different groups that are mentioned in this passage. First, John sees thrones upon which are seated "those who had been given authority to judge." Who are these judges seated on thrones in the Lord's millennial kingdom? To find out, we must compare this passage with the Lord's promise to His disciples: "I tell you the truth, at the renewal of all things, when the Son of Man sits on his glorious throne, you who have followed me will also sit on twelve thrones, judging the twelve tribes of Israel."[8] Jesus says that the twelve disciples will be given authority to judge the nation of Israel—and as we have seen throughout our journey through Revelation, that is a reference to the restored nation of Israel which has played such a crucial role in the last days.

But the twelve disciples are not the only ones who will be judges during the thousand-year reign of Christ. At the beginning of this vision, Jesus told the believers at Thyatira that all "overcomers" will rule with Christ during the Millennium:

> To him who overcomes and does my will to the end, I will
> give authority over the nations—
>
> "He will rule them with an iron scepter;
> he will dash them to pieces like pottery."[9]

The believers of this present age will be allied with Christ during His thousand-year reign over the nations. That is why Paul said to the Corinthians, "Do you not know that the saints will judge the world?" And further, "Do you not know that we will judge angels?"[10] His point to the Corinthians was that the saints who will someday judge angels and nations should certainly be able to settle petty squabbles among themselves!

Then John describes a second group he sees reigning with Christ during the Millennium: martyrs of the Tribulation—"those who had been beheaded because of their testimony for Jesus and because of the word of God. They had not worshiped the beast or his image and had not received his mark on their foreheads or their hands." This is the same group we saw in Revelation 6 and 7, believers who lost their lives in the persecution of the Tribulation, yet who never lost their faith and witness for Jesus Christ. They refused to bow before the Antichrist—and they paid the ultimate sacrifice for their faithfulness to God. They, too, will live again and reign with Christ for a thousand years.

Next John describes a third group. They are mentioned in a parenthesis and are not described in detail. They do not reign with Christ during the Millennium. Of them John simply says, "The rest of the dead did not come to life until the thousand years were ended." These are the unbelieving dead. They will appear before the Great White Throne judgment at the end of Revelation 20.

John concludes his description of these three groups—the saints who return with Christ at His coming, the saints who died in the Tribulation and are raised to life, and the unbelieving dead—with the words, "This is the first resurrection. Blessed and holy are those who have part in the first resurrection." Those who reign with Christ are those who take part in the first resurrection.

The fact that there is a "first resurrection" automatically implies that a second resurrection follows. Our amillennialist friends, however, beg to differ. They say there is only one resurrection. It comes, they believe, at the very end of history, and it therefore must be associated with the Great White Throne judgment. They say it will be one resurrection and one judgment involving both the righteous and the wicked dead.

Of course, that view creates a problem since this passage says there is a first resurrection and that "the rest of the dead did not come to life until the thousand years were ended." What, then, is the a-mills' view of this "first resurrection"? They are driven to conclude that it must have been a "resurrection" of an incorporeal spirit or soul, not a resurrection of the body. But that is an extremely weak position to hold since the word "resurrection" literally means "to stand up again."

The Dutch have a wonderful word for resurrection that captures the meaning exactly: *oopstanding*. A spirit cannot stand up, nor can a soul. They are immaterial. Only a body can stand up. In fact, examine every other use of the word "resurrection" in the Scriptures and you will see that it *always* refers to a resurrection of the body. In light of these facts, the conclusion seems inescapable: "the first resurrection" is a literal raising of the bodies of the dead in Christ.

Jesus, said the apostle Paul, was "raised from the dead, the firstfruits of those who have fallen asleep."[11] So the first resurrection reaches back to include the resurrection of Jesus and those raised with Him.

Matthew 27:52-53 tells us that at the time our Lord was raised,

"The tombs broke open and the bodies of many holy people who had died were raised to life . . . and appeared to many people." Although this resurrection of the saints appears plainly in the Scriptures, many Christians do not seem to be aware of it. These resurrected saints were also among the firstfruits offered to God as a "down payment" on the "first resurrection."

The "second payment" comes when Christ returns for His church at the end of the church age, before the start of the seven years of tribulation. As Paul said to the Corinthians, the resurrection will occur by turns or phases, each in its proper sequence: "Christ, the firstfruits; then, when he comes, those who belong to him."[12] From a human perspective, over 2,000 years lie between the "down payment" and the "second payment"—but there is no time factor in eternal events. Paul continues: "Then the end will come. . . ." That is, the concluding resurrection, the last resurrection before the Great White Throne judgment.

So there are clearly two resurrections taught in Scripture. Jesus Himself referred to a "resurrection of life" and a "resurrection of judgment."[13] The first resurrection raises only those who believe in Christ. That is why John says, "Blessed and holy are those who have part in the first resurrection. The second death has no power over them, but they will be priests of God and of Christ and will reign with him for a thousand years."

The Golden Age

There is a sentence in verse 3 that I passed over without comment. Now I want to return to it. John writes, "After that"—after the Millennium—"he [Satan] must be set free for a short time." The logical question is, "Why? Why set the devil free—even for a 'short time'?"

We have all heard stories of criminals who were furloughed or paroled, only to commit still more heinous crimes as soon as they were free. We expect an imperfect institution such as the criminal justice system to make these kinds of mistakes. But why should God deliberately turn this demon loose upon the earth again, just when things have been going so well for a thousand years?

20:7–10 *When the thousand years are over, Satan will be released from his prison and will go out to deceive the nations in the four corners of the earth—Gog and Magog—to gather them for battle. In number they are like the sand on the seashore. They marched across the breadth of the earth and surrounded the camp of God's people, the city he loves. But fire* *came down from heaven and devoured them. And the devil, who deceived them, was thrown into the lake of burning sulfur, where the beast and the false prophet had been thrown. They will be tormented day and night for ever and ever.*

Someone once asked me, "What reason is there for a Millennium after Jesus comes back? Why not just bring about the new heaven and new earth at that time and be completely done with sin and Satan?" Here is the answer: A thousand years of peace and blessing in a world without Satan is designed to demonstrate beyond question that the Bible's diagnosis of the human condition is true: We belong to a fallen race, and every human being is born with an essentially evil nature!

Very few people today are willing to believe that. Ask most people (particularly those who consider themselves "enlightened") and they will tell you, "I think people are basically good. When they do wrong it's really just because of economic factors or the wrong diet or poor toilet training," or some such excuse. The idea that people are basically sinful is viewed as either quaintly old-fashioned or downright ignorant. Our entire educational system is based on the idea that people are born with a basically good nature, plus some potential for evil.

But that's not what the Scriptures teach. That famous theologian of the 1970s, Flip Wilson, made a career out of the statement, "The devil made me do it!" This has become the standard excuse of man for the evil he has created in the world. Certainly much of the evil in the world does come from the devil. Thus, to inaugurate an era of global peace, God must remove the devil from the scene.

But not all evil comes from the devil. God wants to impress upon humanity what Jeremiah so plainly states: "The heart is deceitful above all things and beyond cure. Who can understand it?"[14] That is why everyone needs salvation. We are desperate and hopeless without it. The evil is not "out there," it's "in here." We have no hope without a Savior.

Before I retired from the pulpit at Peninsula Bible Church, a number of people came up and said a lot of nice things to me. It was almost like getting to hear the eulogy at my own funeral! But I know better. I know all the hidden places of my own heart and my own behavior. I know the malice, the selfishness, the impatience, and other evils that spring from the deceitfulness of my own heart. I experience the same struggles and temptations as anyone else. There are no exceptions to the human condition. The biblical picture of man is accurate—and universal. We are all born with a fallen nature.

The Millennium will prove that to be true. No one will doubt it after those thousand years have passed. No one will be able to say, "The devil made me do it," because the devil will be sealed up in the Abyss.

Certainly, life on earth will be vastly improved once Satan has been removed from the scene. Nations and individuals will live together in peace during the Millennium. As the prophet Isaiah wrote,

> He will judge between the nations and will settle disputes for
> many peoples. They will beat their swords into plowshares and
> their spears into pruning hooks. Nation will not take up sword
> against nation, nor will they train for war anymore.[15]

A beautiful picture of the coming golden age, the thousand-year Utopia. But did you notice that the Lord will be called upon to "judge between the nations and will settle disputes for many peoples"? Why? Because there will still be sin—even when the devil is gone!

The curse will be lifted from nature. The land will produce abundant food and flora. The entire world will be as beautiful as Hawaii—but without the tourists! Animals that are now predators will become herbivores and live in peace with their former prey. "The wolf and the lamb will feed together," says Isaiah, "and the lion will eat straw like the ox."[16]

Man will live long—perhaps as long as the Old Testament patriarchs—700, 800, 900 years or more. "He who dies at a hundred will be thought a mere youth,"[17] says Isaiah, prophesying about this utopian age. Yet, even though death will be a rarity, it will still occur.

And not only death but *sin* will occur. "The sinner who reaches a hundred will be considered accursed,"[18] adds Isaiah. There will still be sin in the millennial age, and that sin will affect the sinner's lifespan. The continuing presence of sin is the reason why Jesus must rule with a scepter of iron. Yet even though sin remains, righteousness obtains.

Today, self-gratification and the selfishness of sin are the dominant philosophy of the masses. Righteousness struggles bravely to exist. But in that day the tables will be turned. Justice will dominate. Evil will be restrained by the iron rule of Jesus.

The Devil on the Loose

But as the text tells us, a time will come at the end of the thousand-year golden age when Satan is loosed from the Abyss. Even in that utopian era, there will be people who resent the Lordship of Jesus Christ, who will hate His restored nation Israel, who will hide themselves as far from the presence of the Lord's throne as they can get—"in the four corners of the earth." Returned from exile, Satan will scour the four corners of the earth to find these renegades and gather them together for one last attempt to overthrow the government of God.

Those who would destroy Israel, even after a thousand years of glorious peace with Israel at the center, immediately respond to Satan's demonic leadership when he is again released into the world. They are called Gog and Magog after Israel's antagonists in the Battle of Armageddon. The individuals and nations which set themselves against Israel, King Jesus, and the government of God clearly demonstrate for all time that there is an evil inheritance locked within man. Until we are born again by the Spirit of God, our nature remains unchanged.

The forces under the dominion of Satan march upon Jerusalem—but they are instantly destroyed with fire from heaven. The devil, the ancient enemy of man and God, is at last thrown down for the final time, consigned along with the beast and the false prophet to the lake of fire. The devil's punishment, and the punishment of all who lived lives of rebellion or indifference toward God, will not last a mere thousand years. "They will be tormented day and night," writes John, "for ever and ever."

It is a horrid picture. But the Scriptures are unambiguous on the subject of eternal punishment. The destiny of human beings is not annihilation or evaporation into nothingness. Our lives had a starting point somewhere in time, but they have no end. We remain alive forever.

Whether we spend the span of eternity in the presence of Jesus or in an abyss of unending despair is a matter of our own choice, here and now.

The Great White Throne

Verses 11 through 15 bring us to the last sobering scene of Revelation 20. It is a scene of final judgment.

20:11–15 *Then I saw a great white throne and him who was seated on it. Earth and sky fled from his presence, and there was no place for them. And I saw the dead, great and small, standing before the throne, and books were opened. Another book was opened, which is the book of life. The dead were judged according to what they had done as recorded in the books. The sea gave up the dead that were in it, and death and Hades gave up the dead that were in them, and each person was judged according to what he had done. Then death and Hades were thrown into the lake of fire. The lake of fire is the second death. If anyone's name was not found written in the book of life, he was thrown into the lake of fire.*

Here is a startling and terrifying scene. Imagine standing on a starship, watching the earth and the planets recede from view, the stars moving against the background of eternal night. That is the vision suggested by John's words, "Earth and sky fled from his presence, and there was no place for them." This suggests that all of humanity will be removed from earth, perhaps from the universe as we know it, to eternity itself, where there is no space and no time. That is where judgment will take place.

The judge is Jesus, not God the Father. "The Father judges no one," said Jesus, "but has entrusted all judgment to the Son."[19] It is Jesus who sits upon the Great White Throne of majesty and gathers all the dead before Him. There will also be some living people from the Millennium, for it must be determined if their names are recorded in the book of life. Judgment will be "according to what one had done." Deeds reveal the condition of the heart. Deeds reveal belief.

All the deeds of mankind are preserved in God's great library. Books are a symbol of the eternal record of our lives. If John were receiving this vision today, the symbol would probably be videotape or computer disks rather than books. The books are metaphors for the record of every life—and the final judgment of every life shall be made on the basis of that record.

Only those whose names are in the book of life can do righteous deeds. Only the deeds of the righteous will survive the fire of judgment. All other deeds will be consumed to ashes. Only those acts that have been done by the power of the Spirit of God and done for the glory of God will remain. Even the noblest and most impressive accomplishments, even acts which have helped many people or changed the course of history—if they were done by the power of the self and for the glory of the self—will vanish without a trace.

If your name is not in the book of life, your evil deeds will be revealed. All the hidden corners of your life will be subjected to scrutiny. Nothing will go unnoticed. Today you may have a reputation for your devotion, your caring, your humility, your abilities—but in that day Jesus will judge the hidden motives behind your deeds. He will know if your real reason for service in the church and the community was to glorify God—or if it was all tainted by selfishness, pride, and the lust for prominence, power, influence, and recognition.

That question that confronts you and me from this passage is the question of the old song:

> Is my name written there,
> On the page bright and fair?

> In the book of God's kingdom,
> Is my name written there?

When Jesus sent out the twelve disciples to minister to other cities and towns in Israel, they returned rejoicing that they had cast out demons with just a word of command. They were amazed at the power of God that was flowing through them, at the wonderful deeds that were being accomplished, at the fact that even the demons submitted to them in the name of Jesus.

"Do not rejoice that the spirits submit to you," Jesus replied, "but rejoice that your names are written in heaven."[20]

That is the central question in life: Is your name written in the Lamb's book of life? Beside this one issue, everything else pales in comparison. Your name is written in that book when you commit your life to Jesus.

No one needs to face the lake of fire. No one goes into the Abyss against his or her own will. It is a choice we all make in this life. If we refuse the Savior, God can only give us the fate we demand.

The issue of eternal punishment raises a problem in the minds of most thoughtful Christians: What about those who have never heard the gospel of Jesus Christ? Isn't it unfair that someone should be condemned to an eternity apart from God simply because he never had the opportunity to hear about Jesus? This is a difficult question, but it is addressed in Scripture. Hebrews 11:6 tells us, "Anyone who comes to [God] must believe that he exists and that he rewards those who earnestly seek Him." God knows the intent and condition of every human being, and He will deal with every individual according to the great declaration of Scripture, "Far be it from [God] to . . . kill the righteous with the wicked, treating the righteous and the wicked alike. . . . Will not the Judge of all the earth do right?"[21]

We know that God only holds us accountable for the light of understanding we have received. Those of us who have received more revelation are responsible for how we respond to that revelation. Scripture does not explicitly tell us the fate of those who have not heard of Jesus, of the cross and the empty tomb, of the grace of God and the forgiveness of sins. But the Bible does tell us that God will deal justly with them.

The question that confronts you and me, since we have received so much of the revelation of God's truth, is this: Have our names been written in the Lamb's book of life? Jesus knows our hearts. Nothing is hidden from His view. If we come to Him, we belong to Him and He to us. We need fear nothing from the final judgment and the second death.

These are sober matters. This is a somber and dark chapter of Revelation. It is painful to write about such things. Yet the darkness of this scene in Revelation provides a clear and unobstructed contrast with the shining and precious gift that Jesus offers us through His sacrifice on the cross. It is a *joy* to announce—particularly against such a dark and ominous background—that there is still time, still hope, and that the grace of God is still available to you. If you have never accepted His grace before, I urge you by the mercy of God to do so *now*.

"God has given us eternal life," said John in his first epistle, "and this life is in his Son. He who has the Son has life; he who does not have the Son of God does not have life."[22] The ultimate issues of life are all settled here. If you belong to the Son and your name is written in heaven, you have life. If you refuse Him, you share the fate of the devil, the beast, and the false prophet. No one can make that choice for you, not even God Himself.

You have been given the choice. What will your answer be?

Chapter Twenty-Five

The City of Glory

Revelation 21 and 22

 television producer for the British Broadcasting Corporation was preparing a documentary about Christianity in England. In the course of his research, he sent a memo to a clergyman who served as an adviser to the BBC on church affairs. The memo read,

> How might I ascertain the official church view of heaven and hell?

The clergyman replied with a memo consisting of only one word:

> Die.

Fortunately, we do not have to die to discover God's truth about heaven and hell. We have already seen much of what the Bible has to say about eternal punishment. Now in chapters 21 and 22 of Revelation we encounter God's revelation of a coming reality called *heaven*.

Throughout much of this book we have seen judgment upon judgment, seven years of tribulation, trials of persecution and martyrdom, earthquakes, plagues, doom in the heavens, smoke and thunder, war, the final judgment, and the lake of fire. Now the scene shifts from images of cataclysm and judgment to images of joy and triumph.

If you are old enough to remember a pre-World War II radio broadcaster named H. V. Kaltenborn, you probably remember the catchphrase with which he began every broadcast: "Well, we've got good news today!" That's the theme of the final two chapters of Revelation: *good news*. The vision of John has taken us through moods of deep sorrow and intense horror and forced us to look at the destruction of our world. But the good news is that God is preparing a new world for us to inhabit after the old world passes away.

George Bernard Shaw once complained, "Heaven, as conventionally conceived, is a place so inane, so dull, so useless, so miserable, that nobody has ever ventured to describe a whole day in heaven, though plenty of people have described a day at the seashore." And you know, the old curmudgeon was right! Remember, he was talking about "heaven, *as conventionally conceived*." And how is heaven conventionally conceived? Look at most movies about heaven and you'll get the picture: Saints who have been transformed into angels with wings and white robes, sitting on clouds and playing their golden harps—all of which is *indeed* conventional, inane, dull, useless, and miserable.

But of course that's not really heaven!

The reason a day in heaven is harder to describe than a day at the seashore is that heaven is a wholly different plane of experience than the seashore. As Peter Toon writes in *Heaven and Hell*, heaven is a reality which is "'outside' the space and time we know" and "must be described in language which of necessity exists for communication within our space and time."[1] And that's the problem.

Imagine trying to explain the concepts of relativity and quantum physics to a child in the second grade. Or trying to explain the technological marvels of the late twentieth century to a man of 2,000 B.C. They would simply have no frame of reference to even begin to grasp what you are saying. And heaven is even more removed from our frame of reference than physics is to a child or the modern world to ancient man. Heaven is not just another place; it is another plane, another dimension.

A New Heaven and a New Earth

The two concluding chapters of Revelation contain virtually all that the Bible has to say about the eternal state of the believer. Certainly there are many passages in the Old Testament that picture a time of great blessing and utopian peace, but these are prophecies not of heaven but of the thousand-year kingdom which precedes heaven.

Heaven, as we discover in these chapters, is an entirely new creation that springs into being at God's command. We catch our first glimpse of heaven immediately after the Great White Throne judgment of Revelation 20.

21:1–4 *Then I saw a new heaven and a new earth, for the first heaven and the first earth had passed away, and there was no longer any sea. I saw the Holy City, the new Jerusalem, coming down out of heaven from God, prepared as a bride beautifully dressed for her husband. And I heard a loud voice from the throne saying, "Now the dwelling of God is with men, and he will live with them. They will be his people, and God himself will be with them and be their God. He will wipe every tear from their eyes. There will be no more death or mourning or crying or pain, for the old order of things has passed away."*

What beautiful words! Nearing the end of the Word of God we come full circle, all the way to the beginning of the Word of God. "In the beginning God created the heavens and the earth," says Genesis 1:1. Now, in Revelation, we see the heavens and the earth of Genesis 1:1 have passed away, and a new heaven and a new earth are coming.

The apostle Peter recorded a parallel description of this scene:

> But the day of the Lord will come like a thief. The heavens will
> disappear with a roar; the elements will be destroyed by fire, and
> the earth and everything in it will be laid bare.[2]

A fiery roar and the earth is laid bare: thus ends the old heavens, the old earth. But the new is coming. In the new heaven and new earth, Jesus will continue His reign. He will be King not only over the earth but throughout the entire reach of the vast universe of God.

Why a *new* heaven and a *new* earth? Four statements in this opening paragraph of Revelation 21 tell us that God has a very definite purpose in mind. The new heaven and new earth are the next phase in His eternal program. There is a strong suggestion in these verses that the New Jerusalem John sees is to be the capital city of the whole new universe.

The new universe will be radically changed from the universe we now know. I don't believe God will eliminate the present heavens and earth, but rather will cleanse and reconstruct the substance of the universe that now is. We see the same principle at work when we become Christians—new creatures in Christ. We are still the same person, but we are also new, changed, and cleansed. So also the old heavens and the old earth will be cleansed. They will be cleansed by fire.

We know that the present universe—even to the farthest reaches we can observe—is governed by the same physical laws that we observe right in our own planetary neighborhood. One of these physical laws is the Second Law of Thermodynamics, the law of entropy, which says that the energy of the present universe is running down. Our ordered systems are tending toward disorder and decay. Given enough time, even the stars will grow cold.

But in the new heavens and the new earth, the law of entropy is reversed. The batteries are recharged, the clock wound up again—only now it will never run down. The new heavens and the new earth will manifest a unity, stability, symmetry, and beauty that even the old heavens and earth—as marvelously ordered and beautiful as they were—never had.

No More Sea

There is an interesting statement embedded in this passage: ". . . and there was no longer any sea." A friend of mine after reading this passage said to me, "I don't think I'm going to like the new heavens and the new earth. I love the ocean!" I understand that feeling. I love the ocean, too. But consider for a moment just why the ocean exists.

Over 70 percent of the surface of our world is covered with salt water. The average depth of the ocean is 2.3 miles. Why does our planet need such a massive covering of salt water? Answer: To cleanse the earth and make life possible. The earth is bathed in God's great antiseptic solution composed of about 96 percent water, 3.5 percent salt, and about .5 percent trace constituents—chlorine, magnesium, calcium, and the like. The salty brine of the ocean purges, cleanses, and preserves our planet, making it fit to live in.

Many of the pollutants and waste we produce get washed out of the soil and into our streams and rivers; others we deliberately dump into the rivers. The rivers wash these materials to the sea. The antiseptic salinity of the sea absorbs, scrubs, and breaks down these pollutants and wastes. The sun heats the sea, causing only pure, clean water vapor to float up into the sky, forming clouds which bring refreshing rain back to the land—a continuous cycle of cleansing and renewal. But in the new heaven and new earth there will be no more pollution, no more decay, no more need for cleansing, and thus no more need for a salty sea.

Though the Scriptures do not suggest this, it is interesting to speculate that there may be large bodies of fresh water, perhaps even larger than the Great Lakes, that we may enjoy in the new heaven and the new earth.

The New City

The second statement in this passage that tells us the purpose of the new heaven and new earth is John's description of the Holy City, the New Jerusalem, "coming down out of heaven from God, prepared as a bride beautifully dressed for her husband."

We all love weddings. The climax of every wedding is that moment when the bride makes her entrance at the beginning of the aisle, beautifully dressed for her husband. All heads turn. You hear that collective intake of breath as every eye is instantly captivated by the literally breathtaking sight of the beautifully adorned bride. In that moment the poor fellow standing at the altar in his rented tux is completely forgotten. It is the bride—so achingly beautiful in her white gown and gossamer veil—that has captured all eyes and every heart.

That's the image we are given of the new city, the New Jerusalem, as it comes down out of heaven from God. Just as the false bride, the prostitute Mystery Babylon, was both a city (Rome) and a woman, this new and pure bride, the New Jerusalem, is also described as both a city and a woman. Mystery Babylon was destroyed for its utter evil and abomination. But the bride of Revelation 21 speaks of true intimacy and purity. And a shining city speaks of community, of many people living together in peace and abundance.

So we are given a picture here of the redeemed of God, each in a new body of glory, empowered with limitless energy. No longer will anyone be able to say, "The spirit is willing but the flesh is weak." Whatever the spirit decides to do, the flesh will accomplish with ease.

I often think of that phrase in John's letters where he says, "It does not yet appear what we shall be."[3] I keep looking in the mirror for signs of change, hoping to see the new body God has promised me. But what do I see? More wrinkles! It won't be like that when we get to the new heaven and new earth. We will have bodies of glory and beauty that will be like the body of the Lord.

There will be such a sense of community, love, and belonging in the New Jerusalem that we cannot even imagine it in this life. We will live in close intimacy not only with the Lord Himself, but with one another.

The Home of God

The third statement in this passage that tells us the purpose of the new heaven and new earth is that the Holy City, the New Jerusalem, will be the dwelling place of God. "Now the dwelling of God is with men," says a loud voice from the throne, "and he will live with them. They will be his people, and God himself will be with them and be their God."

The New Jerusalem will be composed of all the saints. We are the city. The dwelling place of God will be you and me and every other believer! In heaven, the name *Immanuel,* meaning "God with us," will at last be fulfilled. The New Covenant will finally be fully accomplished.

No More . . .

Heaven, as someone has said, will be the place of "no more." No more death. No more sorrow. No more parting. No more pain. No more tears. No more evil.

As a young Christian, I learned a song which still echoes in my soul many years later:

> There's no disappointment in heaven,
> No weariness, sorrow or pain,
> No hearts that are bleeding and broken,
> No song with a minor refrain.
> The clouds of our earthly horizon
> Shall never appear in the sky.
> But all will be sunshine and gladness,
> With never a sob nor a sigh.

That is a wonderful hope—so wonderful it is almost beyond belief. I think the apostle John must have felt that way, too, for in the next few verses he is given words of assurance to help him quell any possible doubts.

21:5–6a *He who was seated on the throne said, "I am making everything new!" Then he said, "Write this down, for these words are trustworthy and true."*

He said to me: "It is done. I am the Alpha and the Omega, the Beginning and the End."

God brackets all of time in that one statement: "I am the Alpha and the Omega, the Beginning and the End." Everything in between proceeds from God. These words are God's seal of truth that help us to believe.

Remember the Lord's last words on the cross? After all the pain, the mocking, the sorrow, the gloom, the darkness, and the anguish of separation from the Father, Jesus cried out, "It is finished!" The basis of redemption was settled. The sacrifice for sin had been made. The foundation for salvation had been fully laid.

In Revelation 21:6 we find a similar statement: "It is done. I am the Alpha and the Omega, the Beginning and the End." The redemption that was begun on the cross has now been completed. The redeemed have arrived home in glory. God's plan has been accomplished. Not one thing is left unfinished.

The Inheritance of the Redeemed

The fourth statement in this passage revealing the purpose of the new heaven and new earth is the statement that it will be the inheritance and the home of the redeemed. In verses 6 and 7 John records the further words of God.

21:6b–7 *"To him who is thirsty I will give to drink without cost from the spring of the water of life. He who overcomes will inherit all this, and I will be his God and he will be my son."*

Heaven will be the home of the redeemed, and the only prerequisite is that you be thirsty. Nothing on earth satisfies—not wealth, fame, pleasure, or possessions. There is only one thing that can quench the deep thirst of the soul, and that is God Himself. People who thirst after God are promised that they shall drink of the water of the spring of life. These are the ones God calls "overcomers." The overcomers will "inherit all this," all that God has newly created.

The apostle Peter tells us that there is waiting for us "an inheritance that can never perish, spoil or fade—kept in heaven for you."[4] Those who have been transformed by God's grace are to be His children forever.

In verse 8, there is a note of contrast, referring back to the judgments we have already witnessed in the book of Revelation.

21:8 *"But the cowardly, the unbelieving, the vile, the murderers, the sexually immoral, those who practice magic arts, the idolaters and all liars — their place will be in the fiery lake of burning sulfur. This is the second death."*

As we have already seen throughout the book of Revelation (and as is apparent throughout the Scriptures), God does not want anyone to suffer this judgment. The apostle Peter writes, "The Lord . . . is patient with you, not wanting anyone to perish, but everyone to come to repentance."[5]

He is reluctant that anyone should be judged, but those who persist in doing such things judge themselves.

In this passage we find three attitudes which result in five forms of visible behavior. These attitudes and forms of behavior mark those who are lost and who will not be a part of that Holy City in the new earth.

First are the cowardly—those who are fearful, unwilling to take the yoke of Christ upon themselves, afraid to confess Jesus Christ, unwilling to be in the minority or on the unpopular side of things. Afraid of the risks entailed in being a follower of Christ, they turn their backs on the offer of life.

Second are the unbelieving, those who willfully refuse to believe what their hearts tell them is true. They reject the evidence because they don't want God to invade their self-centered lives.

Third are the vile, those whose way of life has become foul and abominable. They love the stink of their own sin and would scratch and claw anyone who tried to rescue them from it. They feed their minds with vile books, vile movies, and vile music. They speak vile speech and practice a vile lifestyle.

These, then, are the three deadly attitudes: the cowardly, the unbelieving, and the vile. Out of these attitudes flow evil behavior: murder, sexual immorality, involvement in the occult and demonic arts, idolatry, and lying or hypocrisy. No one who, refusing redemption, gives himself or herself over to such behavior will be found in the city of God.

A Shining City

An angel takes John to a high mountain for a spectacular view of the shining city. John gives us the following detailed impressions.

21:9–14 *One of the seven angels who had the seven bowls full of the seven last plagues came and said to me, "Come, I will show you the bride, the wife of the Lamb." And he carried me away in the Spirit to a mountain great and high, and showed me the Holy City, Jerusalem, coming down out of heaven from God. It shone with the glory of God, and its brilliance was like that of a very precious jewel, like a jasper, clear as crystal. It had a great, high wall with twelve gates, and with twelve angels at the gates. On the gates were written the names of the twelve tribes of Israel. There were three gates on the east, three on the north, three on the south and three on the west. The wall of the city had twelve foundations, and on them were the names of the twelve apostles of the Lamb.*

On reading this description people almost always ask, "Is this a literal or symbolic description?" The fact is, in this as in so many other passages of Revelation, we do not have to make that choice. God loves to use literal things to symbolize deeper truths. Throughout Revelation we have seen the blending of literal and symbolic meaning.

Personally, I believe the city will have a literal dimension. It will be a great, visible city, brilliant and glorious, located somewhere above or within the atmosphere of the new earth. Some commentators have suggested that the New Jerusalem might even orbit the new earth like a second moon. It will be characterized by stability, symmetry, light, life, beauty, and ministry.

But it will also have a symbolic dimension. Let us look at the symbols of this new city and interpret their meaning.

The high wall of the city speaks of separation and of intimacy—separation from what is without, intimacy with what is within. If you want to have an intimate garden party you meet in a yard enclosed within a wall. The wall shuts out the outside and protects the inside, creating a safe enclosure for intimate fellowship.

All through Scripture God expresses a strong desire for what He calls "a people for my own possession." In a sense all that exists is His possession for it is His creation. All animals, all creatures are His. The billions of angels are His. The entire human race is His creation.

Yet He has created human beings with free will, the ability to choose Him or reject Him. Henceforth, only those human beings who choose Him are truly a people for His own possession. The saints alone are His possession, because with them He can share the depths of His heart. They satisfy Him and fulfill Him just as a bride satisfies and fulfills her husband.

The gates symbolize means of entering and leaving the city. There is an amazing verse in the gospel of John where Jesus says, "I am the gate; whoever enters through me will be saved. He will come in and go out, and find pasture."[6] This seems to be a portrayal of the widespread ministry of believers throughout the eternal ages.

The new universe will surely be as big or bigger than it is now—and its vastness is orders of magnitude beyond human comprehension as it is! Billions of galaxies, each containing billions of stars like our own sun, sprinkle the heavens for as far as our greatest telescopes can see. Each of those stars may be circled by planets—perhaps even many earthlike planets. These may be new limitless worlds for us to encounter, explore, develop, and experience. Every moment of eternity will be a new adventure of discovery.

The gates of the Holy City are named for the tribes of Israel. It is a perpetual reminder that "salvation is of the Jews." Access to the city is through Israel—not merely because it was the Jewish nation that gave us Jesus, but also because Israel gave us the Old Testament prophets and the godly traditions and practices of the Old Testament. Many of those brilliant but enigmatic Old Testament passages that now puzzle us will someday come to life as profound jewels of truth. Scripture that once perplexed us will one day lead us to adventures we never dreamed of in this life.

The foundations symbolize those aspects of the New Jerusalem that give it stability and permanence. They are named for the twelve apostles. Judas, who betrayed Jesus, was replaced in the apostolic band by Matthias, as we learn in Acts 1. These foundations speak of New Testament truth and practice. Spiritual realities that we only faintly grasp now will become startlingly clear and meaningful in that eternal plane of existence—and especially those three things which Scripture says will abide forever: faith, hope, and love! "But the greatest of these," says Paul, "is love."[7]

Language is inadequate to express the beauty and truth that is embedded in this description of the Holy City in the fact that the truths of God's Word will never pass away, in the fact that faith, hope, and—above all!— love will never pass away, but will go on and on, enduring beyond this dying and temporary world and crossing the divide into that new heaven and new earth! How can everyday language express a reality that is light-years beyond the reach of our deepest joy and highest exhilaration? Yet it is my prayer, as you read these words, that God would enable the inner eye of your imagination to catch a glimpse of the profound experience that awaits us in the new heaven, the new earth, and that shining new city.

The Measure and Makings of the City

21:15–17 *The angel who talked with me had a measuring rod of gold to measure the city, its gates and its walls. The city was laid out like a square, as long as it was wide. He measured the city with the rod and found it to be 12,000 stadia in length, and as wide and high as it is long. He measured its wall and it was 144 cubits thick, by man's measurement, which the angel was using.*

When God measures, it is a sign of His ownership. The number 12 appears repeatedly in this account: 12,000 stadia, 144 (or 12 squared) cubits, 12 gates, 12 foundations, 12 angels. The number 12 in Scripture symbolizes government. This, then, is the fulfillment of the prophetic words of Isaiah, "The government will be on his shoulders. And he will be called Wonderful Counselor, Mighty God, Everlasting Father, Prince of Peace."[8]

The city is amazingly vast, measuring 12,000 stadia long, high, and wide. In modern measurements, 12,000 stadia equals roughly 1,500 miles—about the distance from Los Angeles to St. Louis or from New York to Denver. For comparison, the moon is about 2,160 miles in diameter. The fact that the city measures exactly the same in all three dimensions does not mean that it is a perfect cube, only that it is a city of perfect proportions and symmetry. It may be intricately formed with spires and domes and graceful buttresses and bridges, or it may be a perfect pyramid. Whatever its shape it will symbolize perfection and it will be the realization of utter beauty.

In verses 18 through 21 John goes on to reveal the materials from which the city is made.

21:18–21 *The wall was made of jasper, and the city of pure gold, as pure as glass. The foundations of the city walls were decorated with every kind of precious stone. The first foundation was jasper, the second sapphire, the third chalcedony, the fourth emerald, the fifth sardonyx, the sixth carnelian, the seventh chrysolite, the eighth beryl, the ninth topaz, the tenth chrysoprase, the eleventh jacinth, and the twelfth amethyst. The twelve gates were twelve pearls, each gate made of a single pearl. The great street of the city was of pure gold, like transparent glass.*

Let your imagination savor this image: a structure of crystalline transparent gold surrounded by a wall of diamond-like jasper, rising from a layered, kaleidoscopic foundation of precious stones of all colors. Light cascades from great jewels embedded in the sides like the light from an intensely bright rainbow. The entire effect is so brilliant and variegated that it can only be described as *heartbreakingly* beautiful. To see it would bring tears to your eyes and a throb in your chest.

The multicolored foundations, as we have seen, symbolize the twelve apostles. They portray the fact that the truths proclaimed by the apostles shine forth with a many-faceted and brilliant light. Paul, in Ephesians 3, says that "now, through the church, the *manifold* wisdom of God should be made known to the rulers and authorities in the heavenly realms." The Greek word in this passage for "manifold" (*polupoikilos*) literally means "many-colored" or "multicolored." The image Paul gives us is like that of the twelve multicolored foundations of the New Jerusalem: God's brilliant, prismatic wisdom flashes forth through the vehicle of the twelve apostles.

Each gate is composed of a single pearl (which suggests the existence of some *very* large oysters!). Despite all the jokes you have heard about Saint Peter standing at the "Pearly Gates" of heaven, there are in fact *twelve* such gates—and we don't see Peter guarding *any* of them!

The fact is that these gates of pearl have a deep symbolic significance. A pearl speaks of beauty born out of pain. The beauty of a pearl comes from the pain of an oyster. A pearl is formed when a tiny grain of sand gets inside an oyster's shell, causing the oyster to become irritated and uncomfortable. The oyster relieves its pain by covering the irritating grain of sand with a soft, lustrous nacre that hardens into a beautiful, glowing pearl.

This is a beautiful picture of how the redeemed have emerged like a beautiful, luminous pearl out of the pain of Jesus Christ. The Lord told a story of just such a pearl. "The kingdom of heaven is like a merchant looking for fine pearls," He said. "When he found one of great value, he went away and sold everything he had and bought it."9 The merchant in the story is Jesus, who gave up everything—His prerogatives as God, the worship that is due Him, and even His mortal life—in order to redeem the saints, which He deemed a pearl of great price. He sold all He had to purchase you and me for Himself.

Because of the sacrifice Jesus made to redeem us, the redeemed will never forget throughout eternity the pain and the shame of the cross of Christ. They will sing forever,

> In the cross of Christ I glory,
> Towering o'er the wrecks of time.
> All the light of sacred story
> Gathers 'round its head sublime.

The Light of the City

The remainder of Revelation 21 describes the transcendent light that illuminates the city.

21:22–27 *I did not see a temple in the city, because the Lord God Almighty and the Lamb are its temple. The city does not need the sun or the moon to shine on it, for the glory of God gives it light, and the Lamb is its lamp. The nations will walk by its light, and the kings of the earth will bring their splendor into it. On no day will its gates ever be shut, for there will be no night there. The glory and honor of the nations will be* *brought into it. Nothing impure will ever enter it, nor will anyone who does what is shameful or deceitful, but only those whose names are written in the Lamb's book of life.*

Throughout Revelation we have seen references to a temple in heaven. That temple remains throughout the Millennium as the original model from which the earthly temple is copied. But in the new heaven and the new earth there is no temple. Why? Because the true temple, of which the one in the old heavens is a symbol, is the True Man, Jesus Christ Himself. God in man is the temple.

That is why Paul says, "Do you not know that your body is a temple of the Holy Spirit, who is in you, whom you have received from God?"[10] If God dwells in you, then you are a part of this heavenly temple. You share the honor of being the dwelling place of God.

The radiant light of truth emanates from this profound truth. People can see all things clearly by that truth. So glorious is it that there is no need for the sun or the moon. It does not mean that there is no sun or moon in the new creation. It simply means that the city is so bright that it needs no additional illumination. It will be lit continuously by the glory of God, which has come to dwell in man.

The gates of the city will never be shut because there is no night, and thus no need for protection. Cities close their gates at night as a defense against enemies. But there is nothing that can harm in the new world that is to come. The kings of the earth will bring their glory in—not to compete with the glory of God but to have it revealed by the light of God. Nothing impure can enter that city, because only the redeemed will be admitted.

The Life of the City

Now we come to the last chapter of the last book of the Bible. John begins by describing the life of the Holy City.

22:1–5 *Then the angel showed me the river of the water of life, as clear as crystal, flowing from the throne of God and of the Lamb down the middle of the great street of the city. On each side of the river stood the tree of life, bearing twelve crops of fruit, yielding its fruit every month. And the leaves of the tree are for the healing of the nations. No longer will there be any curse. The throne of God and of the Lamb will be in the city, and his servants will serve him. They will see his face, and his name will be on their foreheads. There will be no more night. They will not need the*

*light of a lamp or the light of the sun, for the Lord God will give them
light. And they will reign for ever and ever.*

Here is a thrilling picture of abounding fertility, of life on every
side—a river of life, a tree of life, yielding life-giving fruit and leaves for
the health of nations. This description parallels Old Testament passages
such as Psalm 46:4, which says, "There is a river whose streams make
glad the city of God."

Similarly, the prophet Ezekiel relates his vision of a river, wonderful
for swimming, which flows from beneath the threshold of the temple
where God lives forever. Since there will be no eternal temple structure in
heaven, the only temple that could exist in heaven forever is the one
described in Revelation 21:22, which says "the Lord God Almighty and
the Lamb are its temple."[11] Again, this is a parallel image of the crystal-
clear river that flows from the throne of God in the New Jerusalem.

The tree of life that is found by the river in the New Jerusalem is
identified with the tree of life in the Garden of Eden. In Genesis 2:9, the
tree of life is growing in the center of the garden, alongside the tree of the
knowledge of good and evil. The Garden of Eden disappeared from the
earth sometime after Adam and Eve were exiled from it, but in
Revelation 22:2 it appears again in the center of the Holy City.

The river symbolizes the Holy Spirit. Jesus said of those who believe
in Him, "streams of living water will flow from within him," to which
John adds, "By this he meant the Spirit, whom those who believe in him
were later to receive."[12]

The tree is a symbol of Jesus Himself. He is the way, the truth, and
the life—the tree of life. When we obey the Word of God we are feeding
on Jesus, drawing life from the nourishment He offers. The tree of life
gives us spiritual health, enabling us to flourish as we obey His word and
live by His example.

From this magnificent scene of the life of the Holy City flow three
ministries that the redeemed saints will perform:

First, *empowered service.* The saints will joyfully serve God. There is
no greater privilege, pleasure, or joy that you and I could ask than to
spend eternity in service to the God of our salvation.

Second, *intimate fellowship.* The saints will see His face and bear His
name, just as a bride bears her husband's name and sees his face.

Third, *enlightened authority.* The saints shall reign for ever and ever.

Remember George Bernard Shaw's complaint about heaven as an
"inane, dull, useless, miserable" place? Have you ever pictured heaven as
a boring place? You couldn't be more wrong!

What is it that causes boredom? Selfishness! The feeling of, "I want to be gratified, I want to be pandered to, I want to be indulged, I want to be excited, I, I, I!" But in heaven there will be no selfishness. There will be continual excitement, discovery, anticipation, gratitude, praise, and the joy of being a partner in an eternal adventure with God Himself!

"Behold, I Am Coming Soon!"

The rest of Revelation 22 is an epilogue. It is the other bookend that, along with the first bookend, the prologue in Revelation 1, contains and encloses John's vision. It serves not only as an epilogue for the book of Revelation, but as a fitting conclusion to all 66 books of the Old and New Testaments.

The epilogue consists largely of assurances. The first assurance is given by the angel, one of the seven angels of the seven-bowls-of-wrath judgment. The angel, who has been John's guide in his vision of the new heavens and the new earth, gives John the assurance of the truth of what he has seen.

22:6 *The angel said to me, "These words are trustworthy and true. The Lord, the God of the spirits of the prophets, sent His angel to show his servants the things that must soon take place."*

This is God's own guarantee that the words of this vision are to be believed. They are trustworthy and true.

The second assurance comes from Jesus Himself. John records this assurance in verse 7:

22:7 *"Behold, I am coming soon! Blessed is he who keeps the words of the prophecy in this book."*

Many people neglect this great concluding book of God's Word, feeling that it is too difficult or troubling. But Jesus says that the words of this prophecy are to be read, studied, and kept—and that those who do so will receive a blessing. They will be ready to meet their Lord when He comes.

Then John adds a personal word of his own.

22:8–9 *I, John, am the one who heard and saw these things. And when I had heard and seen them, I fell down to worship at the feet of the angel who had been showing them to me. But he said to me, "Do not do it! I am*

a fellow servant with you and with your brothers the prophets and of all
who keep the words of this book. Worship God!"

There is another very similar incident recorded in Revelation 19.
Personally, I do not believe John made the same mistake twice. John is
here referring back to the incident in chapter 19 where he erroneously
began to worship the angel. He is reminding us how he reacted when he
heard and saw the amazing events of Revelation. He is, in effect, recount-
ing his most embarrassing moment and reminding us that the revelation
of God's plan should always lead us to worship Him, not lesser beings,
not lesser things. When you read this book, John says to us in effect, open
your heart and praise the God of glory who gives us such a stirring, exhilarating future as is described in these pages.

Then John records the angel's next words.

22:10–11 *Then he told me, "Do not seal up the words of the prophecy of*
this book, because the time is near. Let him who does wrong continue to
do wrong; let him who is vile continue to be vile; let him who does right
continue to do right; and let him who is holy continue to be holy."

This is a reminder that each of us, throughout each day of our lives, is
moving toward one or another of two distinct destinies. Either we are
growing closer to God, walking with Him, obeying Him, learning from
Him, experiencing friendship and fellowship with Him—or we are
retreating from God and from heaven. It is a sobering truth. And it is one
of the many truths arising from this vision of the future that has powerful
application in our lives today.

We must examine our lives in light of the prophecy of this book,
because the time is near. Are you moving closer to God, expecting the
coming of Jesus Christ—or does the quality of your life reflect a *rejection*
of God's love? No one can answer that question but you.

Next John records another word of reassurance from the lips of
Jesus—and a word of warning.

22:12–16 *"Behold, I am coming soon! My reward is with me, and I will*
give to everyone according to what he has done. I am the Alpha and the
Omega, the First and the Last, the Beginning and the End.

"Blessed are those who wash their robes, that they may have the
right to the tree of life and may go through the gates into the city. Outside
are the dogs, those who practice magic arts, the sexually immoral, the
murderers, the idolaters and everyone who loves and practices falsehood.

"I, Jesus, have sent my angel to give you this testimony for the
churches. I am the Root and the Offspring of David, and the bright
Morning Star."

Following the reassurance of the truth of His promises, the underscoring of His warning that those who give themselves over to sin will
have no part of heaven, Jesus declares His credentials: He is the Alpha
and Omega, the First and the Last, the Beginning and the End. He is God,
the Creator. And He is the Root and Offspring of David. He is also fully
man, the descendant of King David, the Messiah of the Jews, heir to the
throne of His father David, ruler of Israel. And He is the bright Morning
Star—the one who promises to come for His own before the rising of the
Sun of Righteousness.

Again and again in this one concluding chapter Jesus says, "Behold, I
am coming soon!" Many people read that and say, "How can that be?
These words were written centuries ago. Christians in the first century
believed He was coming soon, and He never came. Why should
Christians in the twentieth century believe He is coming soon?" Some
will even say, "The apostles were wrong. The book of Revelation is
wrong. After 2,000 years of waiting, it should be obvious that Jesus is not
coming back."

But if there is one thing the book of Revelation makes clear it is the
fact that John's vision links time and eternity in ways that transcend
human understanding. We look at time as a straight line, marked off in
years like inches on a ruler. We see John's era of the first century A.D. as
being at one point on the ruler, our own era some 2,000 years later, and
the events of Revelation as occurring at some time further along that
ruler.

Properly understood, however, the events of Revelation were no further off in John's future than they are in yours and mine. The final destiny
of a human being, whether lost or righteous, begins the instant that individual dies. Eternity is never more than a heartbeat away, never farther in
the future than one's own death.

It won't be long before both you and I step out of time and into eternity. And when we arrive in eternity, the saints who preceded us in death
by a hundred or a thousand or two thousand years won't say to us, "What
took you so long?" They'll be just like us, new arrivals in eternity, staring
goggle-eyed in amazement at the unguessed-at wonders God has prepared for us.

Jesus is coming soon. He was coming soon in the day of John the
apostle. Even if the events of Revelation do not take place for another

thousand years or ten thousand (though I hardly think that likely!), this statement would still be true: Jesus is coming soon.

"Come, Lord Jesus"

John's vision closes with an invitation and a final warning.

22:17–19 *The Spirit and the bride say, "Come!" And let him who hears say, "Come!" Whoever is thirsty, let him come; and whoever wishes, let him take the free gift of the water of life.*

I warn everyone who hears the words of the prophecy of this book: If anyone adds anything to them, God will add to him the plagues described in this book. And if anyone takes words away from this book of prophecy, God will take away from him his share in the tree of life and in the holy city, which are described in this book.

The invitation is clear: "Come!" This invitation is issued by the Spirit of God Himself, and it is echoed by the redeemed of God (the bride), and by every individual Christian who hears. It is an invitation to every reader of the book of Revelation to come, take the free gift of the water of life, come to Christ and live eternally.

The warning is equally clear: Don't change a word in this prophecy! The book of Revelation is God's truth. Don't add to it. Don't subtract from it.

Certainly a book so rich in symbolism must be interpreted—but it must be interpreted *carefully.* Don't take away its meaning by emphasizing the symbolic at the expense of the literal. Do not destroy its intent by literalizing everything in it and ignoring the meaning of the symbols.

Most important of all: Believe it. Ignore, reject, or distort God's truth and you risk missing out on God's plan; you risk having to endure the terrors described in the book; you risk losing out on your portion of the tree of life and the beautiful Holy City.

Believe it—*because Jesus is coming soon!*

22:20 *He who testifies to these things says, "Yes, I am coming soon." Amen. Come, Lord Jesus.*

Doesn't your heart reverberate with that same poignant prayer? Amen! Come, Lord Jesus! The world is waiting, aching, crying for your return! The church is watching and expecting you! Amen! Come, Lord Jesus!

He is coming soon.

In closing, John leaves us with one last thought. It is a word of benediction. With that benediction, the book of Revelation closes. It is fitting that I close this book with the same words.

22:21 *The grace of the Lord Jesus be with God's people. Amen.*

Notes

Chapter 1: **Behind the Scenes of History**

1. Earl Palmer, author, Lloyd J. Ogilvie, general editor, *The Communicator's Commentary: 1, 2, 3 John, Revelation* (Waco, TX: Word, 1982), p. 97.
2. See Matthew 17 and Mark 9.
3. Isaiah 6:1.
4. Job 1:20-22.

Chapter 2: **Seven Letters to Seven Churches**

1. John F. Walvoord, *The Revelation of Jesus Christ* (Chicago: Moody, 1971), p. 51.
2. Genesis 1:3.
3. Carl Sagan, *Cosmos* (New York: Random House, 1980), p. 246.
4. Encyclopedia Britannica, *Energy, the Fuel of Life* (New York: Bantam/Britannica, 1979), p. 38.
5. Psalm 119:105; Proverbs 6:23.
6. Psalm 43:3.
7. Psalm 37:6.
8. Psalm 27:1.
9. John 1:4-9; 12:46.

Chapter 5: **The Church That Compromised**

1. Isaiah 1:18.
2. Acts 2:14–41 (cf. Psalm 16:8–11; Joel 2:28–32).
3. 2 Peter 2:14-15 (cf. Jude 8-11).
4. See Exodus 16 and Numbers 11.

Chapter 6: **The Worldly Church**

1. See Acts 16:14-15, 40.
2. One example: Sidon was occupied by the Israeli army for two and a half years during the 1980s. After the Israeli pull-out in 1985, the Palestine Liberation Organization moved into the area of Sidon, prompting Israel to launch a series of aerial bombing raids into Sidon in April 1986.
3. See 1 Kings 18:16-19:3.
4. See 1 Kings 21.

5. See Acts 21:8-9.
6. William Barclay, *The Revelation of John*, vol. 1 (Philadelphia: Westminster), p. 134.
7. Earl Palmer, author, Lloyd J. Ogilvie, general editor, *The Communicator's Commentary: 1, 2, 3 John, Revelation* (Waco, TX: Word, 1982), p. 143.
8. See Revelation 20 and 21.
9. Malachi 4:2.
10. Revelation 22:16.

Chapter 8: **The Little Church That Tried**

1. Again, I have to disagree with the New International Version. This phrase should not read, "Since you have kept my command to endure patiently," but rather, "Since you have kept my word of patient endurance." This phrase refers not to the believer's endurance but to the Lord's endurance. Jesus has been waiting for centuries until His enemies be made His footstool. In this verse He is saying, in effect, "Since you have learned to wait just as I am waiting, I will also keep you from the hour of trial that is going to come upon the whole world. . . ."
2. Luke 21:28.
3. J. I. Packer, *Your Father Loves You* (Wheaton, Ill.: Harold Shaw), commentary for December 12.

Chapter 9: **The Rich/Poor Church**

1. Matthew 5:13.
2. Matthew 5:14.
3. 2 Timothy 4:3-4.
4. Matthew 16:24; cf. Mark 8:34; Luke 9:23.
5. 1 Peter 1:7.
6. Isaiah 64:6.
7. Luke 13:34.
8. Matthew 19:28.

Chapter 10: **Supreme Headquarters**

1. Jeremiah 17:12.
2. Genesis 9:13, 15.
3. Daniel 4:17
4. Daniel 7:9–10.
5. Hebrews 12:14.
6. Ezekiel 1:10-11.
7. Eugene H. Peterson, *Reversed Thunder* (San Francisco: Harper & Row, 1988), p. 60.

Chapter 11: **The Great Breakthrough**

1. From *Family Life* magazine (issue and date unknown).
2. Psalm 2:1-2, 6, 9.
3. Hebrews 7:25.
4. Matthew 28:18, King James Version.
5. John 2:25.

6. 1 Timothy 2:1-4.
7. 1 Peter 1:18-19.
8. Philippians 2:9-11.

Chapter 12: **The Riders of Judgment**

1. Daniel 9:26.
2. See Acts 2.
3. 2 Thessalonians 2:3, 8.
4. John 5:43.
5. Revelation 13:17.
6. For a more complete explanation of the relationship and distinctions between time and eternity, see the chapter "Time and Eternity" in my book *Authentic Christianity* (Portland, Oregon: Multnomah, 1975).
7. Luke 23:34.
8. Acts 7:60.
9. Isaiah 2:21.
10. Isaiah 26:10.
11. Hebrews 9:27.
12. John 3:36.
13. Isaiah 23:9.

Chapter 13: **To Jew and Gentile**

1. John 4:22.
2. Matthew 10:5-6.
3. Not including the disputed regions of Gaza, the Golan Heights, and the West Bank (which total roughly 7,000 square miles of territory), Israel covers an area of approximately 8,000 square miles. For comparison, the state of New Hampshire covers approximately 9,000 square miles.
4. Malachi 4:2.
5. Ephesians 1:13; cf. Ephesians 4:30 and 2 Corinthians 1:22.
6. Romans 8:16.
7. Philippians 2:5, King James Version.
8. Genesis 49:17.
9. However, Ezekiel 48 tells us that the tribe of Dan will be given a portion of land in the distribution of the land that takes place during the Millennium.
10. Matthew 24:14.
11. John 3:36.
12. John 3:16.
13. Zechariah 9:9.
14. Matthew 10:5-8.
15. Matthew 10:21-23.
16. Luke 1:32.
17. Micah 4:1-4.

Chapter 14: **Angels of Doom**

1. Habakkuk 2:20.
2. Earl Palmer, author, Lloyd J. Ogilvie, general editor, *The Communicator's*

Commentary: *1, 2, 3 John, Revelation* (Waco, TX: Word, 1982), p. 185.
3. See Luke 1:5-38.
4. Romans 8:34.
5. Revelation 11:15.
6. Matthew 24:21.
7. Ephesians 5:5-6.
8. Quoted by Damon Knight in *Charles Fort: Prophet of the Unexplained* (Garden City, NY: Doubleday, 1970), p. 73.
9. Zephaniah 1:12-13.
10. Jeremiah 51:25.
11. Luke 21:25-26.
12. Habakkuk 3:2.
13. Isaiah 28:21.

Chapter 15: **All Hell Breaks Loose**

1. Luke 8:31.
2. 1 Timothy 4:1.
3. There are growing numbers of court-sanctioned infanticide and euthanasia cases in our society. One of the earliest involved "Baby Doe," born in Bloomington, Indiana, on April 9, 1982. The baby was born with a comparatively mild case of Down's Syndrome, resulting in mental retardation, and an easily correctable deformity of the esophagus. Unwilling to accept responsibility for a Down's child, the parents took the case to court. They won the court's approval to deny food and medical attention to the infant. Thus, with the willing participation of the delivering obstetrician, the baby was slowly and deliberately starved to death. Over a dozen couples offered to adopt the baby, but the parents stubbornly refused. Six days later, the baby died in horrible agony—legally condemned to death by its parents, the obstetrician, and the courts for the "crime" of being born retarded.
4. Hebrews 2:3.
5. Hebrews 4:7; cf. Psalm 95:7-8.

Chapter 16: **The End of Mystery**

1. Deuteronomy 29:29.
2. See Hebrews 6:13.
3. Romans 11:18.
4. Romans 11:25-27.
5. Isaiah 35:3-7.
6. Ezekiel 2:9-3:3.
7. Ezekiel 3:14.
8. In the original Greek this verse literally says, "They said unto me, 'You must prophesy . . .'" It is not clear who the word "they" refers to. It certainly does not refer to the mighty Angel of Revelation 10. I believe this plural pronoun refers to the four living creatures of Revelation 4, because they are the ones who call forth the events of this book.

Chapter 17: **The Last Warning**

1. 1 Corinthians 6:19.
2. Luke 21:6.

3. 2 Thessalonians 2:3-4.
4. Zechariah 4:6.
5. Malachi 4:5.
6. See Matthew 17:1-13.
7. See 2 Peter 1:16-18.
8. See 2 Thessalonians 2:9-10.
9. John Donne, *Holy Sonnets, X.*
10. At this point in the text, the New International Version properly omits a phrase which many other translations contain: "and who is to come." The best Greek manuscripts do not contain this phrase—and for a good reason: At this point in John's vision, He has *already* come!
11. Matthew 25:31-33.
12. Matthew 25:34-40.
13. Habakkuk 2:14.

Chapter 18: **The Woman and the Serpent**

1. William Shakespeare, *Antony and Cleopatra*, Act IV, Scene 14.
2. Psalm 2:6.
3. John 4:22.
4. 1 Corinthians 12:27.
5. 1 Corinthians 12:12.
6. Ephesians 6:12.
7. Romans 8:1.
8. Exodus 19:4.

Chapter 19: **When Men Become Beasts**

1. See Philippians 3:20.
2. See 2 Thessalonians 2:9; cf. 2 Corinthians 11:14.
3. See 2 Thessalonians 2:4.
4. 1 Corinthians 6:19-20.
5. Eugene H. Peterson, *Reversed Thunder* (San Francisco: Harper & Row, 1988), p. 126.
6. See 1 John 4:1.

Chapter 20: **The Time of Harvest**

1. Jude 24.
2. Hebrews 11:6.
3. 1 Thessalonians 4:13-14.

Chapter 21: **Earth's Last Trial**

1. See Numbers 22.
2. Isaiah 6:1-4.
3. Matthew 24:22.
4. See Matthew 8:12; 22:13; 25:30.
5. Rudyard Kipling, *The Ballad of East and West.*
6. 1 Thessalonians 5:1-3.
7. Ephesians 2:2.

8. Luke 21:26.
9. Romans 2:4.

Chapter 22: **The Dragon Lady**

1. Revelation 2:20-23.
2. Eugene H. Peterson, *Reversed Thunder* (San Francisco: Harper & Row, 1988), p. 147.

Chapter 23: **The Rider on the White Horse**

1. Ephesians 5:25-27.
2. Matthew 8:11.
3. 2 Corinthians 5:10.
4. 1 Corinthians 3:12-15.
5. Matthew 24:30.
6. Jude 14-15.
7. Exodus 3:14.
8. See John 18:1-11.

Chapter 24: **One Thousand Years of Peace**

1. Colossians 2:15.
2. 2 Corinthians 4:4.
3. See Luke 11:21-22.
4. 2 Corinthians 4:4.
5. 1 Peter 5:8.
6. Isaiah 24:21.
7. Isaiah 24:22-23.
8. Matthew 19:28.
9. Revelation 2:26-27.
10. 1 Corinthians 6:2-3.
11. 1 Corinthians 15:20.
12. 1 Corinthians 15:23.
13. See John 5:29.
14. Jeremiah 17:9.
15. Isaiah 2:4.
16. Isaiah 65:25.
17. Isaiah 65:20.
18. Isaiah 65:20, alternate rendering of the text as given in a note in the NIV.
19. John 5:22.
20. Luke 10:20.
21. Genesis 18:25.
22. 1 John 5:11-12.

Chapter 25: **The City of Glory**

1. Peter Toon, *Heaven and Hell* (Nashville: Thomas Nelson Publishers, 1986), p. vii.
2. 2 Peter 3:10.
3. 1 John 3:2, paraphrase of King James Version.
4. 1 Peter 1:4

5. 2 Peter 3:9
6. John 10:9.
7. 1 Corinthians 13:13.
8. Isaiah 9:6.
9. Matthew 13:45-46.
10. 1 Corinthians 6:19.
11. See Ezekiel 43:6-7 and 47:1-12.
12. John 7:38-39.

Note to the Reader

The publisher invites you to share your response to the message of this book by writing Discovery House Publishers, Box 3566, Grand Rapids, MI 49501, U.S.A. For information about other Discovery House books, music, or videos, contact us at the same address or call 1-800-653-8333. Find us on the Internet at http://www.dhp.org/ or send e-mail to books@dhp.org.